The Limits of Epistemology

The Limits of Epistemology

Markus Gabriel

Translated by Alex Englander
and Markus Gabriel

polity

First published in German as *An den Grenzen der Erkenntnistheorie*
© Verlag Karl Alber GmbH Freiburg, Munich 2008

This English edition © Polity Press, 2020

Polity Press
65 Bridge Street
Cambridge CB2 1UR, UK

Polity Press
350 Main Street
Malden, MA 02148, USA

The translation of this work was funded by Geisteswissenschaften International
– Translation Funding for Humanities and Social Sciences from Germany, a joint
initiative of the Fritz Thyssen Foundation, the German Federal Foreign Office, the
collecting society VG WORT and the Börsenverein des Deutschen Buchhandels (German
Publishers & Booksellers Association).

ISBN-13: 978-1-5095-2566-9
ISBN-13: 978-1-5095-2567-6 (pb)
ISBN-13: 978-1-5095-2570-6 (epub)

A catalogue record for this book is available from the British Library.

Library of Congress Cataloging-in-Publication Data
Names: Gabriel, Markus, 1980- author.
Title: The limits of epistemology / Markus Gabriel.
Other titles: An den Grenzen der Erkenntnistheorie. English
Description: English edition. | Medford, MA : Polity, 2019. | Includes
bibliographical references and index.
Identifiers: LCCN 2019005170 | ISBN 9781509525669 (hardback) | ISBN
9781509525676 (pbk.)
Subjects: LCSH: Skepticism. | Knowledge, Theory of.
Classification: LCC BD201 .G3313 2019 | DDC 121--dc23 LC record available at https://
lccn.loc.gov/2019005170

Typeset in 10 on 11.5pt Palatino by
Servis Filmsetting Ltd, Stockport, Cheshire
Printed and bound in Great Britain by CPI Group (UK) Ltd, Croydon

For further information on Polity, visit our website: politybooks.com

Contents

Preface to the English Edition

I am particularly pleased that this book, which was published more than a decade ago in German, is now available to an anglophone audience, because I wrote it during my first period as a DAAD (Deutscher Akademische Austauschdienst) postdoctoral researcher at New York University. As Alex Englander began to work on the translation, I decided against updating the book by addressing the (secondary) literature that has been published in the intervening period, as this would drastically change both the course of its arguments and its formulations of central problems. In addition, the work that has appeared over the last decade on issues relevant to the book – on objectivity, the metaphysics of idealism and realism, scepticism, and so on – is so interesting and far-reaching in its own right that it would take at least another book to do it full justice and to adjust some of my arguments to this altered landscape. Hence, I present the book to the anglophone audience in more or less its original form.

Its point of departure is the simple but all too often ignored fact that epistemology claims knowledge. However, its knowledge claims are not quite ordinary, as its object is knowledge as such (its nature and its limits, as the saying goes). This obvious feature of epistemology's knowledge claims tends to be neglected in contemporary epistemology in favour of an investigation into first-order knowledge. Therefore, epistemology is threatened by a blind spot at the level of its own articulation and justification. As long as epistemology remains unaware of the contexts within which it operates as an intelligible enterprise, we are entitled to entertain some degree of doubt concerning its actual success. Accordingly, the book sets out from the question of what it would take to justify the knowability of the kinds of theses advanced by epistemologists. In other words, it is an exercise in transcendental reflection – reflection on the conditions of knowledge-acquisition about knowledge.

Within this framework, it deals with two major issues, which it identifies as hinges of epistemology.

The first issue is *the problem of the world as such*. This problem arises from the erroneous notion that the world is an object of knowledge. In this context, I endorse a specific version of Kant's insight that 'the world' designates at most a regulative idea. In order to make sense of this claim, I distinguish between first-order theories and 'the metatheory'. The role of the metatheory is to make explicit the decisions that guide first-order research, decisions that do not pick out objects in their target domain. The distinction between theory levels serves as an anti-sceptical tool, since it undermines Cartesian-style scepticism about the so-called external world. As a matter of fact, the Cartesian sceptic is on the right track insofar as she implicitly realises that there is no such thing as an external world, but she misconstrues her insight as a commitment to an epistemic asymmetry between an internal world and a domain of external objects potentially beyond our cognitive grasp. To be sure, she is not explicitly aware of the real problem of the world, as is clear from her attempt to treat it as an issue about access: how can we so much as know anything about the external world given that we first need to represent it internally?

The second issue is *the problem of fallibility*. If 'knowledge' is our term for the good case, there has to be something that can go right or wrong. Otherwise, there would be no conceptual space left for the very idea of a bad case. I suggest that there actually is an element common to both the good and the bad case, namely knowledge claims. Knowledge claims are subject to normative evaluation in light of the question of whether they amount to knowledge. At the same time, I argue that this does not mean that knowledge is, as it were, an aperspectival grasp of facts. I wholeheartedly reject the notion that there could be such a thing as 'the view from nowhere'. To know anything whatsoever presupposes the stability of discursive rationality – i.e. of an operation that relies on given parameters that form its context. It simply does not make sense to reboot knowledge claims and to base them on any kind of foundation that (supposedly) transcends the variability of contexts. Much of the book is dedicated to formulating this delicate point without succumbing to the paradoxical, self-undermining expressions associated with the tradition of Pyrrhonian scepticism.

For this reason, I recommend a methodological use of scepticism. Scepticism is integrated into the theory construction of epistemology, which moves from a Cartesian to a Pyrrhonian mode of reflection. In this way, it abandons a model according to which knowledge is a relation between mind and world, or subject and object for that matter. The problem of knowledge should not be couched in terms of a distinction between someone's mere attempt to latch onto a mind-independent reality (the world) 'out there' and the concept of the success conditions of said attempt. We need to overcome the assumption that there is a largely inanimate, material universe 'out there', which serves as the metaphysical foundation of the epistemic objectivity possessed by our mental states. This does not, of course, amount to a denial of specific facts of the matter, including the trivial acknowledgement that we do not make reality up by somehow mentally constituting or socially constructing it. Such a version of overcoming the world (rightly or wrongly associated with Rorty and some time-slices of Putnam's work) remains mired in the mind–world problem insofar as it takes the form of a reduction of the world to the mind, of facts to practices, of conditions of truth to conditions of warranted assertability, or what have you.

Like any other work of philosophy, this book has an autobiographical context. It reflects a range of conversations whose role for philosophical progress lies in putting up rational resistance against our pre-rational, impulsive biases. The view outlined in what follows results from my attendance at Crispin Wright's mind-blowing Heidelberg seminars on scepticism (2004) and the realism issue (2006), which spurred my interest in epistemology. With this inspiration, I decided to spend a year as a postdoc at NYU to work with Crispin while Paul Boghossian was writing his *Fear of Knowledge* and Thomas Nagel was working on the project which became *Mind and Cosmos*. During this time, I profited from constant exposure to sophisticated forms of realism in various areas of theoretical philosophy, and these led me to reassess my earlier idealist inclinations. To be sure, '(absolute) idealism', as I understand it here, has nothing specifically to do with the notion that reality is somehow generally related to the mental; rather, it is a syndrome of epistemological, semantic and metaphysical considerations underpinning the assertion that nothing outreaches 'human inquisitiveness', in Crispin's phrase. According to idealism thus conceived, reality is somehow or other essentially tied to its knowability.

This book is my first systematic attempt to escape the one-way street that leads to (absolute) idealism. I am still convinced that it is not sufficient just to kick a stone and insist that reality obviously outruns knowability, in that it resists conceptualisation. Stamping one's feet on the ground of reality is just not a good move in the attempt to articulate what it means to say that the facts outrun any specific evidence available for warranted knowledge claims. Both realism and (absolute) idealism have to struggle with associated versions of scepticism as they begin to recover their motivation in the form of explicit and reflexive theory construction.

The combination of philosophical styles and sensibilities to be found in what follows will be unusual to some readers. This is largely due to the various historical contingencies that separate different groups of philosophers from one another. In my view, the kind of isolation euphemistically called 'specialisation' does not always serve philosophy's best interests when it comes to dealing with some of the 'big questions' of humanity, including the question of the extent to which reality is knowable and of how to conceive the role of the thinking subjects it contains.

An important characteristic of the book is that it deviates from naturalism in epistemology. It does so on the grounds that there is no epistemically successful way of outsourcing the problem of human finitude to any other science. To put it bluntly, naturalised epistemology in the wake of Quine is a theory failure which stands no real, intellectually honest chance against the most minimal sceptical pressure. Naturalised epistemology is an ostrich-like policy, which explains its 'taste for desert landscapes'.

Unfortunately, the reality of human knowledge acquisition and knowledge is much more multifarious than suggested by the simplified formula 'S knows that p'. In actuality, we only know anything whatsoever in a constellation of contexts whose totality remains forever out of epistemic reach. Downstream, reality contains too much data for it ever to be fully transformed into the kind of information we can handle with a given epistemological model (a first-order case of knowing together with its metatheory). Upstream, the interaction of contexts within which we claim knowledge includes the language we use in coding our thoughts, the socio-economic conditions under which a topic seems worthy of interest to us, the neurobiological preconditions of the human sensory systems, the historical time we live in, our unconscious biases, etc. There is simply no way for us to transcend all of this and to stabilise, once and for all, the ground on which philosophical reasoning unfolds.

Bonn and Paris, November 2018

Introduction

We refer to the objective world *as if* it were essentially independent of the fact *that* we refer to it. This attitude towards the world is described by the concept of objective knowledge, which simply picks out those of our mental states that put us in touch with how things are. By the 'world', we usually understand the totality comprising everything that pre-exists our two most basic epistemic activities: acquiring knowledge of what is the case and securing that knowledge against any possible objections we might encounter. The concept of the world is therefore indispensable to our understanding of whatever it is that we know. For when we know something, such that we can both express what we know in the form of an explicit knowledge claim and defend it in the face of critical questioning, what we usually know is simply how the world is.

When, in our more reflective moments, we try to arrive at a more articulated understanding of this idea, we hit upon a concept of the world as the unified horizon of everything that is the case. On this conception, the world is the object of each successful representation of what is the case. Or, to be more precise: the *states of the world* and precisely not the *world itself* – that is, the world *simply as the world* – are the objects of each successful representation of what is the case. This is the intuitive basis of what Bernard Williams called 'the absolute concept of reality':[1] from the standpoint of our knowledge claims, the world itself assumes the status of the absolute, of that which is independent of and prior to knowledge. Our knowledge claims, by contrast, are subject to the condition that they must either describe how the world is or undergo revisions when confronted with critical objections. Indeed, our reference to the objective world makes us fallible precisely because the world, in whatever way it ultimately exists, is independent of our acts of referring. Take away this independence, and our reference would no longer be fallible. But that just means it would no longer constitute reference to an objective world: to cognise is just to be in a fallible position.

Cashing out these general reflections in the form of a developed theory is a much more problematic enterprise than it may seem at first glance.

For one thing, it is vital to note how we are already operating on two levels. *On the one hand,* we need to understand first and foremost that it is the *world* that we know when we possess empirical knowledge. *On the other hand,* this very assertion already oversteps the boundaries of objective knowledge, of empirical cognition. Indeed, it does so in a twofold sense, because knowing what knowledge is is not itself a piece of empirical knowledge about how the world is, any more than the world simply as the world can ever become an object of empirical knowledge. Otherwise, the putative piece of knowledge whose content is the proposition that the world precedes our knowledge claims would be just as fallible as our knowledge of a determinate state of the world. Yet this seems to be impossible: knowledge of the conditions of knowledge's fallibility operates (at least *prima facie*) at a different theoretical level to the fallible knowledge it thematises. And so, we might think, it must enjoy an exemption from fallibility, else we would be fallible in relation to the very question of whether we are fallible.

It seems, therefore, that the standpoint from which we go about trying to render empirical – and that means fallible – knowledge comprehensible has to differ from the standpoint from which we make empirical knowledge claims. Knowledge of empirical knowledge is not itself empirical. So, since minimal insight into the relation between empirical knowledge and the world cannot itself be subject to inductive verification or falsification, we need to draw a distinction between two theoretical levels: between the level of objective knowledge on the one hand and the meta-level, of knowledge of what objective knowledge is, on the other. However unremarkable this distinction may at first appear, the entirety of the following study is devoted to spelling out its far-reaching implications and to making them fruitful for contemporary epistemology – in particular, for the debate surrounding scepticism. As a theory that investigates truth claims, epistemology itself lays claim to knowledge as soon as it pronounces on how the concept of knowledge should be understood.

However, as an engagement with the problem of scepticism soon teaches us, the knowledge claims of epistemology are far from unproblematic. If the sceptic convinces us that we cannot, after all, know what objective knowledge is, let alone how it is possible, then objective knowledge itself threatens to collapse. For without any epistemic grasp of the very concept of objective knowledge, we can hardly ascertain whether there really *is* any objective knowledge. There is therefore no way around the question of what it really means to know something. The possibility of knowledge is a methodological presupposition of every instance of empirical knowledge ascription, without itself being empirically knowable.

Perhaps the most important methodological insight of modern epistemology since Descartes is that the theoretical stance of epistemology itself is motivated by scepticism. An engagement with scepticism belongs to the very conditions of epistemology: it first makes space for and then sustains the question of what it means to know something. Generally speaking, philosophical questions of the form 'What is X?' acquire their determinacy through being distinguished from what they are not (in this respect, they are just like anything else).[2] And the question of the nature of knowledge is no different: it is comprehensible only given the possibility that there is something we *do not know*, or perhaps even *cannot* know. Knowledge, in other words, acquires its particular conceptual contours precisely in virtue of how we come to distinguish it from its constant companion, ignorance.

This point is echoed in the fundamental epistemological insight recently introduced into the debate by Jonathan Schaffer's *contrastivism*.[3] According to this position, the content of all cases of (propositional) knowledge is respectively determined by its belonging to a class of propositions that is distinguished from a contrast class. Instead of 'S knows that p', we should in fact always read 'S knows that p rather than q'. The contrast class (q) thereby contains all those propositions whose truth implies the falsity of the propositions of the contrast class (p).[4] So, the proposition that I, Markus Gabriel, can now see my notebook in front of me belongs to the class of perceptual propositions. If it were the case that all perceptual propositions were false, such that no one ever perceived anything (because, say, we are only ever dreaming, or we are brains in a vat, or . . .), then the class of dream propositions would be a contrast class of the perceptual propositions.

Knowledge generally contrasts with ignorance. Indeed, the nature of error (ψεῦδος) or ignorance has been one of the central questions of epistemology ever since its origins. It was raised by Plato, especially in the *Theaetetus* and the *Sophist*, and it can hardly be a coincidence that the question of knowledge arose in the context of pre-Socratic metaphysics, which paradigmatically marked a distinction between being and seeming that was at once ontological and epistemological.[5] The development from pre-Socratic metaphysics to the Sophists, against whom Plato developed his theory of ignorance, his 'pseudology', is an historical expression of the fact that, in relying on the determinacy of knowledge, the epistemologist thereby owes a debt to the possibility of ignorance. *Omnis determinatio est negatio* thus applies just as much to the determinacy of the concept as to the objects of knowledge. Whoever claims to know what knowledge is generates an ontological space of opposition within which knowledge contrasts with ignorance, and the continual possibility of the latter becomes the wandering shadow of the former.

I want to elaborate and deepen this connection by pursuing the following thought: scepticism is a *condition of intelligibility* of epistemology. In its continual confrontation with ignorance, epistemology occupies the specific standpoint of a metatheory. From this metatheoretical standpoint, it investigates the question of what (first-order) knowledge is and, in doing so, claims (second-order) knowledge for itself. We have already begun to distinguish first-order knowledge (empirical cognition) from epistemological knowledge by designating the object of the former as states of the world. Since epistemology itself, by contrast, refers both to the successful unity of knowledge claims and the world (knowledge) and to their potential difference (ignorance), it is continually beyond all empirical knowledge. For the world *simply as the world* is no more an ordinary *object* than objective knowledge itself. This, as we shall see, is one of the central insights to be won through our confrontation with scepticism.

The entire first part (Part I) of this study is therefore concerned with the *function of scepticism in the dialectical economy of epistemology*. By 'dialectic', I understand a form of reflection on the connection between the motivation of a theory and its execution. The task of this first section will be to work out the foundational methodological function of scepticism in the construction of (modern) epistemology. Chapters 1 to 4 take up the question of how the concept of the world relates to scepticism. In this context, we will need to draw a distinction between three different conceptions of scepticism, which will be crucial for the arguments to follow. Specifically, we must distinguish between *negative dogmatism*, *Cartesian scepticism* and *methodological scepticism*. The concept of negative dogmatism, I will argue, can be won through an engagement with the sceptical foundations of Kant's transcendental idealism. For, insofar as he attempts to draw boundaries to knowledge, he puts forward negative dogmatic claims: claims to know that there are some things we cannot know.

Specifically, we will have to critically examine Kant's conception of the world against the background of his Refutation of Idealism. Kant's drawing of epistemic boundaries, his negative dogmatism, clearly involves a distinction between two theoretical levels: empirical and transcendental. Nevertheless, the way in which he carries through on the sceptical motivation of his theoretical standpoint does not leave empirical knowledge unaffected: in Kant, the world threatens to vanish into cognition, objectivity into subjectivity. In light of this threat, he seeks to defend his transcendental idealism with the help of the Refutation of Idealism and to show that the objectivity of knowledge, far from being undermined by transcendental idealism, is in fact secured by it. In contrast to a subjective idealism *à la* Berkeley, transcendental idealism is compatible with the assumed existence of things or objects extended in space and time. Nevertheless, Kant's own idealism leads him to over-extend the thesis of his Transcendental Aesthetic. As we shall see, he is ultimately unable (within the context of the Refutation of Idealism at any rate) to mark a distinction between a *spatial representation* and the *representation of something spatial*. Drawing this distinction requires the introduction of a criterion of publicity, and therefore of other subjects in space and time; these subjects must be able both to refer to the same spatial items and to communicate the fact that they can do so.

Throughout the book, I shall be discussing the problematic of idealism in terms of a distinction, due originally to Robert Brandom, between a thesis of the *sense dependence* of objectivity on subjectivity and the thesis of a *reference dependence* of objects on subjects. The distinction guides my arguments right through to the final paragraphs of this study. A concept P is *sense-dependent* on a concept Q, according to Brandom, if and only if we would not understand P if we did not understand Q. Understanding P presupposes understanding Q. By contrast, Brandom explains, a concept P is *reference-dependent* on a concept Q if and only if there would be nothing which fell under P if there were nothing which fell under Q.[6] The concept of 'idealism' can now clearly be understood in at least two different ways: as a thesis of sense dependence on the one hand and as a thesis of reference dependence on the other.[7] Sense dependence idealism merely asserts that we would have no concept of objectivity if we did not distinguish it from our subjectivity. This thesis is a second-order assertion about a condition of our access to the world (and so belongs to the metatheory). Reference dependence idealism, by contrast, asserts that there would be no objects if there were no subjects and is therefore a first-order thesis about what there is – or, rather, about the way in which what there is exists. Kant oscillates between the two assertions. It is certainly true that nobody has operated with a differentiation of theory levels as clearly as Kant does – a fact to which the distinction between the empirical and the transcendental bears ample testimony. Yet his handling of this differentiation is ultimately inconsistent, and he consequently ends up a victim of his negative dogmatism (see chapters 1–2). As we shall see, this reveals itself as the Achilles' heel of the Refutation of Idealism.

Moore's overreaction to Kant's negative dogmatism – his naïve ontology of individuals – forms the next topic of discussion. Moore (quite intentionally) undercuts Kant's reflections and manages to formulate a decisive objection to the Refutation of Idealism, which I shall elaborate in my own discussion of Kant. Yet Moore neglects both Kant's conception of the world and his distinction between theory levels. Moreover, he is unable to defend the fundamental category of his naïve ontology, the so-called physical object, against objections stemming from the conceptual relativity of our access to the world. This clears the path for a remobilisation of Kant's conception of the world without violating the common-sense intuition that all true judgements describe the world as it is in itself – that is, how it is independently of the beings who describe it. Specifically, adopting the Transcendental Dialectic's conception of the world in combination with a rigorous differentiation of theory levels can help dissolve a confusion lying in the concept of the world. In a word: Kant here shows us how we might distinguish between the world as unified horizon and the world as object of our knowledge. It is unfortunate, therefore, that the Transcendental Dialectic's conception of the world plays no role in the Refutation of Idealism, the latter occurring at a systematically unfruitful point in the *Critique*.

At this stage, Cartesian scepticism enters the picture (chapters 5–6). In this context, 'Cartesian scepticism' admittedly stands neither for a sceptical position that Descartes himself advocated nor for the concrete form assumed by his sceptical reflections in the *Meditations*. Nevertheless, as the first to recognise the outlines of its logical structure and to deploy it in a methodologically controlled manner, Descartes bequeathed his name to this variety of scepticism. Before Cartesian scepticism can be developed as a general paradox attending the concept of knowledge or the concept of a justifying reason (chapter 6), we need to set out certain methodological provisos (chapter 5). To this end, I introduce a distinction between *logical* and *dialectical* analyses of sceptical arguments. Both methods can then be put to use in order to better appreciate the impetus behind Cartesian scepticism. Furthermore, we shall see how Cartesian scepticism can best be analysed as a *paradox* – that is, as a set containing seemingly acceptable (and well-motivated) premises, seemingly acceptable (and well-motivated) inference rules, and an obviously unacceptable conclusion.

Our confrontation with the paradox or paradoxes of Cartesian scepticism, however, cannot be restricted to attempts at solving (or dissolving) it. It won't do, say, just to question or replace one of the paradox's premises in an effort to circumvent it. Merely *logical* repair mechanisms will not serve our ultimate purpose here. Rather, we must always ask ourselves questions of another sort: in which theoretical context does the paradox arise? Under which theory conditions can it be introduced – i.e. motivated? In contemporary epistemology, such considerations trade under the name of a 'theoretical diagnosis'.[8] They concern the function of Cartesian sceptical premises in the context of determinate theories and make up the focus of what I am designating *dialectical analysis*. We will test out both methods, logical and dialectical analysis, in the course of a critical engagement with Crispin Wright's ingenious anti-sceptical strategy of *implosion*. However, it will turn out in chapter 6 that, in those cases where the strategy is successful, implosion not only disables Cartesian scepticism but also threatens the very epistemological standpoint from which the strategy is itself developed. For its own standpoint is motivated by premises that lead to the formulation of Cartesian scepticism. Accordingly, the first part of the study then ends by constructing a general paradox of Cartesian scepticism. Since we need draw on nothing more than certain foundational premises of discursive rationality to generate this paradox, it represents nothing less than an intrinsic threat to our rational cognition quite generally.

However, the threat can be averted. By reaching for a *dialectical* manoeuvre, we can restabilise discursive rationality by grounding it in human practice, which is essentially tied to fallible, finite knowledge acquisition. Part II, on *contextualism* and *finitude*, is occupied with the prospects for this manoeuvre. Specifically, it endeavours to rebuild epistemology on a contextualist discourse theory by drawing upon the attempts by Wittgenstein and Sextus Empiricus to draw boundaries to our knowledge. It transpires that there is a common denominator shared by Pyrrhonism and the strategy pursued in Wittgenstein's late philosophy, even though the latter is ultimately *anti*-sceptical and directed against hyperbolic doubt. This common denominator is contextualism, which I understand as a lesson concerning the necessary finitude of objective knowledge. I begin Part II with a systematic outline of Pyrrhonian scepticism (chapter 7), without, however, entering into Sextus' late Pyrrhonism in all of its historical details. My sole concern is to provide a systematic reconstruction of the fundamental operation of self-application, the περιτροπή, the ploy of 'self-refutation' or of 'turning the tables'. This operation consists in applying our insight into the finitude of knowledge to itself and thereby, however paradoxically, in drawing boundaries to our very insight into the boundaries of knowledge.

Chapters 8 to 10 then reconstruct Wittgenstein's contextualism as a theory of assertoric content. It will turn out that the possibility of all discursive determinacy – that is, of all assertoric content – presupposes discursive operating conditions, conditions which discourses cannot have in their self-conscious possession *in ipso actu operandi*. To justify this thesis, I focus especially on the problem of rule-following, while at the same time connecting Wittgenstein's position with certain basic concepts of system theory, primarily of a Luhmannian provenance. Wittgenstein and Luhmann are in agreement insofar as they argue for the necessary finitude of all operations of observation – that is, of all operations of determinacy: whatever can be something determinate for a discursive community counts *as* something determinate only under the presupposition of historically variable parameters, which respectively fix what a community can register. The community constitutes a discourse precisely by fixing hinges upon which all individual moves in the discourse turn. In my reading, this is the most important thesis of Wittgenstein's *On Certainty*, and I will interpret it as an insistence on the necessary finitude of discourse. This insistence, it should be noted, can already be found in Sextus, albeit in a different context.

Chapters 9 to 12 discuss Wittgenstein's private language argument in order to provide a more precise evaluation of the finitude of all discursively communicable knowledge. On my interpretation, which takes its cue above all from Crispin Wright, Saul Kripke and Meredith Williams, the argument tries to prove that all discursively communicable knowledge is finite; knowledge depends upon the stability of a discourse, which has to be fixed as the context of knowledge ascription. Nevertheless, the participants in a discourse cannot determine its foundations *from within* the discourse itself – not without initiating a meta-discourse, which brings along its own presuppositions or operating conditions in turn. One result of this line of thought is that it is impossible to determine when and whether someone knows something from an absolute standpoint. Yet Wittgenstein shows us how we might put this partially sceptical thesis to use in order to develop a contextualism that manages to reconstruct scepticism as a harmless lesson about our discursive finitude.

Chapter 11 then places John McDowell's disjunctivism in this argumentative context, discussing it as an anti-sceptical strategy. Disjunctivism attempts to develop knowledge or cognition under the conditions of a theory of intentionality, understanding the latter as a cognitive relation of mind and world rather than, as in Wittgenstein, as a necessarily social and, in this sense, discursive phenomenon. Following Wittgenstein, I attempt to show that McDowell's disjunctivism faces difficulties as an anti-sceptical strategy, since he fails to integrate the socio-semantic dimension of subjectivity into his approach from the outset. He determines the subject as cognitive intentionality and not as a person in space and time (who is always already socially implicated).

Chapter 12 contains a response to the rule-following problem developed by Kripke in his interpretation of Wittgenstein. It uses some of the conceptual cornerstones of Kripke's suggestion that we might need a 'sceptical solution' in the guise of a community view of rule-following in order to understand how anyone can ever actually follow a rule. I turn this slightly desperate diagnosis into a more positive account of the social nature of thought and theorising. In other words, we need to give up methodological solipsism in epistemology and stop thinking of the problem of knowledge in terms of an attempt of a single knower (typically called 'S') to put herself in touch with objective matters of fact (typically called 'p') by claiming that they obtain. Knowers turn into such individuals only by being singled out from a community of successful knowers. Epistemology should thus return from its self-inflicted Robinson Crusoe-like isolation to the actual context of knowledge acquisition. I call this move 'stage setting'.

Chapter 13 then enquires into the relationship between the concept of representation, which traditionally leads to the familiar sceptical aporia of mental representationalism and Cartesian scepticism. Since Wittgenstein ultimately uses his contextualism to undermine the methodological solipsism of modern epistemology – a position accepted by so many post-Cartesian (as well as ancient) epistemologists – contextualism would seem to offer an escape route from the general paradox of Cartesian scepticism. By uncovering the problem of rule-following and its communitarian solution (which I discuss extensively in chapter 10), the solipsistic I can be shown its way out of the 'fly bottle'.[9] The concept of representation thus disappears – but at a price: our subjectivity and our metatheoretical standpoint, both of which have to be invoked when we talk *about* discourses as such, come under serious threat.

This difficulty becomes especially clear when we take a closer look at Wittgenstein's liberal naturalism (chapter 14). In order to safeguard the possibility of mutual understanding between different discourses (language games), Wittgenstein introduces 'second-nature', which functions as a kind of unifying horizon of all discourses. Humans can communicate with one another because of their shared natural history, and 'very general facts of nature'[10] ensure that there is ultimately nothing alien within the domain of the human. Indeed, Wittgenstein is also explicit that all knowledge comes about only 'by the grace of nature'.[11] This position, however, is incompatible both with Wittgenstein's own motivating contextualism and, as we shall see, with the vital sceptical lesson of finitude. Specifically, it is a position that fails to enquire into the operating conditions of the very discourse in which the claim that our nature is constituted in such and such a way enjoys the validity it does. In other words, Wittgenstein does not think to apply his contextualism to his own reflections (περιτροπή).

As a response to this shortcoming, I endeavour to push Pyrrhonian scepticism through to its logical endpoint while still conceiving of the discourse *about* finitude as a *finite* discourse. This attempt throws up the obvious problem that the resultant metatheory has to concede its own revisability and contingency. To be sure, this does not mean that it has to be false or self-undermining (in the manner of a performative contradiction). But it does mean that it has to be distinguished from an alternative of which it necessarily remains ignorant; it cannot know its own contrast class. Given the principle that all determinacy in logical space generates binary oppositions, applying our insight into the finitude of objective knowledge to itself means erecting a boundary between *this* knowledge and an ignorance that, however indeterminable, is an indispensable assumption.

Lastly, by examining Brandom's interpretation of Hegel, chapter 15 ventures a final attempt to rescue the concept of the world from the contingency of the metatheory. We will see that Brandom's interpretation does not take adequate account of the absolute idealism adumbrated in the *Science of Logic* and, instead, operates with a concept of the world that Hegel wants to supersede. To bring out this point, it will pay to play off some of the basic moves of Hegel's logic of reflection against Brandom's version of an objective idealism. This will finally bring into view the possibility of using Pyrrhonian scepticism to develop a discourse theory whose task consists 'merely' in examining the dialectical consistency of given theories. Once absolute idealism has been liberated from certain absurd prejudices (a task to which this book can unfortunately make only a small contribution), one can understand such an approach as delivering on a Hegelian thesis. Taking our cue from Hegel helps provide a basis for a systematic project: of setting out a methodology for epistemology that does not so much seek to solve supposedly grave sceptical problems as merely to delineate the dialectical topography of their possible solutions. With such a method, we might then evaluate their respective prospects for success.

I see this model of philosophical methodology, generated via reflection on the finitude of knowledge, as a means of inheriting Hegel's talk of 'absolute knowledge', particularly in his *Phenomenology of Spirit*. I therefore conclude with an attempt to show, at least in outline, that the paradigm of philosophy as the unity of method and object – that is, of self-thinking activity in the medium of pure thought – makes an unexpected return within the contemporary scepticism debate in a way that lends renewed impetus to Hegel's programme of absolute knowledge. In this connection, it is already worth noting, even at this early stage, that absolute knowledge is not infinite knowledge. Absolute knowing too has to fail on account of its higher-order immediacy, its own finitude – which is why, of course, absolute knowing does not represent the last word even for Hegel.[12]

Given the length and breadth of what is to follow, the above will have to suffice as a promissory overview. Yet, as an aid to the reader's orientation, it is worth adding that Part I contains a largely *destructive* discussion of the concept of knowledge and possible anti-sceptical strategies, while Part II pursues a more *constructive* project, building contextualism on the ruins of Part I, but without raising objections against the truth of Pyrrhonian scepticism and its lesson regarding our necessary finitude. Epistemology confronts us with our discursive finitude, a finitude we cannot transcend. But, as I try to show elsewhere, this does not rule out metaphysical theories of infinity, provided that these theories conceive their task aright.[13]

A final word on my approach: I work on the understanding that it is legitimate to combine strategies from 'analytic' philosophy – primarily within epistemology, though also from philosophy of mind – with traditional questions of metaphysics and the theory of knowledge. In any case, it is hardly self-evident that the still widespread practice of opposing analytic to continental philosophy is worth sustaining. It would be wrong to classify the arguments that follow by trying to ascertain their respective debts to particular schools; indeed, they do not even presuppose that overgeneralising titles such as 'analytic' and 'continental' allow us to draw anything like adequate distinctions between different methods and schools of thought. The excessive professionalisation of the practice of philosophy in our time does not mean that philosophy itself is a professionalised science that divides neatly into different disciplines, each marked out by its given characteristic methods. For the purposes of classifying the business of modern academic institutions, a strict organisation of philosophical discourse may be acceptable, even advantageous, to a certain extent. But it has the potential to become orthogonal to philosophy as a discursive practice of freedom. For this reason, in trying to determine the function of scepticism in epistemology, I have tried to develop my own position by taking up the approaches of highly diverse thinkers, without worrying about whether I was philosophising within the accepted house style of any particular school.

Part I

The Function of Scepticism

1

Negative Dogmatism and Methodological Scepticism

One of the chief lessons of the sciences is that the world diverges substantially from how we tend to view it as naïve observers. Knowledge acquisition and doubt are therefore not merely compatible – they are not even independent phenomena. We need only consider the all too familiar fact that, with every increase in knowledge, we also acquire knowledge of what we *do not* yet know, of our own ignorance. Indeed, strictly speaking, knowledge in the demanding sense of 'scientific' knowledge is unthinkable in the absence of doubts as to whether the world is exactly as it appears to us to be. Departing from our everyday assumptions is a condition of the very possibility of knowledge *as such* coming into view. Just like anything else human thinkers might investigate, knowledge becomes an object of study only once we have begun to wonder whether and to what extent it actually resembles what we take it to be on the basis of our pre-theoretical assumptions.

As soon as we take even the smallest bite from the fruit of the tree of knowledge, we face the challenge of scepticism: the possibility of knowledge implies the possibility of its impossibility. Knowledge, in short, implies doubt, and the task of alleviating this doubt falls to epistemology.

While scepticism is intimately bound up with the very *possibility* of each and every attempt to achieve theoretical distance from the world,[1] it represents a particular problem for epistemology. By distancing us from our everyday knowledge ascriptions, epistemology too introduces the possibility of scepticism. But by the same token, it implies the possibility of its own impossibility. After all, epistemology is an inherently self-referential enterprise: it strives for knowledge of knowledge. This makes it peculiarly liable to paradoxes. For if it should turn out that such fundamental epistemic concepts as 'knowledge', 'cognition', 'justification', and so on, imply the possibility of scepticism, then epistemology itself comes under threat. And since it depends upon the viability of these concepts no less than any other theory, epistemology has no choice but to face up to the threat to its own possibility from within.

Equipping ourselves with an explicit understanding of knowledge and doubt is evidently an exercise in reflection, an attempt to seek out stable ground in the face of a recognisable threat. Hence epistemology is always a theory of reflection, a theory which has to give an account of the presuppositions governing its own construction. So much follows from its reflexive character, from the fact that it issues in knowledge claims – knowledge claims about knowledge. And since it is a reaction to scepticism, we can understand scepticism in turn as an enterprise that passes from the destruction of individual knowledge claims to the destruction of knowledge claims as such.

It is therefore not merely an historical coincidence that philosophers in the modern period have deployed Cartesian scepticism as a *motivational* theory for epistemology, as an ultimately *anti*-sceptical strategy. This anti-sceptical strategy, first introduced by Descartes himself, amounts to a *methodological* scepticism, the idea being that we can thematise scepticism as a condition of the possibility of reflection. At the same time, this strategy provokes new, second-order sceptical attacks against which epistemology also has to arm itself.

One of the common moves in the defence of knowledge against the inherent possibility of scepticism is the invocation of immediacy, be it nature (Hume), common sense (Reid, Moore), the everyday (Heidegger), the ordinary (Cavell), and so on. This immediacy, however, is thrown into question not only by specifically epistemological scepticism but by the scepticism implied by the sciences too. The latter continually remind us that some part of the world, or the world as a whole, is not *actually* as it appears to be from the (alleged) pre-theoretical standpoint of immediacy.[2] The sciences, that is, exploit the difference between being and appearance no less than philosophy. So if we want to adopt a scientific attitude towards the world, we have to reckon with a potentially considerable difference between how it is and how it appears.

Certain words can convey the impression of picking out a unified phenomenon although, on closer inspection, they in fact do no such thing. Philosophical vocabulary is notoriously guilty in this respect, and positions such as idealism, realism, relativism, and so on, have taken on an often confusing multiplicity of forms throughout the history of philosophy. They can often designate basic options within a certain philosophical subject area, or even fundamental systematic approaches. Indeed, in the eyes of at least some of their representatives, they can sometimes function as descriptions of nothing less than the totality of existence. 'Scepticism' provides another example of a word that promises more unity than it in fact delivers. The history of attempts to provide constructive theoretical solutions to all kinds of philosophical problems runs in parallel to the history of attempts to develop corresponding, destructive counter-programmes aimed at demonstrating their impossibility, and the variety of the latter reflects the variety of the former. The conflict between dogmatism and scepticism, which plays out upon philosophy's 'battlefield of endless controversies',[3] does not even begin with Plato's arguments with the Sophists; it already looms large in pre-Socratic philosophy.

Historically, the phenomena that have been assembled under the label 'scepticism' have depended primarily upon whichever constructive proposals were on offer at any given time, with the result that scepticism has often been 'parasitical' upon dogmatism.[4] Without any further specification, therefore, 'scepticism' is thus just as unclear a term as 'philosophy' or 'science'. Abstractly formulated, 'scepticism' can be regarded as a destructive system of assertions formulated with the intention of systematically dislodging some given piece of constructive theorising. Accordingly, the sceptic philosophises from a position of opposition, following a negative programme that presupposes the existence of a positive programme to be used as a foil. This is why the ancient master sceptic Sextus Empiricus, whom we shall encounter again and again throughout this study, determined the 'activity' (ἀγωγή) of sceptical philosophising as 'an ability to set out oppositions among things which appear and are thought of in any way at all' (δύναμις ἀντιθετικὴ φαινομένων τε καὶ νοουμένων καθ᾽ οἱονδήποτε τρόπον).[5] The sceptic, therefore, avowedly pursues a primarily practical (and thus no longer merely destructive) aim insofar as she attempts to finally make good on the salvific promise of 'tranquillity' (ἀταραξία), just like the adherents of rival Hellenistic schools. Yet she does so by seeking eudemonia not in contemplation of the eternal, as did Plato and Aristotle, but in the life and customs (νόμοι) of the community. These customs do not admit of a *philosophical* legitimation but stand for 'what has to be accepted, the given',[6] as they would later for Wittgenstein.

Although one could cite many contemporary philosophers, such as Richard Rorty, Robert Fogelin or Michael Williams, who self-consciously theorise in the tradition of ancient scepticism, none of these authors seriously take up its soteriological dimension. Yet a much more marked and important difference between ancient scepticism and the contemporary scepticism debate (especially as conducted within analytic epistemology) stems from a feature of post-Cartesian philosophy that I have already mentioned, namely that scepticism came to adopt a systematic function within epistemology.

Since Descartes, that is, it has become customary to incorporate scepticism into epistemology's motivation, a tactic which led Descartes himself to introduce the idea of a constructive scepticism. By a theory's 'motivation', I understand the set of reflections that result in the theory's execution but cannot themselves be justified through the theory's (yet to be established) theoretical resources. *Motivation* is accordingly an operation that conditions a theory, while *justification* – i.e. the giving of reasons – is already conditioned by a theory. Justification always comes after the fact of motivation.

Descartes made a purely methodological use of scepticism in a way that would prove decisive for modern epistemology. He thereby became (among other things) the precursor of what I shall from now on, following

Dietmar Heidemann, label *integrative anti-scepticism*.[7] By this term, I mean to pick out any anti-sceptical strategy that regards scepticism as the *condition of the intelligibility* of the basic question of epistemology: the question of the nature of knowledge. Integrative anti-scepticism sets out from the assumption that the project of modern epistemology can be made comprehensible (intelligible) in the first place – in other words, can be motivated – only given a confrontation with the problem of Cartesian scepticism.

By *Cartesian scepticism*, I understand the project of formulating sceptical scenarios that have the potential to trigger hyperbolic doubt. The relevant scenarios exercise this potential by showing how the world as a whole could be utterly other than it appears, such that most, or even all, of our beliefs about the world would stand revealed as false.[8] Clearly, this sense of 'Cartesian scepticism' does not designate Descartes' own ego-logical or theological anti-sceptical strategy, which instead reverses the pattern described above and attempts to deploy sceptical scenarios as a foil for its own *constructive* programme.

When exploited by an integrative anti-scepticism, Cartesian scepticism functions as a condition of modern epistemological theorising: the strategy in question integrates scepticism into the project of epistemology in the sense that, by making a case for the impossibility of knowledge as conceived by a given philosophical theory, it is scepticism which first opens up the space for epistemology's basic questions. However, the business of highlighting the precariousness of knowledge serves only as a spur to secure it against the spectre of its impossibility, and thus to overcome scepticism. When it plays this role, the problem of Cartesian scepticism is therefore invoked purely as something to be overcome, specifically by casting it in the form of a *methodological* scepticism. The latter arises through the confrontation with the possible impossibility of knowledge and goes on to clarify how knowledge is possible after all. In this way, the possibility of knowledge is to be rendered intelligible in and through the thematisation of its potential impossibility.[9]

This broad anti-sceptical strategy makes room for reflection on the conditions of epistemological theorising by assuming from the start that Cartesian scepticism is a condition of the intelligibility of epistemology itself. It thereby leads to the insight that epistemology is a second-order theory, a theory tasked with thematising the conditions of possibility of first-order cognition. Hence epistemology claims to be reflexive insight into the structure of knowledge and, as such, to constitute knowledge itself – specifically, second-order knowledge. The content of this second-order knowledge is then first-order knowledge, while the content of first-order knowledge, at least in paradigmatic cases of empirical knowledge, is everything that is the case independently of its being known.

This does not mean that empirical knowledge has to be flanked by an explicit epistemology: one can know all manner of things without knowing, in addition, how it is possible to know anything at all. This is why epistemology requires a motivation: there are conditions of its introduction, namely, whichever conditions lead first-order knowledge to reflect on itself. In other words, the transition from a first-order to a second-order theory – i.e. the operation of reflection – always has to be motivated. After all, knowledge is primarily intentional and thus oriented to objects that it does not necessarily have to thematise *as* objects of knowledge. When I know that there is a glass in front of me, I do not *ipso facto* already know that I know that there is a glass in front of me. Taking this further step requires a change in theoretical attitude, and thus a certain provocation.

Since reflection on the very structure of knowledge is not a constitutive ingredient of first-order knowledge, distinctions between different levels of knowledge are drawn only *in* and *for* epistemology. In fact, our everyday first-order knowledge presupposes the absence of epistemological reflection, a feature that Myles Burnyeat captures with the term 'isolation'.[10] As the scepticism debate of recent decades has made clear, scepticism properly belongs to the theoretical conditions of *epistemological* reflection. This, to be sure, does not automatically imply that the epistemologist has to positively advocate sceptical theses (be they of a local variety concerning certain forms of knowledge or of a global variety concerning knowledge as such). When an epistemology is self-consciously motivated as an integrative anti-scepticism, it need not necessarily have sceptical consequences.[11] Nevertheless, we cannot exclude a priori that methodological scepticism will not lead to insights into the boundaries of knowledge, boundaries that first-order knowledge occasionally oversteps. If it turns out that some, or even all, first-order cognition oversteps the boundaries erected by an epistemological metatheory, then that metatheory is entitled to conclusions that will appear to be sceptical from the viewpoint of first-order thinking. At the same time, provided these conclusions do not apply to the metatheory, it need not count as sceptical in its own eyes.

In what follows, our first task will be to draw a fundamental distinction between *methodological scepticism* and another form of scepticism: *negative dogmatism*. As an initial, intuitive approximation, we can say that *negative dogmatism* consists in the thesis that we are not entitled to *assert* propositions of a certain class, and that we are thus not entitled to a set of knowledge claims.[12] It is merely negative in that it attempts to give a systematic proof that there are certain things we cannot know. Accordingly, negative dogmatic propositions always have the following form: that we know that we can know nothing about some X.

By contrast, *methodological scepticism* takes a set of knowledge claims that we cannot renounce without renouncing *all* knowledge or knowledge as such and introduces the spectre of its possible impossibility. It does not put just any old optional class of our beliefs into question, beliefs we may or may not happen to possess, but instead attacks the very foundations of our capacity of belief formation. Crucially, methodological scepticism burrows so deep that we cannot assert it dogmatically without entailing drastic revisions to our epistemic self-understanding.

Whenever an epistemological theory is explicitly constructed in light of an insight into the function of methodological scepticism, I shall, as above, speak of *integrative anti-scepticism*. Integrative anti-scepticism does not attempt to refute methodological scepticism directly. Yet, unlike negative dogmatism, it does not accept local sceptical conclusions either. Moreover, it is important to stress that methodological scepticism does not always have to function as an integrative anti-scepticism: in order to do so, it requires the further methodological insight that, because the project of epistemology requires methodological scepticism as a motivation, it has to be integrated into the theory itself. Given this insight, it is simply imposs-ible to eliminate methodological scepticism without at the same time doing away with the very epistemological reflection that puts it to use.

Unlike methodological scepticism, negative dogmatism develops argu-ments aimed at obtaining specific theoretical results. It commits itself to conclusions to the effect that one can no longer affirm some set or category of knowledge claims to which we previously took ourselves to have an unproblematic and unqualified entitlement. By contrast, methodological scepticism consists of paradoxes – that is, of arguments constructed out of apparently acceptable premises and rules of inference that together support evidently untenable conclusions. Paradoxes constitute a peculiar class of argument: although they conform to the conditions of rational-ity, for a variety of reasons we usually cannot accept their conclusions. Instead, we find ourselves compelled to dissolve them. While *arguments* typically serve to convince us of a particular conclusion, *paradoxes* have conclusions of which we cannot be convinced – or of which we ought to be convinced only in utterly extreme circumstances. Zeno's paradoxes, for example, are paradoxes because they lack the power to convince us (or ought to convince us only in the most extreme circumstances) that nothing moves. Ultimately, it is clear enough that at least some things do indeed move, and, therefore, the way to dissolve paradoxes has to be by asking which properties of the concepts or rules of inference they deploy need to be revised.

Negative dogmatism might assert, for example, that we cannot know anything about God, because the conditions of the possibility of our cogni-tion are incompatible with positive theological knowledge. Pursuing this tack, it can call into question all positive theological knowledge claims – a process which might even necessitate concrete institutional reforms. Yet negative dogmatism does not trade in paradoxes, pursuing instead other paths of reflection to convince us of its conclusions.

Methodological scepticism, on the other hand, offers a lesson about the finitude of our knowledge. It shows, for example, that, since we have no reflective access to the set comprising the totality of the conditions of our knowledge, all knowledge continually depends upon conditions being fulfilled that lie beyond our rational control. It achieves this effect by pointing out that we cannot rationally exclude sceptical scenarios (such as brains in vats) in explicit epistemological reflection because the set of scenarios of this kind is infinitely large. Clearly, if knowing something presupposes that we can first exclude all sceptical scenarios by working through them in a piecemeal fashion, we can hardly provide a guarantee that we know anything at all.

However, this difficulty by no means entitles us to the inference that we have no empirical knowledge – supposing such an entitlement would immediately cancel out epistemology's theory conditions by destroying all of its objects, namely first-order knowledge as a whole. Methodological scepticism formulates paradoxes, arguments with untenable conclusions. But these conclusions are untenable precisely *in virtue of* epistemology's reflexive conditions. Put simply, the paradoxes end up abolishing epistemology itself and, a fortiori, any inferences it might draw about the tenability of empirical knowledge.

The problem is not, as it might at first appear, simply that, by questioning whether we can know anything at all, methodological scepticism threatens our first-order knowledge. The problem is rather that the abolition of our first-order knowledge leads to the abolition of the epistemology that we initially introduced as a reflective theory of that very knowledge. If epistemology led to the result that there can be no first-order knowledge, and this result followed from nothing less than the conditions of intelligibility of epistemology's basic questions, then it would eliminate itself as a cognitive enterprise. Epistemology would forfeit its motivation, and its result – the impossibility of first-order knowledge – would thus end up equally unmotivated. In short, we cannot formulate methodological scepticism as a set of sceptical theses about knowledge without at the same time violating the conditions that allow it to function as a tool for motivating epistemology.

Whatever 'scepticism' means in a given case, and whichever forms of scepticism one might generally wish to distinguish, it is clearly an enterprise that can only ever gain traction within the context of a sophisticated philosophical culture. For it can launch its assaults on that culture only by borrowing from the argumentative measures and standards it provides. Naturally, scepticism comes on the scene when discursive rationality finds its way to a certain boundary of reflection. But, however far removed this might lie from our everyday first-order discursive practices, scepticism nevertheless threatens to undermine them as, after all, we are the same thinkers when we hold something to be true on the first-order level as we are when we puzzle over the nature of knowledge claims on the level of reflection. Scepticism cannot but penetrate down to our everyday epistemic activities. We cannot isolate radical doubt from our mental lives. Yet, since scepticism is just as much a sophisticated product of reflection as any constructive piece of philosophy, it cannot be motivated without first proceeding through a series of arguments that lead us far away from the everyday.[13]

Full-blown scepticism is thus a distinctively philosophical problem, not a natural one. It arises only under the conditions of advanced philosophical reflection, whose results pose a systematic danger either to our pre-theoretical, natural worldview or to our developed philosophical and scientific knowledge. It is for this reason that, time and again, we encounter an opposition between philosophy and nature (the natural attitude). The standard implication of this opposition, found most prominently in Hume, is that philosophy entangles us in the sorts of reflection that we would never countenance in everyday life.

According to Hume, nature itself, in the guise of the necessity to act (and so, in practice, to opt for some particular interpretation or other of a given situation), forces us to make judgements that we cannot justify under the conditions of pure theoretical reflection. Such conditions are, at first glance, irrelevant from a practical point of view.[14] So while Hume the *philosopher* famously doubts the objective validity of causal judgements, having traced them back to an inductive inference that lacks an a priori justification, Hume the *ordinary person* can rest assured that the course of everyday experience will silence the voices of doubt. Yet this distinction is no modern innovation. Many classical sceptics also work with their own preferred versions of such an opposition between *nature* and *reflection*.

The philosophical problem of reflection is commonly distinguished from an attitude of natural scepticism. If you are sceptical about whether the new government, for all its sincere promises, can really solve the country's problems, this does not make you an advocate of scepticism. The everyday use of the predicate 'sceptical' is a very much reduced form of its epistemological counterpart.[15] Yet the everyday predicate still contains echoes of scepticism proper that should not be hastily ignored, suggesting as it does a certain aptitude for criticism. The common reminder to maintain a sceptical attitude implies that, if we are not sufficiently 'sceptical', we run the danger of consenting to things that are seemingly obvious and natural, but which would not withstand the scrutiny of reflective thought. The Greek verb σκέπτομαι in fact means 'to inspect closely' and was opposed by Sextus Empiricus to 'haste' (προπέτεια).[16] Scepticism should therefore not be confused with the pathological *addiction to doubt*, which Karl Jaspers investigated in his *General Psychopathology*.[17] Scepticism might result from some kind of doubt or other, but it is not itself a form of doubt. It is a feature of theory construction that arises at a point in the transition from a natural attitude towards reality to an explicit grasp of the structure of that attitude.

In a somewhat traditional terminology, the opposition of constructive and destructive philosophical programmes can be expressed as the dualism of *dogmatism* and *scepticism*: while dogmatism embodies a philosophical system guided by a constructive theoretical intention, scepticism is its destructive counterpart. As already mentioned, a glance at the history of philosophy shows how variants of scepticism have typically depended upon whichever variants of dogmatism were respectively dominant at a given time. As far as the sceptic is concerned, scepticism is not in the business of producing self-standing philosophical content but, as Hegel in particular emphasised, is instead 'parasitic' upon a given philosophical system.[18] The content of sceptical propositions always depends upon that of dogmatic propositions. Note, though, that the opposition between dogmatism and scepticism does not get a grip when the latter is integrated into an epistemological theory as a methodological scepticism. In these cases, 'scepticism' is no longer scepticism in the traditional sense of a position one might advocate, or even live out. Rather, the scepticism that stands in opposition to dogmatism corresponds to negative dogmatism.[19]

The Hegelian principle of *determinate negation* therefore holds true for classical – i.e. non-methodological – scepticism. We can summarise this principle as follows: the content of a dogmatic position is 'sublated' (as the saying goes) through its sceptical negation in each of the term's three senses: (1) The sceptical negation *imports* the dogmatic content into its own reflection insofar as it (2) seeks to *eliminate* it; it thereby (3) invites a dogmatic reaction, which *sublimates* the original dogmatic content or *enriches* its argumentative resources. This sets up a game of dialectical ping-pong, which Hegel polemically branded as 'the squabbling of self-willed children, one of whom says A, and who by contradicting *themselves* buy for themselves the pleasure of continually contradicting *one another*.'[20] Scepticism as a genre has traditionally drawn attention to the paradoxes and contradictions potentially lurking within dogmatism. Typically, this serves only to provoke a reformulated dogmatism, designed to make good on the original position's weaknesses, and, in this dialectical context, scepticism can have the last word only if it manages to uncover an irresolvable paradox to which any dogmatic undertaking whatsoever is liable. Conversely, dogmatism would win out if it could finally be rid of the sceptic by demonstrating the necessity of dogmatism. Yet as long as dogmatism and scepticism find themselves as dialectical opponents, each threatening and excluding the other, scepticism will always be on the lookout for ever more fundamental paradoxes, while dogmatism will seek out ever more ingenious refutations of scepticism.

Perhaps this conflict between dogmatism and scepticism is itself the problem that needs to be solved. Perhaps the real task is in fact to overcome this very one-sidedness instead of trying either to refine scepticism so that it can continually subvert dogmatism or to reinforce dogmatism so that it builds up a maximal resistance to scepticism. If there is middle ground between dogmatism (philosophy as happy-face theory construction) and scepticism (the articulation of paradoxes that arise from theory construction), it is then imperative to develop a theory that integrates the two. In contemporary epistemology, since methodological scepticism serves the function of articulating the conditions of theorising, it represents just such an attempt. It should therefore be unsurprising that we find constructive theoretical projects in the contemporary philosophical landscape that absorb the destructive impetus of scepticism by including it as an element of their own construction. These projects grant the sceptic her negative intentions but refuse to see these as a threat rather than as a source of useful lessons about the conditions of epistemological theorising. For these projects, what the sceptic says is perfectly in order, only hardly disconcerting; at best, it provides an adequate description of our actual epistemic position.[21]

It is only *methodological* scepticism which can usefully be built into the motivation of epistemology. Yet this does not detract from the importance of negative dogmatism as a form of scepticism: by deploying theoretical arguments to show that we do not really know some or all of what we claim to know, because we *cannot* have knowledge of the relevant kind, it provokes a dogmatic reaction. And, in doing so, it shines a light on the rules governing the to and fro between dogmatism and scepticism that needs to be overcome. All those analyses of our epistemic capacities that intend to show how we are precluded in principle from knowing what we take ourselves to know are negatively dogmatic. Therefore, if we want to pursue the project of integrating scepticism into dogmatism, an engagement with negative dogmatism can clearly have a highly useful function: it can teach us what we are actually committed to whenever we assume that we possess first-order knowledge.

Negative dogmatism sets out to demonstrate that a certain class of propositions is false and seeks to replace them with better ones. It is a variant of scepticism insofar as it thereby intends to prove that a particular system of assertions is untenable on account of the supposed impossibility of redeeming the knowledge claims with which the system is bound up. Negative dogmatism, it should be stressed, is not in the business of arguing that these claims just happen not to be supported, on account of their lacking an adequate justification, say. Instead, it wants to show that there is no way of supporting them *in principle*. It is thus a *revisionist* thesis. It wants to push us to fundamentally reconsider a given procedure of knowledge acquisition by persuading us that our previous way of considering the procedure was guilty of a grave systematic error. And, having uncovered this error, the negative dogmatist intends to replace the procedure with a properly rectified epistemic practice.

We also need to distinguish scepticism in the sense of negative dogmatism from *nihilism*. While negative dogmatism claims to show that some given system of assertions rests upon a systematic error, nihilism asserts that no proposition in a certain system can be true, on the basis that there happens to be nothing that could make them true. At the same time, however, the nihilist cannot exclude a priori that there *could* be a truth-making structure corresponding to the system.

We can distinguish the general form of negative dogmatism from the general form of nihilism as follows:

(a) *Negative Dogmatism: Close attention reveals that a system of assertions is committed to the existence of X, whereby it is either unthinkable that*

> X exists (here, we can give X's value as some concept of knowledge) or
> impossible to acquire any justification for X's existence.
>
> (b) *Nihilism: Close attention reveals that it is conceivable that X exists
> (here, we can give X's value as some concept of knowledge), but X has
> not thus far* in fact *existed and it is unlikely that it ever will exist, even
> though this cannot be excluded* a priori.

Nihilism thus differs from negative dogmatism in that it still accepts the
rules of a given system of assertions and so can attempt to make system-
internal corrections. If you assert a thesis of form (b), you accept the rules
of the system and attempt to demonstrate that the thesis *in fact* fails. Those
who believe that witches neither exist nor ever existed and, moreover,
that it is unlikely or factually impossible that they will ever appear in our
world at some point in the future (given certain natural laws, say) assert
a thesis of form (b). Whoever is convinced that there are witches, the idea
goes, has a false belief and, insofar as she submits to the norm of truth,
ought to revise it.

Negative dogmatism, by contrast, attempts to demonstrate that some
system of assertions fails *in principle*, by showing that it is impossible to
acquire a justification for the assumption that the domain over which the
system quantifies exists. For example, Kant argues in this vein that rational
psychology has no object. He does not set out to demonstrate that there are
in fact no thinking substances to which such predicates as immateriality
and immortality, etc., pertain. Rather, he shows that the conditions of cognitive access to such substances cannot be fulfilled. Rational psychology
conflates the synthesising activity of judgement ('pure apperception')[22]
with an ontologically and epistemologically characterisable object, a soul.

Famously, Kant dissolves the rational psychologist's theory by drawing
a distinction between the *analytic* and the *synthetic* unity of apperception.[23] All representations qua *somebody's* representations are united in
a self-consciousness. They are conceptually determined references to
objects, each of which comprises an event in the cognitive biography of
a thinking being, a self-consciousness. Now, this thinking being cannot
itself be identified with a singular event in its own cognitive biography.
It is not *a* representation that it forms of itself but, rather, the *representing
activity* which brings all representations into an inferentially articulated
whole through subjecting them to conceptual determination. The synthetic unity of apperception, the unifying activity, is thus itself no singular
analytic unity – i.e. no isolated conceptually determined event within
a cognitive biography.[24] By drawing attention to this distinction, Kant
argues that the operating conditions of rational psychology cannot be
fulfilled in principle, since it predicatively determines a substantive soul,
an object, and thus an analytic unity. As a discipline, rational psychology has a self-undermining character: it assumes a substantive soul in
order to guarantee the unity of consciousness while rendering the unity
impossible through that very assumption.

There can be no system of assertions that is not regulated by norms, where norms have the function of distinguishing between correct and incorrect statements within the system. A system in which every proposition is correct would imply, among other things, its own negation; it would lack a prohibition allowing it to declare the negation of the system an invalid move within the system. Once such a prohibition is in place, not *every* assertion within the system will be correct. Accordingly, a system of assertions must consist of permissible and impermissible moves, whereby all permissible moves are correct and all impermissible moves incorrect. This means that genuine discourse always presupposes the possibility of questioning and correcting a given assertion.[25]

It follows that we cannot talk of a negative dogmatism when somebody merely intends to show that some system of assertions cannot fully redeem its epistemic claims. Such negative assertions say little more than that the system contains or implies at least some – and at worst exclusively – incorrect assertions. Yet *all* systems of assertion must be able to contain incorrect propositions, precisely because they are normative systems. If, like the nihilist, we can show that witches neither exist nor have ever existed, we will have successfully refuted a formerly widespread and markedly elaborate theory about these supposed creatures and our dealings with them. But this achievement, just as such, has as little to do with scepticism as does a paradigm shift within an established science, which in some cases may consign an entire system of assertions to history.

We do not need to invoke *scepticism* in order to show that the vast majority of the empirical details of Aristotelian cosmology and biology are irrelevant for the purposes of contemporary natural science. There are not, for example, 55 unmoved movers, and biological species demonstrably evolve before eventually dying out. When some system of assertions is finally put to bed, this will hardly be because the belief caught on that sceptical arguments have managed to demonstrate a priori (i.e. without any modifications to our body of empirical knowledge) that the system in question ultimately rested upon a groundless assumption that was vulnerable to a sceptical alternative. Rejecting a theory instead requires an *error theory*: we need to allow that an entire system of assertions can be found guilty of a *factual* error on the basis that there is nothing, and never has been anything, that could make it either true or false. An error theory convicts some system of resting upon an error at the level of its content.[26] There simply never were 55 unmoved movers to serve as the object of a truth-apt theory, meaning whoever assumes 55 unmoved movers is guilty of an error. This insight, however, is not the result of a sceptical line of thought; it does not lead us towards the idea that belief in the existence of 55 unmoved movers cannot be justified *in principle*, that the very formation of the belief and thus the fundamental rules of the system are ultimately ungrounded. There could well have been 55 unmoved movers, but, as a minimal acquaintance with modern astronomy informs us, there simply are no such entities.

As soon as someone enjoys a sufficient acquaintance with the historical reasons that led to our abandonment of the postulation of 55 unmoved movers, they cannot seriously go on defending it. By contrast, the natural response in the face of a distinctively sceptical attack is generally a defensive reaction.[27] Of course, the assumption of 55 unmoved movers, or of the primacy of masculine form over feminine matter, belongs to a broader systematic context within Aristotle's thought. That context does not itself become obsolete just because some, or even most, of the empirical data evidently speaks neither for nor against it; they are simply not genuine data.

Whether or not there are 55 unmoved movers, or witches, or what have you, is not a question to which we can provide a specifically epistemological answer. Nevertheless, on account of certain vital historical modifications to our overall stock of empirical knowledge and the concomitant substitution of some of our most basic background assumptions, we simply cannot credit a subject with satisfying the norm of truth if they nonetheless persist in assuming that there are 55 unmoved movers, witches, or a heavenly hierarchy of pure spirits. When we maintain that the system of assertions according to which there are 55 unmoved movers, witches, etc., is descriptively empty because there is nothing for it to quantify over, we advocate a *local nihilism*. While the subject matter contested by the local nihilist may well not exist, neither is there any a priori argument against the possibility that a corresponding domain of objects exists. Witches are logically and metaphysically possible; we understand what it means to say that, while there are not in fact any witches, there could well have been some.

The negative dogmatist, by contrast, presents an altogether more fundamental order of challenge to our epistemic situation. In the next chapter, we can begin to get a firmer grip on the nature of this challenge by looking at an especially influential variant of negative dogmatism, namely Kant's, and by examining its lessons concerning the purported object of our cognitive endeavours, the world.

2

Kant's Negative Dogmatism

Negative dogmatism can assume both local and global forms. We can begin to clarify these with the help of our contrast between negative dogmatism and nihilism: whereas nihilism contests the *reality* of a given system of assertions, a negative dogmatism will question its *formal possibility*. More specifically, it will argue that the system under scrutiny cannot be justified, because any successful justification we have to offer has to rely on something in principle unknowable. Clearly, then, negative dogmatism has to argue its case by drawing upon a sceptical thesis.

In modern philosophy, the most prominent representative of a variant of negative dogmatism is undoubtedly Kant.[1] Famously, Kant directs his negative dogmatism against the disciplines of rational theology, cosmology and psychology. In his view, these are suitable targets of his negative dogmatism insofar as they claim to be in a position to know something about the existence and necessary properties of certain substances, namely *God*, the *world* and the *soul*.

It is important to note that Kant does not simply want to shelve rational theology, cosmology and psychology. In other words, he does not set out to show how their objects do not exist, and, in this sense, his negative dogmatism does not represent a form of nihilism. Instead, Kant's essential aim is to shed light upon the semantic structure of these various discourses bequeathed by the rationalist tradition. And, to pursue this self-proclaimed programme of enlightenment or clarification, he explicitly adopts a 'sceptical method':[2] he wants to confront the relevant discourses with a sceptical challenge they will be unable to withstand.[3]

Kant accepts the sceptical challenge of the early modern period (especially in its Humean formulation) and, as the Refutation of Idealism shows,[4] is firmly of the opinion that both Cartesian scepticism and Berkeleyan idealism can be refuted. Yet the key insight motivating his negative dogmatism is in fact derived not from Descartes but from Hume. He developed this into a refined variant of negative dogmatism which – borrowing from James Conant – I shall designate as *Kantian scepticism*.[5]

Kantian scepticism in no way doubts *that* knowledge is possible; rather, it asks *how* (and so not *whether*) it is possible in light of Humean scepticism. In this way, Kant operationalises Humean scepticism to his own ends: he not only deploys Humean scepticism in order to restrict theoretical cognition to the domain of possible experience but also exploits this 'restriction thesis' *in turn* in the service of a transcendental reinterpretation of rational theology, psychology and cosmology. And once they have been suitably reconfigured, these disciplines are supposed to be immune to both negative dogmatism and Humean scepticism.

Kant's own sceptical solution to negative dogmatism therefore consists in a twofold process: firstly, it abolishes rational theology, psychology and cosmology (as disciplines dealing with objects that are straightforwardly reference-independent); secondly, it transforms their basic concepts – God, the world and the soul – into regulative ideas or postulates of practical reason. In what follows, I do not want to discuss this solution in any greater detail. Instead, at this stage, I will restrict myself to clarifying the dialectical structure of Kantian scepticism without yet recommending any competing anti-sceptical strategy.

Modern methodological scepticism introduces the possibility that knowledge as such might be impossible on the basis that we cannot be certain that we know anything even in apparently paradigmatic or 'best' cases.[6] Descartes, Hume and Kant all operate with this prospect of the possible impossibility of knowledge insofar as they turn their focus on the fundamental structure of epistemic purport. We can characterise this structure as follows. When a thinker refers to something with an epistemic intention, she attempts to determine how things are anyway. Things are as they are anyway independently of the fact that someone refers to them with an epistemic intention. That is, we determine whatever we can cognise – i.e. whatever we can acquire objective knowledge about – as something independent of the fact *that* we aim to cognise it.

Crucially for our purposes, it follows from this that objective knowledge cannot be reduced to mere holding-true. As finite thinkers, we do not automatically know everything that we take to be true: only some of what we hold true is, in addition, actually true. I call this difference between truth and holding-true the *contrast of objectivity*. In introducing the contrast of objectivity, we determine the way things are – that is, whatever is the case independently of our epistemic stance of holding-true – by distinguishing them from something whose *esse* is its *percipi*. Accordingly, objectivity is defined by means of our operational distinction between objectivity and subjectivity, where 'subjectivity' refers to domains in which *esse* and *percipi* are identical.

Suppose, for example, I think of a summer's day in southern California. I am neither actually in California, nor do I make any epistemic claim regarding how things really are. In this case, we should not distinguish the *esse* of the imagined summer's day from its *percipi*. It does not matter how I depict the Californian weather when daydreaming: my daydreams are not entertained in light of the contrast of objectivity, while it would be operative in objective thinking about the weather. To be sure, the contrast of objectivity can be applied to the episode of daydreaming insofar as it has specific content: someone (myself included) can be wrong about the content of my daydream. However, the episode itself is not such that its epistemic intention (its content) can potentially diverge from the kind of achievement it exemplifies (holding something true of the actual weather in California).

Now, the problem of objectivity consists in the fact that, insofar as we *determine* objectivity as the negation of subjectivity, we make subjectivity a condition of its intelligibility. In other words, objectivity is objectivity only against the background of subjectivity. Say we construct a theory whose starting point is motivated by this reflection; from the perspective of the theory, objectivity then figures as the negation of subjectivity, such that, without the *concept* of subjectivity, the *concept* of objectivity is simply indeterminate.

To pick up on a helpful distinction of Robert Brandom's, objectivity and subjectivity are thus *sense-dependent*. A concept P is sense-dependent on a concept Q if and only if one can understand P only if one understands Q.[7] Yet, if objectivity is sense-dependent on subjectivity, a certain paradox threatens to ensue: if objectivity is determined by the concept of subjectivity, there is a sense in which it is *posited*. At this point, we have to reintroduce our distinction between different levels of theorising: from the standpoint of every metatheory that grasps the sense dependence of objectivity, objectivity features as essentially posited by subjectivity (the theory construction). By contrast, from the standpoint of the subject engaged in producing first-order knowledge claims, those claims appear to deal simply with objects whose existence is straightforwardly independent of us.

In order to take account of the divergences between these standpoints, we can distinguish three levels. First of all, (1) there are the objects themselves. These can be distinguished only from (2) the perspective of subjectivity. This standpoint can, in turn, be discussed only from (3) the standpoint of a theory that understands objectivity as sense-dependent on subjectivity.

It is in fact by drawing these distinctions that we first obtain the concept of a *metatheory*. If by 'subjectivity' we understand a system of assertions that lays claim to objectivity, once we find ourselves operating from the standpoint of a metatheory, all objectivity seems to be *theory-dependent*. Indeed, from this standpoint the very process of theory construction is isolated and brought into view. Quine draws our attention to just this point in §6 of *Word and Object*: 'Everything to which we concede existence is a posit from the standpoint of a description of the theory-building process, and simultaneously real from the standpoint of the theory that is being built.'[8]

For the metatheoretical standpoint, there is no immediate access to objects. For, from this standpoint, objectivity as such inevitably figures as a posit of subjectivity. A metatheory is a second-order theory, a theory about theories and theory-building. So, by distinguishing subjectivity from objectivity and understanding the relation between them as one of sense dependence, we immediately invoke the possibility of a metatheory. This invocation naturally requires justification. Our metatheory does not grow on trees; it cannot be found among the denizens of the natural order. Kant's own justification involves his particular deployment of methodological scepticism, which, as we have noted, therefore plays a constitutive role in the process of deriving his negative-dogmatic conclusions.

In outlining his distinctive problem of objectivity, Kant thus presupposes methodological scepticism, and it is important to bear in mind that this device was as important to his own theory construction as it was to that of Descartes. Indeed, like Descartes, he turns the possible impossibility of cognition into a motor of philosophical method, appreciating that, without the spectre of this possibility, the business of constructing a theory of knowledge cannot get off the ground. Sceptical arguments are conditions of the very intelligibility of a theory of knowledge, and methodological scepticism is the source of philosophical attempts to answer the question of whether there is such a thing as knowledge.[9] Therefore, in order to get knowledge as such into view, Kant reflects upon scepticism as a condition of the possibility of epistemology, and, in this sense, a version of integrative anti-scepticism animates his negative dogmatism. He integrates scepticism into the motivational structure of epistemology, understood as the project responsible for constructing a theory of knowledge as such. Without invoking scepticism, without considering knowledge to be potentially impossible, we are in no position to introduce a notion of 'knowledge as such' that is supposed to be immune to sceptical attacks. From the standpoint of the metatheory, then, there is no such thing as knowledge as such, as though it were something that could simply be read off the world. Rather, knowledge features as a phenomenon posited within an anti-sceptical theory construction.

Every theory implies a set of theory conditions. In the best case, these conditions are introduced a priori within the theory itself – that is, before we go on to apply it in order to secure possible additions to our current body of empirical knowledge. Some theory conditions are conditions of intelligibility, conditions without which a given theory could not even count as a comprehensible enterprise to begin with. If we have reached a level of theoretical reflection where we start to enquire what knowledge is *as such*, we clearly operate at a certain distance from knowledge itself. So much so, in fact, that knowledge threatens to elude our grasp, which is why epistemology puts its own conditions of intelligibility in danger. Scepticism is the most visible symptom of this process, since its arguments problematise knowledge as such (as opposed to a given local knowledge claim about a particular subject matter). It is then no historical accident that these arguments belong to the canon of epistemological theorising:

epistemology acquires an explicit structure through its exposure to scepticism and its attempts to find adequate anti-sceptical measures.

With this in mind, we can borrow from the jargon of post-Kantian idealism and distinguish between dogmatism and criticism: *dogmatic* theories of knowledge are those which do not integrate scepticism into their own construction, while *critical* theories are precisely those which ground their theoretical approach with the help of an integrative anti-scepticism.[10] Dogmatism's metatheory fails regardless of the apparent plausibility of its first-order declarations about knowledge, for it has no control over the introduction of its central concept, that of knowledge as such. This is why it is not sufficient just to stamp your feet when confronted with scepticism. The sceptic is justified in forcing us to respond to her question as to how we have derived our concept of 'knowledge as such'. Where does it come from? After all, it is the sceptic herself who provides the original impetus behind whichever reflections lead us to the notion that there might be such a thing as knowledge.

Kant takes over the problem of knowledge's possible impossibility from Descartes and Hume, giving, in Luhmann's words, 'a formulation of the improbability of the probable, of the questionable nature of what we always already know'.[11] If the prospect of this possible impossibility lacks a convincing motivation, nothing prevents us from simply bypassing the Kantian project. Accordingly, everything turns on providing a particular formulation of the possible impossibility of knowledge, which can then function as a criterion of success for the epistemological undertaking. If we are already convinced that Humean scepticism is an inevitable problem for the philosopher, we will struggle to avoid Kant or transcendental arguments in general.[12] It therefore makes sense to turn to the fundamental structure of Humean scepticism in order to understand how and why Kant came to reconfigure the problem of objectivity within the framework of transcendental philosophy.

To begin with, let us reduce Humean scepticism to the following basic insight: *to confront an objective reality, finite epistemic beings have to collate data (impressions) that they have not themselves produced, and process it into information (ideas)*. Finite epistemic beings are faced with the task of establishing unity and coherence among their representations, since the sheer volume of data they confront always transcends what they can actually process. In other words, finite epistemic beings have to construct doxastic systems, going beyond the empirical data at their disposal at any given time and assigning it a position within an overall worldview. A worldview is therefore a horizon of knowledge. It can never be exhaustively mapped, since one of its primary functions involves anticipating further information.[13]

Since the world itself is incomplete, insofar as it has an as yet unrealised future, a worldview too has to be incomplete. Hence its function of continually anticipating further information on the basis of given data. The necessity of this function explains why inferential connections must always play a role in the realisation of a stable objective world for finite epistemic beings. In virtue of their finitude, such beings have to establish conceptual connections determined by relations of predicative inclusion and exclusion. Remove these conditions and there can be no objective world for them.

As Hume showed, however, obtaining a licence for those inferences that enjoy a foundational, world-constituting status involves a certain vicious circularity, because we *already* make use of them in our information-processing. We thus face a dilemma: either we have an a priori licence for our unity-conferring inferences or they are arbitrary assumptions which, logically – if not practically – speaking, are replaceable.[14] Hume, of course, grasps the latter horn. Yet insofar as he regards all causal inferences as arbitrary and, thus, replaceable assumptions, he paradoxically undermines our access to an objective world. Hume draws our attention to those access conditions of which we are usually unconscious when we refer to objects *intentione recta* – i.e. on the level of first-order knowledge claims – claims directed at objects that would have been the way we discover them to be had we not tried to discover them. And he introduces the possible impossibility of objective knowledge precisely via an appeal to those access conditions – therein lies the essence of Hume's sceptical strategy. The sceptical paradoxes of Humean scepticism therefore result from a tension between the objective world and our conditions of access to it: the ontological and epistemological orders do not present a continuum that guarantees us an a priori path to the safe haven of the good epistemic case. Hence the fallibility of finite beings.

By drawing such a distinction between the objective world and our access conditions, Hume points to the possibility of transcendental philosophy, of a metatheory tasked with investigating the conditions of possibility of first-order theories. The content of our first-order theories is the objective world, and, from the standpoint of everyday theory construction, this world appears to be ontologically self-sufficient ('mind-independent', as the saying goes). Kant thus builds upon the foundations laid by Hume and uses transcendental arguments to show how a metatheory can step in where our ordinary information-processing fails – namely, in giving an account of its own conditions of possibility. Yet Kant's debt to Hume does not end there. He also concedes to Hume that certain discourses are in fact empty precisely because of their inability to generate a contrast of objectivity.

Besides proving that there are synthetic judgements a priori, one of Kant's central intentions in the *Critique of Pure Reason* is 'to deny *knowledge*, in order to make room for *faith*'.[15] The knowledge that he wants to deny is not just *any* piece of knowledge. Kant is no *global sceptic*, let alone a global fideist. Rather, the knowledge he wants to deny contains a series of metaphysical assumptions about God, the world and the soul. According to Kant, our being rational subjects means we are unavoidably inclined to add these entities to the ingredients of our overall metaphysical belief systems.[16] In so doing, we confuse a condition of objectivity with an entity to be found in the objective world – i.e. in the structured information space to which we have access thanks to the very structure of our cognitive apparatus.

Kant's negative dogmatism builds upon two sceptical premises that he inherits from Hume and subjects to a critical reinterpretation:

> $Hume_1$) *We have no immediate access to the world because we can refer to the world only by means of our impressions.*

If we want to refer to the world, we relate not directly to it but first and foremost to our impressions. The world in itself is potentially hidden behind our representations, meaning that we philosophers have no choice but to investigate our representations and their various modes of connection (in other words: we have to investigate our access conditions to the world). To do justice to the contrast of objectivity, we have to reckon with the potential divergence of our representations of the world from the world itself.[17] Now, we cannot know the extent of this divergence a priori; having no immediate access to the world in itself, there is no position from which we might investigate the conditions of any actual divergence.

> $Hume_2$) *We not only enjoy no immediate access to the world without the mediation of our representations, but we also have no choice but to* interpret *our representations.*

Hume's famous application of this principle has it that, while we undeniably have representations of the succession of two events, this does not grant us an immediate entitlement to think of these representations as causally connected. Without any further justification, we interpret a psychological *post hoc* as an ontological *propter hoc*. According to Hume, we cannot make any legitimate inference from the epistemological facts of experience to the structure of any ontological order.

Yet, we can give a general formulation of this principle independently of its Humean application. We need only make the observation that our representations need to be connected. Our representations do in fact build a temporally ordered nexus, in which they refer to other representations by means of their propositional content and thus stand to them in inferentially articulable relations of inclusion and exclusion. Kant draws upon this very point.

In this context, he accepts $Hume_1$) and $Hume_2$) with important modifications which, in his view, serve to assuage Humean scepticism:

> $Kant_1$) *If we can in fact relate to the world only by means of our representations, it no longer makes sense to assume the existence of a world in itself, which first has to be compared with the world of our*

representations in order for us to think of them as grounded in the ontological world order.

Talk of a *world in itself* needs to be exposed as a false interpretation of a structural property of the world of our representations. Further, ascribing objective reality to our representations does not require us to think of them as standing in relation to a world that we in turn have to conceive as existing independently of our representations. In order for us to have knowledge, we cannot ground the objective reality of our representations by momentarily stepping outside of them and investigating which relations would have to obtain between the world in itself and our representations of it.[18] If it is impossible in principle to relate to the world in itself without the mediation of representations, talk of a world in itself loses all sense for us: it cannot possibly be an object of any justified beliefs. The upshot of Kant's modification is thus that he accepts the Humean challenge and suggests that we overcome it by *internalising* the distinction between the world and our representations. And, as a result, the world turns into a regulative idea.

Despite initial appearances, Kant rejects mental representationalism on the basis that it ultimately boils down to a bad theory of intentionality. His occasionally misleading terminology notwithstanding, he in fact thinks of the distinction between representation and represented as falling *within* the purview of representation. The alternative would be to incur all the problems of an impossible sideways-on view, which attempts to determine what corresponds to a representation without itself making use of any act of representation.[19] Yet, as Davidson emphasised, it is impossible – and so unnecessary – to get outside our own skins in order to observe the world as it is independently of our observations.[20] Whenever we determine what corresponds to our representations, we have to make use of a second-order representation, a representation of a representation. A representation of a representation is precisely what Kant calls a concept:[21] without concepts, we would be in no position to test whether an extra-mental correlate corresponds to our representations. So any intelligible distinction between representation and represented must be explicable in terms of the *modus operandi* of the act of representation itself – which is, to repeat, not to say that there is nothing representable that has not always already been represented.

Kant thus avoids mental representationalism, the sceptical consequences of which had been exposed by Hume. He also avoids a variety of subjectivism that conflates represented and representable and so falls victim to the 'notorious ing-/ed-distinction'.[22] The subjectivism at issue arrives at this fatal conflation on the basis of the following piece of reasoning: from the intentionality of representation, which must always have an intentional correlate, it infers that we still represent something even when our representation has no *extra-mental correlate* but only an *intra-mental intentional correlate*. In such a case we would represent a correlate, albeit a merely intentional correlate. Yet this line of thinking immediately leads us into the aporia of representationalism. For every representation, we would have to assume that it could relate directly only to its intentional correlate and only indirectly to its extra-mental correlate.[23] Given our need to explain the contrast of objectivity, we have to distinguish the represented from the representable, and reducing the latter to the former is not an option if we want to do justice to the fallibility of finite epistemic beings.

Mental representationalism transfers the content of a representation into the object that caused it, thereby reifying the contrast of objectivity which characterises epistemic intentionality. This reification consists in mistaking sense-dependent objectivity (which is thus essentially related to subjectivity) for a world in itself in order to secure the world's onto-logical and epistemological independence from our holding-true. But the representationalist thereby fails to see our representation of the world as a *representation* that we have. In this way, a kind of intentionality that seeks to explain its own objectivity ends up placing the world at such a remove from intentionality itself that it constructs a sheer 'boundary' [*schlechthin scheidende Grenze*] between the two that 'completely separates them'.[24] Crucially, however, Kant understands this absolutely dividing boundary (whose reified form is the substance dualism of *res extensa* and *res cogitans*) as reason's own necessary *self*-bounding: it functions as an element of a self-referential theory of intentionality, whose task is to clarify how precisely the contrast of objectivity is located within the conceptual archi-tecture of our representational capacities.

We bump up against an absolutely dividing boundary between mind and world only as long as we try to construct an account of success-ful epistemic claims under the theory conditions of representationalism. Representationalism, though, is implicitly committed to there being no *criterion* for successful epistemic claims, and it thus becomes clear that its theory construction collapses to the extent to which it fails to explain the very possibility of representational content. Since we do not possess any material criterion of truth, we of course cannot know a priori which epis-temic claims succeed or fail. We are generally dependent upon data we have not ourselves produced. Yet *that* we are thus dependent is precisely something that we can know a priori. And it is in reflecting on this piece of a priori knowledge that we come to understand just why, in virtue of our epistemic finitude, we cannot possess a material criterion of truth. We thereby clarify a basic feature of our cognition.[25]

According to Kant, we cannot know anything of a world in itself. However, this in no way means that we are somehow epistemically defi-cient beings, as Kant takes being related to representations to belong to the concept of the world. The world is a concept that does not permit of ostensive designation. In this respect, it differs from a table, for example: whereas we can point to a table if we want to prove that the table exists and that the concept 'table' is therefore not empty, we cannot likewise point to the world in order to show that the concept 'world' is not empty. The ground of this difference is the idea that the world is a totality that can never be given in an intuition, because all intuitions are intuitions of something determinate *within* the world. The determinacy of an object of intuition entails that we can distinguish it from other objects, and it is not at all easy to say what we could distinguish the world from, at least not without entering the realm of the unsayable.[26] Put slightly differently, the world as the totality of facts cannot be an object of perception, because it is a condition of the perceivability of objects. It is only because they belong to a whole that objects can be more for us than the partial aspects they present to us at any given moment, and this whole can only be anything for us given our investment of concepts (categories and ideas). These first bestow coherence on the world of representation, lending it a structure and unity that only obtains because we establish and maintain it through time. This activity of establishing and maintaining coherence and structure – i.e. their identity in time – is what Kant calls 'synthesis of representations'.[27]

Again, if the *world* is the sum total of determinacy, there could not be a world for us were it not for a structuring (unifying) activity that distinguishes something from something else and thereby relates different elements to one another. Everything in the world is what it is only insofar as it differs from everything it is not. Now, what distinguishes something from what it is not are its properties. Properties, in turn, are universal because they usually pertain not only to one but to several of the world's contents, and, since the properties of the world are universal, we can accordingly explicate them *predicatively*. When we make a judgement and ascribe a property to an object as a predicate, the property is determinate for its part only thanks to its membership in a differential nexus in which it hangs together with other properties. This differential nexus is not itself found in the world, as this would undermine the notion that we can infer something from something else on the basis of a *logical* nexus. We do not *find* the logical structure of our metatheory (including inference rules, theory virtues such as coherence and simplicity in comparison with rival accounts, etc.) as we go about our investigations of the objects (and their connections via properties and laws) we do find in the world.

In a famous footnote, Kant invokes different unities of consciousness to account for the determinacy of representations. On the one hand, he ascribes the representation of an isolated property to the *analytic* unity of consciousness; on the other hand, he ascribes the representation of the determinacy that this representation possesses in virtue of its connection with others, to the *synthetic* unity of self-consciousness. As the very meaning of the word 'synthesis' suggests, the activity consists in putting something together with something else. Without synthesis, no predicate can be determined, which means that synthesis must precede analysis:[28] we have to put two and two together in order to open up a space for different analyses, such as the analysis of two and two into four times four.

More generally, we have to place objects together in a unified system of representations in order to learn anything about their objective relations. The objects of our representations cannot themselves tell us how to put them together, else we would have to accept a wild metatheory according to which any representation of any object occurring to any subject automatically represents how things are.

Kant shows that analytic unity presupposes synthetic unity. For instance, if we ascribe the property 'red' to an object, we thereby acknowledge that it can or could be ascribed to further objects. In being aware of what one is doing in judging something to be red, one can become aware of the further fact that other objects might be red too. It would be a very strange coincidence – given what we know – if there were only one red object. But even if there were just one red object, this would not entail that there could not be more red objects, for the properties that we perceive acquire their determinacy in virtue of being predicates of possible judgements. The unity of predicates refers us to a variety of unities (objects) to which they could be assigned. To be sure, the range of possible objects to which a given predicate could be applied is not present to a thinker in the sensory mode through which she gets in touch with the given perceived properties that ground the introduction of predicates. Rather, the vital point is that, on this account, the supposedly simple unity of perceivable properties reveals itself to be their mediated universality: individual representations refer to a totality against the background of which they acquire their determinacy in the first place. When we refer to an individual as having this or that property, this background is only dimly present. Yet the cognitively relevant presence of individual objects always relies upon the absence of the totality implicitly at work in our cognitive activity. We get specific objects in view by not having absolutely everything in view. Yet we can always integrate what we do get in view into a larger worldview precisely because the 'world' as the sum total of all objects sets no upper boundary to knowledge acquisition.

The activity of synthesis is guided by a striving for determinacy. Were it not for this striving, we could not explain why we find ourselves in the search for knowledge to begin with – that is, in the incessant search for appropriate predicates and connections. This striving aims to discover the world as a thoroughly determined nexus which, to be sure, can never be fully given: the world is far too differentiated for it to fall within our complete conceptual grasp.[29] It cannot, that is, be an object of first-order knowledge, grounded entirely in sensory encounters with what there is.

Although Kant himself might suggest the very opposite, our theory of synthesis has to start out from the idea that synthetic activity keeps on running precisely because the world in itself is too complex. We can grasp it under an unsurveyable number of descriptions and order it in innumerable ways. And we cannot determine the elements of our various orderings independently of the concepts we bring to bear. This is precisely not to deny that the world consists of distinguishable elements – it is simply to issue a reminder that we have no conceptually unmediated access to those elements – i.e. to any alleged elementary facts. The sheer complexity that the world presents to our conceptual activities proves an incessant impetus to persist in our efforts to bring it within our cognitive grasp. The intelligible order of things stems from the demand to bring order to what Luhmann calls the world's 'noise'.[30] It follows that determinacy is *contingent* complexity reduction: because concepts other than our own are possible, all determinations could be otherwise.

The metatheoretical insight into the difference between already catalogued and as yet unfathomable, unsuspected predicates presupposes the world as an ultimate nexus. Kant calls this the *omnitudio realitatis*. This nexus merely regulates our search for knowledge: since it is precisely that which vouches for the difference between our knowledge and our (current) ignorance, it can itself be neither sought nor found. The world as the condition of possibility of the determinacy of objects cannot itself be a determinate object. Its indeterminacy is a condition of the thoroughgoing determinacy of the objects connected by way of our syntheses.

Our epistemic orientation within the world of representations therefore presupposes a world that both contains all contents and is independent of all and any individual representations. While this is not a presupposition capable of empirical verification or falsification, it is what allows us to embark on the search for knowledge to begin with.[31] The idea of a world is nothing we might stumble upon *in* the world (it is, as we have seen, not an object of intuition). The world cannot be a *content* of the world either – i.e. a way to think of it. In a catchphrase: the world is not of this world.

In short, Kant thinks of the world as a necessary assumption of enquiry, not as an object of discovery. We might also make the point by saying that we confront a world of conditioned things only insofar as our cognitive endeavours are oriented towards something unconditioned. There are no properties we could ascribe to this unconditioned something that would allow us to distinguish it clearly from anything else.[32] The world is thus the ultimate condition of the possibility of the objective reality of our representations: our representations have content if and only if they refer to something that transcends them, something that they discover and do not invent – else they are not subject to the contrast of objectivity. The world enters into the process of our knowledge acquisition as a consequence of our need to articulate the contrast of objectivity. For Kant, this rules out thinking of the world itself as a big object 'out there'; the concept of the world comes into play only when we try to make sense of the unity of our judgements. No judgements, no world. This does not mean that our judgements create the objects about which we judge. But, had there been no judgements, there would not have been an ultimate ground for regulating our inquisitiveness, and that ground is the world.

To be sure, Kant attempts to do justice to the contrast of objectivity primarily with his concept of intuition. On his account, intuitions would have no content without sensations. Yet he nowhere makes it entirely clear where the content of sensation comes from. If it straightforwardly came from the thing in itself, Jacobi's famous objection would hit its target: despite his restrictions on cognition, Kant would have ascribed causality to the thing in itself. Famously, he ascribes causality to appearances and claims that appearances do not exist as extra-mental correlates of representations. Appearances are conceptual representations and, as such, embedded in syntheses. They can therefore hardly be the cause of our sensations having a content which *requires* synthesis. Yet things in themselves cannot be the cause of sensations either, else they would stand in a thoroughgoingly determined causal nexus. Needless to say, this would render Kant's practical philosophy impossible and would in any case contravene his restrictions on cognition, according to which we cannot ascribe any properties to things in themselves, as we cannot cognise them.

It is therefore at the very least puzzling where the content of sensation is supposed to come from. Kant's apparent lack of clarity on this score has triggered the familiar and interminable debates surrounding the ontological status of things in themselves. Here, I do not want to offer yet another *exegetical* contribution towards solving this problem. Instead, I want to make a twofold suggestion. Firstly, we should take over Kant's conception of the world as we have been interpreting it thus far; by availing ourselves of this conception, we can steer clear of hypostatising the world. Secondly, we should assume, *pace* Kant, that there is a world, which our representations straightforwardly and unproblematically grasp in those cases in which our representations are true. The world grasped by true representations of the relevant kind is not *produced* by our representations. Rather, it is the domain of things actually known by us. It differs from the wider domain of the Kantian world, which consists of all knowable objects. The world known by us is, quite trivially, not a candidate for a domain consisting of potentially or even analytically unknowable things in themselves. It is populated by knowable objects, which we can call 'appearances'.

The coherence and structure of the world of representation testifies to the necessary assumption of a representable world, of a world that potentially diverges from our representations. We can accordingly distinguish between the *represented* world and the *representable* world, where the latter is the world we grasp in true judgements, in judgements that assert what is the case. In this way, the *represented* world, in the sense of a domain comprising known objects and facts, is essentially tied to the practice of human knowledge acquisition. Kant, by contrast, reduces the representable world to its function within the epistemological economy of finite beings in a way that forfeits its ontological independence. He leaves open the theoretical space for taking the decisive step towards representationalism, towards equating the world of appearance with the world of representation. Taking this step potentially revokes the very objectivity we originally hoped to gain with the help of Kant's promising conception of the world. For the world is not a representation but, rather, the totality of the representable, the totality of that which features in our discourse whenever we make true judgements. It is worth emphasising here that this position implies neither a naïve form of direct realism (whatever exactly 'naïve' might mean in this context) nor any kind of unwarranted epistemological optimism. It implies neither that we can cognise the world in the absence of conceptual mediation nor that the world as a whole is an object of knowledge just because we can indeed correctly represent some of the ways things in fact are.

Further, from the mere fact that we cannot determine how things are independently of judgements, it does not follow that what is the case is reference-dependent on the existence of beings with the capacity to judge. Nor does it follow from the fact that true judgements describe the world correctly that we necessarily make true judgements about *which* of our judgements are true and which are false.

Since we have no unmediated access to the world in itself, we are dependent upon the practice of making judgements. As we shall see in due course, the 'game of judging'[33] is constitutively social in virtue of the normativity of the logical space we inhabit as objective thinkers. We cannot and need not pierce through to the world in itself in order to ascertain which of our judgements are true: true judgements are not simply results of the successful establishment of a binary relation between mind and world but have to be recognisable from within the game of judging. Acknowledging the sociality of the game is not an invitation to give up on the idea that true judgements have to describe the world in itself. The price of denying this idea is succumbing to the aporetic view that our predicatively mediated access to the world is necessarily distorting. Such a view tends to lead to the absurd doubling of the world into a thing in itself on the one hand and a world of appearances on the other. (It is notoriously a matter of ongoing debate whether or not Kant himself advocated such a 'two-world' view. In light of the reconstruction of his account of the world offered in this chapter, I find such an attribution fairly doubtful.)

Remaining true to the spirit of Kant's conception of the world, we can insist that the world is distinct from the world of our representations. Yet we can also maintain that it is so distinct only given our assumption of a world that is always more than any individual we happen to represent at any given time. This assumption is a condition of the possibility of our having the kind of representations that characterise us as objective thinkers. If Kant himself does not think that there is a world in itself independent of the 'Idea of absolute totality',[34] then neither should we think of the *omnitudio realitatis* as incompatible with the existence of a representable world. Otherwise, we would face the serious threat of a subjectivism that reduces the representable world of first-order theories to the world of representation. The latter, however, is only a concept of the metatheory. Understanding 'the world' as the totality of the representable by no means entails that we should hypostatise it, *pace* Kant's justified provisos. The cost of hypostatisation is a purely causal model of experience, which regards all cognitions of individuals as isolated episodes and fails to take into account that individuals come into view only against the background of a totality that does not itself count among the representable individuals. Since it is not another already determinate object waiting for us to come along and establish cognitive contact, this background remains cognitively unavailable and cannot possibly affect our sensibility.

According to Kant, the meaning of a concept is its 'relation to the object'[35] – i.e. its reference. There can be no reference, however, unless the object is given in a determinate way; that is, there is no meaning without (Fregean) sense. We can therefore see knowledge acquisition as the task of establishing the identity of reference in spite of the multiplicity of sense. This task presupposes the thoroughgoing determinacy of a world order that is in principle open to further discovery. From the fact that the world is given to us in a determinate fashion – i.e. as a field of sense – it does not follow, however, that it does not exist independently of its being so given.[36] On the contrary, the plurality of sense presupposes the singularity of reference, at the risk of erasing the contrast of objectivity. While objectivity is certainly sense-dependent on subjectivity, this does not mean that subjectivity constitutes, let alone produces, objects. Rather, sense dependence merely commits us to the minimal insight that we would have no concept of the objective reality of our representations were these unequipped to represent anything that potentially diverged from them. We have to assume this potential divergence when we try to account for the fallibility of those representations that make epistemic claims to empirical knowledge. Our multiple modes of access to the world constitute subjectivity as a field of sense, and the singularity of the world therefore functions as their decisive contrast-concept. It serves the function of accounting for the unifying pole of reference under conditions of plural access, without thereby turning into a given object of enquiry. This is why the world differs from the universe in the sense of the big object studied by the scientific discipline of modern-day cosmology.

The strength of Kant's anti-sceptical strategy against Cartesian scepticism resides in his concept of the world as a prerequisite of objectivity. As we have seen, he obtains this concept through analysing the conditions of possibility of a semantically stable world of representations. The Cartesian sceptic implies that the world is an aggregate of ready-made objects. Given how our access to it is necessarily mediated by representations, she believes that we can put the existence of this world into question. Yet she thereby misses the problem of the world and remains committed to a naïve ontology of individuals: she thinks of the world as an aggregate of individual objects and thus as a kind of super-object, of which only segments are ever present to us. A misguided theory of representations thus follows from a misguided theory of the world: any theory of intentionality that results in the external *world* problem – i.e. in a doubt directed at the existence of an object named 'the world' – has already fallen victim to an unreflected concept of the world. 'The world' is no object but, at best, the name for a *horizon* within which objects can first be encountered. Kant draws the right consequence both from the external world problem and from the antinomy he located within the very concept of the world, which is precisely why he subjects it to a transcendental reinterpretation.[37]

In Kant's hands, *res extensa* turns into the spatiotemporally extended world of appearances. These are necessarily related to our representations and, as he explicitly asserts, have no existence outside of representations.[38] Yet, even if we reject Kant's problematic (if not downright inconsistent) form-content dualism, we can retain his insight that the world cannot be given in an intuition – i.e. as a content of the world.

Our assumption of a world as the totality of representables is in fact a condition of the possibility of our cognitive projects. Therefore, we should not conceive the world on the model of an object metaphysically external to our representations (as the physical universe of the 'scientific image', for example). Modelling the world as a super-object leaves us entangled in irresolvable theoretical difficulties, all of which stem from conflating a condition of the possibility of constructing content-involving theories with the object of a theory.

This lesson is the positive consequence of Humean scepticism for the concept of the world, the very scepticism which awoke Kant from his dogmatic slumbers. Hume clarified the aporia of mental representationalism, and it is therefore no coincidence that Kant variously attributes this awakening both to Hume and to the antinomy of the world.[39] Nor is it a coincidence that the first *Critique*'s methodological scepticism, which he himself dubs a 'sceptical method',[40] plays a central role in his treatment of the concept of the world.[41]

Kant's reduction of the concept of the world to a regulative idea implies his transcendental idealism. This doctrine asserts that there is no mind-independent world in the sense of a large whole, extended in space and time and populated with individuals. The world, for Kant, is not independent of the existence of finite epistemic beings who refer to objects with the intention of cognising how they are. His concept of the world is therefore negative-dogmatic insofar as it deprives rational cosmology of its object domain: according to Kant, were we to operate under the theoretical conditions implied by the thesis that the world is a thing in itself, it would be impossible to cognise the world. The assumption of a reified world in itself, that is, implies that our cognition of the world, in the best case, encompasses what is independently so. Kant understands such a thesis as 'transcendental realism'.[42] In what follows, I shall follow Putnam in labelling this position 'metaphysical realism'.[43]

3

Metaphysical Realism and the Naïve Ontology of Individuals

By 'metaphysical realism', I understand a position that conceives the world a priori as the totality of all modally robust facts. It is important to stress right away that, insofar as she puts forward a *metaphysical* view, the metaphysical realist is not interested in keeping an open mind about whether the world really is such a totality; this is what I mean by saying that her worldview is a priori. Her worldview cannot be corrected by anything she encounters in the world because she limits the scope of all legitimate investigations to the domain of modally robust facts. This restriction follows from her conception of objectivity, her belief that only one specific kind of object is the genuine article, namely, the knowledge involved in modally robust facts. By a *modally robust fact*, I mean a fact that would still have obtained had nobody ever been around to make any epistemic claim about it; the fact would still have been the fact that it is, independently of our establishing any kind of cognitive relation to it. The supposition that there are modally robust facts seems to follow directly from the epistemological difference between actual knowledge and mere holding-true – that is, from what I have been calling the contrast of objectivity. For whatever it is that we come to know must have been the case 'already' or 'anyhow' before we integrated it to our overall body of knowledge.

Strictly speaking, of course, this implication does not apply across the board – that is, for all species of knowledge; it applies only for objective knowledge. We have knowledge about ourselves as subjects, of social objects such as governments and institutions, of the bundle of self-descriptions favoured by the societies we happen to belong to, and so on and so forth. The respective contents of such instances of knowledge, however, do not comprise modally robust facts. Governments, artworks, societies and life plans do not qualify as modally robust facts because their existence essentially depends on the fact that someone knows something about them: had no one ever noticed that there are governments, there would not have been any governments. And while we might of course quibble over particular cases, it is important not to over-extend the case of standard objective knowledge: there clearly are cases where we possess knowledge of objects that would not have existed had we not known them to be the way they are.

Nevertheless, it has proved a widespread assumption in the history of philosophy that the content of our entire knowledge of the world has to be precisely of 'what is there anyway'. Bernard Williams famously dubbed this assumption *the absolute conception of reality*. He elaborated this conception in the context of an analysis of the concept of knowledge, according to which the world, in the sense of a totality of all modally robust facts, is 'the object of any representation which is knowledge'.[1] This concept of knowledge is, then, far from innocent; it seduces us into entertaining the notion of a world that obtains independently of any epistemically motivated referential activity on our part. Yet two difficulties immediately follow from this supposition.

First of all, as I have already insisted, there are facts that are not modally robust. And we should surely not want to expunge these non-modally robust facts from the world by defining 'the world' just as the totality of all modally robust facts. It is, after all, not only facts about history, ourselves as minded beings, the state, the future, (perhaps even) the past, abstract (e.g. mathematical) entities, etc., which belong to this set; it also, crucially, includes the fact (the thought) *that* the content of our knowledge is exhausted by the totality of all modally robust facts. For if we define the content of all knowledge of the world as a subset of the totality of all modally robust facts and claim to know, in addition, that this satisfies the concept of knowledge, then this piece of second-order knowledge is not *itself* knowledge that has a modally robust fact as its content. Quite trivially, our knowledge as the object of a knowledge claim would not have existed had there never been anyone around to refer to it with epistemic purport. So whenever we determine the relation between world and knowledge in such and such a way, this determination (i.e. the thought that the relation is such and such) clearly cannot itself be a modally robust fact.

One evident difficulty for the metaphysical realist is that, if she wants to keep the phenomena of mindedness anchored in the 'world', she has to take on the task of understanding those phenomena in terms of modally robust facts. But, as we now see, this is far from the only difficulty facing the metaphysical realist: her truly fatal problem concerns the assertability of her own theory. For, on its own assumptions, this theory cannot amount to a claim to knowledge unless it is itself defined as a modally robust fact. If the metaphysical realist truly knew that the content of all knowledge was a subset of the totality of all modally robust facts, the content of her own knowledge (i.e. first-order knowledge) would have to be a modally robust fact too. In that case, this particular content would be something that would have existed independently of anyone's ever referring to it as part of a knowledge claim – which is clearly absurd. The concept of knowledge is just not something that we find among the denizens of the world of modally robust facts.

The concept of first-order knowledge belongs to epistemology. It describes how such knowledge can enjoy the status of objectivity. Whenever I know something about a modally robust fact, the concept of a modally robust fact is thus instantiated while also having other instantiations – namely, all other instances of first-order knowledge. Yet the crucial point is that the concept of first-order knowledge is itself not an object of first-order knowledge but, rather, the object of epistemological theory construction and its knowledge claims. So, according to the stated criterion, first-order knowledge cannot be an object that is itself characterisable in terms of modally robust facts. In other words, it is misguided to assume that first-order knowledge is a natural kind. First-order knowledge does not constitute extra-mental bedrock, even if it remains true that we have to recognise some extra-mental bedrock if we want to understand how instantiations of the concept 'first-order knowledge' can possibly be objective. But there is no need to throw the baby out with the bathwater: we can hold on to the notion that there is objective knowledge of modally robust facts without identifying this particular instance of knowledge with knowledge as such.

Secondly, metaphysical realism implies a form of mental representationalism. It maintains that, whenever we know something, we thereby know how things are 'anyway', and how things are anyway cannot depend on our knowing it. Yet we can only have any empirical access to what is the case anyway because it is, by hypothesis, prior to our epistemic activities. Further, it is clear enough that epistemic claims do not necessarily have to hit their targets but are constitutively subject to conditions of success and failure. It is for this reason that we are epistemically fallible: we can always take false steps and err in our judgements. Now, since the metaphysical realist asserts that she knows a priori that the world is the totality of all modally robust facts, it follows that she can possess only empirical knowledge. Yet if she can possess only empirical knowledge, she cannot know a priori that she can possess only empirical knowledge: she can *know* precisely nothing about the world a priori. If she knows a priori what it takes to have objective knowledge, she should not conclude that what she thereby knows also applies to her knowledge claim. But that just means that she does have to be open-minded about other forms of knowledge after all and cannot hold on to the view that knowledge as such is essentially about how things are anyway.

The epistemological position underpinning metaphysical realism therefore proves to be dialectically unstable. *By presupposing that we can only ever have cognition of limited sections of the world, on the basis that the world is the totality of all modally robust facts, the metaphysical realist overlooks the epistemic claims bound up with her own unexamined conception of the world.* If the world did consist exclusively of modally robust facts, our knowledge of knowledge itself could not feature as one of its elements. However, in that case, what could 'making a knowledge claim' possibly mean? It surely cannot mean that epistemic agents 'inhabit' some further space besides the world, and that they raise their knowledge claims from out of that space, so to speak. It is hard to see how such beings could ever direct their thoughts towards anything in the world, at least not without being taken by surprise by the disconcerting fact that they have to belong to the very domain from which they had previously (and needlessly) excluded themselves – indeed, from which they had excluded themselves *in order* to make knowledge claims.

In light of these pitfalls for metaphysical realism, it pays to consider an aspect of G. E. Moore's objections to Kant's idealist alternative. Moore objected to Kant's replacement of metaphysical realism with transcendental idealism on the basis that this brand of idealism represents a sceptical position, namely, that there is no world in itself. Against Kant, he famously argued that the reality of the world is independent of consciousness by first stretching out his hands and then concluding from the ostensibly evident existence of at least some objects (viz. his hands) that physical objects, and hence the external world, exist. In this argument, the operative criterion for the existence of an external world is accordingly the presence of at least one physical object.[2]

Such a 'demonstration', though, does not do justice to Kant's motivation in formulating the problem of the world, and so it misses its negative-dogmatic import. Nevertheless, Moore's objections do have a bearing on Kant's Refutation of Idealism and, indeed, succeed in undermining the argumentation of that particular chapter of the first *Critique*. At the same time, certain details of Moore's argument help us better understand Kant's basic insight concerning the concept of the world, which we began to discuss in chapter 2. In this way, Moore's justified critique of the Refutations of Idealism provides us with the tools for understanding Kant's own intentions in adding this chapter to the *Critique*. Further developing the outlines of Kant's notion of the world, using Moore's critique as a kind of *via negativa*, will occupy us for the following two chapters. But, to begin with, we need to get the main elements of that critique on the table.

First of all, Moore attributes the following two equivalences to Kant, both of which underlie the overall argument of the Refutation of Idealism:

(1) '[T]he existence of things outside of us' is equivalent to 'the objective reality of outer intuition'.[3]
(2) '[T]hings external to our minds' is equivalent to 'things which are *to be met with in space*'.[4]

According to Moore, trading on these two equivalences serves Kant's project in the Refutation of proving the existence of the external world.[5] The essential idea is that, if we can demonstrate that one of the two sides of the equivalence is necessarily instantiated, we thereby demonstrate that the other side is also instantiated. So a demonstration of the objective reality of our representations a priori by means of transcendental

arguments amounts, according to Kant, to a demonstration of the existence of things outside of us. And if we can prove that things encounterable
in space and time necessarily exist if there are to be representations at all,
we also prove the existence of things external to our consciousness, as
there are representations of things external to our consciousness. Kant
thus infers that there must be things outside of us from the fact that there
are, in any case, *representations* of things outside of us.

With his reinterpretation of the concept of an external world, Kant wants
to show that our representations of things in space correspond to something
we have not ourselves produced. And his strategy here is to argue that
this is a condition of the possibility of self-consciousness – that is, of self-
conscious description of the activity of synthesis. Kant thinks of the sensibly
given manifold as the condition of synthetic activity, and by means of this
manoeuvre he tries to show that what corresponds to our representations
of things in space is not an extra-mental substrate that itself stands in spatial
relations. Instead, against the background of the Copernican revolution, we
have to think of what is given to us subjects as itself related to representations: as the sensible manifold given in space and time.

In the Anticipations of Perception, Kant introduces the notion of the
'real of the sensation',[6] and in his treatment of 'actuality' in The Postulates
of Empirical Thought in General, he simply uses the term 'sensation'.[7] The
receptive finitude of the cognitive subject belongs constitutively to subjectivity, the actuality of which is simply its synthetic activity: to our concepts
of things in space there corresponds a manifold on the side of sensibility,
which the subject posits *as* not posited by her. This manifold is a condition
of the possibility of empirical self-consciousness, of the actualisation of
synthesis, which can only be performed on given material. For Kant, this
means that the existence of a given manifold follows from the very fact of
self-consciousness. In this context, self-consciousness is not an object in the
world but a description of the theory-building process that is Kant's investigation into the structure of reason. And this investigation is committed to
sensations as the material of synthetic activity. It does not follow from this
that Kant engages in any kind of (transcendental) psychology. His task is
not to describe the workings of the human mind under everyday conditions. Rather, 'self-consciousness' is the particular deployment of rational
thought in which we reflect on the constitution of knowledge claims. It is
within this framework that we are entitled to introduce (to posit) sensations
as the material upon which first-order knowledge claims draw, without
thereby succumbing to an empiricist picture of human psychology.

Moore does not delve into the details of Kant's theoretical presuppositions. Instead, he asks whether he succeeds in proving the existence of
things outside us without begging the question. In particular, he wants
to undermine the second equivalence stated above, by attacking Kant's
identification of things outside our consciousness with things encounterable in space. According to Moore, Kant thinks that things which can be
met with in space are necessarily *representations* of things which can be

met with in space. Kant's own premises in fact preclude the assumption of any direct epistemic access to things in themselves, which take up determinate locations in space and time independently of our subjective modes of registration.[8]

The problem is that we can have representations *as though* we were encountering something in space, such as hallucinations or after-images. There are thus many 'objects' that we represent as though we were encountering them in space, even though they are not actually in space, as we can infer from other people's inability to see them. For the visibility of whatever can be met with in space cannot be restricted to visibility to a single person; such objects are necessarily public. After-images, for example, might be regarded as being represented in space – or, more precisely, spatially – without therefore being encounterable in space. We thus need to mark a difference between things 'presented in space' and things 'to be met with in space' – a difference which Kant fails to take into account in his Refutation of Idealism.[9] While things presented in space can be either veridical representations or hallucinations/illusions, things to be met with in space are public objects (if we exclude, for the time being, the possibility of collective illusions).

Kant goes to great lengths to debilitate a forerunner of Moore's illusion argument, and not by coincidence: if he cannot rebut it, his Refutation of Idealism fails. Yet, in this context, he flagrantly begs the question. In the third note of the Refutation, he exploits an empiricist abstractionist theory to explain the contents of hallucinations and delusions, stating that the imagination can never freely produce its own content but generates content 'merely through the reproduction of other outer perceptions'.[10] Since, as the Refutation is to have shown, these 'are possible only through the actuality of outer objects',[11] the illusion argument is meant to have been repelled. But this just means that Kant, from the very outset, clearly presupposes the success of the Refutation in order to disable the illusion argument. The problem is that the possibility of abstracting contents given to us from an external world is precisely what the illusion argument is designed to put into question. Kant's argumentation against the illusion argument is therefore viciously circular: his appeal to an abstractionist theory already assumes that the argument has been refuted, since it understands illusions as abstractions from veridical representations.

Be that as it may, the negative-dogmatic import of Kant's concept of the world eludes Moore. And his alternative to transcendental idealism is therefore of limited appeal, since it ultimately consists in a naïve ontology of individuals – that is, a conception of the world as the totality of what he labels 'physical objects'. As examples of physical objects, Moore names 'my body, the bodies of other men, the bodies of animals, plants of all sorts, stones, mountains, the sun, the moon, stars, and planets, houses and other buildings, manufactured articles of all sorts – chairs, tables, pieces of paper, etc.'[12]

These objects are in fact public in a broad sense, and we certainly ought not to confuse them with representations. Tables are, at the end of the day, not representations, because representations are not tables, where tables are the kinds of items produced in factories, supported by legs, etc. Yet, this does not mean that they are 'physical' in a precise sense. To my knowledge, neither hands, nor tables, nor chairs, nor cats belong to the object domain of physics as it is currently taught and practised at most universities and scientific research institutions. If 'physical object' means as much as 'object studied by actual physics', Moore gets into trouble. The expression 'physical object' is therefore at the very least misleading insofar as Moore's own examples of physical objects do not in fact feature in physics. In another passage, Moore himself concedes that he is unable to define the concept 'physical fact', but he assures us that this is hardly problematic; everyone will surely understand what he means anyhow.[13]

At this stage, we might well confront Moore's list of physical objects with the *problem of conceptual relativity*. This problem has driven several contemporary rehabilitations of Kantian insights, especially in the work of Goodman and Putnam. Say two sufficiently educated and competent observers (two British common-sense philosophers at the beginning of the twentieth century, for example) find themselves presented with a selection of Moorean physical objects at a given place and time. When asked *which* objects are present at that location, it is fair to assume that they ought to agree in their responses.

The situation becomes more complicated, however, when we add a physicist, an artist and an adherent of a religion who ordains that at least one of the items must be treated as a fetish object. If we ask the physicist, for example, which physical objects are present, none of the items on Moore's list would feature in her answer. The artist will also certainly see objects that none of the other participants had noticed, as she will direct her attention at, say, the fine structure of the given materials. The religious believer, meanwhile, will place yet further objects on his own list.

The relevant lesson is that, while *something publicly available* (in Kant's terms = X) is indeed present at the location in question, it is not possible to state what that something is independently of the conceptual preferences of a given group or individual. The question of *which* public objects there are at a given location (i.e. objects distinct from hallucinations or after-images) can only be answered by specifying the meaning of 'object' relative to a set of assumptions concerning what it is for something to be an object in the first place.

At this point, one might object that, while all the participants in our metaphysical debate – the common-sense philosopher, the physicist, the artist and the religious believer – really do agree that they are confronted with physical objects, each ascribes them different properties to those favoured by the partisans of alternative conceptual schemes. Yet this objection presupposes that worldly things are first and foremost physical objects which then exhibit further, *additional*, properties that depend upon an observer's constitution. But whether that is so is precisely what is at stake. Moore's hands or his body are not physical objects in any obvious sense insofar as they are considered *as* Moore's hands or *as* his body. At best, one might say that Moore's hands *consist* of physical objects (of particles of some kind or another).

The concept of 'physical object' as used by Moore belongs to a particular genre of philosophical fiction, which imagines a basal world of primary (and for Moore also secondary) qualities to which we enjoy unproblematic, everyday cognitive access.[14] Remarkably enough, such perplexing objects as artworks, galaxies, physical particles, the nervous systems of elephants, or epistemology seminars never seem to feature in the narratives that play out in this purportedly mundane world. Instead, our actual experience is reduced to an epistemological model on which we are primarily and unproblematically in contact with 'boring' mesoscopic objects. Of course, nobody doubts that many mesoscopic objects are what they are independently of our conceptual preferences. However, large-scale agreement concerning the fact that there are some modally robust facts or other should not mislead us into inflating this consensus into a world picture according to which, say, the world is a big physical object composed of physical parts.

Nobody lives in the world imagined by the alleged realism of the common-sense philosopher (physicists included). On most days at least, a large section of humanity deals almost exclusively with artefacts, which are in any case not what and as they are independently of our concepts and interests. What is more, many people (such as serious believers in Hinduism, for example) instead believe that life is really a dream and that metaphysical realism is therefore quite fundamentally flawed.[15] In fact, a conception of life as a dream is a component of practically all religious traditions. *Philosophical* common-sense realism lacks an empirical basis: it invents a 'common man', the supposed representative of 'common sense', without caring to investigate what people actually believe. Yet common sense is a problem, not a datum to which one can appeal.[16]

The common sense of contemporary epistemology is nothing more than a philosophical invention designed to establish the epistemological superiority of one particular worldview, where what we really have is a standoff. The notion is ultimately invoked in reaction to sceptical paradoxes, and it represents an attempt to fend them off through a would-be anti-sceptical strategy. Against this move, Kant had already pointed out that common-sense philosophy's retreat to a supposed *consensus gentium* represents a 'naturalism of pure reason', behind which lurks nothing less than a species of 'misology'. As he correctly noted, common-sense philosophy finds itself forced to determine the moon's size and distance from earth-bound observers by means of rough visual estimates.[17] Science, which teaches common sense that the world in fact diverges from appearances, already implies the possibility that we will have to submit most of our pre-scientific beliefs to sceptical questioning. Scientific research leads 'to a considerable extent to the delegitimization of everyday knowledge'.[18]

Kant rightly insists on the incompatibility of so-called common sense with scientific knowledge. The project of constructing a notion of 'common sense' to use as a yardstick for measuring the truth or falsity of philosophical theories founders on the simple fact that the sciences exist. What is usually called 'common sense' tends to get by with countless illusions; more often than not, it is a diffuse set of beliefs without any significant common denominator. If we try to discredit methodological scepticism by appealing to common sense, we lose the very critical distance that first puts us in a position to note that the world is not necessarily as it appears to be to a putative naïve observer. Without entertaining at least a minimal difference between being and appearance, there would be no science.

Defining the world as an aggregate of physical objects in space and time does not represent a promising anti-sceptical strategy. Pointing out that we have hands, and that there is therefore an external world, is no way to refute scepticism. I will continue to label the view that the world is such an aggregate of physical objects (in the Moorean sense) a *naïve ontology of individuals*. Typically, advocates of a naïve ontology of individuals rely on a default perspective on things, to the effect that there is exactly one true description of the world, namely the one that breaks it down into objects embedded in modally robust facts.[19] This default perspective reflects a certain metaphysical conception of the world and its constitution which, as we have seen, is put into question by the simple observation that Moore's hands can be physical objects (i.e. mesoscopic individuals) for Moore, a configuration of particles for the physicist, potential aesthetic forms for the artist, and a fetish object for the religious believer.[20] We cannot say what Moore's hands are independently of this conceptual relativity. And without making any conceptual choice among a series of potential candidate descriptions, there is nothing to be said in favour of the notion that the world is, say, a big physical object. The contents of our assertions about the world do not allow of context-independent determination, where a context is individuated by a range of conceptual decisions – conceptual decisions which, as we shall have occasion to discuss extensively, do not themselves have to be transparent within the context itself (see Part II). Quantum physics, Aristotelian cosmo-theology, Spinoza's *Ethics*, and the art and religion of each and every epoch and society are all related to the world; but we cannot just straightforwardly say *what* the world is independently of a conceptual frame of reference. There simply is no such generally shared public object corresponding to what Habermas calls 'the deep knowledge which forms the background of our lifeworld' [*lebensweltliches Hintergrundwissen*].[21] It is conceptual frameworks that first fix how the world is to be conceived, by fixing what counts as an object. The conceptual framework supplied by the background assumptions of a given lifeworld has always already done its work in determining the constitution of whatever objects we can encounter.

4

Conceptual Relativity and the World

In attempting to adopt a position beyond any particular standpoint, we might endeavour to abstract from all conceptual decisions. But this will just mean that we can no longer determine anything at all. The world slides fully out of view. Such a 'view from nowhere' is bound to be descriptively empty, as it leaves us unable to distinguish options from a specific range of possible alternatives; specific alternatives can come into view only given a decision to focus on something rather than something else. Taking a particular conceptual decision immediately establishes one among several possible ways of referring to a logical space and thereby opens up a domain of alternative conceptual decisions. All conceptual decisions (that is, choices of a conceptual frame of reference) are *contingent* – which does not mean that they are arbitrary. Yet we always need to have taken conceptual decisions in order to determine something *as* an individual in the first place, and doing so involves a commitment to a determinate conceptual frame of reference: it is frames of reference that establish what we can so much as register.

Any act of reference to individuals determines a logical space, a domain of objects, over which it quantifies. The act cannot *itself* immediately determine anything about its object domain, as this would require the establishment of a higher-order domain: we would need, by means of a further act, to make the object domain over which the original act quantifies into a further individual, and this individual would accordingly exist in a broader domain. So much follows from the function of the existential quantifier in our reality-directed thought: the quantifier allows us to refer to items within an object domain, but not immediately to the domain itself, at least not without introducing a higher-order domain.[1]

This insight is in fact nothing other than an inheritance of the crucial Kantian thesis we have discussed in the previous two chapters: namely, that the world is the ultimate horizon of our quest for knowledge and, as such, functions merely as the regulative 'Idea of absolute totality'.[2] Without this 'Idea', our ongoing endeavours to articulate the properties of things in and through our practices of predication would grind to a halt. At the same time, however, we ought not to lose sight of the fact that the world is always given to us in a determinate manner. We never have a sense-free, purely referential mode of access to the world in itself, and for this reason it can only ever function as a necessary assumption; it can never exist as some kind of 'super-object', given to a point of view *we* cannot occupy.

At this point, however, we need to take account of two potential objections:

(1) It bears emphasising that accepting conceptual relativity in no way implies that we somehow produce the world by means of our conceptual preferences. On the contrary, having a conceptual framework for our worldly encounters is a condition of the possibility of our discovering the world to begin with. Establishing a conceptual framework is how we decide *what* it is we want to discover and so what ought to *count as* a discovery. Conceptual relativity is therefore compatible with an 'internal realism' that contests the unity of the world in favour of the plurality of versions in which it appears.[3] Thus, in contrast to *metaphysical* realism, *internal* realism asserts that there is no absolute world. Yet this denial does not entail that objectivity vanishes into subjectivity: the fact that conceptual decisions have to be made and then honoured is just what provides a guarantee for objectivity. Objectivity is sense-dependent on subjectivity, which, again, does not mean that subjects produce objects.

A conceptual decision establishes the conditions under which some particular discourse is governed by a norm of truth, a norm which can then be fulfilled or contravened. It is because our conceptual decisions first afford us access to what there is that facts enjoy an independence from our conceptual decisions. Indeed, it would not even be possible for us to seek out anything determinate whatsoever in the world unless such decisions had already been taken. It belongs to the very nature of our concepts that whatever satisfies our quest for knowledge has to be independent of them – at least in some way such that we can make sense of the potential divergence of mere knowledge claims and actual knowledge. As a consequence, we have to do justice both to the world's independence and to its function as the inexhaustible horizon of our cognitive endeavours. Without conceptual decisions, embarking on these endeavours would be impossible. All epistemic projects ultimately rest upon decisions that establish what counts and what does not count as a successful instance of cognition, and the plurality of our conceptual decisions corresponds to a plurality of worlds, in the sense of a plurality of *discourses*. This plurality, to repeat, does not put the unity of the world under threat: insofar as they stand under the condition of the contrast of objectivity, all discourses occur in *one* world and make reference to *one* world.

The important point about conceptual decisions, therefore, is that without them there would be no *determinate* states of the world for us at all. Yet as soon as there are determinate states of the world for us, we can be sure they owe their determinacy to those concepts of which we have become competent users. And, to reiterate, this does not mean that the existence of these states depends on us in the sense that they would not exist if we did not exist; it does not compromise their status as modally robust. Of course, there would be no thoughts, and thus no concepts, were there nobody capable of having thoughts and so of deploying concepts. Our own existence as finite epistemic beings is clearly not a product of our own conceptual preferences. Indeed, being a competent user of the concept 'world' means understanding that the world would still be conceptually determin*able*, and so think*able*, were there nobody around to determine it conceptually. We cannot seriously question this assumption, even if we happen to be committed advocates of some variant of subjective idealism or Leibnizian monadology. Even a subjective idealist like Berkeley thinks there are independent facts about the connection between our information-processing equipment on the one hand and God (who feeds us the information) on the other, and thus still believes there are modally robust facts about what we represent at any given point in time. Both idealism and realism have to start out from the idea that the world is independent of our holding-true. Only it would be wrong to infer from this independence that we can determine what is the case independently of our conceptual preferences. (Note, of course, that this vital distinction between our conceptual determinations and the conceptually determinable is no invitation to metaphysical realism: as we saw in the previous chapter, not all facts are modally robust, and we must accordingly be wary of conceiving of 'the world' as the totality of all modally robust facts.)

Given how even the idealist has to take account of a potential divergence between holding-true and truth,[4] we should not understand the dispute between idealism and realism as though what was up for debate is *whether* the world exists or not. Rather, the dispute centres on the question of *what* the world is: the world would still exist even if all that existed were, say, an evil demon and our minds, with the former manipulating the latter and supplying it with a continual stream of impressions. In this scenario, the world would consist of the evil demon and a number of finite minds, together with their representations. Such a world may well be a less comforting prospect than the familiar world of our everyday assumptions – but it is a world nevertheless. The potential divergence between truth and holding-true is thus a tenet shared by both realists and idealists, even by Cartesians and Humean sceptics. Consider how the evil demon argument itself exploits this potential divergence insofar as it allows truth to differ completely from what we hold to be true.

The finitude of human beings is manifest in the problem of truth. The problem first arises because the contents of the human understanding have to be given; it does not produce them itself. Indeed, this is just what it means for human thinking to be finite thinking. One consequence of this reliance on the given is that the understanding can err in its thinking about objects. Hence thoughts can be true or false. Yet, in virtue of its finitude, the finite understanding cannot avoid claiming that it has operated correctly: it establishes claims to truth, knowledge and validity, despite (and *because of*) the fact that in doing so it is always fallible. Part and parcel of our making epistemic claims to truth is the presupposition that *what* we hold to be true is distinct from our holding it true, such that our holding-true can be true or false.

Now, while Cartesian and Humean scepticism attempt to demonstrate an unbridgeable divide between truth and holding-true, they do so by helping themselves to the concept of the world, in the sense of that which our holding-true potentially misses. This concept of the world corresponds to the metaphysical realism that Cartesian scepticism continually exploits across its multiple formulations. Both Cartesian and Humean scepticism, that is, operate with the difference between the unity of the world on the one hand and the plurality of frames of reference on the other, where it is frames of reference that first make reference to the world possible by fixing what is to count as an element of reference – i.e. as an object. Hence scepticism and metaphysics have always been close companions.

(2) The fact that there is a plurality of referential systems implies neither that they are all equally *warranted* nor that we can simply *choose* between them. So, diagnosing a thoroughgoing conceptual relativity need not bring relativism's notorious problems in tow. In order to take that diagnosis as the basis for an 'anything goes' relativism, we would need an additional argument to the effect that there are no good reasons to prefer one referential system over another in some particular case (or in all cases).

Nor need a highly general thesis of conceptual relativity be the immediate consequence of abandoning the naïve ontology of individuals. In this context, it might be helpful to consider the concept of an object as it features within various aesthetic discourses. In the world of art, we obviously do not find physical objects in the Moorean sense. Instead, we find artworks. If somebody thinks of an artwork as a physical object, we will hardly be inclined to say that she understands it *as* an artwork; rather, we would claim that she has failed to grasp what she is actually confronted with. This basic insight was elevated to programmatic status by so-called abstract art. Famously, Malevich exhibited his *Black Square* (1915) as a representation of the unrepresentable that, according to him, art, religion and science all try to capture but necessarily distort through their conceptual (formal) decisions.[5] In this work, Malevich captures the thing in itself within the image, so to speak, and so manages to lend objective form to a theoretical insight into conceptual relativity. Of course, this particular insight was never the exclusive property of abstract art. Among the great lyric poets of the previous century, Rilke exhibited a peculiar sensibility to the concept of an object. In his *Dinggedichte*, and especially in his *Duineser Elegien*, he guides us towards the question of how the unrepresentable is nevertheless manifest in poetic representations of objects. Such poetic representations compete with the naïve ontology of individuals insofar as they advocate the primacy of the enchanted world over the world of 'numbers and figures' (Novalis) – that is, over the world of physical objects in the strict sense. The idea that art and science spar not only over the concept of an object but also over that of the world finds a celebrated illustration in Novalis's poem *Wenn nicht mehr Zahlen und Figuren* (1799/1800):

Wenn nicht mehr Zahlen und Figuren
Sind Schlüssel aller Kreaturen,
Wenn die, so singen oder küssen,
Mehr als die Tiefgelehrten wissen,
Wenn sich die Welt in's freie Leben,
Und in die Welt wird zurückbegeben,
Wenn dann sich wieder Licht und Schatten
Zu echter Klarheit werden gatten,
Und man in Märchen und Gedichten
Erkennt die ewgen Weltgeschichten,
Dann fliegt vor Einem geheimen Wort
Das ganze verkehrte Wesen fort.

When numbers and figures
Are no longer the keys to all creatures,
When they who sing, or kiss
Know more than the deeply learned,
When the world itself reverts again
To free life and to a (free) world,
When light and shadow too
Are wed again unto true clarity,
And one recognizes in fairy-tales and poems
The (ancient) true histories of the world,
Then, there flies away before a single secret word
This entire inverted existence.[6]

In *Being and Time*, Heidegger had already attacked the misplaced concept of the world supposed by the naïve ontology of individuals. It is no accident that when, in his later thought, he wanted to separate out the concept of the *thing* from that of an *object* of representation, he sought truth in poetry and aligned himself with Hölderlin and Trakl, as well as with Rilke and Novalis.

Yet we hardly need advert to aesthetic treatments of the concepts of 'object' and 'world' (which, of course, I have merely touched upon here) in order to see that their treatment at the hands of the naïve ontology of individuals is as problematic as it is seemingly natural. As we noted in the previous chapter, the concept of the world as the spatiotemporally extended totality of Moorean physical objects does not overlap with that of modern physics; in the domain of investigation of modern physics we will not find mesoscopic objects such as G. E. Moore (at least not understood in the way Moore understands physical objects). That Moore cannot simply retreat to 'the everyday' is something we can also learn from Heidegger: the concept of the world perpetuated by the naïve ontology of individuals represents a phenomenologically inadequate portrayal of our everyday engagement with the world. The 'everyday' is a complex philosophical problem, of which common-sense philosophy does not even begin to give an adequate formulation.

Therefore, there is nothing paradoxical in the assumption of a thoroughgoing conceptual relativity. It need by no means imply that we have no criteria for individuating objects. All it says is that there are no overall – maximally general – individuation facts. Local individuation relative to domains is sufficient for objectivity. Far from leading us to any unacceptable conclusion, it is an indispensable feature of our actual engagement with the world. And, as such, it is not a phenomenon we can afford to ignore. Yet, when we reduce that engagement to a purely theoretical attitude, it is a phenomenon that is liable to slip from view.[7]

The thesis of a thoroughgoing conceptual relativity does, however, presuppose the unity of the world as the ultimate object of our acts of reference, even if we can never encounter this world *in propria persona*, as it were.[8] We cannot encounter the world itself in space and time. Following Kant, we can call the objects we encounter within a determinate conceptual framework 'appearances',[9] where these contrast with the world in itself or *the transcendental object*[10] – that is, the world we have to assume in order to secure the commensurability of a multiplicity of conceptual frameworks. Accordingly, the transcendental object here assumes the function of a final unity to which all predications are related: in playing this role, it designates nothing further than an empty objectivity, which only ever appears to us in the form of determinate things. Once we make this distinction, the concept of the world functions as the ultimate background or 'dimension of distinctions' of different determinations.[11] The *transcendental object* is therefore the label for what is represented in our representations without ever appearing as a determinate representation among others. This is not to say that it is located in any sense beyond, behind or outside of our representations – if it were, we would be led back to the aporia of mental representationalism. Rather, it is always represented under some description or another. Thus understood, it is an object of our proto-reference, so to speak, something we strive to represent, but cannot. As the transcendental object, it is at once present and absent; while we certainly represent it, we can never grasp it – and so represent it – independently of a determinate description.

In Frege's example of the evening star and the morning star, which he famously employs to explain his sense/reference distinction, the transcendental object would be the common referent of evening star and morning star, without our ever attaining a sense-free mode of access to it. There is no access to the transcendental object independent of a determinate description. Even if we introduce the proper name 'Venus' for the referent of 'evening star' and 'morning star', the reference still figures for us under a determinate description, namely *as* Venus. It belongs to the conceptual history of Venus that it appears as the morning star on the one hand and as the evening star on the other hand, which is evidently not true of either the morning star or the evening star. The concept 'Venus' is thereby distinguished from the evening star and the morning star and so represents what they also represent under a different description. The point is that, whichever descriptions we might wish to use in place of these expressions, it is impossible to describe something without marking some conceptual preference. This is just what the *thesis of conceptual relativity* amounts to. Yet the thesis presupposes the assumption of a world in itself, our transcendental object, to serve as the reference of all meaningful expressions.

As in Kant, the transcendental object functions first and foremost merely as a restriction on sensibility. That is, it is a means of distinguishing our representations of the world from the world they represent, and there can be no mode of access to the latter whose veridicality is guaranteed automatically simply in virtue of its being the mode of access that it is (which, note, does not mean that our representations distort the world). The transcendental object (which Kant also calls the 'noumenon in the negative sense') is 'therefore merely a **boundary concept**, in order to limit the pretension of sensibility'.[12] It is that something of which all we can know is that it is a necessary assumption of our cognition; it is what ensures that our *representations of the world* are distinguishable from the *world represented*. In other words, the world is a necessary assumption of the metatheory that refers to the contrast of objectivity between subjectivity and objectivity, the contrast deployed by every first-order theory and, therefore, by pre-theoretical consciousness as well. Accordingly, we should regard the assumption of a world in itself as a consequence of the contrast of objectivity: wherever the contrast of objectivity applies, a world in itself is presupposed.

If we want to be able to draw a distinction between empty representations and representations with content, we have to acknowledge a possible divergence between representation and the world. The transcendental analysis of our representations should therefore never lead to the absurd result that all representations are true. Of course, our metatheory can never step outside of representations altogether and compare them with the world in itself. Yet, since the distinction between representations and the world in itself belongs merely to the metatheory, it is not a statement of any first-order theory which has the world itself as its representable object.

Adopting a different terminology, we can say that the assumption of a world in itself is ontological, not ontic: it does not describe what is the case anyhow but, rather, illuminates *how* we can refer to what is the case anyhow. We can guarantee the objective reality of our representations, their 'worldliness' so to speak, only by qualifying what we represent as something whose being does not simply merge into its being observable – i.e. through some conceptual frame of reference. As Luhmann continually underlines, the world 'is the blind spot of observation – that which one cannot observe when one has decided to make an observation with the help of a specific distinction.'[13]

In our metatheory, therefore, the position assigned to a world (to what is supposed to be independent of and represented by our representations) has to be occupied a priori. That is to say, it is a necessary component of our conceptual repertoire. What the world is like, however, cannot be specified a priori, meaning that the world finds its way into our meta-theory at best as a transcendental object. The assumption of a world in itself is a consequence of the structure of our representations of the world; these are wrung from us in such a way that they appear as representations *of something*, such that this something can never be fully represented.[14]

According to Kant, it is as a result of this structure that we are essentially knowledge-seeking or fundamentally heuristic beings tasked with trans-lating the world into representations, with determining the determinable. In going about our cognitive tasks, we are oriented towards a something that we can never completely grasp. At any given point, at pain of jeop-ardising the objectivity corresponding to the contrast of objectivity, we have to contemplate the possibility that the empirical distinctions in terms of which we observe the world might prove inadequate. Yet, for it to be so much as intelligible that the world potentially encompasses more than we currently know, we have to reckon with a noumenon in the negative sense. This can never become an object of our cognition but is merely a necessary constituent of the 'universal search field' [*universelles Suchfeld*] within which we hope to make an 'assertoric find', to use another expres-sion of Wolfram Hogrebe's.[15]

In short, we can embark upon the search for knowledge only because there always remains something as yet unknown. Because this insight is a priori, we can build it into the 'architectonic of pure reason' as a condition of the possibility of objectivity. The 'something' to which all our representations refer, without itself being *representable*, must therefore be *thinkable*. It is a concept we have to possess in order to develop a satisfac-tory concept of potentially content-bearing representations.

In my view, this line of thought operates in the background of Kant's Refutation of Idealism. We can gain a better understanding of this laconic chapter (which, if taken in isolation, is barely comprehensible) if we read it as invoking nothing less than a version of the distinction under discussion, namely between our changing representations and their persisting transcendental object which, qua persisting, is 'substance'.[16] Reconstructing Kant's highly elliptical argument in the Refutation would require an extensive account of the role played by the 'world' in ground-ing the distinction between contentful and empty representations. And this would itself require a lengthy piece of Kant exegesis which I cannot undertake here. My present concern is only to show how the Kantian concept of the world and the Refutation of Idealism belong together. For Moore's critique of Kant certainly hits its target *provided* we take the Refutation of Idealism in isolation. And given how Kant claims that the Refutation is indeed comprehensible on its own terms (it consists, after all, of a theorem and its 'proof'), it is admittedly a grave problem that, as we saw in the previous chapter, its argument is ultimately circular.

So that Kant's own wording is not fully lost from view, it should be noted that, strictly speaking, the Refutation of Idealism concerns only the concept of substance (the persistent) and not that of the world. Substance, for Kant, would be inconceivable without the distinction between a '**thing** outside me' and 'the mere **representation** of a thing outside me'.[17] Unfortunately, Kant makes no explicit reference here to the transcendental object.

Moore's argument against Kant appeals to how the Transcendental Aesthetic is already supposed to have shown that things outside of me must be things in space. Yet things in space are things intuited in space. Now, the intuition of space is itself not a thing [*Ding*] but a condition [*Bedingung*] of there being things for a subject; for space is a pure form of intuition, which we must always already have supplied in order to be confronted with anything that occupies a different location from ourselves. Whatever is intuited in space is so intuited that it is not where something else is; and in order to learn that something is located somewhere other than something else, we already have to come equipped with space as a form of intuition; we cannot first learn about this form (a posteriori) by being told that something has a different location from something else. And, consequently, the concept of space is prior to the concept of multiple locations (of restricted space) in the same way that the concept of the world is prior to the concept of a determinate object.

The problem now is that, according to Kant in the Refutation of Idealism, everything that is intuited outside of me is an object. So, Moore's first equivalence (see chapter 3, above), between *the existence of things outside of us* and *the objective reality of outer intuition*, applies here. Yet, as Moore insists, many things are intuited in space without in fact having a spatial location. Kant himself registers this potential difficulty in the third note on the Refutation and dismisses it as unproblematic for his argument. But, as we have seen, his dismissal involves an unfortunate appeal to a highly questionable abstractionist theory to explain the contents of dreams and hallucinatory states (and, whatever problems this theory faces on its own account, its empiricist basis makes it systematically adequate in the context of the *Critique*). An uncontrolled function of the imagination (i.e. a function cut off from its usual relation to the world) would draw its contents 'merely through the reproduction of previous outer perceptions, which, as has been shown, are possible only through the actuality of outer objects.'[18]

Kant thus helps himself to a contention that would in fact first have to be demonstrated against the argument from illusion. His appeal in the note to the informational sources of dreams remains viciously circular: it asserts that representations as if p, such as we would have under the conditions of a Cartesian sceptical scenario (e.g. of being a brain in a vat), would be possible only had we already had the opportunity to record representations that p at an earlier stage in our cognitive biographies. Kant does explicitly confront the objection that our representations might only be dreams or that we might intuit certain things in space via halluci- nations, without their actually existing in space. Yet his argument already presupposes the Refutation of Idealism, which is precisely designed to show that we could not have representations of objects without there being objects outside of us. But things outside of us are things in space. Things in space are, in turn, things intuited in space, since space is a form of intuition, and there can be nothing outside of us that cannot be intuited outside of us. Consequently, hallucinations are also things outside of us, if being intuited in space is sufficient to satisfy the concept of being a thing outside of us. Kant evidently fails to take specific account of the necessary conditions of the *publicity* of things in space, and this is what makes room for Moore's objection that hallucinations too would be 'things in space' in Kant's sense.

We thus have to distinguish *representing something as spatial* from *representing something spatial*. When someone represents something spatial, they represent something that is publicly accessible, although, as cases of dreams and hallucinations testify, not everything that we represent *as* spatial can be represented by others. We cannot infer a priori that there actually is something persistent in space from the mere fact that some- body is representing something spatially; something persistent, which is represented spatially, is something that, as spatial, is publicly accessible.

To be sure, publicity is not yet a sufficient criterion for a representation of something spatial; we also have to represent the relevant others who themselves refer to the putatively public object as spatial. What we repre- sent spatially is not necessarily something spatial that we represent – so, if we did take publicity as a criterion, we would need another criterion of publicity for our criterion of publicity and find ourselves caught in a vicious circle. Nevertheless, the publicity criterion is an element of our concept of what it means to represent something spatial, for it is ulti- mately the criterion we apply in order to distinguish true from illusory representations of something existing in space. To acknowledge this is not to introduce publicity as an anti-sceptical criterion; it is simply to point to its necessity for distinguishing between a representation of something in space and a spatial representation – a distinction ignored by Kant's Refutation of Idealism.

At most, Kant's Refutation shows the possibility of distinguishing between the production and reproduction of spatial representations. This distinction belongs to transcendental philosophy; it is an element of the metatheory. However, the Refutation does not prove that there are *in fact* reproductions; it merely insinuates that there are. As already mentioned, since Kant presupposes an empiricist abstractionist theory of the content of dreams, hallucinations, and the like, he already assumes that there are reproductions. Contrary to Kant's explicit claim, then, the Refutation demonstrates neither the 'existence of things outside of us'[19] nor the existence of a persisting substrate of our representations. And if all he succeeds in showing is that there could be reproductions of representations, then he has hardly given us what he claims: namely, objections to either the Cartesian sceptic or the Berkeleyan idealist.

Kant's transcendental philosophy does not always operate with a sufficiently clear distinction between different levels of theorising.[20] In my view, this failure is responsible for the persistent and notorious ambivalence that attaches to the concept of the thing in itself, or to talk of things outside of us, of substance, and so on. On the one hand, Kant seems to introduce the thing in itself as a necessary element of the metatheory. On the other hand, though, he denies it an independent existence insofar as he maintains that all determinate existence is categorially determined and thus constituted through subjectivity. The key question is thus whether objectivity and subjectivity are merely sense-dependent or whether they are also reference-dependent.[21] If they are only sense-dependent, it means that the concept of objectivity presupposes that of subjectivity. This insight would have to be asserted within the metatheory, where the distinction between thing in itself and representation (appearance) is drawn. Yet no reference dependence follows from this – that is, no thesis to the effect that there would be no objects were there no subjects. Proving reference dependence would require an additional argument.[22]

Kant himself, at any rate, does not give us an unequivocal account of how to distinguish first-order theories, which have objects as their contents, from the metatheory, which has first-order theories as its content. I would therefore suggest we confine the distinction between thing in itself and representation to the metatheory and accordingly argue for the thesis that subjectivity and objectivity are only sense-dependent. This puts us in a position to say that true representations represent the world in itself, which is simply to articulate a basic assumption deployed in all first-order theories that contain statements about states of the world. The metatheory, by contrast, operates from a standpoint of theorising, which remains unavailable to the first-order theories themselves. It explains how there can be incommensurable, mutually irreducible theories in the first place only if we mark a distinction between representations and the world. This distinction, as we have seen, is induced by methodological scepticism, which is responsible for motivating the original switch from a first-order theory to a metatheory (which I shall henceforth call a 'theory-level transition').[23]

This means that we can comfortably assume a world in itself without indulging any of the subjectivist tendencies that might otherwise tempt us towards reference dependence. At the same time, the thesis of conceptual relativity enables us to avoid metaphysical realism insofar as it understands the world not as the totality of all modally robust facts but as the dimension of distinctions. Since we can grasp this dimension only under a determinate description, it is determined in and through all true judgements without ever being completely describable. The sense dependence of objectivity and subjectivity ensures that some brute facts are inaccessible to us.

With his Refutation of Idealism, Kant claims to have shown that we could have no semantically stable representations at all if there were no substance (if everything were a hallucination, for example). But what if the 'substance' underlying our representations were a world inhabited by ambitious scientists who feed our disembodied brains with a constant flow of information, so that we merely hallucinate a world of things outside of us? In such a scenario there would be things outside of us (scientists, their machines, the world we inhabit, and so on), and these things would even be the causes of our representations, such that our representations alter while the things outside of our representations persist. The Refutation of Idealism is thus compatible with any sceptical hypothesis you like, as long as it contains something or other that counts as persistent. Since we can concoct potentially infinitely many sceptical hypotheses of this kind, in which all our beliefs save one (namely, that there is a substance) are false, the outlook seems bleak for Kant's Refutation insofar as it aims to be an anti-sceptical strategy against Cartesian scepticism.

Kant's retreat into the world of representation (through his versions of $Hume_1$ and $Hume_2$; see above, p. 32) cannot be reversed by the Refutation of Idealism alone. We can learn this much from Moore. Nevertheless, when confronted with Moore's argument, every Kantian will surely feel an irresistible urge to protest. And in the broader context of his system, Kant's Refutation certainly does take on a different aspect: seen in context, it is clear that he has more resources at his disposal to make an a priori distinction between the world as representation and the world in itself. He just fails to make it clear that this distinction derives from a sceptically induced shift to the metatheoretical level, and this lack of clarity brings numerous ambiguities in its wake. One of the crucial tools at his disposal is his concept of the world, which, unfortunately, tends to be neglected discussions of 'external world' scepticism. These discussions frequently neglect the issue of the *world* in favour of the question of the existence of familiar contents (objects) *in* the world. This is certainly true of Moore's argument that an external world must exist if his hands exist, since hands are objects and the world is composed of objects (the account of the world we have designated as the *naïve ontology of individuals*). Yet Kant owes his awakening from his dogmatic slumbers not only to Hume but also to his engagement with philosophical cosmology. It was through this engagement that he gained his lifelong attachment to the distinction between *mundus sensibilis* and *mundus intelligibilis*. Far from abandoning this distinction after his critical turn, he simply subjected it to a subtle reinterpretation.[24]

Yet, in the Refutation itself, Kant fails to address a central sceptical problem. This is the problem that arises if we accept that the world of our representations could *seem* to be just as coherent and object-related even if there were no objects – that is, if the world in itself diverged completely from the world of representations in all its determinations. The insufficiencies of the Refutation thus derive from its failure to achieve an adequate focus on the very problem it sets out to solve. And this difficulty certainly hangs together with the fact that Kant's theory as a whole constitutes a 'refutation of idealism', given how it aims to distinguish a priori between empty and contentful representations. The weaknesses of the Refutation in the narrow sense are not reproduced in Kant's global project, or at least not in the same way.

According to Kant's metatheory of representation, the concept of a transcendental object 'remains not only admissible, but even unavoidable, as a concept setting limits to sensibility.'[25] Under the Humean sceptical conditions that form Kant's point of departure, without the 'unknown something',[26] we would be left with nothing but solipsism: we would be trapped in our representations as if p, without any grounds entitling us to the assumption that at least some representations as if p *must* be representations that p.[27] That, however, would amount to a triumph for the sceptic, to the 'scandal of philosophy and universal human reason that the existence of things outside us (from which we after all get the whole matter for our cognitions, even for our inner sense) should have to be assumed merely on faith, and that if it occurs to anyone to doubt it, we should be unable to answer him with a satisfactory proof.'[28]

In order for us to come to know anything objective, there must always be something unknown. We continually have to determine this unknown something without ever being able to bring our determining activity to any kind of ultimate conclusion. As finite beings, our epistemic lives consist essentially in the undertaking to comprehend the world, and this finite, discursive existence would come to an end if we somehow reached a point at which the search for knowledge finally attained its goal of achieving complete knowledge of reality. It is for this very reason that Pyrrhonian scepticism recommends continually extending our pursuit of knowledge (ἐπιμονὴ ζητήσεως), a pursuit which cannot be interrupted by setting any definitive limit to our cognitive possibilities. Sextus Empiricus accused negative dogmatism of trying to establish just such a limit: 'And if everything is clear, there will be no such thing as investigating and being in an impasse about something. For a person investigates and is in an impasse about a matter that is unclear to him, not about what is apparent. But it is absurd to do away with investigation and impasse.'[29]

Moore would surely be unimpressed if it were pointed out to him that the 'external world' in fact functions as a necessary assumption within a broader philosophical account of the possibility of veridical representations. Yet we cannot allow him any direct reference to physical objects at the metatheoretical level. Introducing the distinction between the world in itself and representation at this higher-order level is an attempt to pay tribute to the Kantian insight that the 'unknown something' does not exist as some mysterious magnitude external to our epistemic intentionality but serves merely as a necessary assumption if we want to secure the contrast of objectivity from a metatheoretical standpoint. The thing in itself, on this understanding, is epistemologically necessary (indispensable for any stable metatheory), without representing extra-mental bedrock.

By his own admission, Moore is in no position to understand Kant's distinction between the thing in itself and things that can be encountered in space (appearances).[30] In failing to grasp this distinction, however, Moore misses at least two points: first, the role played by Kant's concept of the world in determining his concept of an external world; and, second, the significance of sceptical arguments for conceptual relativity. Arguments for conceptual relativity first make us aware that we have no unmediated access to the world in itself, and, as a consequence, it is only once we allow for conceptual relativity that we can introduce the distinction between thing in itself and appearance.

Accordingly, the thing in itself functions as a boundary concept, which stands in for the unity of the world (of reference) over against the multiplicity of our various modes of access. As we have seen, the distinction between thing in itself and appearance is motivated by a sceptically induced shift to second-order theorising. Indeed, it is only from the standpoint of a second-order theory that the distinction has intelligible applications, meaning that deploying the distinction is an altogether different enterprise from establishing a revisionary first-order theory of what does and does not exist. The thing in itself is thus not one thing that exists alongside others. It is, as it were, the name for the circumstance that we can refer to determinate items only by selecting and quantifying over an object domain. In this sense we can agree with Quine that 'being', in the sense of existence, is the value of a bound variable (namely of the existential quantifier). The dimension of distinctions as such – i.e. the world – is itself not some determinate thing which might occur in a particular object domain.

It will therefore make sense, in what follows, to equate the thing in itself with the world and accordingly to speak of the 'world in itself'. This is not to postulate the world as a mysterious super-thing which we cannot cognise. In Kantian terms, the world is not a noumenon in the positive sense. By 'world', I merely understand the fact that our different modes of access are always modes of access to something – namely to the world. When we succeed in making true judgements about what is the case, we grasp how the world is via conceptual mediation (that is, under a determinate mode of presentation). There is thus no unbridgeable chasm gaping between truth and the world built into the very notion of a world. The world is introduced in the metatheory in order to make sense of the contrast of objectivity, but it makes no appearance on the first-order level of object-directed cognition. We perceive concrete objects, but not the world.

For Kant, the world is the idea of a totality that comprises everything determinate, the *omnitudio realitatis*.[31] He therefore integrates the representation of a world in itself as an 'idea' into the world of representation: the idea of a world serves to orient our dealings with our representations when we ascribe objective reality to them. We have determinate representations – that is, representations of determinate items – only when we can distinguish them from other representations in some specifiable fashion. For Kant, an isolated representation can have no propositional content and so fails to be a representation of anything.

However, to maintain this kind of position about determinacy, we have to reckon with a totality of relations between all possible contents, and this is what Kant calls the 'world'. When introducing a Kantian concept of the world, it is important to keep hold of the idea that it is neither necessary nor possible to cast aside the veil of representation and gain a glimpse of how things unfold behind appearances. In order to guarantee the objective reality of our representations, it suffices to join Kant in setting out a sufficiently thorough and detailed analysis of the logical structure that characterises the (transcendental) conditions for representations to bear propositional content. Given such an analysis, for representations to be veridical, the propositional content of all representations must be a function of their totality. This holistic idea is supported by the principle that the determinacy of a propositional content is its difference from all other contents. In other words, it is supported by the idea of the world as something that transcends any given positive content, in that it can never be positively grasped as one item among many.

> Kant₂) The determinacy of representations is conceptual and explicated in judgements. There are no determinate representations without judgements and therefore no determinate representations without conceptual content.

The method of transcendental philosophy, which Kant explicitly owes to his engagement with Humean scepticism, also provides him with a solution to the sceptical problem of causality.[32] This problem derives from the thought that, although we certainly assume that the world is causally constituted, we can only infer this from our representations. Being finite, these only ever present us with a limited range of cases from which we have to infer an organising law, meaning our inference to the causal constitution of the world is inductive and thus fallible. For our purposes, Kant's procedure in addressing this problem is of particular interest. He attempts to show that we necessarily interpret our representations such that what they represent stands in causal connections. To be more precise, Kant maintains that we can have no representations of the world without connecting them in such a way that they can be brought into an objectively ordered series by means of the concept of causality.

In the present context, the details of Kant's individual arguments are less important than his general anti-sceptical strategy, which, as we discussed in chapter 2, functions as an integrative moment of his negative dogmatism. This overall strategy consists in drawing an inference from reflection on the structure of the conceptual determinacy of representations to the order of the representable world. A central element of Kant's argumentation here is the thought that we could not even have representations were they not already interpreted: 'Thoughts without content are empty, intuitions without concepts are blind.'[33] For Kant, the capacity to have representations implies the necessity of applying a determinate set of concepts to combine them (specifically: pure concepts of the understanding, *alias* 'categories', and concepts of reason, *alias* 'ideas'). In order to have so much as propositional content, our representations must be connected.

Further, given the *principle of determinacy through difference*, the propositional content of a representation is its differential connection with all possible propositional contents. Now, causality belongs to the set of concepts that guarantee a thoroughgoing connection of all states of the world. At the same time, without the concept of a causal order obtaining among worldly states, there would be no objectivity at all and thus no propositional content. For without the concept of causality we would not be able to make intelligible how the order of worldly events differs from the psychological order of our apprehension of worldly events – i.e. from the temporal succession of our representations.[34]

In order to establish the general thesis that there can be nothing in the objective world that does not stand in relation to everything else, we have to reach out in thought to the world as a whole. The idea of the world, for Kant, is accordingly the ultimate condition of the possibility of our capacity for representation, since representations have to possess an intentional propositional content in order to be determinate. To this end, though, they have to be related to the totality of possible propositional contents, the *omnitudio realitatis*. *For us*, this totality is only a horizon; yet, *in itself*, it is a thoroughgoingly ordered nexus. We presuppose the world as a horizon in order to guarantee the determinacy of the representable and thus the objectivity that goes hand in hand with the fallibility of finite knowers.

Since our judgements can be wrong, we have to allow that the world in itself can always be other than we represent it to be. How it really is cannot be ascertained a priori, but only through empirical investigation; we cannot determine the truth and falsity of our representations without recourse to experience. Yet in order to make the need for such recourse intelligible, we must take the world into account as a horizon, where this horizon cannot itself be any kind of determinate object that represents a possible candidate for objective knowledge. In other words, the world is not a fact for us but the sum total of factuality; it is what guarantees that everything is thoroughgoingly determined. What is in fact the case is a determination of the world in itself, and we can know something of this world only when we decide to participate in the game of judgement and begin to raise knowledge claims.

Contrary to Kant's tendency to reduce the world solely to its function as epistemic horizon, it seems to me vital to insist, firstly, that true judgements describe the world in itself and, secondly, that the concept of the world as horizon belongs to a metatheory that clarifies our access conditions to, not the states of, the world in itself. The concept of the world as horizon thematises the world as a condition of the possibility of objectivity, whereas the world is the content of all true judgements made within first-order theories, the totality of objects and their constellations. Expanding the concept of the world in this way does not imply any kind of 'two-world' doctrine, with the world as horizon and the world as a totality of everything that is the case on different sides of an ontological divide. Each concept of the world belongs to a different level of theorising, and so we need not entertain any dubious doubling of the world. From the fact that objectivity is possible only against the background of an always elusive horizon, it does not follow that there would be no objects were there no horizon (and thus no subjects). The concept of a world is an intelligible part of a metatheory only insofar as we are interested in drawing a distinction between objectivity and subjectivity; but, given its epistemological indispensability to finite knowers, an interest in the distinction is inevitable.

Kant thus accepts variants of both Hume$_1$ and Hume$_2$. He aims to make a virtue of Kantian negative dogmatism from the necessity of Humean scepticism: he conjures a positive thesis out of the dilemma that results from conjoining two genuinely Humean premises, namely that (1) we are imprisoned within a world of representations, which (2) we are forced to interpret, even though we philosophers know that the interpretations we produce lack an objective anchoring. According to Kant, however, we are not *imprisoned* within the world as representation, because it is senseless to talk of a world outside of the supposed prison. In saying as much we have already situated the world within the prison walls. And if we knew that we were locked into our representations, we would know *ipso facto* that there was an external world.

Nevertheless, insofar as Kant's transcendental idealism conflates the world with its function as a regulative idea, it compromises the commonplace idea of a world in itself, of that which acts as a truth-maker for the judgements of first-order theories. Kant reduces the world qua totality of all objects and object constellations to the idea of a regulative unifying horizon. But we can avoid this reduction if we disambiguate the concept of the world – world in itself/world as representation – across different theory levels. We can first posit the world in itself as thoroughly determined and explain how its relevant determinations are what are discovered by first-order theories; and we can then recognise how *this* insight is elaborated within a metatheory, a theory within which the distinction between world in itself and representation functions as a necessary assumption for making the contrast of objectivity explicit. Only the metatheory contains the insight that, for us, the world in itself is always a horizon.

As we have already mentioned, however, this insight need imply only that objectivity is sense-dependent on subjectivity, not that objects are reference-dependent on subjects. As noted above, to arrive at the stronger thesis of reference dependence would require an additional argument for construing the insights of the metatheory as statements of a first-order theory whose content is the world in itself. If Kant's negative dogmatism ultimately denied that there is a world in itself and instead restricted the concept of the world to the realm of representations, this would indeed approximate to the error of interpreting a metatheoretical insight as a negative ontological statement to the effect that something or other – in this case the world in itself – does not exist. Yet Kant merely shows that the concept of the world fulfils an irreplaceable function in our access to an objective reality. Accepting this does not mean accepting that there is no world in itself. It does not mean denying the existence of a thoroughgoingly determined total nexus comprised of states which, unproblematically, can appear as the contents of ordinary first-order theories.

In contrast to Hume, Kant operates at a metatheoretical level insofar as he no longer reckons with a given yet unknowable objectivity, a transcendent world in itself, but instead thematises the contrast of objectivity as such – that is, the source of the subjectivity/objectivity distinction. There is thus a crucial insight in Kant, which it pays to hold onto. We can formulate it as follows: *The assumption of objective being (in the sense of being-the-case) depends on the possibility of its appearance. Appearances are truth-evaluable, true or false, and hence require truth itself as a norm.* This formulation accounts for what Anton Friedrich Koch describes as the *phenomenal aspect* of the concept of truth.[35] For us, being and appearance together belong to truth because the plurality of appearances indicates the unity of the world. This is just what is expressed by the norm of truth, which determines the standard for the identity and difference of being and appearance. What is true is not identical to what we take to be true. In order for such a distinction to be applicable to our mental lives as knowers, something has to play the role of that which can potentially mislead us. And given that the truth cannot potentially mislead us in the required way, we are entitled to introduce a concept of appearance. It is appearances that let us explain the notion of error.

In the course of expounding his negative dogmatism, Kant also provides an elaborate error theory to explain how we come to conflate concepts that play a functional role in the constitution of the world of representation with meta- or, rather, hyperphysical entities (God, the soul and the world). These entities are pure concepts of reason, concepts necessary for the structural formation of representations bearing potentially objective content, but they are not objective contents themselves. In chapter 2, I reconstructed Kant's thesis that the concept of the world is a regulative idea, a concept that fulfils a unifying function. The regulative roles of God and the soul, by contrast, transcend the scope of theoretical philosophy. We can set them aside here, given how our present topic is the motivation of Kant's negative dogmatism in the dialectic of Cartesian and Humean scepticism.

It would take us too far afield to provide anything like a systematically and exegetically adequate account of Kant's entire error theory and the details of the underlying doctrine of 'transcendental subreption'.[36] My concern here is merely to set out the basis of Kant's anti-sceptical strategy because it represents an especially clear example of negative dogmatism. Suffice to say that, by 'transcendental subreption', Kant roughly understands the fact that finite epistemic beings tend to construe the conceptual framework necessary for having representations as itself a further representation. This move is recognised only indirectly by the finite knowers who commit the error, as is betrayed by their tendency to bestow a particular eminence on this representation.[37]

Kant's philosophical resolution of this conflation consists in reducing the supposedly eminent *ontological* status of our representations' conditions of possibility to a functional status within transcendental philosophy, so that we can operate safely with categories and ideas under immunity from scepticism. Kant believes that his restricted error theory, which interprets the 'Ideas' as regulative concepts, helps stave off an incomparably more fatal error theory (i.e. a nihilism), according to which 'God', 'world' and 'soul' are simply not subjects of rational discourse at all. Kant therefore takes a metaphysical *façon de parler*, which falsely lays claim to a right to hyperphysical assertions within a first-order theory and replaces it with a transcendental diagnosis of the organisational concepts that lie behind our usual, non-philosophical talk of 'God', 'world' and 'soul'. He thereby opposes the prominent (especially French) Enlightenment conception of his day, which in his eyes led to atheism, fatalism and materialism, and aimed to revolutionise not only political but also philosophical tradition.[38]

In summary, the negative-dogmatic result of Kant's 'paradoxical reinterpretation'[39] of Humean scepticism is the verdict that our metaphysical concepts of God, the world and the soul should not be interpreted as factual knowledge. We cannot *know* anything about such entities since they are simply not objects qualified for objective knowledge. For Kant, we can positively exclude the idea that we can know anything about hyperphysical entities.

Since it culminates in a negative dogmatism, Kant's anti-sceptical strategy leads to a variant of scepticism. This is not to say that Kant's efforts are in vain. He is no sceptic in the common sense of the word. Viewed from the perspective of our overall argument, Kant is instructive for seeing how a philosophical system can be constructed under sceptical conditions without having to reject the sceptic's premises completely. The programme of a critique of pure reason runs through scepticism and, in so doing, manages to do justice to the *prima facie* plausibility of certain premises without which the sceptic could not begin to unsettle our everyday knowledge claims. At the same time, Kant's critical philosophy draws the sting from scepticism. Far from leading to a 'scandal' for philosophy, scepticism holds reason's excesses in check and keeps it from straying into domains where we have a tendency to make knowledge claims even though there is no objective knowledge to be had.[40] In his own way, Kant interprets scepticism as a lesson regarding the necessary finitude of objective knowledge. Like Hume before him, he stands in the tradition of Cartesian methodological scepticism, which he expressly holds to be 'rational and appropriate for a thorough philosophical manner of thought'.[41]

In calling the variant of scepticism deployed by Descartes *Cartesian scepticism*, I am not of course making the historical claim that Descartes himself drew the very consequences of the form of scepticism that I have been outlining here. Cartesian scepticism designates a form that threatens to remove our entitlement to a range of assumptions that we cannot give up without sustaining heavy epistemic losses. This form of scepticism, unlike negative dogmatism, cannot simply be affirmed, a fact which accounts for one of its distinctive peculiarities: that is, there can be no corresponding Cartesian *sceptic*, no *advocate* of the position labelled 'Cartesian scepticism'. And this alone means that Descartes himself could not have been a Cartesian sceptic. Rather, he integrated 'Cartesian scepticism' into his theory construction in order to motivate a philosophical standpoint that should then in fact *repudiate* its sceptical motivation.

In confronting Cartesian scepticism, the philosopher's task is thus to show *how* we can be entitled to assumptions to which we *are* in fact entitled, in spite of a set of reasons that apparently deprive us of that entitlement. Using James Conant's distinction, we might also say that the confrontation with Cartesian scepticism in the development of modern philosophy has ultimately led to the conclusion that scepticism represents not so much a *position* as a *dialectical space*. In other words, it should be seen as the whole comprised of both the motivation and the construction of a certain class of philosophical theories, namely those that self-referentially integrate scepticism as a condition of their own possibility and proceed to determine their theoretical options against this background.[42]

The reason why Cartesian scepticism does not represent a position one can advocate is that it ultimately comprises a family of paradoxes, and paradoxes culminate in conclusions that cannot possibly be endorsed. There are, of course, different ways of reacting to the phenomenon, yet, as long as we accept that Cartesian scepticism presents a serious threat to some or all domains of discursive rationality, we have no choice but to come up with at least the following: (1) an anti-sceptical strategy and

(2) an explanation of why Cartesian scepticism has such frustrating consequences. This implies that Cartesian scepticism signifies a provocation, one to be taken seriously and rationally confronted. And, as we shall see below, the reason it acts as the sort of provocation it does is because it can be formulated as a quite general epistemological paradox.

Before we can develop an anti-sceptical strategy, however, we first have to clarify the structure of Cartesian scepticism and its role in the dialectical economy of epistemology. By the *dialectical economy of epistemology*, I understand the entire theoretical motivational apparatus of epistemology together with the fundamental parameters of its execution. In other words, the dialectical economy of epistemology consists in the totality of its conditions of intelligibility and rules of conduct. Now, one of these rules states that Cartesian scepticism may assume merely a *methodological* function and is thus forbidden, in principle, from pushing us towards a global negative dogmatism – i.e. to a conclusion to the effect that objective knowledge is impossible, *tout court*. Such a negative dogmatism would not only introduce a range of semantic antinomies and fatal confusions into the everyday practice of making knowledge claims; it would also be dialectically inconsistent insofar as it would eliminate a decisive condition of epistemology's own possibility qua knowledge claim about knowledge. For the task of epistemology consists in explaining what knowledge is and how knowledge is possible. If it fails, epistemological theorising itself becomes untenable. Accepting Cartesian scepticism thus presupposes that we can transform it into a useful theoretical insight. But this means avoiding the temptation to treat scepticism's conclusions as legitimate parts of whatever good arguments it otherwise provokes. The global negative dogmatist is guilty in just this respect, however, and creates a second-order paradox for epistemology – a paradox which, in turn, needs to be resolved in a further metatheory. We must therefore be careful to avoid eliminating epistemology by extrapolating a negative dogmatism from the problem of Cartesian scepticism: doing so amounts, *prima facie*, to a scenario in which epistemology succeeds in destroying itself by simultaneously reviving itself at a higher level of theorising.

The analysis of the logical structure, and thus of the impetus, of sceptical arguments represents a *sine qua non* of modern epistemology. There are at least good, if not compelling, reasons for this. To be sure, thinkers who proudly parade the title of being a (Cartesian) sceptic are hard to come by these days.[43] Engagement with scepticism has instead become part of the *methodological* reflection that forms a necessary component of epistemology. For epistemology is never just a theory of the objects of our knowledge but always a second-order theory that asks what knowledge or cognition of objects actually is (*the problem of definition*) or which classes of knowledge or cognition there in fact are (*the problem of classification*). Epistemology does not therefore lay claim to knowledge that occupies the same theory level as its object. Its object, first-order knowledge, does not know *as such* anything about epistemology, a business to which it is by and large (and quite rightly) indifferent. Hence epistemology has to apply different classifications to its own knowledge and to the knowledge claims it thematises when it investigates ordinary knowledge ascriptions.

In short, the kind of cognition investigated by epistemology is not identical with the kind of cognition it itself exemplifies. Of course, since it addresses the question of what knowledge is, epistemology tends not to deal with itself but with an object, first-order knowledge. Yet it is certainly wise, at least from time to time, to reflect on the standpoint that we occupy in our capacity as epistemologists. We shall see that such reflection constitutes a decisive step towards answering our guiding question: how does scepticism function in the dialectical economy of epistemology?

5

Direct and Indirect Sceptical Arguments: The Path to Semantic Nihilism

Philosophy provides us with at least two different methods for investigating theories or systems of assertions.

Firstly, we can test a system for its straightforward *logical* consistency and coherence. This kind of investigation involves examining the system's component concepts and propositions with respect to their inferential structure. The aim is to see whether it reveals any logical incompatibilities when subjected to analytical scrutiny, where logical incompatibilities are present if a system explicitly or implicitly commits itself to asserting the conjunction p and ~p. Specifically, *logical analysis* is the explication of a philosophical theory's presuppositions and implications with a view to testing it for consistency and coherence. Before subjecting a system of assertions to any deeper form of logical analysis, we have to determine whether its component statements betray any surface inconsistencies – i.e. inconsistencies at the level of their explicit formulation.

Secondly, we can investigate a system with reference to its conditions of possibility. In this case, the question is not whether the relevant statements are true given an established theoretical framework; that is, when conducting such an investigation, we are not interested primarily in whether or not the statements are true in light of conditions to which someone who accepts the rules of the theory subscribes anyhow. Instead, an investigation of a theory's *dialectical* conditions of possibility enquires into the theoretical attitude that a proponent of the theory has to possess and, in particular, how she motivates this attitude. We can therefore call this kind of investigation *dialectical analysis*.[1]

More specifically, a dialectical analysis of a system of assertions studies the *connection between its motivation and its construction*. This connection cuts deeper than a theory's merely logical consistency, because, while a theory's motivation introduces and grounds the basic elements that play a role in its execution, none of the relevant motivating considerations need play any explicit role in the course of the execution itself. A theory cannot introduce its basic elements once the conditions of its construction have already been established. At best, it can attempt to recover them retrospectively.

Every theory is the result of the pursuit of knowledge, and as such it requires both a *target projection* (an anticipation of the knowledge sought) and a *provisional method* (an ideal conception of how to work towards the projected target). The theory's target projection and provisional method are usually edited out of its execution – i.e. from the act of theory construction itself. Indeed, it is often even a condition of a successful theory that it not refer explicitly to its own conditions in the process of its execution. All theories that are not purely self-referential – that is, all theories whose success does not consist exclusively in investigating their own conditions – betray a tendency to conceal the epistemological dimension of *seeking* knowledge in favour of the dimension of *securing* knowledge.[2]

Naturally, the dialectical analysis of a theory will sometimes employ a logical analysis of the theory's component assertions in order to make its dialectical presuppositions explicit. Conversely, a logical analysis can become implicated in a dialectical analysis, even though the logical analysis as such cannot issue in any properly dialectical pronouncements. For example, when a logical analysis stumbles upon a paradox (and not merely a logical error), it usually pays to check whether the paradox can be dissolved at the dialectical level by articulating its motivation.

An important part of any dialectical analysis of a set of sceptical arguments consists in evaluating its particular 'dynamic'. In other words, it is crucial to examine the connection between its *motivation theory* on the one hand and its *theory construction* on the other. Every theory is motivated: something counts as evidence in its favour; foundational assumptions are generated by generalising on experience; certain logical principles are accepted as axioms; problems are identified that need to be addressed in an inferentially disciplined manner; etc. Yet, executing the theory represents a significant step beyond merely motivating it and always involves some level of revision of the motivating vocabulary. Theories are never just 'mirrors of the world'. Their explanatory power resides in the distance between what is accepted as given and what is recognisable as claimed. And as we shall see when discussing Wittgensteinian manoeuvres to avoid theorising, theory is inevitable. On the level of our metatheory, it is true that nothing is merely given. What is given to a first-order theory is a consequence of a construction of its metatheory.

In what follows, we will see how this insight can be turned into an anti-sceptical strategy. When confronting a sceptical paradox, we often have to ask not only which logical error is involved but why we regard it as a *paradox* to begin with, rather than just as a false inference: that is, we have to ask why we regard its premises and rules of inference as plausible (as motivated). When investigating a sceptical paradox, we should never lose sight of the perplexity it provokes. As will become clear, the peculiar advantage of dialectical analyses of sceptical paradoxes is precisely that they do not merely attempt to negate this or that premise but, instead, enquire into the paradox's underlying motivation.

It seems to be a general characteristic of Socratic questions of the 'What is X?' variety that they bring along innocent motivational presuppositions: to pose such philosophical questions, we must have come to adopt a particular attitude to both the world and ourselves that now suddenly prevents us from epistemically negotiating everyday life (whatever that might actually be) in our accustomed manner. Initiation into philosophical questions of the 'What is X?' variety, that is, presupposes a *break with the illusion of the everyday*. The theoretical attitude indispensable to philosophy is thus a form of alienation; without it, nobody would ever take up the purely theoretical standpoint of reflection characteristic of philosophical thought.[3] The practice of problematising the everyday and its routine operations already occupies a space outside or above, while still apparently occurring within, the everyday, and this ambivalence alone explains the formation of reflexive scientific treatments of these problems – i.e. the emergence of philosophy and science. It is also why we cannot embark on the business of subjecting our smooth-running linguistic practices to philosophical scrutiny – practices that, as Wittgenstein says, are conducted 'blindly'[4] – unless we take on scepticism as a chief liability.[5]

In concrete, everyday situations, someone may well ascribe knowledge to both herself and others with perfect competence but still find herself suddenly forced to ask what knowledge really is. When she does so, however, she has to reckon with the possibility that, ultimately, her question has no answer. In order to begin the project of epistemology, that is, the would-be epistemologist must have discovered that her epistemic dealings with the world somehow no longer proceed with the same frictionless innocence as before, else everything she previously accepted without question would not suddenly seem so dubious. The epistemologist must therefore have been led to *wonder* at the fact that there can be anything like knowledge at all. And, furthermore, when she goes about answering her question, she will have a chance of clarifying what knowledge really is only if she truly holds out hope for a positive answer.

If we regard the project of epistemology in the light of dialectical analysis, our primary aim cannot be to establish a series of valid propositions within the framework of an already established epistemology. If I provide logical analyses of epistemological arguments in what follows, it is not because I mean to restrict myself to the moves of any generally accepted game or to legitimise innovations based upon predefined rules. Rather, I want to bring out how logical analysis serves the *dialectical* aim of rendering transparent the conditions of possibility of epistemology *as such*.

To anticipate: we will come to see how a variety of scepticism – whose structure we will have to determine more precisely in the course of our investigation – belongs to the very conditions of possibility of epistemology. Note, however, that this result should not be confused with a thesis that has found prominent advocates in Barry Stroud and Michael Williams. They argue that scepticism is a necessary *result* of adopting the epistemological attitude to the world, oneself and others.[6] My own thesis will not be that epistemology *presupposes* a theoretical attitude that cannot resist the allure of scepticism and ultimately ends up ensnared. Instead, I want to demonstrate the very opposite: far from scepticism being a *consequence* of epistemology, there is an indispensable variety of scepticism that *conditions* initiation into epistemology in the first place.[7] Scepticism thus precedes epistemology as its condition of intelligibility. It is not a consequence of epistemology but its driving force.

It is hard to imagine that, in order to enquire into the nature of knowledge, epistemologists have to effect a complete break with their normal epistemic dealings with the world. This is because epistemologists cannot fully neutralise the object of their investigation, not even under the antiseptic conditions of epistemology. Instead, the epistemologist has to maintain contact with the knowledge she customarily ascribes to both herself and others. From the standpoint of epistemological theorising, we tend to get a distorted view of how things were before epistemology came on the scene, of paradise before the fall, even though its topic is supposed to be nothing less than the knowledge with which we ordinarily credit ourselves and others.[8]

For this reason, a common move in epistemology's battle with scepticism is to appeal to our usual competence in trading knowledge ascriptions, a competence we exercise without having at our disposal an uncontested concept of just *what it is* we thus ascribe.[9] Epistemological reflection therefore finds itself in dialectical conflict with the world of habit and custom (the 'lifeworld'), making it all the more unsurprising that some philosophers have taken up the cause of habit and custom in the hope of leaving epistemology behind; epistemology, the idea goes, inculcates an unnatural attitude, the fruits of which are scepticism's scandalous excesses.[10]

To step outside the world of habit – and so to begin to see knowledge as a problem – we need sceptical arguments. This is especially clear in Descartes' *Meditations*, which are committed to a declared methodological scepticism. To lead the reader to self-knowledge, Descartes first of all sets aside the certainties of the world of habit with the aid of various – now canonical – sceptical arguments. The construction of his positive contribution presupposes his methodological scepticism.

Therefore, epistemology and scepticism cannot be isolated from one another: knowledge becomes a problem only if we can show that it is systematically *under threat.* Knowledge is not threatened simply when we become convinced that some particular set of claims we previously held true are in fact invalid – that is, in our terms, when we advocate a local nihilism. One can assert, for example, that all positive statements about witches or phlogiston are false if they presuppose the existence of these entities. In certain once prominent domains of 'knowledge' there would then in fact be nothing to know. This observation as such, however, has nothing to do with scepticism. A truly sceptical problem first comes on the scene only when we formulate legitimate reasons to infer from such an observation that *all* our knowledge might possibly turn out to be as good as witchcraft.

The epistemologist continually has to strike a balance between two tendencies, both of which are constitutive for her project: on the one hand, there is the methodologically necessary scepticism that allows her to thematise knowledge or cognition as a problem in the first place; on the other hand, there is the need to keep our everyday practices of knowledge ascription in view so as not to renounce them altogether. Both tendencies are inscribed in the very project of epistemology itself. And insofar as they evidently point in opposite directions, they display the dialectic of epistemology and its potentially antinomic constitution.[11] From now on, I will designate the two tendencies as *scepticism* and *conservatism* respectively. While scepticism puts our naïve knowledge claims on display, conservatism consists in the attempt to secure the conditions of our naïve, everyday knowledge ascriptions *in spite of* epistemology's sceptical tendencies.

We can also express this idea as follows. Epistemology's provisional method (scepticism) stands in dialectical tension with its target projection. This tension is dialectical rather than logical because it is not immediately visible at the level of sceptical and anti-sceptical *arguments themselves*, however much they are always already – incognito, as it were – at work in them. So, to render epistemology's motivations transparent, one has to relate the observational standpoint of metatheoretical reflection to its own conditions of construction and success.[12]

This motivational set-up not only lies behind Descartes' project but also – and especially – governs contemporary epistemology. Indeed, the latter would be unthinkable without methodological scepticism. Most contributions to epistemology, that is, begin with a logical analysis of sceptical arguments before, in a second step, going on to cast doubt on one or more of their premises or inference rules. This tends to be the usual strategy for making progress in epistemology.[13]

A classical means of generating a *systematic* threat to our knowledge is to generalise from the fallibility of our holding-true – i.e. from knowledge claims. This tack leads to the formulation of a *Cartesian scepticism*. Given that we often go astray in our dealings with the world, it is seemingly only natural to ask whether we possess a criterion that allows us to make a systematic distinction between cases of knowledge and cases of error. This reflection stands behind *Descartes' rule of prudence*, not to trust anyone who has already deceived us in the past.[14] For whoever has deceived us once may possibly deceive us a on a second occasion and therefore – given a simple inductive operation – in the worst case, on every occasion. The problem of a systematic threat to our knowledge becomes ever more pressing when the Cartesian sceptic selects a best case of knowledge (usually unproblematic empirical knowledge) as the object of her doubts. If we cannot even succeed in defending trivial knowledge claims against the sceptic, then our more extravagant knowledge claims will a fortiori seem to be null and void.

Yet, notoriously, an inductive generalisation of our everyday fallibility does not on its own suffice for generating Cartesian scepticism. A few additional considerations are needed. These come into play once the sceptic has shown not only that we might frequently err in our judgements but that this possibility disrupts the smooth running of our everyday practice of knowledge ascription to an untenable degree. The possibility of a continually recurring error is intelligible at least *prima facie*, and it already leads to the questions of what knowledge is and how it is possible.[15] Generalising from our everyday fallibility certainly leads us to philosophical questions, though not ones that we should in any sense regard as unanswerable or liable to paradox. However, the prospect of the possible impossibility of knowledge forces us to engage in reflections geared towards guaranteeing the possibility of knowledge. These reflections have to lay claim to knowledge of knowledge and are therefore the preserve of a metatheory, of a theory (knowledge) that has theories (knowledge) as its content.

As is well known, Descartes makes use of two classical arguments in order to motivate the possible impossibility of knowledge and to sharpen the problem of fallibility into a genuine paradox: the *dream argument* and the *evil demon argument*. These arguments constitute the implicit methodology of his own metaphysical project in the *Meditations*.[16] Neither show – nor are they meant to show – that knowledge is *in fact* impossible, merely that it *might* be impossible. For all we know, knowledge is not what it seems (why else would there be epistemology?). In this way, Descartes introduces solipsism and global scepticism (negative dogmatism about knowledge in general) as possibilities, the rejection of which is supposed to provide our knowledge with an absolutely certain foundation.[17] Accordingly, Descartes himself does not advocate any kind of negative dogmatism, which would require him to assemble arguments for knowledge's impossibility. Rather, he avails himself of sceptical arguments in order to motivate the transition from our everyday engagement with the world to epistemology (i.e. from a first-order to a second-order theory).

Each of Descartes' arguments possesses a different logical structure. To analyse them, we can follow Crispin Wright, who distinguishes between *indirect* and *direct* sceptical arguments.[18]

(1) *Indirect argument*: Suppose that we were currently dreaming. Our dream state, moreover, is phenomenally indistinguishable from our waking state. In that case, our beliefs about the current goings on in our environment could not be justified by relying on the causal connection between mind and world that we usually take for granted when we believe, for example, *that* we see a table *because and just because* there actually is a table where we see one.

At the same time, it would be possible for us to have accidentally true beliefs, ideally about everything that is the case; for dreaming that such and such is the case is not incompatible with such and such really being the case. We can thus imagine someone who continually dreams the world to be exactly as it really is but without thereby standing in any identifiable causal relation to it. The person who dreams that someone is entering his room when someone is really entering his room does not necessarily dream *that* someone is entering his room *because* someone is entering his room (although there are cases of this kind). An argument along these lines is *indirect* because it does not doubt the existence either of the world or of knowledge of the world. Indeed, the existence of a world and the actuality of knowledge of the world are presupposed. The argument merely shows that we lack a criterion for determining whether we, here and now, actually fulfil the conditions necessary for acquiring knowledge of the world. It by no means shows that we might in fact have no true beliefs, merely that we could possibly have only *accidentally* true beliefs.

(2) *Direct argument*: Suppose someone were deceived by an evil demon: she maintains a set of her everyday beliefs about an (external) world, other minds, the reality of the past, and so on. But these are merely things she has been tricked into believing. Since the evil demon creates only the illusion of a world, the poor, deceived victim does not stand in any relation to anything external to her consciousness or mind. Such a scenario presents a greater and more obvious epistemic threat to the afflicted subject than the indirect argument: because the epistemic subject can no longer even be sure of the contents of her own consciousness, the direct argument presents a total threat to the practice of knowledge acquisition. While indirect sceptical arguments generate an *external* world problem, direct arguments generate an *internal* world problem. They isolate the epistemic subject from herself.

And therein lies the difference between the *dream argument* and the *evil demon argument*: the evil demon argument imports the sceptical problem into the internal world. A sceptical argument that leaves the fact of our otherwise indeterminate existence as thinking subjectivity as our sole refuge can surely be counted as a triumph for the sceptic. If we wind up at any point in our theory construction with a theorem according to which we really are a 'transcendental ego', a 'pure thinker', who does not know whether the 'I' in 'I think' refers to an embodied animal, we have already given in to methodological scepticism.

While the direct argument confronts us with the problem of *solipsism*, the indirect dream argument is compatible with our having acquired knowledge in our waking state on sufficiently many occasions to know that there is a difference between wakefulness and dreaming – in particular, such that other subjects (persons) exist outside us in the external world.

According to Crispin Wright, (1) and (2) are distinguished by their dialectical structures. The structure of 1) classifies it as an *indirect sceptical argument*. Following Wright, this structure can be analysed as follows.

(A) Firstly, the sceptic introduces a *sceptical hypothesis* whose truth value cannot be ascertained *in principle*. Accordingly, we can classify the hypothesis as evidence-transcendent *in principle*.[19] This kind of evidence transcendence means it is impossible (at least for the subject trapped in the sceptical scenario) to acquire any kind of information that would allow her to introduce a rational decision procedure for determining the truth or falsity of the relevant hypothesis. It matters little whether the hypothesis postulates that we are dreaming right now, or that we are under the influence of drugs that have us hallucinate the world as it actually is, and so on and so forth. It hardly takes a great effort of the imagination to come up with an indefinite number of sceptical scenarios that are (a) evidence-transcendent in principle and (b) logically compatible with everything that is the case. It suffices that the subject trapped in the scenario be cut off from the commonly assumed *causal origin* of her beliefs.

(B) The sceptical strategy now consists in showing that the beliefs of the affected subject are not adequately justified unless the sceptical hypothesis is demonstrably false. To be sure, this presupposes that the reasons for our beliefs must be knowable in principle. Now, since i) we must be able to justify the reasons for our beliefs when faced with a sceptical hypothesis that motivates their possible impossibility, and ii) it is *ex hypothesi* impossible to justify the reasons for our beliefs in light of a sceptical hypothesis, we forfeit the grounds for our beliefs.

The following holds for (A) *and* (B): when confronted with an appropriate sceptical hypothesis, a subject who accepts she has reason to believe that a table is in front of her (that she is not merely hallucinating, etc.) is forced to take a stand; she has to show that the hypothesis is either irrelevant or demonstrably false. But as there is no decision procedure for determining the truth value of the hypothesis – it has, after all, been purposely constructed to have a truth value that is evidence-transcendent in principle – any attempt at an ad hoc rejection of the sceptic will fail.

If, by contrast, one appeals to the *irrelevance of the sceptical hypothesis*, one of course has to show why a hypothesis incompatible with one's beliefs should be discounted as irrelevant. It is not enough to dismiss the hypothesis on the grounds that it is merely the product of epistemological theorising and so formulated under 'unnatural' conditions. This ploy requires drawing a distinction between a naïve use of knowledge ascriptions on the one hand and their philosophical thematisation on the other – a distinction for which there is notoriously little philosophical justification. The contexts of philosophy and of everyday discussion are obviously different. The question 'Does she really know what she is saying?' will naturally provoke a very different reaction in a philosophical context to when it is posed, say, in an emergency meeting of military high command. Yet we cannot simply dismiss philosophical contexts as irrelevant *as such* – not without appealing to a kind of reflection that possesses the inconvenient self-referential property of being philosophical itself.[20]

However, the most significant problem facing appeals to relevance is that asserting the irrelevance of all sceptical hypotheses to everyday life, while conceding their relevance to epistemological contexts, ultimately leads to an untenable stance.[21] *For the claim that we can distribute the relevance or irrelevance of sceptical hypotheses over different contexts has itself to be made in some context.* We are really dealing with three contexts here: (1) The context of everyday knowledge-ascription (C_E); (2) the context of epistemological, philosophical knowledge-ascription, viz. the position from which sceptical threats are handled (C_P); and (3) the epistemological (contextualist) context (C_C), within which one can draw the distinction between (1) and (2). C_P and C_C are therefore not identical: because it is a context in which sceptical alternatives are taken seriously (i.e. are relevant), one cannot claim to know that p in C_P. By contrast, C_C claims neutrality in respect to the conflict between sceptical reflection and the everyday. If we now place ourselves in C_C, we must be in a position to assert that both $C_E(p)$ and ~$C_P(p)$ can obtain without contradiction. Therefore, in C_C we assert that $C_E(p)$ and that ~$C_P(p)$. In the contextualist context, we know that we know that p in the everyday context because no sceptical hypothesis is relevant there, while we know at the same time that we do not know that p in the epistemological context, where all logically consistent sceptical hypotheses are relevant. Accordingly, since we know the conjunction of $C_E(p)$ and ~$C_P(p)$ in the contextualist context, it follows both that $C_E(p)$ and that ~$C_P(p)$; otherwise we could hardly expect to draw any anti-sceptical advantage from the distinction between relevant and irrelevant hypotheses. After all, this distinction establishes that sceptical hypotheses are irrelevant under standard conditions but relevant in sceptical (and thus in epistemological) contexts.

However, knowledge is a *success* state, meaning that it is true that p if it is true that somebody knows that p. One cannot know something that is false (other than in the sense that one knows that it is false). And, since knowledge is a success state, it follows from the truth of $C_E(p)$ – to which we are committed in C_C – that p. In C_C, we thus know that p. This means, however, that C_E and C_C claim knowledge with the same content. Yet we know in C_C that we do not know that p in C_P and, if we know this, we can then confidently assert that we do not know that p in C_P. We therefore assert, at the same time, both that p and that we do not know that p.[22]

This results in a grave problem for contextualism. For, if p is true, then p is true *tout court*, since, although C_C certainly implies a form of contextualism for knowledge ascriptions, it does not necessarily imply a form of relativism about truth. But if p is true and, moreover, we know that p is true, then the sceptical hypothesis loses the relevance it was *ex hypothesi* meant to have for us in C_P. Therefore, C_C cannot make good on the initial contextualist promise, namely, of distributing relevant and irrelevant alternatives between different contexts. Since it follows from C_C that C_E is true, every sceptical alternative must be false. If, conversely, the contextualist were to position herself on the side of C_P, she could not then assert that p. In short, we cannot eliminate the epistemological relevance of sceptical hypotheses by appealing to their irrelevance to everyday life. The contextualist standpoint is not a neutral one.

To see the kind of havoc that indirect sceptical arguments can wreak, we can take its paradigmatic instance, the dream argument.

> (1) Supposing a given subject x at a given time t has no good reasons (G) for the assumption that she is not currently dreaming (D): ~Gxt(Dxt).[23]
>
> (2) Supposing further, that dreaming that p (e.g. that a table is in front of me right now) is incompatible with being able to provide any (e.g. perceptual) good reasons for p: Dxt → ~Gxtp.[24]
>
> (3) Since we can have no good reasons for the claim that we are not currently dreaming, and since it thus follows that we have no good reasons for our perceptually based beliefs, it follows that: ~G~~Gxtp. That is: we have no good reasons for the claim that it is false that we have no good reasons for p.
>
> (4) Yet because of the elimination rule for double negation, this is equivalent to: ~G(Gxtp). That is: we have no good reasons for the claim that we have good reasons for p.

The problem is that, under the conditions set in place by a sceptical scenario with the logical structure of an indirect sceptical argument, we lose any reasons for relying on the justificatory procedures we usually apply in our epistemic dealings with our worldly surroundings. Yet having no reasons for the claim that we possess reasons for a certain set of beliefs seems to be just as irrational as having no reasons at all – especially on the internalist assumption that someone who has reasons for their belief does not accept these in turn without reason.[25] But anyone who tries to deploy *philosophical* arguments to rescue their threatened trust in perceptual reasons – i.e. tries to acquire reasons for it – is committed to this belief. That is, if we react to an indirect philosophical argument by developing a scepticism-resistant theory of perception, we thereby accept that, should it come under sceptical attack, we need reasons for our trust in perceptual reasons. And, by that same token, we therefore accept a *second-order internalism about justification.*[26]

As soon as we accept a second-order internalism about justification, we are already operating on Cartesian terrain. The position assumes that trust in our everyday dealings with the world requires theoretical support, for the internalist has already conceded that we need good reasons for our reasons if we want to defend our entitlement to our beliefs in a rational manner. And this potentially leads to an infinite regress: someone could demand good reasons for any good reason as soon as they have concocted an arbitrary sceptical alternative that makes the reason appear worse than we assumed.[27]

We can now turn to the *evil demon* argument. Since its strategy embodies a *direct sceptical argument*, it exhibits the following structure.

(A) As in the case of indirect sceptical arguments, the sceptic first introduces a sceptical hypothesis that is evidence-transcendent *in principle*. Yet, unlike in the indirect case, were *this* hypothesis true, it would follow *directly* and *immediately* that all our beliefs were false because, quite simply, there would not be any truth-makers. This is the danger posed by the *evil demon* hypothesis, as well as its modern avatar, the *brain in a vat*. Say Descartes' *evil demon* implanted all of our mental contents, presenting each mind with a world that has no existence beyond its presentation, while all that in fact existed were disembodied minds together with the *evil demon*; there would be nothing to make our beliefs about the world true or false. For our beliefs about the world are so constituted that we have to suppose some minimal contact with it, such that, in the case of true beliefs, we have the beliefs we do only because the world is in fact how our beliefs take it to be. Were there no objects, but only pseudo-perceptual fragments fed to us by an evil demon, we could not do justice to that supposition (and thus to the contrast of objectivity). Our beliefs would no longer have any ontological correlate besides their intentional content. In this way, the *evil demon* argument radicalises the danger of solipsism: the isolated judging subject is thrown back upon herself, unable to find a way out of her solipsistic representational intentions – representations which reach out into nothingness and, therefore, do not really even reach out at all.

(B) Since we cannot, in principle, have any good reasons for maintaining the falsity of a direct sceptical scenario, we cannot possess any good reasons for continuing to trust our own beliefs. The strength of a direct sceptical argument thus resides precisely in how its preferred sceptical scenario seems immediately to undermine our beliefs. Were the sceptical hypothesis true, an unnervingly large set of our beliefs would be false. And, because we cannot know that it is false, we cannot know whether our beliefs can be true in the way we previously held them to be.

It is important to note that the firepower of *an individual* direct sceptical argument does not depend upon its particular formulation: just as in the case of indirect sceptical arguments, it is possible to construct an indefinitely large set of direct sceptical arguments. So if we want to evaluate the impetus of Cartesian scepticism, we need to avoid becoming preoccupied with its concrete manifestations and their particular conceptual conditions. Descartes himself commits this very error when he merely undertakes to show that, given a certain (or even necessary) concept of God, it would be impossible for there to be an evil demon who deliberately plies us with delusions of a world and its governing eternal truths. Showing this, supposing he can, is still quite different from showing that we could not be brains in a vat, or that we are not in fact hallucinating the world as the result of some mass hysteria that has suddenly broken out in the realm of immaterial spirits, and so on and so on. Fixating on one scenario is a blind alley, even though they all share the same logical structure. Descartes' concept of the world is thus of little help if we want to show that we are not brains in vats or purely immaterial beings with no causal relation to the world (Leibnizian monads, say). You cannot think you are safe from the hydra just because you have cut off one of its heads. And if the hydra cannot in fact be killed, by far the best strategy is to lure it onto your side – in other words, to integrate scepticism into the construction of your own theory as a methodological device.

Following Michael Williams, it is often emphasised that, if we really want to understand the connection between scepticism and epistemology, we first have to obtain a *theoretical diagnosis* of the logical structure of sceptical arguments.[28] Such a diagnosis is supposed to spare us from having repeatedly to do battle with arbitrarily chosen instances of a general logical structure; for refuting the errors of a *particular*, determinate sceptical scenario does nothing to immunise ourselves against the direct argument as such.

For example, we might compare life to a long dream (and thus accept a particular sceptical argument) without seeing that this same idea equally invites a comparison between life and *The Matrix*, or with a conspiracy plotted by aliens, in which each and every detail of our personal lives is a part of some bizarre experiment. In short, as direct sceptical arguments only sometimes offer serious alternatives to our factual epistemic situation (if it is approximately as we believe it to be), they do not automatically represent a substantial threat to our overall cognitive situation. While it might be shocking to hear that we quite possibly have no good reasons for rejecting the assumption that an evil demon governs the world, the world just being part of his wicked game, it is perhaps less unsettling to learn that we are in fact pure spirits whose representations arise not through causal contact with the world but through internal mechanisms of projection. The latter scenario merely encapsulates a neo-Platonic belief that has been vitally important throughout the history of philosophy (it operates, for example, in the background of Leibniz's monadology). And the idea that the world is merely a dream granted us by God is a religious conception with a considerable pedigree, playing an important role above all in Hinduism. In certain representations of Shiva, the god dances on the back of the dreaming human being, feeding him representations from behind his back. To be sure, it is highly questionable – to say the least – whether direct sceptical arguments should convince us of any such picture of our actual metaphysical situation – particularly so, when we realise that sceptical arguments are paradoxes with a general logical structure and that we cannot fight them on their own terms.

Let us call *Descartes' failure* the mistake of attacking only an *instance* of a (direct or indirect) Cartesian sceptical argument, instead of dealing with the logical structure itself. Descartes himself, as noted above, commits this error insofar as he refutes the *evil demon* hypothesis by appealing to God's goodness. Yet God's goodness, however great, does not help us one bit; we can go on to construct a further sceptical hypothesis to the effect that there could be an evil demon who tricks us not only regarding our representations of the world but also regarding our concept of God's goodness. And even if we could show that a determinate, even a necessary, concept of God could free us from the *evil demon* hypothesis, we would not yet have shown that there can be no benevolent spirit who, precisely in virtue of her goodness, reveals herself to us by having us believe there cannot be an evil demon, even though there actually is one. The good spirit might, for example, want to protect us from the consuming fear the evil spirit would doubtless inspire if we caught on to his existence.

And even if we could disable this peculiar hypothesis too, there would always still be a stock of sceptical hypotheses in reserve, ready to exploit empirical possibilities that cannot be disabled a priori (including with the help of rational theology). One can imagine, for example, that just a few minutes ago every one of us took a drug that has the property of making its consumer immediately forget that she has taken it, while having her hallucinate a world identical to the actual world in every last detail. We would then continue to have seamless practical dealings with the world while being simultaneously robbed of the epistemic responsibility we usually bear for our judgements – i.e. when we are not under the influence of the drug.

Wittgenstein seems to succumb to Descartes' failure in *On Certainty* when he claims: 'The argument "I may be dreaming" is senseless for this reason: if I am dreaming, this remark is being dreamed as well and indeed it is also being dreamed that these words have any meaning.'[29] Wittgenstein's rejection of the dream argument here is somewhat too quick. Of course, we have to put it in the context of his philosophy of language and mind before determining how much anti-sceptical potential we can really credit it with. Yet it seems that he commits Descartes' error by presupposing a specific concept of 'dream' in order to combat Cartesian scepticism. For it is not immediately obvious why the meaning of the words I deploy when trapped in a Cartesian scenario should depend on my not dreaming. Even if we advocate a version of social externalism according to which expressions can have propositional content only given their acquisition within a social game (which therefore has to include other subjects), no objection to Cartesian scepticism immediately follows. Ultimately, the influence of other members of my speech community, my fellow participants in the language game, might also be dreamed: from the perspective of someone outside the dream, who knows that I am dreaming and, in addition, is quite well informed of the truth of social externalism, my words may well have no meaning. But this does not mean it is merely *dreamed* that my words have meaning.

Besides, we can contrive a variant of the dream argument in which I cannot know at any determinate point in time whether or not I have just fallen asleep and happen at this very moment to be dreaming precisely what I would experience were I awake. Nothing about this scenario presupposes that I might possibly have never been awake. This means, however, that I could well have been a member of a community for long enough to receive the linguistic training necessary for me now, in my dream, to apply my words perfectly correctly. So merely verbalising the dream argument does not immediately amount to its performative self-refutation: I can by all means think of a dream state in which I am a competent speaker and thinker, whatever conditions I in fact have to take as fulfilled in order to be a competent speaker and thinker. The argument for social externalism could itself ultimately have been dreamed.[30]

Wittgenstein's remark belongs in the context of his dissolution of solipsism. Yet, at bottom, solipsism is merely a symptom of Cartesian scepticism. It is not enough to convict solipsism of semantic deficiencies, since solipsism is not the origin of Cartesian scepticism. Clearly, scenarios such as the *Truman problem* (how do you know you are not in *The Truman Show*?) can be developed without solipsism in the strict sense; Truman is trapped not in his representations (understood as representational intentions without ontological correlates) but, at best, in a web of false beliefs. For this reason, it is also insufficient to reject solipsism if we want to solve the problem of Cartesian scepticism. Solipsism is merely the outcome of some sceptical scenarios, not their overall presupposition.

Moreover, none of this means that sceptical scenarios can withstand social externalist objections only if they accurately depict the true nature of dreams. Generally, we should not understand the debate with Cartesian scepticism as a debate about substantial metaphysical possibilities.[31] Invoking a social (or causal) semantic externalism to oppose the dream argument does not even bring us close to winning the debate with Cartesian scepticism: we will only find ourselves confronted with ever more refined sceptical scenarios. That is, it will not do merely to show that we are not dreaming, where by 'dreaming' we understand what we usually do by the term (i.e. without wanting to imply any complicated theory of dreams). We could ultimately be dreaming*, where a dream* differs from a dream by exhibiting the necessary characteristics of a sceptical hypothesis. Cartesian paradoxes do not depend on the possibility that we might be dreaming; it suffices that we might be dreaming*.

Nevertheless, semantic externalism has rightly drawn attention to the problem that Cartesian scenarios bring into question not only our epistemic but our entire semantic situation; they thereby threaten intentionality qua relation to anything determinate whatsoever, thus raising the prospect of *semantic nihilism*.[32] The worry, in other words, is that, in a Cartesian scenario, we cannot even ensure that our reference to intentional correlates is so much as truth-*apt*. While indirect arguments raise the question of whether our beliefs are *true*, direct arguments confront us with the possibility that there may not be any truth-makers for our beliefs at all. The concept of representational intentions then begins to unravel precisely because representational intentions, by their very nature, seem to aim at representing something independent of the act of intending itself. In short, if we could not even ensure that there are intentional correlates (and thus truth-makers), our representational intentions would collectively amount to a hopeless grasping in the void.

As I've already hinted on several occasions, the epistemological progress achieved by more recent engagements with scepticism lies in the discovery that we need to treat sceptical arguments not as expressions of substantial philosophical programmes but, rather, as paradoxes.[33] By analysing sceptical paradoxes, we can uncover the consistency or inconsistency of fundamental assumptions that we traditionally attach to the concept of knowledge.

A particularly sophisticated logical analysis of sceptical paradoxes has been offered by Crispin Wright. At the same time, he gives us a strategy for overcoming Cartesian-style paradoxes by way of what he calls an 'implosion'. In the next chapter I will argue that his analysis unwittingly reveals a deep dialectical feature of scepticism – a feature that will serve as a guiding thread for the rest of our investigation.

6

Crispin Wright's Implosion of Cartesian Scepticism and its Dialectic

---

Crispin Wright has developed a range of highly sophisticated anti-sceptical strategies aimed at refuting both direct and indirect sceptical arguments.[1] In this chapter, I will be focusing on one of his most subtle strategies, the strategy of *implosion*, and showing how it ends up by upsetting the delicate equilibrium between the competing tendencies that, as we have seen, characterise the project of epistemology. The result is that, while Wright's attempts to liberate our knowledge ascriptions from the clutches of sceptical paradoxes certainly amount to a set of logically cogent analyses, they simultaneously undermine the dialectical presuppositions of his own approach. In other words, my aim is to demonstrate that we can occupy the epistemologist's observational standpoint, the standpoint Wright occupies in conducting his analysis, only given a vital supposition: namely, that we can *motivate* the very sceptical paradoxes that Wright's own anti-sceptical strategy sets out to dissolve. So, far from dissolving the fundamental Cartesian sceptical paradox, Wright's implosion serves only to increase its power. He therefore shows, *malgré lui*, how to formulate a general Cartesian paradox that grounds nothing less than a form of semantic nihilism.

Wright's implosion works by detecting a contradiction lurking between the motivating theory behind sceptical paradoxes and their actual execution. This strategy, it should be noted, applies exclusively to Wright's *implosion* of Cartesian scepticism. He develops his general treatment of the problem of scepticism within the context of his theory of warrant acquisition, where he operates quite self-consciously with sceptical arguments of another kind. We should therefore bear in mind that, just because the *Cartesian scepticism treated in Wright's analysis* does not serve primarily to shine a light on our mechanisms of justification, this is not to say that a more general form of scepticism might not perform this function instead. In the second part of this study, I shall be considering this more general form under the heading of *Pyrrhonian scepticism*.

In this chapter, my aim is not to show that Wright's anti-sceptical strategy of implosion is *logically* unsound but, rather, to demonstrate that it is *dialectically* incompatible with the execution of a particular project in epistemology. We should see this as an indication of a general dialectical instability inscribed within the distinctively modern project of pursuing epistemology as a foundation for *prima philosophia*. This instability finds expression in how, on the one hand, the epistemologist's treatment of knowledge ascriptions from an observational standpoint implies the possibility of scepticism while, on the other hand, it is supposed to establish how the thematised knowledge is itself immune to scepticism. The Cartesian sceptic, therefore, has to be banished from the realm of knowledge as a disruptive gadfly. We seemingly have to refute her in one form or another, by proving that her arguments are indebted to a range of premises we are not compelled to share. Yet rejecting Cartesian scepticism undermines our ability to adopt an *observational standpoint* on our everyday practice of knowledge ascription. The problem is thus not, as it might seem to be at first glance, that paradoxes threaten our everyday epistemic practice but, rather, that adopting an observational standpoint on that practice betrays two dialectically incompatible tendencies. We can label these *conservationism* and *scepticism* (see above, p. 77): on the one hand, epistemology is tasked with explaining our everyday acts of knowledge ascription, and thus the concept of knowledge. It has to render intelligible how it is so much as possible for us to know how the world is, without eliminating its object – first-order knowledge – in the process. On the other hand, because scepticism belongs to epistemology's motivation, it is in continual danger of losing sight of its object insofar as it approaches it under sceptical theory conditions.

In his fascinating essay 'Scepticism and dreaming: imploding the demon', Wright develops a more powerful version of a classical anti-sceptical strategy: that which convicts the Cartesian sceptic of holding a self-contradictory stance. The first step towards understanding his strategy is not to treat 'scepticism' as we would a specific doctrine or theoretical position that various philosophers advocate and defend. Such a doctrine or position would include a range of particular beliefs that, collectively, would be incompatible with some set of knowledge ascriptions to which we usually take ourselves to be entitled. Instead, says Wright, we should think of 'scepticism' as a class of paradoxes. These paradoxes appear in the guise of sceptical arguments, and we can classify them according to their different dialectical structures.

Each class of sceptical paradoxes comes with a range of presuppositions and putatively valid rules of inference. More precisely, each sceptical paradox qua paradox consists of a set of apparently plausible premises, apparently acceptable inference rules, and an obviously unacceptable conclusion. In general, paradoxes are valid arguments with premises that can be rationally motivated and conclusions that we would not accept without deep reservations, since accepting them would mean losing our entitlement to an indispensable class of beliefs. A paradox, therefore, has at its disposal all the necessary and sufficient conditions not only of a valid (i.e. logically correct) argument but of a sound (i.e. true) argument too. Nevertheless, it manages to present (in the best case) a local or (in the worst case) a global threat to our discursive rationality.

Paradoxes are often deliberately employed in order to induce a kind of rational paralysis. This manifests as follows. A paradox is a structured set of premises – say (1) and (2) – and a conclusion (3), thus: {[(1), (2)] → (3)}. When a paradox is presented, the common reaction is to negate the conclusion. This reaction, though, is incompatible with retaining the premises, since a paradox is *by definition* a valid argument. If we want to negate the conclusion but maintain the premises, we will find ourselves assenting to the conjunction of {[(1), (2) → ~(3)]} and {[(1), (2)] → (3)}, and thus to a contradiction.

The kind of cognitive paralysis that a paradox generates is not a matter of struggling to decide which of its premises we ought to give up so that we can then go on to negate the conclusion without fear of inconsistency. For, in trying to solve paradoxes, it is always easy enough to formulate a counter-argument beginning with the negation of the conclusion. The paradox and its counter-argument then have the same *prima facie* plausibility. A simple example can serve as an illustration.

> 1 Scepticism [SC]
> (1) If I am currently seeing my hands, then I am not a brain in a vat.
> (2) I do not know whether I am a brain in a vat.
> (3) Therefore, I do not know whether I am currently seeing my hands.

The counter-argument begins with the negation of the conclusion of (SC):

> 2 ~SC
> (1) I know that I am currently seeing my hands. (= (~3))
> (2) If I am currently seeing my hands, then I am not a brain in a vat.
> (3) Therefore, I am not a brain in a vat.

So far, both (SC) and (~SC) are equally unmotivated. What matters here is simply that both possess equal *prima facie* plausibility. (SC) presents a paradox precisely because it produces an equipollence between two arguments – in classical terms: an *isostheneia* situation (ἰσοσθένεια τῶν λόγων).[2] If deciding which piece of reasoning we found cogent were just a matter of preference, we would place our confidence in (~SC).

Supposing, though, that we could formulate a *global* sceptical paradox and motivate its premises; we would then be compelled in virtue of our discursive rationality to a comprehensive suspension of judgement. Such a paradox would bear the force of a discovery that we have to dismiss our discursive rationality on account of our discursive rationality. Theoretical diagnoses of sceptical paradoxes are thus not inconsequential exercises of epistemological ingenuity: they are our discursive rationality's reflexive defence against itself.

Now, Cartesian scepticism presents us with the possibility of just such a global sceptical paradox. Indeed, since, as we shall see, it puts discursive rationality as such into question, it can result in total cognitive paralysis. Cartesian scepticism, that is, allows us to formulate and motivate a general sceptical paradox that leads our discursive rationality right up to its own limits. This general paradox, however, presupposes that we have already made our way through the implosion.

Generally speaking, we can classify anti-sceptical strategies according to whether (a) they draw on external resources in order to prove how the premises of the sceptical argument in question are untenable, or whether (b) they bring down the argument with the aid of its own premises. Wright calls the refutation or rejection of one, several, or all of the premises of a sceptical argument an *explosion*, whereas an *implosion* involves the dissolution of a sceptical paradox by deploying its own resources. An implosion should thus show how a paradox cancels out its own motivation, without our having to invest any external conceptual resources.

If we suppose, in addition, that sceptical paradoxes are in a position to threaten certain domains of our discursive rationality only because they are *arguments*, it makes sense to interrogate a given sceptical argument in terms of its general logical and dialectical structure. We might call this operation a *theoretical diagnosis* of a sceptical problem. A sceptical problem does not arise simply because someone points out, for example, that our thoughts might be controlled by aliens or that our representations might have been inserted into our minds by an evil demon. In such cases, we need only point out the abstruseness of the suggested scenarios before continuing to go about our usual epistemic business. Neither Hollywood movies nor arbitrary fantasies can, just as such, present a genuine sceptical problem, a problem that would require epistemological rather than, say, psychiatric therapy. We therefore have to draw a distinction between, for example, the delusion of having seventeen noses and the sceptical hypothesis that our lives are merely elaborate dreams, or that we are brains in a vat, and so on.[3]

The relevant difference cannot consist (exclusively) in the idea that sceptical hypotheses are of a seemingly more serious philosophical nature. Heraclitus asked what the difference was between the state of being asleep and the state of being awake, between being sober and being drunk, and used such questions as a basis for discovering fundamental structures of rationality.[4] Schopenhauer even compared life affirmatively with a dream, while Plotinus believed that our sensible representations result from a kind of intoxication of the soul.[5] And, no less significantly, the works of a host of artists would have us view life as a kind of dream, or nightmare.[6] Sextus Empiricus, for example, loved to quote from Euripides when generating his sceptical arguments in favour of a global relativism.[7]

However, serious engagement with, or even affirmation of, the sceptical hypotheses of the philosophical tradition should not hide the fact that sceptical arguments are not bound to their concrete realisations. This is why it is possible, in principle, to generate an indefinite number of sceptical arguments, which can nevertheless be traced back to an identifiable class of logical forms. Thus, a theory of dreams, for example, that empirically investigates and enumerates the differences between wake and sleep – be it psychologically, neurologically, etc. – cannot count as an anti-sceptical strategy, especially as one of the points of the dream argument is precisely to put into question the reality of empirical concepts quite generally. If our objection to the dream argument is that, in some particular respect or other, we do not in fact experience dreams in the same way as we do the conditions of waking life, we only rehearse Dr Johnson's misunderstanding when he sought to refute Berkeley's idealism by kicking a stone.

Cartesian scepticism traditionally seeks to show that our representations *as if* p, despite their representational purport, might generally be representations of nothing at all. It thus attempts to show that our representations have an intentional content to which, however, there need not correspond any extra-mental correlate, any correlate that exists independently of the act of representation. The dream argument is supposed to show that every judgement of the form 'X seems to me to be F' is logically prior to the corresponding judgement of the form 'X is F'. It has to show that our epistemic access to the world, and thus all *is-talk*, is secondary in relation to our access to our representations of the world, and thus to all *seems-talk*. What is at issue, therefore, is a reduction of being to seeming, of reality to appearance.[8] That X seems to me to be F is certain, even though it is quite doubtful whether the appearance as though X is F corresponds to anything independent from it. This line of thought is a version of Descartes' original declared intention of showing that our mind is better known (*notior*) to us than the world it seemingly represents.[9] Cartesian scepticism first of all serves to lock us into a theatre of representations or sense data to which we enjoy privileged, albeit strictly private, access.[10] In this way, it guarantees that the subjective (our representation *as if* p) has an epistemic advantage over against the objective (p), such that the latter can be grounded on the former.

To be sure, Descartes' own aim is to steer a course between the Scylla of solipsism and the Charybdis of scepticism, so that the position he ends up establishing might avoid both dangers. But he cannot justify his anti-sceptical strategy without first introducing scepticism. This is what paves the way to his 'discovery' of an *epistemological asymmetry* between mind (the subjective) and world (the objective), which can easily lead to an interiorisation or alienation of the subject from her world, and thus to a renewed scepticism.[11] Descartes – together with post-Cartesian epistemological foundationalism – sees the benefit of this supposed discovery in the idea that the kind of privileged, immediate access we have to our own states (the subjective) enables us to extract the objective from the subjective: according to Descartes, an appropriate investigation of the subjective will lead back to the objective, since the certainty of one's own existence and of God's existence, together with the predicates supposedly contained in the concept of God, prevent *methodological* solipsism from transforming into a substantial *metaphysical* solipsism.[12]

The paradox underlying Cartesian scepticism presupposes a seemingly innocent principle which, following Wright, we can call *Descartes' principle*:

> In order to know any proposition P, one must know to be satisfied any condition which one knows to be necessary for one's knowing P.[13]

Cartesian scepticism thus makes use of a certain understanding of iterativity: when one knows *something*, one must also be able to state that one *knows* it, at least when this knowledge seems to be under threat – i.e. insofar as one is in a position to ask oneself whether one knows it.[14]

'To know' is a success verb. Therefore, from 'S knows that p' it follows that p. To know that p thus means to know that p is true. If p were false, one could not know that p. And so, when it is true that S knows that p, it is *ipso facto* true that p. To challenge a given knowledge claim, it is sufficient to introduce an alternative in which p is false. If the challenged subject is unable to dismiss the alternative, then they seemingly do not know that p. Indeed, given that we adhere to this claim in our everyday practice of giving and asking for reasons, we might justly regard it as a basic discursive norm. To *assert* something is to commit oneself to the truth of the asserted proposition. Yet, as we can challenge an assertion by presenting an alternative in which p is false, the claimant to knowledge has to revoke the assertion just in case she cannot provide any warrant to defend her belief.

If we accept this quite general line of thought, we find ourselves landed straightaway with the by now canonical formulation of Cartesian scepticism. This can be stated as an argument with two premises and a conclusion.

> (1) Someone can know that there is a table in front of them only if they know that a given sceptical hypothesis (i.e. an alternative in which the knowledge claim is not true) is false, at least when they are confronted with a sceptical hypothesis.[15]
> (2) Sceptical hypotheses have the property that their truth values are evidence-transcendent in principle, and, as such, nobody can know whether they are true or false.[16]
> (3) Therefore, nobody can know that there is a table in front of them.[17]

Premise 1 implies the validity of the *principle of closure* for a set of propositions that fall within the scope of the epistemic operator 'knows'. The
principle of closure asserts that we must know all the implications of
a known proposition, at least if we know that the proposition implies
them. This entails that, if a subject S knows that p and that p implies q,
then (*ceteris paribus*) S also knows that q.[18] *Descartes' principle* is, as is fairly
clear, an instance of the principle of closure, since it demands that we
assume the negation of a sceptical hypothesis q to be justified insofar as a
set of ~q obviously follows from every p (in our case, that there is a table
in front of us).

To ward off the danger of scepticism, we cannot just give up the principle of closure ad hoc, since the principle has at least the following two
indispensable functions in our epistemic economy.

(1) Firstly, the principle of closure is a condition of those advances
    in our knowledge that make use of the rational tool of deduction.
    Every rationally controlled advance in knowledge works by elab-
    orating the implications of the knowledge we already possess:[19]
    'The core idea behind closure is that we can add to what we know
    by performing deductions on what we already know.'[20] Of course,
    this is not to say that every advance in knowledge works with
    rational means. The actual logic of invention exhibited by our
    cognitive life functions mostly without any recourse to rational
    control mechanisms that lead us in a structured fashion from one
    belief to the next. The presentation of a theory *more geometrico*
    is secondary to the creative impulses that led to its discovery,
    impulses which seduce us into thinking 'abnormally' – that is,
    differently. Orthodoxy is never really creative, and innovation
    requires going beyond current modes of expression and insight.
    In fact, genuine innovation presupposes precisely that we do not
    merely form deductive chains of reasoning based on our already
    secured beliefs; rather, it assumes that our pre-existing beliefs
    have come under pressure and so have to be replaced by new
    ones. Authentic scientific discoveries generally begin with a flash
    of inspiration or a vague inkling that gradually creeps up on us,
    and these can only be lent a rational form *post festum* (if at all).[21]
    We should therefore avoid confusing the rational presentation
    of a theory with its explicit or implicit provisional method (see
    chapter 5 above): while the former tries to secure knowledge
    within a *context of justification*, the latter emerges from the search
    for knowledge in a particular *context of discovery*.[22] Nevertheless,
    the principle of closure is a *conditio sine qua non* of those advance-
    ments in our knowledge that unfold the implications of what we
    already know.

(2) The second function of the principle of closure is to ensure that
    someone who knows something must be able to defend their

knowledge in the face of justified critical questioning: they have to be able to react to a given challenge by stating what they necessarily take to be good reasons for their knowledge claims.[23] For they know not only what they know, but also that they know it – i.e. in the sense that they have to be able to defend their knowledge. This is why statements such as 'she knows that p, but she does not know that she knows p' have a paradoxical complexion.[24] It also lies behind the ancient Platonic demand that knowledge be more than true belief (ἀληθὴς δόξα). A knower will react to threats to her body of knowledge with a defence of her knowledge claims. Plato calls such a defence 'logos', which we are entitled to translate as 'justification'. Knowledge is thus *at least* true justified belief (ἀληθὴς δόξα μετὰ λόγου), where everything of course turns on finding the right concept of justification.[25] And it is important to emphasise that we cannot spell out this concept by seeking criteria that amount to *guarantees*: because of the discursive aspect of knowledge, the aspect which refers us to the game of giving and asking for reasons, we can at best specify *authorising* criteria, which establish when we are to *count* something as a good reason for a knowledge claim.[26]

An intuitive basis for the insistence on iterativity is thus that we can always demand of a putative knower that she defend her knowledge against relevant objections. This intuition lies behind the Socratic apologia the λόγον διδόναι.[27] Following Plato, we can speak of an *apologetic dimension of knowledge* motivated by the principle of closure: it belongs to knowledge's apologetic dimension that it can be defended against relevant objections.

Without the apologetic dimension of knowledge, we could not connect the concepts of *belief* and *responsibility* in the way that we usually do when it comes to counting potential knowers. We are prepared to recognise a subject as epistemically responsible only on the condition that she responds to rational critiques of her beliefs by engaging in critical reflection. Obviously, it does not follow from this that a putative knower has to change her beliefs as soon as she is confronted with the critic's objections, even if she cannot respond to them immediately. Yet we would surely be within our rights to convict her of a breach of fundamental discursive norms if she refused even to reconsider her reasons for belief when confronted with serious objections.[28]

There are, however, several objections to the iterativity thesis as motivated by knowledge's apologetic dimension, and thus to the second function of the principle of closure. One of the most persuasive objections appeals to the fact that we often, rightly, stick to our beliefs when challenged, even though we do not have any good reasons for our beliefs at our immediate disposal. No one will think it irrational to concede to a critic that they have indeed presented reasons which count against some

belief. But not all good reasons are overriding reasons and not all seemingly overriding reasons really are overriding. We are therefore often
quite right to rely on our ability to come up with good reasons for our
good reasons at a later stage, or with a refutation of the seemingly good or
overriding reasons that put our knowledge claims into question.[29]

If, for example, somebody is confronted for the first time with one of
Zeno's paradoxes, she will hardly simply concede that she does not, after
all, know whether anything moves; even if she does not yet have any proposal at hand for resolving the paradox, she will retain her belief that she
lives in a world in which some things move while others remain stationary. The same goes for somebody who is taught that the proposition 'the
sun moves' is incomplete without defining a frame of reference in which
the sun moves relative to some object or objects that remain stationary.
Even when we learn in a physics seminar that 'motion' stands for a more
complicated phenomenon than we realised, we will not suddenly refrain
from asserting that the sun moves. When it comes to science, and indeed
philosophy, we suppose that 'true statements imply the prior testing and
rejection of their potential untruths.'[30] However, the observation that this
criterion by no means applies to everyday knowledge ascriptions is of
course the *raison d'être* of contextualism and provides the source of its
anti-sceptical impetus. Ultimately, philosophical or scientific innovations
cannot unsettle the epistemic economy that regulates everyday interactions with the world. And this is why the wiser course of action is often
to trust that we will sooner or later hit upon good reasons for our beliefs.

Philosophical reflection on the structure of our everyday knowledge
ascriptions must therefore do justice to the fact that our everyday *practices
of justification* are not philosophical in nature. In certain circumstances,
we can integrate this observation into a sceptical or anti-sceptical position
as a dialectical parameter. Epistemology is always entitled to strive for
an equilibrium between its two tendencies, of legitimating our normal
practices of knowledge ascription while acknowledging that it was their
vulnerability to sceptical pressures which motivated the dialectical necessity of their justification in the first place. Yet if we place too much weight
on the former tendency, the tendency towards securing knowledge, we
always invite the danger that we render the standpoint of the epistemological observer superfluous. It is therefore a *dialectical* error to judge
epistemological theories from the outset according to whether or not they
promise to deliver an anti-sceptical strategy; we can determine the prospects for holding onto our everyday knowledge ascriptions only once we
have made our way through the theory.[31]

A basic rule of *philosophical* debate states that we must temporarily
renounce a theory if we cannot defend it. This rule distinguishes philosophy as a discursive practice from many of our non-philosophical,
everyday methods of justifying beliefs – which is not to say that philosophical beliefs, once put into question, cannot be reaffirmed later on. The
least that we can demand of a vulnerable belief when it is successfully

challenged is that it be temporarily withdrawn and placed on hold. So, since Cartesian scepticism is a philosophical problem and not a problem of everyday life, we are entitled to apply the iterativity principle to philosophically challenged knowledge, despite the fact that our everyday practice of knowledge ascription might be subject to other standards.[32] Thus even if we try to show that differences between everyday and philosophical standards of justification mean that we cannot motivate the Cartesian paradox for everyday knowledge, and so have to restrict it to epistemology, we still confront a grave difficulty: namely, that we cannot arrive at a *metatheoretical* understanding of what it means to make a knowledge ascription.

This makes our common practices of knowledge ascription seem problematic: we would no longer have a definite grip on these practices if epistemology generated a general paradox that, thanks to a second-order internalism about justification, it could not dissolve. If we cannot use epistemology to defend or clearly determine our everyday knowledge within, then we cannot claim to know what knowledge is. But if we cannot know what knowledge is, if we cannot formulate epistemological success conditions that avoid the paradoxical dissolution of our knowledge, then we can hardly assert that we know anything in particular. How could we still be competent users of the knowledge predicate if, in the philosophical game of giving and asking for reasons, it has lost all conceptual determinacy?

If we cannot show within epistemology that our everyday knowledge ascriptions are warranted by good reasons, the sceptic will have already won. Scepticism does not have to permeate everyday life in order to be effective. As a primarily philosophical problem, it is not redundant simply because we might not *de facto* pay it any attention when going about our everyday business. If epistemology cannot refute scepticism or 'domesticate' it in some other way, we will be unable to determine our everyday knowledge ascriptions, on account of our inability to make them the object of a consistent metatheory.

A metatheory is always a theory of knowledge tasked with thematising knowledge as such. It thus takes knowledge ascriptions as its object. Should this prove impossible, we could not know what it so much as means to know something – and if we cannot know that much, neither can we know whether we know anything at all. As soon as we find ourselves occupying the epistemological standpoint, we face the threat of a general cognitive paralysis.

One might object that, because knowledge is a success verb and depends partly on the world, we are not usually in a position to know whether we know p. If the world changed without there being any covariance with our body of available information, we could continue to believe that we know p without really knowing that p. Think, for example, of somebody who knows at a given point in time that there is a certain building in his neighbourhood. After leaving his house one day to go travelling, the building burns down. But being on holiday, with no access to local news, he does not know that he no longer knows that the building is in his neighbourhood, since knowledge is a success verb, and it follows from his knowledge that p, that p.[33] Accordingly, the subject does not know that an alteration in worldly states has unexpectedly converted his knowledge into a false belief.

Yet formulating the iterativity principle with reference to the concept of knowledge allows us to evade the objection.[34] That is, if we formulate the demand that knowledge has to be iterative as the demand that a knower has to be able to defend her claims against relevant alternatives, or to be open to alternatives showing that the putative knowledge is not (no longer) knowledge, then this objection from the factivity of knowledge no longer functions. The assumption of iterativity implies that the person whose knowledge is on trial has been confronted with a relevant alternative. It is not shaken by sudden alterations in worldly states. We see whether the man in our example knew that there was a building in his neighbourhood by whether or not he changes his belief when confronted with the information that it has burnt down.

This sensitivity condition for knowledge, first introduced by Robert Nozick, does not require that someone alter their beliefs whenever the world unexpectedly alters; otherwise we could never know any contingent empirical proposition. The truth conditions of such propositions can, after all, alter unnoticed at any time. But since the greater portion of the knowledge relevant to our lives and survival consists precisely of empirical, contingent propositions, some sensitivity condition or other must do justice to this fact. The condition must therefore be formulated as a counterfactual conditional stating that someone knows something only provided that they would adapt their belief accordingly when informed about pertinent worldly alterations.

Someone able to defend their knowledge must be able to state good reasons for standing by their claim and not renouncing it. In order to defend themselves, they will also cite good reasons for the good reasons they consider themselves to possess. Knowing something, that is, is not simply taking it on faith. Rather, knowledge is bound up with its possible justification, and since someone who knows something has good reasons for something, they must also be able to present good reasons for their good reasons should someone cast doubt on their initial justification.[35]

As we now know that every Cartesian sceptical argument depends upon the evidence transcendence of its sceptical hypothesis, we already have the following two premises for an initial formulation of a Cartesian paradox.

> (P1) We have no good reasons for the assumption that we are not dreaming: $\sim Gxt\ (\sim Dxt)$.
> (P2) We have good reasons for the assumption that we are not dreaming if we have good reasons for p: $Gxt\ (Gxtp \rightarrow \sim Dxt)$ (an

instance of *Descartes' principle*, where p must here be a proposition for which we can have good reasons at t only if we perceive that p).

The apparently plausible inference rules that we need in order to motivate a Cartesian paradox are:

(IR1) If we have good reasons for p, then we have good reasons for everything that follows from p insofar as we know that it follows from p (principle of closure).[36]

(IR2) If we have good reasons for p, then we also have good reasons for the belief that we have good reasons for p (principle of iterativity).[37]

With these rules we can formulate the following paradox:

(1) We have no good reasons for the assumption that we are not dreaming: $\sim$Gxt ($\sim$Dxt) (=P1).

(2) Suppose that we had good reasons for p: Gxtp.

(3) Then we also have good reasons to assume that we have good reasons that p: Gxt (Gxtp) (from (2), principle of iterativity).

(4) We have good reasons to assume that we are not dreaming, if we have good reasons for p: Gxt (Gxtp → $\sim$Dxt) (= P2).

(5) Since we have good reasons for everything that follows from p (for we have good reasons for p and we know, in accordance with IR1, that we must have good reasons for everything that follows from p insofar as we are aware that it follows from p); and since it follows from p that we are not currently dreaming that p, we must have good reasons for the belief that we are not currently dreaming – Gxt ($\sim$Dxt) (principle of closure from (3) and (4)).

(6) It is therefore true both that we have no good reasons for the belief that we are not dreaming and that we have good reasons for the belief that we are not dreaming, which is a contradiction (conjunction of (1) and (5)).

(C) As a consequence, we have no good reasons for p, since, if we accept all premises and rules of inference, a contradiction follows from the assumption that we have good reasons for p.

Put simply, we fall into the trap laid by the Cartesian sceptic's paradox as long as we assent to the conjunction of the following *prima facie* plausible principles.

(1) Whoever knows something also knows that their knowledge excludes all circumstances that would stand in the way of their knowing what they do – at least when they have been confronted with such circumstances. Therefore, if they know that they are

currently *perceiving* something, they must know that they are not dreaming. If someone knows that there is a table in front of them, they must also know that they are not merely dreaming that there is a table in front of them.

(2) But no one can know that they are not currently dreaming, because it is possible to find oneself in the phenomenal state of representing a table, even though the table is merely dreamed. The representation of a table does not as such contain any sufficient indication of its causal pedigree, even when it does in fact have an appropriate causal pedigree.

(3) Because no one can ever exclude the possibility that they are merely dreaming what they take themselves to perceive, no one can ever know whether they really know what they believe they know. One would have to precede every claim to perceptual knowledge with an indefinitely long series of conditionals such as 'If I am not dreaming', 'If I am not a brain in a vat', etc. And this would be absurd.[38]

It should now be clear that motivating a Cartesian sceptical paradox presupposes a series of general steps, and that these can in fact generate an indefinitely large number of paradoxes. So we are finally in a position to establish the general form of a Cartesian sceptical paradox.[39]

(P1) Principle of indistinguishability: We (x) have *hic et nunc* (t) no good reasons (G) for the assumption that we are not in a sceptical scenario (SC) that is phenomenally indistinguishable from the state in which we take ourselves to be: $\sim Gxt\ (\sim SCxtp)$.

(P2) We have good reasons for the assumption that we are not in a sceptical scenario if we have good reasons for p, where p is a proposition for which we could have no good reasons were we in a corresponding sceptical scenario: $Gxt\ (Gxtp \rightarrow \sim SCxt)$.

The seemingly plausible inference rules needed to motivate the general Cartesian paradox are:

(IR1) Principle of closure: If we have good reasons for p, then we have good reasons for everything that follows from p, insofar as we are aware that it follows from p.

(IR2) Principle of iterativity: If we have good reasons for p, then we also have good reasons for the assumption that we have good reasons for p.

The form of the general Cartesian sceptical paradox is thus as follows:

(1) Supposing we had *hic et nunc* good reasons for p: Gxtp.

(2) Then we would also have good reasons for the assumption that

we have good reasons for p: Gxt (Gxtp) (from (1), principle of iterativity).

(3) We have good reasons for the assumption that we are not in a corresponding state SC, if we have good reasons for p: Gxt (Gxtp → ~SCxt (= P2).

(4) Since we have good reasons for everything that follows from p, insofar as we are aware that it follows from p (= IR1); and since it follows from p that we are not merely SCing (i.e. dreaming or hallucinating, etc.) that p, we must have good reasons for assuming that we are not currently SCing that p: Gxt (~SCxtp) (from (2) and (3), principle of closure).

(5) We have no good reasons for the assumption that we are not in a state SC: ~Gxt (~SCxt) (= P1).[40]

(6) It is therefore true both that we have no good reasons for ~SC and that we have good reasons for ~SC, which is a contradiction: ~Gxt (~SCxt) ∧ Gxt (~SCxt) ((4) and (5), conjunction).

(C) Therefore, we have no good reason for p, since, if we accept all of our premises and rules of inference, a contradiction follows from the assumption that we have good reasons for p.

The formalised version of the general Cartesian paradox therefore looks like this:

(1) Gxtp
(2) Gxt (Gxtp)
(3) Gxt (Gxtp → ~SCxtp)
(4) Gxt (~SCxtp)
(5) ~Gxt (~SCxtp)
(6) ~Gxt (~SCxt) ∧ Gxt (~SCxt)
(C) ~Gxtp.

It obviously requires little heuristic effort to contrive a sceptical scenario for any given proposition, and thus for any given belief, allowing us to construct a *global scepticism* on a Cartesian basis. This scepticism, it should be noted, does not destroy all beliefs *at once* but, rather, all beliefs *one at a time*, which is why it does not fall victim to the straightforward objection that its very formulation involves a simple self-contradiction. Deploying the general structure of Cartesian scepticism in order to put any given proposition into question (without *ipso facto* putting them all into question at once) does not mean committing to any kind of semantic antinomy – i.e. assertions that would deprive themselves of their own assertive force, such as: 'all statements are false' or 'everything can be doubted'. Wright's implosion presupposes an incomparably more subtle formulation of Cartesian scepticism, one which enables us to attack all beliefs distributively without putting all beliefs into question collectively.

Let us take a state, SC, which rules out not only the possibility that we are currently experiencing anything at all but also our ability to competently exercise our discursive rationality. The SC in question might be an LSD trip or clinical psychosis: someone on an LSD trip can never be sure that what she thinks she perceives is independent of her perceiving it. But, at the same time, being in the state means that her discursive structures are sufficiently disrupted that, however rational she may think she is, she is unable to follow chains of consistent reasoning and so indulges in wild associations. We thus get the following two premises.

> (P1*) We have no good reasons for the assumption that we are not currently on an LSD trip, in which things are phenomenally indistinguishable from the state we take ourselves to be in (LSD): ~Gxt (~LSDxt).
>
> (P2) We have good reasons to believe that we are not on an LSD trip if we have good reasons to believe that p, where p is a proposition for which we could have no good reasons if we were in a corresponding sceptical scenario, because p presupposes that we can think rationally: Gxt (Gxtp → ~LSDxt).

(1) But we now have good reasons for the conjunction of both premises. For both premises have so far been motivated by a series of considerations that lend each of them a *prima facie* plausibility: Gxt (P1* ∧ P2).

(2) If we have good reasons for the conjunction of both premises and accept their conjunction, we cannot possibly be on an LSD trip: if we were, we could have no reasons for anything at all. Yet since we can accept both premises only on the basis of a series of motivating considerations (we cannot just suddenly grasp them out of the blue), it follows that we have good reasons for the assumption that, if both premises are true, we are not on an LSD trip: (P1* ∧ P2) → ~LSDxt.

(3) Since we have good reasons for the conjunction of the premises, it follows from the principle of closure that we have good reasons for the negation of P1*. The paradox therefore eliminates its own premises, as it presupposes that we can *understand* it: this would be impossible if we were on an LSD trip – i.e. if one of its premises were true. And, with this result, the implosion is complete.

Just as there are indefinitely many consistent instances of the general structure of Cartesian scepticism, the implosion would have it that there are also indefinitely many instances that are self-undermining, resulting in a contradiction between their motivation and their explicitly assumed premises. So taking one of the consistent instances with the general structure of Cartesian scepticism to be a valid and sound argument (and therefore not a paradox!) means abdicating our entire rationality. We end up having to commit ourselves to indefinitely many contradictions, since these follow from the motivation of whichever particular instance we accepted. The implosion thus seems finally to present us with a suitable weapon for defeating Cartesian scepticism – at least as far as Wright is concerned.

However, instead of dissolving Cartesian scepticism, the implosion in fact drives it to an extreme by generating a general Cartesian sceptical paradox of its own. In doing so, it *strengthens* the paradox. For what conclusion could be more sceptical than that we not only cannot know whether we are currently dreaming or perceiving something, but that we *also* cannot know whether we are even in a position to process reasons for the belief that we do not know whether we are currently dreaming or perceiving something? The implosive instances of Cartesian scepticism are therefore themselves paradoxical. More precisely, they generate an *antinomy of discursive rationality*: if they can be motivated, they cannot be motivated, because, when we try to understand their motivation, we have to reckon with the possibility that we are not in full possession of our rational faculties – which then makes it impossible to understand the motivation.

This paradoxical self-reference arises in any situation in which we ask ourselves whether or not we are in full possession of our rational faculties in posing the question. If we manage to convince ourselves that we are not in fact in full possession of our faculties, then we do so using those very faculties. This does not of course amount to a proof that we are in possession of our rational faculties, else nobody who was in fact in full possession of their rational faculties could ever ask themselves whether they might, on occasion, be experiencing a lapse in rationality. Part of being in full possession of one's rational faculties is being able to wonder from time to time if one is indeed in possession of them. And we can also believe that we are when, in fact, we are not.[41]

The implosive instances of Cartesian scepticism thus simply serve to reveal a further paradoxical property, which, at least at first glance, does not pertain to its non-implosive instances. We can celebrate them as a genuine implosion of Cartesian scepticism only if we *presuppose* that we are in full possession of our rational capacities in the very moment that we run through the paradox. There are thus two options: either we do understand the motivation of an implosive instance of Cartesian scepticism, in which case we are in full possession of our rational faculties and are not on an LSD trip – but then we cannot exclude being on an LSD trip; or we do not understand the motivation of the implosive instance because we are not in full possession of our rational faculties – but then we do not satisfy the conditions necessary to understand the paradox in the first place. If we understand the paradox, we have to reckon with the possibility that we have not really understood it, as we would not be in a position to understand anything at all. If some such sceptical scenario were true, it would not follow that it was false, merely that we found ourselves in the unfortunate position of being unable to determine its truth value.

It is part and parcel of the concept of discursive rationality as a mental capacity that we can ask ourselves whether or not we are exercising it in a way that would so much as allow us to understand the motivation of a paradox. And this question is itself an instance of the paradox insofar as we can take it as a basis for developing implosive instances of the general paradox (such as the LSD scenario).

If we have good reasons for anything at all, then we must have good reasons for the belief that certain sceptical hypotheses are false. But we cannot ensure that we have any good reasons whatsoever without undertaking a series of reflections, and these reflections will themselves be fallible. One way of making this fallibility comprehensible is to entertain scenarios in which we merely have the impression of being in full possession of our faculties. This exercise could well fail insofar as its details prove to be unwarranted. But it could also fail insofar as we just happen not to find ourselves at the height of our rational powers, or simply, for reasons unbeknown to us, insofar as we never attain the rational threshold necessary for formulating true thoughts about our mental powers' modes of operation.

In short, reason's self-examination presupposes its own fallibility, and this means that we cannot secure our own rationality by simply insisting that we have, just now, in the course of our apparent reasoning, been fully rational. In a given situation, it is always empirically possible that we might not be in full possession of our faculties, even though we falsely believe that we are. The possibility of a genuinely paradox-engendering error truly exists and cannot be disabled by any anti-sceptical argument.

Wright's dialectical argument shows that Cartesian scepticism combines a series of premises that a rational – that is, discursively competent – being ought to accept. If it is true that these premises, in virtue of their *own* motivation, commit us to the idea that we can have no good reasons to be rational at all, this would only be all the more devastating for our discursive rationality. Remember, the general structure of Cartesian scepticism does not deploy any external premises that a rational thinker cannot accept but, rather, exploits certain consequences of our discursive rationality. It shows how we, as rational beings, cannot not be in a position to cite good reasons for the belief that we *are* rational beings.[42] The Cartesian evil demon hypothesis is just one way of bringing out how the exercise of our rational faculties might be impeded in some manner beyond our grasp. We would then collapse into a cogito, a kind of awareness that might perhaps never extend as far as formulating true thoughts about itself; its occasional momentary intuitions would never allow it to arrive at any conceptually articulated self-description, let alone one which might afford it some understanding of its own activities.

In short, if we are rational beings, we can formulate indefinitely many sceptical scenarios (the dream argument, the evil demon, etc.) that commit us to assuming indefinitely many paradoxes incompatible with the proper functioning of our discursive rationality: all paradoxes of the LSD type teach us that we could be in a truly desperate state to the effect (1) that this state is phenomenally indistinguishable from the more epistemically favourable state we suppose ourselves to be in and (2) that this condition means we cannot even understand that we cannot understand anything in it. Attempts to understand what follows from the fact that we could be in such a condition are condemned to fail *because* we might be in such a condition. We could be in a condition that is so epistemically fatal that we can no longer attack it with rational tools. And we would not even be in a position to understand quite how damaging it would in fact be for us to be in it. When we consider these consequences, the ground begins to slip from beneath our feet. Yet if the sceptic has managed to entrap us in this situation by presenting us with a series of ever more deadly paradoxes (beginning with the dream argument, say, and ending up with some variant on the LSD argument), then she has clearly succeeded in destroying far more than we originally bargained for when we first lent her a reluctant ear.

The implosion refutes the sceptic only if we impute to her a commitment to discursive rationality. As Michael Stack notes in his essay 'Self-refuting arguments':

> The believer in knowledge begs the question by trying to impose the concept of good argument on the sceptic. The sceptic need not be bound by this. Since his opponent accepts the concept of good argument, it is perfectly in order for the sceptic to use this concept and show that the concept of good argument is self-defeating: if there were any good arguments there wouldn't be, which is what a reduction is all about.[43]

The implosion thus strengthens rather than refutes Cartesian scepticism – but this is only a regrettable result at first glance. To see why, we need only consider some of the dialectical consequences of a potentially successful implosion argument that would turn out to be more damaging for epistemology than general Cartesian scepticism. Borrowing from Richard Fumerton, we can make a distinction between a *formal* and an *epistemic self-contradiction*.[44] We are confronted with a formal self-contradiction when the premises of an argument are incompatible with its conclusion. Presumably, no serious sceptical argument is guilty of this. Wright is therefore correct to try to show that Cartesian scepticism is guilty of an *epistemic* self-contradiction, whereby the motivation of the paradox implies that we are not in a position to understand the paradox itself. Hence Wright suggests that scepticism cannot undermine the very discursive rationality it tries to make use of. But we can concoct a range of cases in which the self-contradiction exhibited by a sceptical argument swallows up not only the argument itself but also the knowledge claim under attack, and thus, in the most extreme case, discursive rationality as a whole.

Suppose there is an entire culture that finds it rational to consult an oracle whenever they cannot resolve some particular question. The oracle can answer only 'yes' or 'no', and, supposedly, it never lies. Imagine too that there is a local oracle sceptic who argues that the people should stop consulting the oracle if they want rational answers to their questions; far better, she maintains, to remain in a state of uncertainty. Say the locals are uncertain about the sceptic's claim; obviously, it would be epistemically self-contradictory for them to have the sceptic ask the oracle if she is correct. But the sceptic questions the oracle anyhow: she asks it whether it is a reliable source of information and whether it arrives at its results in an epistemically controlled manner, even if its methods remain opaque to the questioner. Even after several reruns of the experiment, the sceptic consistently receives the answer 'no'. Where does this leave the oracle's followers? They would be ill-advised to claim that the sceptic has no right to question the oracle in order to test her oracle scepticism. Nor will it get them any further to point out that, when she questions the oracle, the sceptic is guilty of an epistemic self-contradiction along the lines that she appeals to the oracle in order to receive confirmation that no one should appeal to oracles when they want to know something.

The oracle sceptic therefore generates a paradox for the adepts in the very same way that the evident epistemic self-contradiction of implosive instances of Cartesian scepticism generates a paradoxical situation for discursive rationality. Proving an epistemic self-contradiction in our sceptical paradox does not necessarily lead to its solution. Rather, we further boost the power of the paradox if we can show that its general formulation has logically and dialectically consistent instances on the one hand and epistemically self-contradictory instances on the other. That the latter threaten to rob us of our discursive rationality altogether in no way alters this result.

The implosion presupposes that Cartesian scepticism essentially cannot be *eclectic*: one cannot doubt, say, the existence of a representation-independent external world without putting into question the existence of the past, or of other minds, say, because the motivation of the one doubt suffices to motivate the others.[45] The foundation of Cartesian doubt is a general structure. But by committing to the soundness of an instance of a general logical structure, we commit ourselves, whether we like it or not, to all other instances of that structure. However, if there is another instance that is not sound, since it cancels out its own premises, then the structure itself is fragile.

Wright suggests that, if Cartesian scepticism is to constitute a serious, well-grounded, epistemic threat, its motivation must be thoroughly epistemically transparent.[46] So, in order for Cartesian scepticism to present an *epistemologically* relevant problem, it cannot launch its various attacks unmotivated: it has to produce a series of considerations capable of leading to a suspension of judgement, to justified doubt, or (in the worst case) to semantic nihilism – i.e. to acceptance of the possibility that all our thought might be empty, that no articulated thought ever manages to put us in touch with an independent reality.

Wright himself remarks that it might seem fairly shocking to claim that his implosion argument allows us finally to put dream scepticism to bed.[47] And in this he is surely correct. Were the claim true, the implosion would rob us of one of the key methodological exercises of the philosophical tradition. Whenever we were confronted with a sceptical scenario recognisable as an instance of Cartesian scepticism, we could confidently set it aside. But this would mean losing a piece of critical apparatus that we deploy not only in philosophy but whenever we are 'sceptical' in the ordinary, non-terminological sense. We should therefore think twice before all too hastily renouncing Cartesian scepticism: it is a vital element of our critical sensorium, an element which functions only as long as we can take a step back from our everyday judgements in order to evaluate and test them *as such*. Scepticism is, if nothing else, a radicalised form of critique inherent to the exercise of judgement. If discursive rationality is on trial, we can exclude from the very outset the possibility that, at the boundaries of its self-examination, it generates a form of semantic nihilism.

Consequently, the strategy of specifying the problem of Cartesian scepticism by rationally constructing the general Cartesian paradox is one that we should only push so far. We need to avoid assigning all sceptical scenarios – including those we encounter in the visual arts, in film and literature, and so on – a merely epistemic valence in the narrow sense.[48] The phenomena that take the form of arguments and paradoxes in contemporary epistemology also possess undeniably existential, indeed religious components. The existence of the world and the problem of other minds are both classical problems of philosophy and religion. The debate surrounding the problem of Cartesian scepticism in contemporary epistemology tends to skip over how this variety of scepticism represents a particular stage in the history of subjectivity and how the series of meditations within which Descartes himself introduces it possess a partly theological significance. The investigation of one's self and one's cognitive capacity does not go back just to the Delphic γνῶθι σαυτόν; it also has a religious pre-history, which culminated in the 'sceptical' scenarios of Greek tragedy.[49] Indeed, insofar as it *reduces* scepticism to an epistemological problem, the contemporary renaissance of scepticism is based upon a forgetfulness of the tradition. It is then no accident that great sceptics such as Montaigne, Friedrich Schlegel and Nietzsche are wholly lost from view, given how they refuse from the start to play along with discursive rationality's criteria of consistency. Against these criteria, they advocate a kind of sceptical thinking that faces up to its own paradoxes in and through its literary form, specifically, as an ironic reaction to a scepticism that cannot be staved off by the resources of mere epistemology. When talking about Cartesian scepticism, we only impoverish our discussion if we lose sight of such attempts.

Transitions from being to appearance, from judgements of the form 'S is P' to 'S seems to be P', are what allow us to establish epistemic distance. While a judgement of the 'S is P' form implies, qua assertion, that one stands behind the judgement and so commits to S *being* P, asserting the judgement 'S seems to be P' merely implies that one has reasons to assume that S is P, but that these do not suffice to assert 'S is P' without reservation. Seems-talk thus performs a critical function, which Cartesian scepticism exploits by devising an argument schema with indefinitely many instances that reduce judgements of the 'S is P' form to judgements of the 'S seems to be P' form. Faced with these arguments, we need to adduce reasons to defend the original judgement against its phenomenological reduction. Under non-sceptical conditions, reference to possible appearances (illusions, deception, dishonesty, etc.) thus performs a critical function, which is then deployed by sceptical scenarios of all kinds (the evil demon, Dretske's zebras, Goldman's barns, etc.) to put into question discursive rationality as a whole.[50]

It is only because we do not always grasp the full import of our words, thoughts and actions that we are triggered to the critical reflection that potentially grants us a more determinate understanding of them. In the most extreme case, this critical reflection induces sceptical despair. It might be tempting to circumvent this possibility by ruling out the use of harmless sceptical scenarios, and thus the critical distance from our everyday beliefs that they encourage, on the basis that they represent instances of an implosive argument and are thus untenable. But it is, rather, this defensive strategy which is untenable. For we could not even embark upon the search for knowledge if it were not for the fact that our cognitive endeavours play out within a dimension of ignorance. If we want to know what we are really doing when we make knowledge ascriptions – that is, if we want to secure the right concept of knowledge – we have to place our prior knowledge in (at least) temporary suspension. The usually unproblematic (indeed, heuristic) ignorance implied in the search for knowledge first becomes a *philosophical* problem when it is generalised. We might insist that this generalisation ultimately has to fail because it is undergirded by an unstable dialectical structure. But we then rule out any chance of establishing a *philosophical* relation to our fallibility and of specifying criteria for successful knowledge ascriptions.

Epistemology (and ultimately all philosophy) is driven by a critical impulse – an impulse that certainly merits the label 'sceptical'. Yet, if nothing remained of scepticism besides a precarious dialectical structure with self-contradictory instances, our critical capacities would evaporate into an empty acquiescence in our everyday linguistic practices, into the bloodless quietism that Wright wants to combat in his attempts to destroy Cartesian scepticism with rational resources.

Wright's favoured 'sceptical solution' points to how large swathes of our linguistic practice rest upon groundless yet necessary presuppositions: hinge propositions. These propositions are harmless, because indispensable, though unjustifiable presuppositions of all cognitive projects. To arrive at this solution, we first have to be able to *stage* sceptical scenarios, so to speak. This does not mean that we have to go along with the general paradox and its indefinitely many instances, in the sense of taking some or all of them as valid and sound arguments. We need accept no obviously false conclusions. But if we could immediately dispel *every* Cartesian sceptical doubt by adverting to its implosive consequences, we would deny ourselves any possibility of casting a critical eye over our cognitive prospects. And this really would lead to a 'bloodless quietism' or to a blind acquiescence in our equally blindly conducted linguistic practices.[51]

The first step to introducing the implosion was the thesis that we have to see Cartesian scepticism as a family of paradoxes, which can be classified according to their logical structure. So far, we have shown only that the generalised logical structure of *Cartesian* paradoxes is dialectically self-undermining: their motivation is incompatible with their execution. An unmotivated manifestation of Cartesian scepticism presents no problem for epistemology. A motivated paradox, by contrast, leads to a general paradox, which threatens discursive rationality as a whole. And the implosion, as we have seen, cannot help us evade this threat, since it endangers the very critical sensorium that we employ in our capacity as epistemologists.

The implosion presupposes that we have to concede the relevance of Cartesian scepticism only when it consists of at least two aspects: (1) a motivation theory, which establishes the plausibility of a series of premises, and (2) an argument with premises, rules of inference and a conclusion. The conclusion here is not unacceptable because we cannot but be irritated when we hear that our lives might be only dreamed, hallucinated, etc. It is unacceptable because it commits us to the thesis that we are not entitled to assume *any* empirically contentful proposition: for each class of empirical propositions there exists a corresponding sceptical scenario that undermines the acquisition of good reasons for the class to which the assumption belongs.

A distinguishing characteristic of Wright's analyses of sceptical arguments is that he generally investigates them within the context of a theory of warrant.[52] Since it is hard to diagnose a case of knowledge when the putative knower is unable to adduce the required justification for his belief in principle (Descartes' principle again), it seems obvious to treat the problem of scepticism as a problem about the justification or warrant for knowledge ascriptions. This presupposes in turn, however, that we can *consider* the acquisition of justification as problematic, else we could not even initiate any kind of theory-building process. No one will construct a theory of veridical perception, for example, without having at some point been confronted with some variant of Cartesian scepticism. Yet if we reach the end of the implosion argument and throw away the ladder which led us there, we then find that we have blocked the way to the positive enterprise of developing a theory of justification.

Wright's own theory of the connection between warrant, truth and objectivity therefore represents a comprehensible enterprise only provided his readers have not already been informed about the downfall of Cartesian scepticism. The implosion is itself paradoxical because it consists of a series of seemingly plausible premises, seemingly acceptable inference rules, and the obviously unacceptable conclusion that we cannot be *warranted* to any *motivation* of a direct or indirect Cartesian sceptical argument. Were we entitled to the motivation of *a* Cartesian sceptical paradox, we would thus *eo ipso* be entitled to the motivation of *all* Cartesian sceptical paradoxes. However, this class of all Cartesian sceptical paradoxes has the implosive property of being epistemically inconsistent: some Cartesian sceptical paradoxes are not paradoxes at all insofar as, for a given argument to count as a paradox, our discursive rationality has to be able to register them as a threat to its own functioning and integrity. Wright implies that the motivation of sceptical paradoxes must be epistemically transparent, at least potentially. But some Cartesian sceptical paradoxes rob us of the modes of registration necessary to understand a paradox at all, and thus to understand it *as* a paradox. As a result, there is no consistent class of Cartesian sceptical paradoxes – precisely because they are paradoxes. This is the logical result of implosion, which clearly raises important dialectical questions about the construction of epistemological theories. Many of these have been taken up by Wright himself in subsequent work.[53]

Positive contributions to epistemology first assume a determinate shape against the background of a methodologically necessary scepticism. This scepticism cannot of course consist in holding all at once that the general form of Cartesian scepticism is plausible, that all its premises are acceptable, and that its conclusion is true (and thus also acceptable). If we formulate the problem of Cartesian scepticism as a genus of sceptical paradoxes with indefinitely many instances, we cannot resist the apparently logical consequence that *all* instances are unstable provided the genus has at least one epistemically contradictory instance. Wright's argumentation for the implosion is suspicious not only because it denies us an indispensable critical sensorium but also because it rests upon the assumption that Cartesian scepticism is not *permitted* to abrogate discursive rationality. One of the implosion's presuppositions, after all, is that there cannot be a sceptical paradox that operates with the impossibility of discursive rationality – i.e. through invoking a scenario that involves the suspension of our cognitive competence. Wright thus argues as though such a paradox could not be motivated, because its motivation would anyhow presuppose the possibility that we understand it. Yet, say Cartesian scepticism could bring us to a point where we could no longer even be sure of possessing the logical competence required to understand it, let alone to believe that we could oppose it with an intelligibly structured series of thoughts: in that case, while it would certainly have defeated *us*, it would by no means have defeated itself.

In order to make explicit its own presuppositions, its own motivation, scepticism has to be *consciously* integrated into the construction of an epistemological theory. In the best case, this integration will result in the theory retrieving and redeeming its own presuppositions. Scepticism thus makes an appearance not only among the objects of epistemology – i.e. in the domain of first-order theories; it also belongs primarily to the motivation of epistemology itself.[54]

Faced with the conclusion that placing our discursive rationality under philosophical conditions generates paradoxes and commits us to the irrational assumption that discursive rationality *as such* is an inconsistent presupposition, it can seem that our best bet is to refrain from placing our discursive rationality under philosophical conditions.[55] This decision, however, leads to the problem of quietism, the renunciation of philosophical theory. Yet those facing the challenge of scepticism can hardly be satisfied with such an extreme measure; they are already too deeply involved in epistemological theorising simply to turn their back on philosophical reflection and make a leap into silence. At this stage, it is only right to demand either a rational solution to the paradox or an argument that explains why we are not in fact obliged to confront it in the first place.

Part II

Contextualism and the Finitude of Discourse

I have so far been observing a distinction between (at least) two varieties of anti-sceptical strategy. On the one hand, there are strategies that impute a hidden *epistemic self-contradiction* to the sceptic. These strategies deploy the methods of logical analysis and their associated solutions. Wright's implosion of the Cartesian sceptical paradox, which we investigated in chapter 6, clearly belongs in this category. On the other hand, there are strategies that impute a *dialectical* inconsistency to the sceptic, an inconsistency between theory motivation and construction. The Greek term of art for such strategies is περιτροπή[1] –that is, self-refutation or, as it is often translated, 'turning the tables'.[2] When it came to examining Wright's arguments, however, we saw how his implosion involves not only logical but also dialectical analyses of Cartesian scepticism. After all, one of its key diagnoses is of a tension between the *motivation* and the *execution* of a Cartesian sceptical paradox in its most general form. According to Wright, it is just this tension which leads to the implosion.

On my view, however, the tension in fact leads to a semantic nihilism which only serves to strengthen the original impetus of the paradox. And since all it takes to motivate the general Cartesian paradox is to invoke our fundamental (and indispensable) epistemological concepts, we now confront a new question: under which operating conditions does knowledge function *in spite of* its ultimate impossibility? How can we acquire knowledge given that we can never provide a complete account of how we can acquire any knowledge (including knowledge about knowledge)? Accordingly, my task in this second part of this study will be to provide an analytic of discursive finitude – to answer the question of how discourse can manage and organise its blind spots (and thus its potential instability) such that meaning can so much as emerge.

Because Wright himself does not distinguish between logical and dialectical analysis, a dialectical problem arises for the implosion; for it simply *presupposes* that discursive rationality is essentially debarred from being deployed against itself. In the last chapter we showed how this presupposition only begs the question against the general Cartesian sceptical paradox. As we saw, the structure of the implosion turns out to have a decidedly awkward property: contrary to its original aim, it manages to motivate the insight that we cannot ascertain whether we are in full possession of our rational powers in and through exercising those very powers. The following part of this study can be read as an attempt to respond to this insight by providing a diagnosis of the necessary finitude of discursively communicable knowledge. This diagnosis will ultimately become clear in the *peritrope* that arises at the metatheoretical level once the metatheory draws the consequences of *epistemic* finitude for *epistemology* itself. After all, there is no reason why the metatheory should be exempt from the theory conditions that are otherwise valid for all discursive projects as such. For our investigation, the most significant point is that these conditions always generate a structure of presuppositions that is necessarily opaque to the discourse it determines. And, for this reason, all discursive projects are subject to a dialectically grounded condition of revisability: because their initial conditions cannot be redeemed as the discourse develops (precisely because the *terminus a quo* of theory construction is not yet itself subject to the theory conditions to be established), all discursive projects are finite, including epistemology.

'Finitude' should here be understood in the sense in which Heidegger alleges that Kant's theoretical philosophy is finite in *Kant and the Problem of Metaphysics*: namely, as the thesis that human cognition is finite because it always depends on acquiring information that it does not itself generate through its processes of information acquisition. While Kant explains the finitude of human cognition within the framework of his theory of sensible receptivity, discursive finitude in general need not arise from our specifically *sensible* receptivity: it is inherent to every mode of registration we might deploy to justify an epistemic claim. Kant's assertion that human cognition is finite in virtue of its sensibility is selective; it exempts reason's self-investigation from the rule that objective knowledge is fallible. But why should reason's self-investigation be any less liable to error than investigations that depend upon receiving information via the senses – i.e. on information about the 'external world'? The finitude of human cognition is much more general than the finitude of sensible cognition. The latter is finite because the former is finite, and human cognition is finite because *every* form of discursive rationality is finite.

As we will see throughout the course of Part II, the arguments of *Pyrrhonian scepticism* function as they do because they possess a peculiar paradoxical property: that they cancel out their own epistemic status in the course of making good on their motivation. These arguments are dialectically unstable, but that does not mean that they cannot function as directives for constructing a *finite epistemology*. We will have to address the worry that dialectical instability derives from Pyrrhonian scepticism's combination of its self-cancelling character with a misguided conception of absolute knowing. Yet, as we will see, there is no reason to think that the self-cancelling property in question is incompatible with an insight into the *prima facie* plausibility of Cartesian-style sceptical paradoxes; rather, Pyrrhonian scepticism makes use of strategies of implosion in order to show that knowledge claims, taken to their reflexive extremes, tend to collapse under the pressure of meta-reflection. Their plausibility does not exclude the possibility that they implode upon closer inspection. As our investigation progresses, we will see how Pyrrhonian scepticism, however surprisingly, is the rightful candidate for pursuing the project of an integrative anti-scepticism. This is of course somewhat paradoxical, because it means reinterpreting the Pyrrhonianism developed by Sextus Empiricus as an *anti*-sceptical strategy – a strategy that rests upon a stable, self-referential acknowledgement of finitude.

In chapter 1, I introduced a distinction between *negative dogmatism, methodological scepticism* and *Cartesian scepticism*. It is worth recapitulating this distinction in light of what we have established so far. Negative dogmatism aims to change our attitude to a determinate set of supposed knowledge claims by showing that no element of this set is qualified for the status of knowledge; by contrast, Cartesian scepticism erects a logical structure that generates an indefinitely large set of paradoxes. A Cartesian sceptical paradox is so constructed that it is impossible to go along with its conclusion unless we want to pay the price of sacrificing all first-order knowledge – and so of denying that we possess something that we do in fact possess. Direct Cartesian arguments not only attack knowledge but deny that we can have good reasons for our beliefs about the world. This results in the threat of semantic nihilism, as we end up unable to understand how we can so much as refer to worldly objects and states of affairs *as though* they were substantially independent of our acts of reference.

Because it constitutes an internal antinomy in the concept of knowledge, it is impossible to accept Cartesian scepticism as the result of a motivated process of deliberation. The antinomy is based upon the fact that the ability to claim objective knowledge involves taking on a commitment to defend that knowledge, and it thus depends upon the ability to cite good reasons. Since these are never truth-guaranteeing, but at best authorising grounds, the finitude and contingency of good reasons threatens knowledge with implosion. This means that Cartesian scepticism, far from being a substantial theoretical option, is ultimately an unwelcome consequence of the concept of knowledge itself. It is therefore not surprising that contemporary epistemology often tries to redefine this concept in a way that allows us to dismiss the danger of Cartesian scepticism.[3]

Cartesian scepticism presents a series of considerations that result in an untenable conclusion; the conclusion is incompatible with most or all of the beliefs that we possessed before we were confronted with Cartesian scepticism. It seems that we could liberate ourselves from the clutches of Cartesian scepticism if we could only find an epistemological self-contradiction in its logical structure.

In this context, the debate with the Cartesian sceptic is pursued in the name of our discursive rationality, whose essential machinery comes under threat if the sceptic can expose such concepts as 'knowledge', 'justification', 'warrant' and 'good reasons', as well as such operations as induction, *modus ponens* or the principle of closure as mere ungrounded assumptions. This provokes the desire to find a ground for discursive rationality without already relying on its full-blown functionality. However, how is it ever possible to find a not yet fully rational ground of discursive rationality? This is a question for Pyrrhonian scepticism, which results precisely as a response to the apparent lack of grounding for our trust in reason.

Because the confrontation with Cartesian scepticism unavoidably leads to a refinement of our anti-sceptical strategies, it suggests the possibility of a *methodological scepticism* that intentionally introduces sceptical scenarios that lack any philosophically substantial content. It opens up a space for constructing sceptical paradoxes as an epistemological exercise, an exercise whose end is to teach us something about reason's capacity for engaging with itself. It thereby allows us to integrate scepticism into the method of epistemology, whose primary goal is to uncover and make explicit the right concept of knowledge – that is, the concept of knowledge that is at the same time knowledge of knowledge. The aim of this kind of (methodological) scepticism is to lead us to reflect on the logical structure of Cartesian scepticism: the point is not that we cannot *know* whether we are dreaming or whether there could be an evil demon but, rather, that applying the concept 'knowledge' generates presuppositions that sceptical scenarios bring to our attention – precisely by painting situations that undermine them.

Say the motivation of Cartesian scepticism did in fact imply a self-contradiction. In that case, if making good on that motivation (developing sceptical arguments) requires that the sceptic draw on the fundamental concepts and operations of discursive rationality, we are entitled to demand that she execute her sceptical programme without implying any contradictions. And if it then turned out that a being who shared our discursive rationality would be irrational if it acquiesced in Cartesian scepticism, that form of scepticism would, seemingly, no longer present any serious problem for our discursive rationality. We could always rest assured that we have a right to ignore Cartesian sceptical arguments to the extent to which they undermine discursive rationality and, accordingly, that we can continue to go about the business of cognition without first having to refute them. But this is not a viable strategy. The sceptic challenges us to show that we are not under an illusion generated by the mere *impression* that we are rational. Discursive rationality needs to be able to get a hold of itself without simply rejecting the very idea of a potentially mad use of reason. We still need a reason for believing that our discursive rationality actually works roughly in the way we characterise it in stating some of its most fundamental argumentative/logical principles, such as *modus ponens*.

One of these constituent elements of discursive rationality is the principle that a paradox implodes if one of its instances is self-contradictory. One need only motivate *traditional* (non-implosive) instances of the Cartesian paradox in order to go one better and introduce instances that cast doubt on discursive rationality as such: if there is a paradox stating that it is quite possible that I cannot even understand its motivation because it is quite possible that I do not understand *anything*, this hardly means that the paradox disappears. If I could understand its motivation, I could not understand it anyhow. The paradox thus shows that I might not be able to understand anything, not even the paradox. And say it does not really manage to show this – on account of the fact that someone who cannot understand anything can hardly be *shown* anything – the paradox has still had its desired effect: you do not have to *convince* somebody who does not understand anything that they do not understand anything. Yet if it does manage to show this, then it also shows that it is superfluous to motivate the paradox to begin with – which does not mean that our epistemic situation is any less unfortunate: if we found ourselves in such a ruinous epistemic condition that our discursive rationality could not even secure its own basic functionality, it would hardly require the subtlety of *paradoxes* to cast us into the abyss of reason. The lesson we should draw, therefore, is that the implosive character of certain sceptical paradoxes is by no means the Achilles' heel of Cartesian scepticism; instead, it points to its very epicentre. This epicentre manifests itself primarily in a form of *Pyrrhonian scepticism*, the form of scepticism which, in what follows, I shall integrate into the construction of our metatheory. Doing so will allow us to see how Pyrrhonian scepticism is the true agent of epistemology, a fact which is also becoming ever clearer in the contemporary scepticism debate.[4]

Negative dogmatism and Cartesian scepticism by no means exhaust the sceptical repertoire. The *Pyrrhonian scepticism* that is now up for investigation represents a further variant. From an historical point of view it is in fact *the* prototypical variant of scepticism, while from a systematic perspective it is the most sophisticated. And, as I have been stressing, it can be integrated into positive (although not dogmatic) theory construction. Since the Pyrrhonian sceptic explicitly accepts that the *peritrope* poses a valid objection to her argument and, insofar as she raises this objection *herself*, even sees this as the very point of her scepticism, it is worth taking a more systematic look at Pyrrhonian scepticism in order to explore how it bears on the possibility of epistemology.[5] Cartesian scepticism is unstable, at least on the interpretation that presents its logical structure as a paradox. Yet we still require a variant of scepticism to save the project of epistemology from its dialectical implosion. To this end, it is Pyrrhonian scepticism which will give us the tools for a more precise determination of the relationship between logical analyses of sceptical arguments on the one hand and their dialectical function within epistemology's overall theoretical economy on the other.

7

Pyrrhonian Scepticism as the Agent of Epistemology

The history of scepticism teaches us that we cannot reduce it, in any of its guises, to an exclusively theoretical problem. It assumes other shapes besides that of a philosophical paradox. The most developed versions of scepticism as a purely theoretical, or logical, problem are still just derivative products of an original mode of enquiry, which we should not just dismiss dogmatically as 'unphilosophical'. Indeed, from an historical point of view, this mode of enquiry was responsible for the first formulations of methodological scepticism, and thus for the foundation of epistemology.

The origins of scepticism are clearly traceable in the development of Greek philosophy, and we can make out the steps of a process leading up to the formation of Pyrrhonian scepticism. The significance of this variety of scepticism for contemporary epistemology, which has been made particularly clear thanks to a series of important recent studies,[1] derives from how it puts our discursive rationality under pressure as a whole: faced with this form of scepticism, we can longer take for granted our previously established and accepted conditions of rationality and restrict ourselves merely to the task of maximising their coherence by minimising any residual irrational elements. For this form of scepticism works by turning the brute fact of rationality against rationality itself: there is evidently no justification for our discursive rationality that does not already presuppose our discursive rationality as its justification. The *rational*ist game of giving and asking for reasons is ultimately revealed as groundless (ir*rational*) and so, in the final analysis, as arbitrary. Borrowing from Schelling, we can capture Pyrrhonian scepticism's original guiding concern in the question: 'So why *is there* reason, why not unreason?'[2]

Michael Williams has argued that Pyrrhonian scepticism is a 'scepticism without theory',[3] whose definitive characteristics can be brought out by way of a comparison with methodological scepticism. Methodological scepticism deploys doubt within an *already established discipline* as a methodological tool for constructing the concept of knowledge. By contrast, the goal of Pyrrhonian scepticism is to disrupt the establishment of any such discipline from the outset. One of the cornerstones of philosophy's traditional debate with Pyrrhonian scepticism is the critical question of whether attempts to justify discursive rationality as such land us in a *virtuous* or a *vicious* circle. After all, the groundlessness of reason does not in and of itself imply the impossibility of theory.

Although the comparison has yet to be developed in much detail, it is frequently stressed that there are important *systematic* parallels between Wittgenstein's anti-sceptical strategy in *On Certainty* and Sextus' Pyrrhonian scepticism.[4] Both philosophise under extreme sceptical conditions, with the intention of putting the enterprise of philosophy into question while simultaneously wanting to do justice to our ordinary (linguistic) practice or to everyday phenomena. Wittgenstein and Sextus share the goal of showing how philosophy as a theoretical project is uninteresting in general because inconclusive in principle. And both attempt to construct an inference from the impossibility of a universal philosophical theory to the idea that there is an ineliminable deficit in philosophical reasoning as such.

As we shall see, the seemingly *anti*-sceptical strategy that Wittgenstein deploys to reject the hyperbolic doubt of Cartesian scepticism does overlap to a considerable degree with Pyrrhonian scepticism. Indeed, Wittgenstein's anti-sceptical strategy exhibits several of Pyrrhonian scepticism's systematic traits. It follows that Wittgenstein is a sceptic in a certain sense, even though he sometimes presents his most convincing reflections on rule-following, the impossibility of a private language, and the groundlessness of our (linguistic) practices as anti-sceptical strategies. Especially in *On Certainty*, he clearly tries to show that the Cartesian sceptic strives to formulate questions outside of any sufficiently determinate context. In this regard, Wittgenstein directs his objections exclusively against Cartesian scepticism, but it is nevertheless vital to see how, by the principle of determinate negation, he needs to treat this form of scepticism as a foil that allows his own position to come into view.

The common denominator of Pyrrhonian scepticism and Wittgenstein's anti-sceptical strategy (which will occupy us throughout the remainder of this study) is the connection between *contextualism* and *naturalism*. At this stage, it is worth giving a provisional, anticipatory sketch of these two positions.

(1) The *contextualism* common to both Pyrrhonian scepticism and Wittgenstein is based on the idea that we can motivate and formulate versions of Cartesian scepticism only if we ignore the context-sensitivity of knowledge ascriptions or, more generally, of cognitive projects that process information with objective purport. Cartesian scepticism seems to presuppose the *possibility* of the absolute certainty of our beliefs: if we know anything at all, we know it with absolute certainty. Yet the absolute certainty of my belief that, say, there is a table in front of me disappears in at least one context: namely, the supposedly context-free context of Cartesian scepticism's motivation. The impression of a paradox derives

from how the premises of Cartesian scepticism are valid in a certain context but lose their validity as soon as we find ourselves beyond its scope. It follows that our beliefs forfeit their absolute certainty as soon as they are placed in the supposedly context-free context of epistemology, revealing Cartesian scepticism as an epiphenomenon of the epistemological attitude. So, if we can show that that attitude is ungrounded or even unreasonable by its own lights, we will be in a position to liberate ourselves from Cartesian scepticism without having to dissolve its paradoxes.

Say someone is sitting on the New York subway. They know they are travelling on a line that runs to Columbia University, and they also know to state as much if challenged. Yet say this passenger is on their way to a Descartes seminar and is discussing Cartesian scepticism with a colleague: they suddenly lose their entitlement to their knowledge claim, because, under the conditions determined by this epistemological context, they do not even know whether the subway system exists. If knowing something always presupposes the ability to exclude anything that would make that knowledge impossible – specifically: that one can do so as soon as one becomes aware of the threat – they do not know whether they really know what they think they know. Now, it would clearly be absurd to take this as a basis for seriously denying that somebody knows something, and this suggests that something or other is awry with the epistemological context. Having an adequate entitlement to the belief that one is travelling on the subway line that leads to Columbia University in no way implies that one retains one's entitlement in all contexts or given any systematic background whatsoever. If we want to describe knowledge, we have to be on our guard that we do not depart from the context in which a given knowledge ascription is valid. Otherwise, we will be guilty of the classic error of *misidentifying object domains* (μετάβασις εἰς ἄλλο γένος).

Contextualism is a variant of the age-old idea of *relativism*: it claims that some particular warrant is not valid in all contexts, because a 'warrant' is only ever a warrant relative to or within a given context. Searching for an *absolute* warrant is therefore a senseless enterprise. In Sextus' words: 'since everything is relative, we shall suspend judgement as to what things are independently [ἀπολύτως – i.e. literally, ab-solute] and in their nature [ὡς πρὸς τὴν φύσιν]'.[5] Both Sextus and Wittgenstein exploit a variant of contextualism to refute the form of epistemological foundationalism according to which there is a range of absolutely certain beliefs to which all non-foundational and derived beliefs owe their certainty. And they thereby oppose the assumption of an epistemic asymmetry of mind and world. In light of the apologetic dimension of the concept of knowledge (see above, p. 95), we cannot maintain that there is a class of absolutely warranted beliefs; the putative class would not constitute knowledge if we could not defend its members under critical questioning, and items of knowledge that have to be defended are not absolutely warranted. Rather, since they are relative to a context, they possess the validity they do only against the background of that context. All justification makes use of operating conditions that cannot themselves *all* be justified in the process of justification. Every procedure for making the warrant of a process of justification explicit will draw on some conceptual resources or other that resist being made explicit through that particular procedure. In this regard, knowledge acquisition remains incomplete, which is why there is always a way in for Pyrrhonian scepticism.

(2) *Naturalism* is the (anti-)sceptical strategy deployed most famously by Hume in his *Treatise of Human Nature*.[6] This strategy does not argue that Cartesian scepticism is untenable in virtue of some logical or dialectical error. Rather, Hume accepts that scepticism represents the only rational system. Yet, so it would seem, no one imports Cartesian scepticism into their everyday life – indeed, it would be impossible to do so, and, as Descartes already noted, it is this impossibility that distinguishes Cartesian scepticism from madness.[7]

Because of certain 'very general facts of nature',[8] human beings are evidently so constituted that they develop a steadfast reliance on a certain range of assumptions, even though we cannot obtain any rational justification for them. Finite epistemic beings such as we are can formulate sceptical hypotheses and demonstrate how there can be no absolute justification for our fundamental beliefs (such as the uniformity of nature or the existence of an external world). At the same time, however, life compels us to decide against the force of our arguments and to hold onto more beliefs that we are really entitled to from the perspective of a strictly theoretical attitude. Some entitlement is epistemically blind, including the kind of warrant we acquire in epistemological reflection. Engaging in epistemology is just more human activity and does not transcend the limits of the everyday: there is no extraordinary, god-like point of view onto our epistemic practices. Epistemology cannot reboot our entire system of knowledge claims so as to implement an idealised operating system that is somehow immune to the Pyrrhonian halting problem. And naturalism claims that this does no harm to local, finite knowers once they realise that they are entitled to isolate their local claims from the misguided assumption that they ought to be better grounded than they ever possibly could be.

We can find naturalism in this sense both in Wittgenstein and, more prominently, in Sextus. Wittgenstein's naturalism revolves around the ideas of a 'natural history', 'life' or 'forms of life'. Sextus also speaks of 'life' (βίος) and of the 'guidance of nature' (ὑφήγησις φύσεως). One of the most famous naturalistic passages in Sextus deserves to be quoted in full on account of its programmatic clarity:

> Thus, attending to what is apparent, we live in accordance with everyday observances, without holding opinion [ἀδοξάσως] – for we are not able to be utterly inactive. These everyday observances seem to be fourfold, and to consist in guidance by nature [ἐν ὑφήγησει φύσεως], necessita-

tion by feelings [ἐν ἀνάγκῃ παθῶν], handing down of laws and customs [ἐν παραδόσει νόμων τε καὶ ἐθῶν], and teaching kinds of expertise [ἐν διδακαλίᾳ τεχνῶν]. By nature's guidance we are naturally capable of perceiving and thinking. By the necessitation of feelings, hunger conducts us to food and thirst to drink. By the handing down of laws and customs, we accept, from an everyday point of view, that piety is good and impiety bad. By teaching kinds of expertise, we are not inactive in those which we accept. All this we say without holding any opinions [ἀδοξάσως].[9]

Both contextualism and naturalism are results of a series of sceptical arguments, which receive particularly clear formulations in Sextus' work. Strawson has underlined an important parallel between Humean and Wittgensteinian naturalism, while both Kripke and Fogelin have shown the extent to which we can read Wittgenstein's reflections on rule-following as providing a sceptical solution to a sceptical argument.[10]

Pyrrhonian scepticism is based on a certain promise of salvation: when we reach the edge of rationality, the senselessness of the search for knowledge will dawn on us, and the resultant insight should induce a kind of self-conscious *seconde naïvité*.[11] Now, under the conditions of Pyrrhonian scepticism, we cannot even affirm any empirical proposition with absolute certainty, meaning that an assertoric, theoretical promise of salvation a fortiori lies beyond the scope of Pyrrhonian discourse. Instead, Sextus counts on a dialectical effect that should set in automatically following an exhaustive confrontation with Pyrrhonian scepticism. He explains this process in a frequently cited simile:

A story told of the painter Apelles applies to the sceptics. They say that he was painting a horse and wanted to represent in his picture the lather on the horse's mouth; but he was so unsuccessful that he gave up, took the sponge on which he had been wiping off the colours from the brush, and flung it at the picture. And when it hit the picture, it produced a representation of the horse's lather. Now the sceptics were hoping to achieve tranquillity [ἀταραξία] by deciding the anomalies in what appears and is thought of, and being unable to do so, they suspended judgement. But when they suspended judgement, tranquillity followed as it were fortuitously, as a shadow follows a body.[12]

Accordingly, Pyrrhonian scepticism is a system of assertions that, in the final act of its construction, pulls the rug from under its own feet. The Pyrrhonian sceptic's concern is not, therefore, to develop a constructive system but, rather – to speak with Wittgenstein – to see the world aright.[13] But, for this kind of sceptic, seeing the world aright means giving up on every form of justification of our fundamental beliefs that steps beyond the context of our given (linguistic) practices. The parallel between Wittgenstein and Sextus in fact runs so deep that both exploit the famous metaphor of a ladder that we must first ascend so that we might then ultimately discard it. We find this image not only at the end of the *Tractatus* but also at the climax of the eighth book of *Against the Mathematicians*:[14]

> And again, just as it is not impossible for the person who has climbed to a high place by a ladder to knock over the ladder with his foot after his climb, so it is not unlikely that the skeptic too, having got to the accomplishment of his task by a sort of step-ladder – the argument showing that there is not demonstration – should do away with this argument.[15]

Wittgenstein and Sextus' common project is to purify forms of life to the end of attaining a philosophically unencumbered worldview. This has at least two implications.

(1) It is possible to draw a clear dividing line between the non-propositional acceptance of given forms of life and their distorting philosophical interpretations.[16] Affirming this dividing line also implies the verdict that, while our everyday (linguistic) practice is for the most part *legitimate*, any demanding attempt to *legitimate* it will lead to irresolvable sceptical paradoxes and is thus condemned to failure. It transpires that, generally speaking, we are entitled to a host of beliefs, without our *entitlement* to them requiring their prior *justification*.

(2) The only statement made by the Pyrrhonian sceptic that is bound up with an assertoric claim is that it is *nature* which compels (not obligates) us to accept beliefs that we cannot rationally justify. On closer inspection, this statement succumbs to the verdict delivered in (1), meaning it is no ordinary statement: while it looks to all intents and purposes like an ambitious philosophical claim, it can be put forward only once we have in fact renounced all and any strictly philosophical claims. The affirmation of naturalism as an anti-sceptical strategy revokes its own status as a statement capable of theoretical legitimation.

These two implications produce a problem: Pyrrhonian scepticism lacks the philosophical tools to make any philosophically substantial claim about human nature. Under contextualist conditions, that is, nature is available to theory at best as a kind of *promise* in which we have to keep faith, at least if we are to carry on with our habitual ways of engaging with the world.

At this stage, we have to bear in mind for what follows that anything Wittgenstein, Sextus and other naturalists say about the everyday and the extra- or non-theoretical life are elements of theory construction. This means that it is *theory* that has to keep faith in the smooth running of everyday practice. Blind trust in the assurance that nature shows us the way out of scepticism is itself a purely theoretical promise of salvation; it is not simply coextensive with the supposedly frictionless course of everyday life and its justificatory practices. If we accept contextualism as a lesson learnt thanks to our exchanges with the sceptic – i.e. as a lesson about the necessary finitude of our (justificatory) discursive practices – we have clearly already gone too far if our aim was to deploy the immediacy of the natural without any further conceptual mediation. The *plurality* of contexts forced upon us by scepticism can no longer be absorbed into the *unity* of human nature if the natural, for its part, is something that can be made available only conceptually (theoretically).[17] Incoherent relativism is contextualism's ever-present shadow, which always has to be suppressed by any means possible; and if we find ourselves forced to stave off its unwanted side-effects and contradictions by introducing nature as a unifying concept, we must have already exited the allegedly 'natural state' of reflection.[18] The idea that there are smooth operations of ordinary knowledge acquisition, which come under threat at the hands of scepticism, is itself a theoretical move designed to keep the sceptic at arm's length. On closer inspection, naturalism's 'nature' turns out to be a loophole of theoretical reflection rather than a state that thinkers can ever be in under 'normal' conditions.

Setting out from the idea that Pyrrhonian scepticism represents the true agent of epistemology, my aim in the remainder of Part II is to show how both Wittgenstein and Sextus are committed, for rigorous conceptual reasons, to both (1) and (2) – i.e. to a version of contextualism and a version of naturalism. Unlike Sextus, Wittgenstein's presentation of his position conceals the methodological function served by sceptical arguments, despite the fact that, as Stanley Cavell has convincingly shown, his philosophy 'is everywhere controlled by a response to skepticism'.[19] As a result, Wittgenstein does not face up to how the conjunction of contextualism and naturalism is dialectically inconsistent with the arguments that first lead to each of these positions, and thus to how their conjunction issues in a paradoxical naturalism.

Moreover, I shall be arguing that Wittgenstein is ultimately incapable either of drawing a dividing line between everyday (linguistic) practice and its philosophical distortion or of seeing the paradoxical nature of naturalism. In other words, I want to uncover a dialectical instability in his (anti-)sceptical strategy, which ultimately arises from an underlying failure to account sufficiently for the function of scepticism in the dialectical economy of epistemology.

By contrast, Pyrrhonian scepticism in its original form operated at a high level of dialectical self-consciousness. Hegel was therefore very much on the right track when he attempted to use Pyrrhonian scepticism as the agent driving dialectic *as a metaphysical* theory.[20] In fact, as we shall see towards the end of our investigation, Pyrrhonian scepticism not only represents the pure form of scepticism, and thus a kind of archetype, but can also be deployed against its own intentions to motivate the construction of an ambitious metatheory. Such a metatheory can ultimately lead us back to metaphysics as first philosophy (though I shall only be able to hint at the prospects for such an enterprise within the framework of this study). Scepticism should thereby help us to dislodge epistemology from its status as *prima philosophia*, without falling into a negative dogmatism that asserts the impossibility of *metaphysical* knowledge as such.

Our first task will be to present the sceptical arguments that encourage *contextualism* on the one hand (chapter 8) and *naturalism* on the other (chapter 14). We can then turn to arguing that the *conjunction* of contextualism and naturalism is unstable in virtue of how the arguments that motivate the former are ultimately incompatible with the formulation of the latter (chapter 14). It is impossible to be an (anti-)sceptical contextualist while making an appeal to human nature. However, we can grasp this difficulty only by returning to Pyrrhonian scepticism, which *self-consciously* endorses the very dialectical instability I want to highlight. We will then be able to see, by way of contrast, how Wittgenstein neglects to view the tension between contextualism and naturalism as an impetus to metatheoretical reflection on the foundations of his own project.

Ultimately, we should gain an insight into the necessary finitude of epistemological discourse – and into why, in principle, it is no less fallible than any of the first-order knowledge it examines. Epistemology is bound to context-sensitive (and historically variable) parameters which it can never fully thematise within its own discourse. In this regard, it shares a common feature with the first-order theories whose context-sensitive epistemology derives from an account of the justification conditions of knowledge. In spite of itself, Pyrrhonian scepticism thus teaches us a vital lesson about the finitude of epistemological discourse, since its attempt to dissolve the sceptical paradox through a conjunction of contextualism and naturalism results in failure – a failure stemming from the very finitude, the diagnosis of which lay behind its own original motivation.

A key result of these reflections will therefore be that *all* objective knowledge is finite. Of course, this assertion cannot simply be made without qualification – it must itself be subject to revision. We therefore need to settle on a methodologically circumspect form of reflection on our finitude. Otherwise, we run the risk of introducing a putative piece of absolute knowledge whose (virtually empty) content would just be the idea of that very finitude. The insight into finitude cannot be a replacement for a more contentious form of absolute knowing; this would hardly be a plausible tactic for overcoming the fantasy that real knowledge must dispense entirely with perspectival elements in order to be objective. We should instead dissolve the conflict between finite knowledge claims and the success case of actual knowledge by recognising the possibility that knowledge itself is finite – i.e. bound to a contextually shaped standpoint.

Contextualism in the wake of Wittgenstein has certainly been aware of the paradoxical structure of Pyrrhonian scepticism. Yet, by and large, its representatives are still after an epistemology that would avoid the fate of self-cancellation at the hands of an epistemological paradox, and as a result they tend to withdraw, whether explicitly or implicitly, to a form of Academic scepticism.[21] Our task must instead be to give an account of everyday knowledge ascriptions without making use of any putative knowledge to which our necessary finitude denies us an entitlement.

Of course, all this raises the question of whether this approach is compatible with Wittgenstein's concerns. For Wittgenstein, like Sextus, is well known for questioning the very possibility of a philosophical theory and, *ipso facto*, the possibility of epistemology.[22] Nevertheless, as I hope to show, if we combine the rule-following considerations with certain lessons from his campaign against solipsism, we have the basis for an interesting contextualist position.

In the following chapters, we will therefore begin by running through Wittgenstein's actual and implied arguments for contextualism (chapters 9–10). In doing so, it will be especially important to give a reconstruction of the private language argument, given its constitutive role in justifying contextualism. We will then turn to the relevant parallels with Sextus so that we finally have at our disposal a generalised formulation of a Pyrrhonian contextualism. This will allow us to determine whether contextualism really does bring into view an appropriate strategy for combating Cartesian scepticism.

The origin of contextualism in modern philosophy is Pyrrhonian scepticism. The latter, I would argue, shines through in Wittgenstein's manner of treating everyday knowledge claims. But, if this is correct, we can expect that sceptical difficulties will emerge within more recent strategies that align themselves with Wittgenstein's anti-sceptical naturalism. So, by tracing the latent Pyrrhonism in Wittgenstein, we will be in a position to see how various difficulties emerge for those more recent anti-sceptical programmes that align themselves with his liberal naturalism. Such programmes understand the finitude and sociality of reason in terms of a second nature realised within first nature (see chapter 14 below). The anti-sceptical role of liberal naturalism is meant to consist in treating human nature as a guarantee of the possibility of meaning in order to ward off the sceptical threat that emerges from contextualism's original motivation. But, in order to set out Wittgenstein's arguments, let alone assess them, we first of all need a little more clarity about the concept of 'contextualism' itself.

Contextualism, Normativity and the Possibility of Discursive Determinacy

One possible line of response to Cartesian scepticism is to show how the principle of closure can be restricted. At first glance, this seems to be a hopeless strategy. After all, the principle allows of a universal formulation and at least seems to rule out any exceptions. It states (see above, p. 94) that, if a subject S knows that p, if p implies q, and if S is aware of this entailment, then (*ceteris paribus*) S also knows that q. Now, every proposition implies the negation of all propositions incompatible with its truth. So, for all true perceptual judgements, for example, it follows that making such a judgement implies that the judger is not dreaming, is not a brain in a vat, and so on. Consequently, every class of propositions implies a contrast class, whereby the truth of the propositions contained in the latter class is incompatible with the assertion of those of the former class. It would clearly be an absurd demand to place on a putative knower that, before asserting any proposition with a full-fledged epistemic intention, she first run through and negate all and any implications incompatible with the truth of the proposition she intends to assert.[1] We must therefore have an a priori warrant to a certain set of assumptions (i.e. a warrant that requires neither reflection on all the implications of an asserted class of propositions nor any increase in our stock of empirical information) that make determinate empirical projects possible in the first place. These assumptions divide up a logical space into true and false propositions without our having any explicit reflective access to this operation. There are, that is, certain beliefs that need to be presupposed by any epistemic project geared towards the acquisition of new information. For example, we simply assume that a *solipsism of the present moment* is false. And we assume that we can make assertions about the immediate future without having to appeal to specific arguments or additional empirical information to rule out the possibility that the world might undergo radical alterations in the very next moment. Insofar as they assert contingent matters, these are substantial assumptions; it is, after all, not logically impossible that the universe sprang into being only five minutes ago together with traces that suggest a much more extended pre-history to us fallible and relatively young Earthlings.

If, in what follows, we can successfully show how we are necessarily finite as epistemic agents, then we can sap the power of Cartesian scepticism by reducing it to a harmless lesson about our epistemic finitude.[2] As necessarily finite epistemic beings, we have no choice but to rely on our information-processing mechanisms – provided, of course, that no modifications or reparatory measures happen to be required by the lights of our finitude. Fundamental epistemic norms determine which assumptions have be excluded in principle, and we can take their truth for granted without having to subject them to any explicit decision-making process. Instead, these norms form the background of our information-processing. It is thus a concomitant of our finitude that, in the course of exercising our epistemic powers, we have to rely on the idea that whichever contingent decisions allow us to process information function as necessary presuppositions. Strictly speaking, each epistemic project is constitutively dependent on a class of underlying propositions, and it would be misleading to say that we ultimately have to place our 'blind trust' in these propositions – in fact, we have no attitude to them at all. It is only in a metatheory that they stand revealed as operating conditions of a given epistemic project; the project itself is in no position to establish a properly theoretical attitude to its conditions from out of its own resources. The object-level theoretical attitude neither takes them for granted nor places any kind of blind trust in them; they are simply absent from its functioning operations.

Seen in this light, scepticism merely serves the function of leading us to a vital insight into our epistemic situation: namely that, in order for us to be justified in our beliefs, we have to be entitled to forgo subjecting *all* the implications of our otherwise warranted beliefs to serious deliberation. Scepticism seems to be such a destructive threat only as long as we allow ourselves to be persuaded that we have to be able to achieve something more than we can ever possibly achieve as necessarily finite epistemic beings – that is, insofar as we accept that, before we are permitted to assume any entitlement to our beliefs, we must have actively defended them against all thinkable objections.[3]

This kind of anti-sceptical strategy, which sees the true lesson of scepticism as the need to content ourselves with the finitude of objective knowledge, contrasts with a direct solution to sceptical doubt (with a *refutation* in any straightforward sense of the word). We might even label it a 'sceptical solution'.[4] But, in order to find this sceptical solution attractive, we clearly need an argument for the necessary finitude of those epistemic beings who are capable of arriving at the strategy – i.e. formulating a version of methodological scepticism. And since *we* are such beings, what is needed is an argument for *our* necessary finitude. If we want to show that all knowledge and all justification are necessarily finite, then we also have to demonstrate how there can be a self-knowledge of finitude that is not in turn subject to the defeasibility indissolubly bound up with the finite.[5] Since the concepts of 'knowledge' and 'justification' would themselves have to be used in an argument for our necessary finitude, we are threatened with an apparent paradox: we are dealing with an argument that asserts that *all* justification is finite and thereby asserts the finitude of its own justification. It might seem hard to understand how we can possibly make a general assertion about the concept of justification while conceding the defeasibility of the assertion.

In any case, the self-reference of finitude, and thus our epistemological self-knowledge, evidently leads to a *peritrope*. So, at first glance at least, an assertion about the finitude of human knowledge cannot be understood as finite in the same way as the knowledge whose finitude is asserted.[6] If we want to construct epistemology on a scaffolding that is so vulnerable to paradox, then everything depends upon finding the right concept of finitude and thus on the question of whether it is possible to avoid the familiar 'dialectic of the boundary' that sets in when we see how drawing an epistemological boundary between finite and infinite seems to require knowing both sides of the boundary – and so already being beyond it.

As I mentioned in the previous chapter, Wittgenstein's *On Certainty* stands in the background of the anti-sceptical strategy that I here want to designate as *contextualism* (in Michael Williams's sense of the term). In what follows (chapters 8–10) I will be reconstructing Wittgenstein's arguments for the necessary finitude of our justificatory practices and discourses that are concentrated around the rule-following considerations and the associated problem of a private language.[7] In the course of my exposition, it will emerge that a version of Wittgensteinian contextualism was already advocated in antiquity, by Sextus, with the important difference that Sextus' position turns out to be unassertable on account of the *peritrope* it involves. Sextus, to be sure, sees this as a virtue of his theoretical procedure, not as a drawback, and therefore turns his back on the striving for absolute self-knowledge that characterised classical Greek metaphysics. This striving is manifest not only in its attempts to disclose both true reality and our cognitive access to it through philosophical reflection but also in its negative-dogmatic counterpart – viz. the attempt to demonstrate that such an undertaking is impossible on account of how our finitude stands in the way of attaining genuine metaphysical knowledge. With his contextualism, Sextus opposes *any* form of ultimate grounding, be it positive (dogmatism) or negative (negative dogmatism). Instead, he argues that we should acknowledge an infinite, because ultimately undecidable, difference of opinion (ἀνεπίκριτος στάσις). And because this includes his own view, he intends to capitalise on its resulting self-cancellation.[8] This position, however, can be won only through an exchange with philosophical positions that come to us with constructive theoretical offers. Pyrrhonian scepticism is thus dependent on the existence of the dogmatist (including the negative dogmatist). Without her constructive efforts, it could not pursue its destructive programme.

By *contextualism*, I understand the following thesis: it is possible to evaluate the validity of a given statement only provided it has already been placed within a set of distinctions, where this set forms a presupposition of some contexts, though not of others. Since these distinctions are not without alternatives, they are contingent. Accordingly, contextualism in this sense represents a *thesis about the contingent conditions of the validity of statements*. On a contextualist account, there is no overall context of all contexts whose preconditions are necessary for any kind of empirical enquiry whatsoever. The position asserts that a statement is only verifiable given a determinate frame of reference (a context) against the background of which it can be evaluated.

The first step towards motivating contextualism is the observation that it is impossible so much as to *begin* a truly presuppositionless evaluation of a statement. Even the judgement that some given event presents us with a linguistic or non-linguistic expression presupposes a linguistic context – i.e. a language. A language, though, is already a complex frame of reference, as a mere glance at the grammar of any natural language reveals. The meaning of a language's expressions can be determined only with recourse to a complex, differential system of rules, such that the classification of an event as a linguistic sign and thus as a *semantic* event – including the conditions of the possibility of understanding this event – presupposes a stable frame of reference. Without such a frame of reference, we could not even *register* an event as a linguistic act and so could hardly evaluate its content. Of course, not every speaker has access to all the contexts that develop in the context of a language. Every living language, like the world itself, continually offers more possibilities than we could ever begin to fathom and a fortiori provides more possibilities than could ever be realised.[9] Logical space (what is possible) far exceeds the world (what is actual).

A frame of reference reduces complexity by establishing distinctions that divide up the world into what is and is not available within some particular context. It thereby dictates the selection of elements that compose it as well as their possibilities of recombination. This does not mean that the elements precede the frame of reference, as though the latter could subsequently be composed out of the former; rather, elements obtain as *determinate* elements only as elements of a frame of reference. For it is the frame of reference which determines what gets to count as an element. In order to understand the elements, therefore, we require a prior familiarity with the frame of reference, just as we need to be familiar with the elements in order to apply the frame of reference.[10] In this way, language is established as a system distinct from the world, which thus becomes the system's environment. The world is distinguished from language as the object of our talk, as what we talk about, and it thus becomes a totality of elements – i.e. the absolute environment of the language system. This environment is not simply available without further ado, that is, without forms of discursive mediation that are always liable to paradox. It follows, once again, that 'the world' cannot be an element of theory construction; it cannot be an ordinary object that might feature as the subject of our statements. Its being any such thing would be incompatible with the implication of a totality of elements that comes into play as soon as we understand that statements are subject to selection mechanisms that can never select everything at once. Picking something is always picking something out from a domain that cannot itself be chosen. And this domain is the world in the sense of a merely implied totality, a totality that can never turn into an object of fully articulate *de re* knowledge.

Linguistically regulated contexts erect boundaries between the world, on the one hand, and possible statements about (or actions within) it, on the other. They thus enable 'the gradual elimination of the arbitrary, the reduction of informational burdens, and the restriction of possibilities for forging connections; and this all takes place against the background of conceding the fact of self-reference – i.e. in the knowledge that everything could be otherwise.'[11] Therefore, a context necessarily marks distinctions, both between context and world and between itself and other contexts. The delineation of the boundaries in question is not something that can be completely thematised within the context itself. The attempt to do so would both disrupt its own smooth functioning and lead to a further context which, for its part, would introduce a set of distinctions, and it could not process these as information without leading to a new context . . . and so on *ad infinitum*.

Every assessment of a statement involves standards – i.e. norms for determining what count as correct and incorrect moves once a set of rules has been presupposed. Rule-governed (linguistic or non-linguistic) behaviour – behaviour which can be described using a set of rules for distinguishing between correct and incorrect moves – can be called a *practice* or a *discourse*.[12] In the following, I will use the concepts of *practice* and *discourse* respectively, depending upon whether the context at issue is a system that could not be understood without some *concept of action* or a system that could not be understood without some *concept of assertion* – that is, without that of an epistemic claim. In a still more general sense, I will simply call actions and assertions 'moves' within a discourse. Moves within a discourse are performances that have a certain temporal duration and that can either conform or not conform to the relevant discursive rules.

As we shall see, one of Pyrrhonian scepticism's central results is a specific variety of contextualism. We should distinguish this from two other versions of the doctrine: from a trivial contextualism and from a contextualism focused on concept of knowledge. The latter asserts that the semantics of 'knowledge' imply non-trivial context-sensitive conditions.[13] Trivial contextualism, by contrast, merely draws our attention to how all knowledge ascriptions are situated: that is, they have a relation to a constellation of facts, to some determinate set of worldly conditions. Insofar as trivial contextualism does not entail any sweeping revisions to, but can still be accommodated by, classical truth-conditional semantics, it falls outside the scope of our present concerns.[14]

Contextualism about the concept of knowledge asserts that the evaluation of knowledge ascriptions varies with the *standards of the ascriber.* A knowledge ascription can therefore be true or false according to the standard of whoever ascribes it. By contrast, trivial contextualism asserts that the truth of an asserted proposition varies with the *facts*. In the case of indexical expressions, this has led to the introduction of two-dimensional semantics, but it still does not require any significant revisions to the assumption that truth is a relation between a fact (the world) and a proposition. Instead, in the case of two-dimensional semantics, the introduction of contextual parameters serves to provide a better understanding of the traditional concept of a proposition and, with its help, of the function of indexical expressions.[15]

Unlike both knowledge-specific and trivial contextualism, *contextualism tout court* asserts that there can be no context-free evaluation of an event, and thus of any piece of information. From this assertion, it infers that the concept of a fully determinate world in itself cannot make any contribution to semantics: meaning is a normative concept and has no application conditions whatsoever in the absence of some practice for evaluating the meaning of an event (a statement, a road sign, the changing of the seasons, etc.). According to contextualism, we should no longer understand linguistic meaning in terms of the *expression of propositions* that are eternally true or false – i.e. true or false in virtue of how the totality of all facts is eternally fixed, and thus fixed independently of their application in an informative context and practice of evaluation. Further, contextualism draws our attention to the *creative dimension* of all practices and discourses, which consists in the fact that all practices and discourses *produce* at least some of their own operating conditions. A discourse does not exist as a modally robust fact independently of the practices of finite epistemic beings, who are the creators, not the discoverers, of discourses.

Contextualism represents the direct negation of Platonism, if we understand 'Platonism' broadly enough so that it encompasses any theory built on the following two assumptions: (a) there is an eternally stable realm of meanings (Frege's 'thoughts', Plato's 'ideas'); and (b) insofar as we understand anything determinate whatsoever, we must have cognitive access to these meanings. This eternal realm of meanings contains all true and false propositions, which retain their truth values eternally. As soon as we ascertain which proposition a statement expresses, its truth value is fixed – though this does not mean that we are necessarily in a position to evaluate it. For example, it is eternally true or false that there are an even number of stars at a given time t in a specific region r. If we assert that the number of stars at t in r is even, we commit ourselves to the truth of a proposition and thus say something either true or false, independently of whether there will ever be a cognitive being capable of ascertaining the truth value of the proposition *that the number of stars at* t *in* r *is even.*

Contextualism doubts the utility value of a metaphysical commitment to propositions and a corresponding totality of facts (the world).

It attempts to argue that neither propositions nor non-discursive facts have normative force in the sense that they could establish what *ought* to count as correct and what as incorrect within a discourse. As to the question of the existence of propositions and of the concept of the world as the absolute totality of all facts or states of affairs, it prefers to withhold judgement. The general form of contextualism is thus committed to the semantic primacy of ought over is – that is, to the totality of norms over the totality of facts. Among other things, this implies a primacy of justification over truth and of practice over theory for the metatheory. Contextualism thus seems to contrast with certain variants of naturalism that would want to reduce ought to is, norm to nature. It is therefore no accident that it is often seen as a bulwark against those varieties of reductive naturalism, naturalised epistemology or meta-ethical naturalism that assert that knowledge, morality, etc., should be reduced to natural processes, processes that can be better investigated by cognitive science and evolutionary theory than by philosophy.[16]

Contextualism is a general theory of the verifiability of both our (linguistic and non-linguistic) practices and our discourses. It maintains that no move within a discourse can be evaluated without norms – i.e. without social rules.[17] Norms are accordingly *norms-in-context*, in the sense that they always depend upon the stock of information possessed by a subject and her communicative community. Information cannot be gathered and compiled without presupposing a set of rules that are independent of all individual acts of compilation, where 'independent' just means that these presuppositions cannot for their part be processed as information without stepping outside of the context and into a meta-discourse. Every process of information acquisition within a discourse presupposes norms, and these norms cannot be evaluated by the discourse itself – or, to be more precise, on the same discursive level within the same context. For no piece of information within the discourse can speak decisively for or against the validity of the relevant norms. But without these norms there can be no information gathering or compilation. In other words, without these norms it would be impossible to initiate any investigation. The norms thus facilitate information acquisition, and, as such, they are conditions of the possibility of the search for knowledge.

To borrow a term from Hogrebe, the search for knowledge brings a series of *meta-pragmatic* presuppositions into play.[18] To see the impossibility of avoiding meta-pragmatic presuppositions, we need only contemplate how someone might try to avoid them: the putative knower would still have to *embark* upon their cognitive enterprise at some point or other, and so assume a set of meta-pragmatic presuppositions *in ipso actu operandi*. It is impossible in principle for beings who depend upon acquiring knowledge – that is, finite beings, who can never have all information at their disposal at once – to make explicit all of the conditions of possibility of a putative cognition and thus to bring the process of securing knowledge to a definitive conclusion. Contextualism investigates this finitude before drawing the inference that there can be no absolute certainty – hence its tendency to trade in seemingly sceptical arguments.

Specifically, contextualism appeals to the following condition of the possibility of knowledge acquisition (for finite epistemic beings): *in order to take up and maintain a conceptually communicable (and thus discursively usable) attitude to anything in the first place, it is necessary (a) that we always make certain presuppositions, even though (b) we can have no access to these presuppositions at the same theoretical level.*[19] This insight is not exempt from itself insofar as it too has to imply meta-pragmatic presuppositions that it cannot fully retrieve. (Full retrieval would be possible only if we could acquire an insight whose very acquisition consists in making the totality of its presuppositions completely available; and this would require the construction of a self-referential theory exhibiting a virtuous circular structure. Such a self-referential theory would, of course, involve fundamental logical laws, which cannot be grounded without already being presupposed. Yet, from the fact that they cannot be grounded without already being presupposed, it hardly follows that they are *un*grounded.)

Contextualism quite generally draws our attention to how every practice (every discourse) generates its own a priori. Whenever we make some move in a practice or discourse, we generate a set of conditions under which the move can be assessed as such and such a determinate move. Now, *this* observation (about the conditions of discursive moves) can only be made within a philosophical discourse theory. This is just to say that the descriptive vocabulary we are using here, including terms such as 'context', 'norm', 'discourse', etc., belongs to an epistemological metatheory whose objects are first-order discourses or practices. The object of theories that are themselves objects of the metatheory is the world, which plays a different role across different first-order discourses. These roles can then be determined in a second-order epistemological discourse, which brings the concepts of *representation* and *truth* into play. The object of the metatheory is thus not the world but our relation to the world, or that of first-order theories to the world.[20] Accordingly, our relation to the world as subjects who raise knowledge claims and form beliefs about it is determined by the possibility of truth.

The totality of norms-in-context that condition a given discourse cannot be made explicit *as* such conditions within the discourse itself. This follows from a familiar regress that sets in as soon as we assume that norms-in-context have to be made explicit in order to be valid. Yet suppose the norms of some system of assertions had to be explicated *in toto* in order to be valid. Such an assumption might recommend itself on the basis of the following idea: making a norm explicit comes with the advantage that we can compare it with each of its applications in order to establish whether some *supposed* application is a *genuine* application. Since norms divide logical space into possible agreements and contraventions, making norms explicit seems to have the advantage that it allows us to interpret a set of relevant events as cases of conforming or non-conforming behaviour in light of the norm. Now, norms do not interpret themselves. And supposing all discourses are conditioned by norms-in-context that can be made explicit, in order to interpret a norm correctly (a prerequisite of comparing it with a putative application), we would require a further norm to determine what should count as correct and incorrect applications of the first norm, and so on *ad infinitum*. It follows that making norms explicit does not of itself contribute to improving our ability to engage in a discourse (however much limited meta-discursive correction mechanisms might well have their uses). Any explication of norms-in-context is finite, meaning that they lead at best to a change of discourse – i.e. a transition from a first-order to a second-order theory that, for the sake of brevity, I will henceforth simply call a *theory-level transition*.

Whenever the explication of norms within a discourse$_1$ leads to another discourse$_2$, whose object is no longer the world, *tout court*, but the world as it appears in discourse$_1$, we are dealing with a theory-level transition. Every theory-level transition thus leads away from the world as it *is* for a determinate discourse by thematising this as a world as it *appears* within the discourse. Theory-level transitions are thus the fundamental move in any practice of achieving epistemic distance, of transitioning from being to seeming. In particular cases, achieving such distance can mean acquiring a critical overview of our practices. Therefore, a theory aiming at self-reference, and thus at an ultimate theory-level transition, will always strive to 'break through the illusion of normality'.[21] With Luhmann, we can label this *phenomenological reduction*. Far from being the exclusive property of transcendental philosophy or Husserl's phenomenology, this characterises every theory that transitions from being to seeming.

Theory-level transitions can easily provoke sceptical arguments, as is especially clear in the case of moral scepticism (or relativism). Moral sceptics mostly appeal to the apparent relativity of moral norms across various communities or across various groups within a community. From the fact of moral plurality, they infer that we should analyse the validity of moral norms not as an objective cognitive relation between a discursive practice and independently obtaining values but as a relation between the ultimately arbitrary values of a restricted group and the behaviour of its members. They accordingly consider moral phenomena *from the outside*. They refrain from adopting the perspective of a particular group and from making an argument to the effect that the moral norms of other groups do not merely diverge from one's own but, in virtue of that divergence, are in fact false, morally reprehensible. The seemingly neutral moral sceptic undertakes a theory-level transition insofar as she does not determine the world as thus and so from within a moral discourse (for example, as characterised by moral values) but, rather, remains undecided about how the world is. She directs her attention to the world's multiple appearances within the multiple discourses of multiple groups and communities and infers that there is no independent authority or entity (*the* moral truth in the eminent singular) to which we might appeal so as to decide between the plurality of discourses. *Neutralism* is the thesis that a theory-level transition necessarily leads to a neutralisation of the validity claims of its object theory. As the case of moral relativism shows, this need not always be the case, for moral relativism is itself a morally engaged standpoint.[22]

Of course, not *all* theory-level transitions are building blocks of scepticism. In the course of a conversation, for example, someone might refer to the conditions of the conversation in order, say, to provoke a disagreement or, conversely, to clear up some fundamental misunderstanding. Theory-level transitions can therefore also function as harmless mechanisms of reflection. They mark a form of self-reference or self-observation for practices and discourses, albeit not the only possible form.

Not every form of self-description is apt for generating sceptical arguments. Yet, while not all theory-level transitions are sceptical, all sceptical arguments are theory-level transitions. This is the central insight of the contextualist thesis that all forms of scepticism arise as a result of a change of context. Consequently, the debate with scepticism has to be conducted at least in part within the framework of a suitable analysis of the general dialectical structure of theory-level transitions.

Fundamentally, sceptical arguments reduce being to seeming: they impute to a first-order discourse, for which the world *is* thus and so, a range of optional norms, such that the world of the first-order discourse only *seems* to be thus and so for the sceptic. In this way, sceptical theory-level transitions maintain a 'distance to their object and thereby trivialise its code'.[23] These transitions are a function of freedom to the extent that they establish distance from the given (being) and thus transform it into a phenomenon. That which is given (immediate) for a first-order theory is revealed by the transition to be a function of deploying certain norms, norms which are ultimately optional (at least for the sceptic). For norms are valid only in a mode of virtual reality, that of recognition: they depend upon events being recognised as behaviour and assessed as moves in a particular practice. And, as such, they are not modally robust facts. This means, however, that the existence of norms depends upon events that are recognised as behaviour, where this recognition rests upon a *creatio continua*, upon a community's decision to validate authorising criteria for classifying certain events as actions.[24]

Scepticism is an expression of epistemic distance from a given discursive operation. The (philosophically) relevant sceptical reduction of being to seeming always makes use of an operation, the upshot of which is that we cease to observe the world in terms of some particular distinction – e.g. between the domain of ethical and the domain of non-ethical statements. So, instead of observing what *is*, the sceptic observes what is *observed* and seeks to discern an incompatibility between the observed and the observation. The sceptic wants to draw our attention to how the epistemic conditions of the observation are not necessarily identical with the ontological structure of the observable.[25] Our modes of registration have alternatives and are thus contingent; and, insofar as we observe the world with their help, we have to reckon with the possibility that the world is closed off from us precisely because we are trying to observe it by means of some particular mode of registration. We introduce the world into our theories because we work within a framework based on an assumption of totality, and this means that we cannot ever apprehend it completely under individual descriptions. In other words, the world enters our theories given an operative distinction between the plurality of discourses and that which remains constant throughout discursive variability. This explains the (misleading and ultimately illusory) tendency to think of the world as an eternal object, as something that might be observed *sub specie aeternitatis*, even when it is conceded that we cannot possibly adopt such a standpoint, a 'view from nowhere'. We cannot proceed from the assumption that the 'world' is a given, as though the only remaining question were how we are able to cognise it. This assumption overlooks that epistemology originally introduces the world as an element within a specific explanatory context that articulates the connection between truth, knowledge and objectivity. Because we cannot catch sight of the mechanisms of selection we use to describe the world (e.g. in a sensorily limited fashion), we do not *encounter* it as one more given, stably appearing individual object among others, as though it had been secretly frozen in a crystalline eternity.

In the *Phenomenology of Spirit*, Hegel investigates various forms of relation between the observable and the observed by examining different shapes of consciousness (discourses, contexts, practices) with reference to the distinctions they try to draw between truth (the 'in itself') and certainty ('for-consciousness'). In so doing, he continually considers how this succession of shapes unfolds 'for us', for the at once observing and observed reader who, together with the phenomenological subject, 'merely looks on'.[26] Unlike for scepticism, however, there is no triumph here of seeming over being. Hegel pays explicit attention to how scepticism too is a conditioned phenomenon, such that 'scepticism's lack of thought about itself' is to vanish.[27] Just like Luhmann in our own day, Hegel attempts to construct a universal and thereby self-referential theory that the sceptic cannot outbid with yet further reflection on the theory's underlying conditions. How he goes about this concretely, let alone whether he succeeds, is something I cannot go into here;[28] I mention Hegel and Luhmann in this context merely in order to point out that engaging with scepticism as a variety of theory-level transition is a widespread theoretical move and that it therefore pays to get a clearer view of its dialectical structure.

Two examples can help to further clarify, first, the structure of theory-level transitions and, second, the *regress problem* that will play an equally important role throughout the remainder of this study.

(1) <u>Theory-level transition</u>: A frequently discussed theory-level transition is that from science to sociology of science. This has opened the door to forms of relativism that convict the sciences of a constitutive blindness.[29] Central here is the *discovery of latency* (Luhmann): the real conditions

of knowledge are just as latent in the production and accumulation of knowledge as the real conditions of capitalism according to Marxism or the real conditions of consciousness according to psychoanalysis.[30] Once we investigate the historical and social conditions of the emergence of the sciences and their vocabularies – in a word: their genealogy – we lose our previously unshakable trust in the objectivity of their results. In the extreme case, this loss of trust can lead to the untenable relativism of which, rightly or wrongly, Rorty, Feyerabend or Kuhn are often accused.[31] The transition from *context of justification* (validity) to *context of discovery* (genesis), or from the conditions of securing knowledge to the conditions of seeking knowledge, shows that scientific results depend partly on historically contingent parameters, which are liable to present us with a certain mythological picture of a supposedly pure registration of facts.

Luhmann is aware of the epistemological problems bound up with the sociological standpoint, and he therefore suggests a corrective to classical or, as he puts it, 'academic' epistemology. This corrective consists in observing the observational standpoint of the epistemologist, a move that corresponds to what in chapter 5 I labelled *dialectical analysis*. Luhmann works on the premise that every observation is of something determinate which it has to distinguish from something else unobserved (without this meaning, of course, that everything not under current observation can actually be observed). That which is not observed is not observed *as* the very thing that is not observed – after all, it is not observed. That which is not observed is present only *de dicto* (under the description just given) and never *de re*. 'Latency' is the name Luhmann gives to that which goes unobserved precisely so that what is observed can be observed. Therefore, observation always occurs as a dual operation: of both making a distinction and simultaneously indicating only one side of this distinction while screening out the other. These two selections serve to delimit an object domain. However, the distinction that conditions *all* indications of an object domain – i.e. the choice of one of the two sides of a selected difference – cannot be observed in and through this observation itself *in ipso actu operandi*. That would require a change of schema and a second observation – i.e. a theory-level transition – for which the distinguishing activity that precedes *it* is in turn necessarily opaque or latent.[32] We simply cannot make everything explicit, as this would undermine the operating system we rely on in directing knowledge claims at objects in a suitably local domain.

Every observation thereby reconstitutes its own blind spot. Now, if *this* observation – viz. that the distinction necessary for any observation at all is itself unobservable – is not to lead to an infinite regress of metatheories, we need to construct a theory in which observation and theory construction coincide. What such a theory might look like is something we shall have to address in chapters 14 and 15 below. For the moment, our task is merely to clarify the notion of a theory-level transition, since it is the key notion underlying contextualist discourse theory. We thus need to ask whether such an observation is possible and to what extent it holds out the prospect of an anti-sceptical strategy.

A whole range of epistemic projects relies on theory-level transitions and would thus be threatened were these to fall under general suspicion. Most so-called humanities disciplines rest upon theory-level transitions insofar as they are not first-order discourses, for which the world *is* thus and so, but, rather, second-order discourses, which investigate how the world *appears* to the first-order discourses under examination. The art historian, for example, cannot say which artwork was 'necessary' at which time, something that artists often claim of their own productions. She can merely investigate what artists or consumers have considered to possess a certain aesthetic necessity in a certain period. The point of view afforded by a second-order theory forbids any immediate engagement in the business of aesthetic evaluation, which is not to say that evaluation is categorically excluded. Further, a second-order viewpoint can often turn out to be particularly enlightening; a theory-level transition can lead to the result, say, that all of the first-order discourses that fall under its examination are guilty of an egregious error. This result would itself be an evaluation, just as moral relativism represents a moral position despite being a second-order theory. When a theory-level transition has been effected, it does not at all follow that the second-order standpoint it motivates is necessarily neutral in relation to the observation schema of its object theory. Sceptics, of course, like to contend otherwise, coating their positions in a veneer of neutrality or impartiality.[33]

Certain theory-level transitions are also built into the concept of scientific progress. Consider a simple example. Suppose two parties find themselves in a serious disagreement over whether the sun orbits the earth or vice versa. Both parties operate with an elaborate theoretical system which includes its various arguments and background assumptions. Now say that, in the course of their dispute, they arrive at the position that motion is relative to a frame of reference, meaning that there are simply no absolute facts about what does and does not move. The sentence 'the sun moves' expresses the proposition 'that the sun moves relative to frame of reference X', such that the apparently contradictory statements (1) 'the sun moves' and (2) 'the sun does not move' are compatible because (1) and (2) are relative to different frames of reference. The discourse generated by the encounter between the two parties thus only seems to contain contradictory statements; it suppresses an important component, which, at the second-order logical level, reveals itself to be a condition of the possibility of genuine discourse about movement.

(2) <u>The regress problem</u>: In a forest (say the Odenwald), S encounters a signpost in the form of an arrow pointing to the right.[34] The signpost bears the inscription 'Heidelberg – 7km'. Since S is on her way to Heidelberg, she will doubtless take the path to the right. After all, according to the sign, it leads to her destination. However, there is no *fact* between heaven

and earth that establishes that a signpost with an arrow pointing to the right shows, implies, that one ought to turn to the right if one wishes to interpret it correctly. For we could easily imagine a culture, for example, that reads right to left, and so interprets arrows 'backwards'. There is no underlying conceptual necessity that renders our conventions necessary. If we were to suggest to S, without adducing any further reasons, that the signpost perhaps recommends turning left, she would quite rightly express incomprehension, wonder why we would say such a thing, and continue on her habitual way to the right. S will hardly orient her actions via reflection on the arbitrariness, and thus contingency, of conventions. To be sure, *we* might think of S's behaviour in this way when describing it as rule-governed; for we can deploy a vocabulary that lays bare the contingency of the rules she follows. Yet this no more means that S can follow the signpost only because she is a competent user of a descriptive vocabulary than that someone is able to speak a language only once they have studied its grammar.

It would be even more absurd to postulate that S is able to follow the signpost only because she has already been informed of the rule stating that one has to read signposts in continental Europe (or in whichever context is familiar to S) from left to right. That is, if we suggest that the capacity to explicate a rule is the condition of the possibility of following one at all, there would be no reason to reject the assumption that a further explication, and thus a further rule, would *ex hypothesi* be required to understand the vocabulary originally used in formulating the rule.[35]

Notoriously, the assumption that S follows an explicit *interpretation* of the signpost thus leads to a vicious infinite regress. And, as is equally well known, in order to avoid it, we need to formulate a theory that makes room for the assumption that S follows the signpost and not her interpretation of the signpost. When we insist that there has to be an explicit norm in order for S's behaviour to be intelligible as conforming to a rule at all, we forget that this norm *ex hypothesi* also has to be interpreted. It would thus, for example, first have to be recognised *as* a norm, and its linguistic formulation would in turn rely on a number of linguistic presuppositions, and so on and so forth. Therefore, the reasons which lead us to demand that all norms must be explicit if we are to secure a *definitive* interpretation generate an infinite regress. To avoid such a vicious regress, we have to suppose that there is 'a way of grasping the rule which is *not* an *interpretation*',[36] whatever this grasp might consist in.

With the notion of a theory-level transition and the regress problem both in view, we can attain a clearer grasp of the basic idea of contextualism. It generally consists in supposing a series of parameters that are implicit in our assertoric behaviour, without having to be made explicit. These parameters fix what can be meant by a certain statement – i.e. what is to count as an application of a certain rule. These parameters are non-propositional, in the sense that, as Wittgenstein says, they 'are indeed not doubted'.[37] This does not mean that we explicitly and consciously consent to them. When we behave in such and such a way, we act within parameters to which we need not have any intentional (propositional) access; the attempt to examine the parameters (to justify or defend them) leads to a vicious infinite regress.[38] Wittgenstein's observation is how all discourses always have to make a host of implicit assumptions in order to be able to state anything at all. Much has to remain fixed if other things are to move. The discourse itself thus has to generate stability-guaranteeing presuppositions. Qua norms-in-context, they are not modally robust facts but virtual entities that are pre-*supposed* [*voraus*-gesetzt] in the mode of retrospective causality.[39] Their being is their repetition.

The individuation conditions of a context are the rules that first have to count as valid within it before we can go on to test the validity of any of its further statements. These rules are a priori in the sense that, because they are what first enable a possible investigation of a statement's valid-ity, they are not liable to either empirical verification or falsification. But they are not a priori in the sense of supplying us with a universal matrix for all discursively engaged subjects. To be more precise: not all rules qua norms-in-context are a priori in the sense of being operating conditions of theoretical subjectivity as such. There may well be something a priori in the classical sense; but, as we learn from the rule-following problem, there is also a contextual a priori. And it is only the latter, context-sensitive a priori that interests us here.

We can initiate 'empirical enquiry' – i.e. controlled, information-processing investigations (first-order epistemic projects) – only when something or other remains fixed relative to the investigation being undertaken. In the context 'astrophysics', for example, the assumption that the world, together with all its manifold traces of an extremely exten-sive past, was not created *ex nihilo* five minutes ago functions as an a priori assumption in this sense. One cannot put this assumption into doubt without overstepping the boundaries of the context 'astrophysics'. And, likewise, the context 'travel' currently excludes the proposition that we can be teleported from Australia to Finland within a single minute. 'That is to say, the questions that we raise and our doubts depend on the fact that some propositions are exempt from doubt, are as it were like hinges on which those turn.'[40] The parameters of a context are therefore hinge propositions for the metatheory. And it would run counter to the foun-dational pragmatic idea governing contextualism if the validity of these propositions required their explicit articulation in the form of expressions with propositional content.[41]

In other words: as finite epistemic beings, we find ourselves in pos-session of a certain variable stock of information, which we continually have to modify in light of new input. Whoever, or whatever, processes information does this by means of a certain mode of registration that will not be suitable for processing *all* information – there *can* be no mode of registration able to process all information. Modes of registration *are necessarily finite: they selectively process information that they have to acquire and cannot produce.* What can count as information depends upon a given mode of registration, and not everything counts as the same information to every such mode.[42] For a mode of registration to function, several parameters need to be fixed, and these cannot be shifted without damaging the functionality of the mode in question. These parameters generate an information filter that is just as contingent – i.e. variable – as the parameter itself.[43]

The existence of thermometers provides a simple example. A thermometer shows the temperature, but not the time. Yet, when it shows the temperature, it does not show that it does not show the time. When we read a thermometer, we do not first check to see whether it might in fact be showing the time, and so whether it is really a clock rather than a thermometer. This is something we just have to presuppose, else we would also have to check whether it shows the distance between the sun and the moon or between the Eiffel Tower and the tip of our nose. In addition, it is important that the thermometer is not seriously damaged and thus unreliable. Now, supposing that, one summer's day in Barcelona, somebody has the impression that it is uncommonly cold. She looks at the thermometer and, exercising all the commonly required expertise for reading thermometers, reads that it is 39 degrees Celsius. She can then either infer that the thermometer is damaged or come up with some hypothesis to explain why it seems to be a cold day in spite of the high temperature that the thermometer clearly registers. There is, however, no possibility of concluding that 39 degrees Celsius has become colder than it used to be before that particular summer's day, or that 39 degrees Celsius is colder in Barcelona than it is in Paris or Madrid. While she investigates what has gone wrong in such a situation, Celsius as a measure remains fixed.

Or say an astrophysicist looks through a telescope and suddenly discovers a new star, never previously registered. According to all the rules of science, she ought to confirm her finding with a second observation, perhaps even with another telescope. Yet she will not check whether telescopes are the appropriate mode of registration for processing information about the stars.[44] Such a revision to astrophysical practice would be necessary only under quite extreme conditions – for example, if we were to discover that the physical conditions in our solar system mean that all the telescopes within it deliver false information about distant solar systems. A datum that could lead us to such a revision of our current beliefs about telescopes might be, say, that the materials we use to construct telescopes undergo relevant changes when transported to other solar systems, such that, in our solar system, the information they deliver us about distances has merely a local validity. Yet, however we might make this discovery, it would doubtless lead us to find an alternative to basing our beliefs about distant solar systems upon telescopic observations.

Note, however, that these observations motivate only a version of discourse-theoretical internalism, not relativism. Discourse-theoretical internalism asserts that every modification of a discourse must also be *internally* motivated. There can be system-immanent reasons for this, which are, to be sure, not absolute in the sense that they would be reasons immanent to every system. Modifications to a discourse cannot just be imported from outside without further ado. A *discourse-theoretical relativism*, by contrast, asserts that all reasons for modifying a discourse are not only system-immanent but *eo ipso* ungrounded, because there cannot be reasons for playing off one discourse against another. Reasons for and against a discourse-theoretical relativism have to be weighed in the context of two questions: to what extent can one motivate a global relativism and what exactly does it assert? As a starting point, one might point out that the telescope example of belief revision can indeed become an element of a relativistic diagnosis; but it is not sufficient for this diagnosis in and of itself without an additional demonstration that there can be system-immanent reasons only if there are absolute reasons. Yet this assumption is highly questionable.[45]

Discourse-theoretical relativism thus asserts that all the discourse-internal beliefs taken to be valid by the discourse's justificatory standards are ultimately ungrounded because there are no absolute reasons for the justificatory standards themselves.

Discourse-theoretical internalism, by contrast, contents itself with noting how discourse-internal mechanisms of justification function and, like relativism, points to the impossibility of absolute, truth-guaranteeing reasons. If absolute, truth-guaranteeing reasons are impossible, but we are nevertheless in a position to demarcate discourse-internal mechanisms of justification, then, as far as internalism is concerned, we are entitled to the assumption that these mechanisms are warranted in any available sense of the term.

If there are no absolute reasons, there cannot be any argument for the thesis that *all* discourse-internal standards of justification are arbitrary. This could only be established with the help of absolute reasons. Yet, if there are no absolute reasons, they can hardly be necessary for our practices of justification. Relativism therefore overlooks how all rational grounding is finite; it quantifies over all discourses without reflecting that its own assertion *ex hypothesi* occurs within a discourse and is consequently finite too.

We can regard discourses quite generally as information-processing, social modes of registration that produce (among other things) discourse-internal information. This information too, to be sure, has to be processed; nothing alters the foundational insight that discourses have entry conditions that they cannot consciously examine *in ipso actu operandi*. This means that information still has to be processed in both a Lockean empiricist and a Berkeleyan or Leibnizian universe, otherwise we would have to change our diagnosis that discursive entry conditions are necessary objects of philosophical investigation. When conducting such an investigation, where the information comes from plays no role; we simply investigate different mechanisms of information-processing by enquiring into how discourses differ from one another. Discourse-theoretical analysis of modes of registration is thus neutral vis-à-vis the question of the relation between being and thought or cognition, and especially vis-à-vis the question of whether or not knowledge presupposes the existence of an external world in the sense of a naïve ontology of individuals (see chapter 3 above).

Rather, in this kind of analysis, realism and idealism themselves appear as distinct discourse theories, and we can observe their conditions without having to make any (implicit) decision about the 'reality of the external world', however one might construe this. The metatheoretical investigation of the finitude of discourse is not indebted to any specific metaphysics because it is not in the business of constructing a first-order theory about what exists. It merely investigates what it means for something or other to exist for a first-order theory.

For an internal modification of an information-processing system to result in a corresponding modification to its stock of information, it must be registered by the system itself (in the case of a conscious system: apprehended and conceptually determined). Now, since discourses themselves are information-processing systems, they too participate in the universal finitude of such systems. In other words, no information-processing system can initiate determinate processes for modifying its overall stock of information unless it relies blindly on the orderly functioning of its modes of registration. Again, this is not to say that it can establish anything like a cognitive relation, or even a relation of trust, to its conditions, as these are constitutively latent. That is, it is impossible for a discourse to examine all the conditions of its own functioning, because it cannot process any information incompatible with the functioning of its modes of registration. In the case of discourses, this means that they can never thematise the presuppositions they generate without remainder so as to justify them in the course of their operation.

From now on, I will follow Wittgenstein in calling the general operating conditions of discourses (Hogrebe's meta-pragmatic presuppositions) their *hinges*. To a certain extent, the hinges of a discourse can be registered within discourse theory as hinge propositions, which does not mean that, in order to exercise their function, they have to appear as *explicit* propositions, assertions or statements within the discourse. Rather, since we can regard them as the indispensable blind spot of an object theory, they can be registered, if at all, only within the metatheory.

Hinges are constitutive of a discourse in the sense that they govern which information can be processed in the first place. An illustrative example: suppose we had daily encounters with extra-terrestrials who had decided to blend into our society in order to study our behaviour. Though indistinguishable from humans, they all possess a distinguishing characteristic that allows them to identify one another, some particular way of tying their shoelaces, for example. Given our current general stock of information, we are not in a position to establish a truth-apt discourse about these extra-terrestrials; the hinges of our discourse, as they currently stand, are incompatible with focusing upon signals that we could process as information about their presence. The same goes for miracles, witches, phlogiston, time travel, unknown natural and psychological laws, and much more besides – although the existence of information that would be confirmation of the presence of such entities and phenomena, for *other* modes of registration, is of course not logically impossible. Our finitude thus consists in our ineliminable need to rely on particular operations for processing information. Were it not for the latency of these operations, we could not even begin to initiate any information-processing. Indeed, it follows from the very grammar of modes of registration that we are creatures fated to have to process information; we are inescapably dependent on acquiring given information and incorporating it into a broader horizon – a horizon that, for its part, can never be fully available for information-processing.

Where we acquire this information *from* is another question, the question fought over by metaphysical realists and metaphysical idealists. A realist may assert, roughly, that our information is supplied by a world of independent objects. We have access to this world thanks to our sensible, and thus causal, anchoring within it. An idealist, by contrast, may assume an encompassing mind in which we participate as finite minds. Yet neither contests our finitude in the sense at issue.[46] Each associates a different metaphysical world picture with their preferred explanation of the state transitions effected within our modes of registration. It would be absurd, though, to assume that we might have an infinite stock of information at our disposal. The very fact that our information stocks change testifies to the need to reckon with something that (a) transcends them at any given time and is therefore (b) responsible for any changes.

In this context, I understand the 'world' as that which is responsible for such modifications. Therefore, quite trivially, how the world is at any given time cannot be observed independently of the operations of an observer – which does not entail that the world is reference-dependent on the existence of observational operations. Finitude by no means implies that the (epistemological) conditions of the possibility of observation are at the same time (ontological) conditions of the possibility of the observed. Though one might assume as much from reading Kant,[47] we should of course immediately note that the observed in Kant are 'appearances' and not 'things in themselves'. His transcendental idealist thesis of an interdependence between conditions of the possibility of observation, on the one hand, and of conditions of the possibility of the observed, on the other, is not an ontological statement about the world whose *being* thus and so is the content of all first-order theories (see chapter 3 above).

We must also be wary of supposing that the presupposition-structure of finitude implies a further dubious idea, namely that we are trapped within a world of information elicited from something in some sense independent of and external to the information it contains. Our finitude implies merely that we can have no semantic access to the world unless we can count on our operations having a certain stability – a stability which cannot (and need not) be guaranteed independently of these operations. The attempt to trace back our cognitive operations to a *fundamentum inconcussum* necessarily fails: the attempt itself generates presuppositions without which it could not even be carried out as an epistemic project, and thus as an operation. Our information-processing operations are necessarily blind vis-à-vis their own conditions; indeed, this is a condition of their possibility.[48] Whether our epistemic finitude has consequences for the concept of the world – i.e. how one should determine the relation between epistemology and ontology – is a question to be posed only after we have run through epistemological arguments for the necessary finitude of information-processing modes of registration quite generally. In order to be able to infer from the structure of our understanding to the structure of the world, however, we always need an additional argument that transcends a mere analysis of the structure of our understanding.[49]

Our finitude is Janus-faced. (1) On the one hand, we are *a parte ante* restricted to processing information we can register. The set-up or attunement of our discursive modes of registration presupposes that in play is a determinate set of hinges, which discriminate between valid and invalid information a priori by fixing what can so much as count as a unit of information. (2) On the other hand, we rely *a parte post* on our always incomplete stocks of information when anticipating alterations to those stocks in both the near and distant future.

As discursive beings we are inductive beings. This means that sceptical attacks on the very possibility of inductive inference have a particularly deep effect on our discursive rationality.[50] Because having a justified belief always presupposes an entitlement to rely on rules that cannot themselves be justified by their own lights, we need the concept of a non-inferentially acquired entitlement; we must be entitled to assume the validity of a certain set of rules in order to have any justified beliefs at all: '[B]ecause claimants and challengers share justificatory burdens, epistemic questions always arise in a rich informational context. This context will be constituted by background beliefs that are currently not up for grabs, some of which will have the status of default entitlements.'[51] We also have a non-inferential entitlement to assume propositions that we could never even suspect of being constitutive of our discourse. The stability of discourse thus depends decisively on its potentially unstable parameters. We might even say with Nietzsche that discourse as such is 'clinging in dreams, as it were, to the back of a tiger'.[52]

Whatever we claim about beliefs and their propositional content, it nevertheless seems clear that beliefs can be justified only given established parameters entitling us to trust in a certain discursive stability.[53] Say both our consciousness and the world kept vanishing at utterly irregular intervals before popping back into existence with fresh representations and worldly states, and say, moreover, that we had no good reasons to suspect this was the case. Somebody who was informed about this metaphysical schizophrenia (God perhaps) could judge that the beings who dwell in this on–off world can have no justified beliefs at all, as any stability would be sheer illusion. Participants in every discourse have to be granted an entitlement to certain presupposed rules, and these cannot be made explicit if we want to keep the discourse running.

The parameters of a discourse are variable. But it follows neither that they are arbitrary nor that there are no absolute hinges that have to be in play if discursive rationality exists. An apparently paradox-inducing candidate for an absolute rule would be the rule of finitude we have been formulating: that all discourses can have only relative and variable parameters. At first glance, it might seem that the principles of philosophical, discourse-theoretical reflection themselves have to be exempted from the flow of history, else one would have to contextualise the standpoint of the discourse-theoretical observer, of contextualist discourse itself. One of the questions that will occupy us time and again in what follows, therefore, is whether there is in fact a systematic method that would allow us to acquire a warrant for the conditions of the possibility of discursive rationality as such. With such a warrant, we might initiate a critical examination of factual discourse or practices, without thereby suggesting a revision to our guiding claims about revisability.

Were there only a single context, it would be impossible to determine which hinge propositions, and thus which rules, fix its parameters. For these rules are for the most part inexplicit, and, were there only one context, we could not reflect on them – i.e. make them explicit. If rules are to be made explicit, they must first lose their sheen of naturalness; they must lose their status as the taken-for-granted background of our discourse and become conspicuous *as* rules.[54] The conspicuousness of rules is not initially given, as following a rule means following it blindly'[55] – that is, 'without thinking'.[56] 'But *entirely* without thinking? Without *reflecting?*'[57]

As I have been emphasising, following the rules of a given discourse involves accepting that some things remain fixed, forming the background against which other things can be mobile. What 'moves' is our stock of information, behind which our modes of registration operate on some particular setting that remains partially opaque. We thus know that some particular epistemic set-up or other is in place, without necessarily being able to extrapolate quite what it consists in from the process of expanding our store of information itself.

We cannot, in short, know all of the presuppositions that have to remain securely in place in order for anything to appear to us at all. Kant's project in the *Critique of Pure Reason* comes to grief on just this point: he is confident of discovering reason's universal setting via an appeal to given forms of judgement and inference. As logic has since made precisely the kinds of advance that Kant thought impossible, it would be very unwise for anyone simply to suppose that there is some single determinate catalogue of logical forms. We can also understand Wittgenstein's remark (directed against Russell) in the *Tractatus* along these lines: 'Logical forms are *without* number. Hence there are no pre-eminent numbers in logic, and hence there is no possibility of philosophical monism or dualism, etc.'[58]

In order for rules to be conspicuous *as rules*, they have to be over-stepped, forcing corrective mechanisms (e.g. sanctions) to come into play. What a rule prescribes becomes explicit only thanks to acts of contravention, because we have to be confronted with the rule qua rule in order to be in a position to understand it as such. In this connection, Wittgenstein speaks of an 'entanglement in our rules'.[59] He sees this entanglement as containing the seeds for the emergence of philosophical problems: 'Here the fundamental fact is that we lay down rules, a technique, for playing a game, and that then, when we follow the rules, things don't turn out as we had assumed.'[60]

Scepticism, and thus philosophy, first emerges where the possible impossibility of establishing corrective mechanisms reveals itself as a problem. Philosophy initially entertains the apparent possibility of an infallible discourse, of a basic layer of reality that necessarily appears to any thinker whatsoever. Yet this ploy turns out to be discursively problematic, as it is unclear how one could articulate the contents of one's original vision of the being/appearance distinction without thereby advancing defeasible claims. It was the discursive conditions of philosophical enquiry at the pinnacle of pre-Socratic speculative physics which provoked the first sceptics to point out that we might not be able to infer the ground of being from how reality happens to appear to finite thinkers. It is then no accident that early scepticism arose together with metaphysics, that an enterprise that tried to fix the being/appearance distinction once and for all attracted systematic forms of doubt from the start.

In Hegel's terms, the possibility of sceptical reflection arises in times of 'diremption' or 'dichotomy' or 'confusion'.[61] In his view, characteristic historical conditions for the emergence of sceptical movements are periods when existing discourses come under maximal external pressure. In our own time, encounters with previously distant cultures and traditions, as well as the virtual availability of a practically infinite number of contexts, act as catalysts for philosophical enterprises that serve to fuel all manner of sceptical tendencies. In his essay 'Des tours de Babel', Derrida even went as far as to construct a plural of the famous tower of Babel in order to exploit the extreme collision of contexts for his own translation scepticism.[62] The virtual availability of an unsurveyable number of modes of registration leads to an inevitable confusion; because of the different kinds of measurement operations constitutive of each discourse, it piles up ever multiplying stocks of information. This confusion in turn provokes theory-level transitions that aim at confining the confusion to a metatheoretical level.

A context is the framework of a discourse, its *frame of reference*. An established *discourse* is a system of assertions in which each assertion defines a series of possible predecessor and successor assertions. The set of possible predecessor and successor assertions for a given proposition is individuated by rules implicit within the discourse, rules which commit its participants – i.e. those who make assertions – to differentiate between correct and incorrect, however specified (true and false, good and evil, beautiful and ugly, etc.). A statement or move in the discourse is thus essentially the kind of thing that can be correct or incorrect.[63]

When a participant within the discourse makes a particular move, its validity can be evaluated and thus tested. To be sure, a move within a discourse has by no means to be an assertion. A question, tacit agreement, a fit of anger, a command or even the abrupt ending of a conversation can all be part of a discourse just as much as a gesture or an action; all count as moves that are either correct or incorrect. Nor need talk of discourses or contexts imply that assertions enjoy any kind of primacy.[64] The normativity of a discourse, that is, does not always have to be determined by assertability conditions. Not all norms realise their regulations in terms of the code true/false. It is no part of my aim here to replace truth with warranted assertability: assertability is only one possible instance of a normativity-constituting difference.

The phenomenon of intertextual reference in literary history (or indeed any form of citation within any artistic medium whatsoever) has nothing to do with truth or falsity – and neither is it governed by assertability conditions. Art as a variety of discourse, together with its panoply of sub-discourses, is every bit a system containing permissible and impermissible moves.[65] Anyone, for example, who tries to work in the tradition of abstract expressionism or impressionist poetry in 2019 will struggle to find a receptive audience. What counts as an artwork depends upon the conditions established by a given artistic discourse, and no putative artwork can circumvent these conditions if it is to be registered as such. As Wittgenstein puts it, the institution of art presupposes an 'entire culture', and we can hardly reconstruct this culture as a totality of true propositions.[66] In contrast to the discourse theory accepted in the mainstream of contemporary analytic philosophy, it is important to emphasise that truth is not the goal of *all* discourses and that assertion is not therefore the foundational function of language. There is no foundational function of language independent of the context of particular discourses.

We can allow that a sentence can (unproblematically) be permitted in one discourse and proscribed in another without drifting into an impermissible – because ultimately inconsistent – relativism. Even the propositional content of an assertion can be context sensitive (although it does not have to be). Take a simple example. Suppose on Blackpool beach you hear the statement 'Ayer's rock is fantastic.' You will presumably understand this as an assertion about the sticks of rock sold at Mr Ayer's sweet shop. But if you hear the statement at *Ayers Rock* in Australia, you would instead interpret it as a statement about the large sandstone formation in front of you. Things would get complicated if you heard the statement on a bus on the way to *Ayers Rock*, where the bus journey has (however improbably . . .) been organised for promotional purposes by Mr Ayer's confectionery company. And things become more confusing still when you overhear the statement in a philosophy seminar on Ayer's epistemology. Is someone suggesting that Ayer manufactured sweets? The statement 'Ayer's rock is fantastic' is clearly neither correct nor incorrect, *tout court*, as without any relation to a determinate discourse we cannot even determine its propositional content. This does not mean that the proposition has to be covertly indexical, where this implies relativity to a context such that, according to context, 'Ayer's rock is fantastic' expresses the proposition *that Ayers Rock is fantastic relative to the context C*. The context does determine the propositional content of the expression 'Ayer's rock is fantastic', but this does not imply any relativity of the proposition *in* a discourse itself. It merely implies a relativity of our determination of the proposition *to* a particular discourse. Truth is as absolute as it gets, but it arises only under contextually constrained discursive conditions.

Therefore, since assessing the validity of a statement presupposes the determinacy of a discourse, validity is discourse-dependent. As we could not even ascribe any content to a statement independently of its relation to a given discourse, no statement can be valid unless its validity is possible to assess *in principle*. The relativity of statements to a particular discourse means that all *statements* (but not the propositions thereby expressed) are covertly indexical, in the sense that they always contain an implicit or explicit reference to a discourse in which they are evaluatively embedded.

It is therefore important to maintain a distinction between *statement relativism* and *proposition relativism*. A statement relativism for 'knowledge' asserts merely that the statement 'S knows that p', for example, does not and cannot express a proposition unless it is embedded in a context in which it first takes on a meaning and allows of assessment. By contrast, a proposition relativism for 'knowledge' asserts that the proposition expressed by the statement 'S knows that p' would be true in some contexts and false in others; the semantics of 'knowledge' therefore implies that all sentences of the form 'S knows that p' have the propositional content *that S knows p relative to a (or in a) discourse*.[67]

A move's reference to a context is a minimal condition for registering something as determinate. The matter of what something is can come up for discussion only within a discourse. To know what something is thus includes being able to explain to others that it is not something else,[68] and, in order to be able to draw this distinction between something and something else, certain statements must be proscribed and others permitted qua discourse-internal moves. Conceptual determinacy therefore presupposes the testability of a statement, which means, however, that the statement to be tested must admit of being correct or incorrect.

I call this condition *minimal verificationism*. If this condition is not fulfilled – i.e. if we find ourselves confronted with something in principle undecidable – we are simply not dealing with any content.[69] Decidability in turn presupposes information-processing that cannot be realised independently of modes of registration, where these, for their part, are finite. We can ground minimal verificationism by way of a *contrast theory of meaning*, according to which a predicate X can be meaningful only provided we exclude the existence neither of objects to which X pertains nor of objects to which X does not pertain.[70] The determinacy of the predicate is differential, meaning that semantics is a theory of difference. The differences between predicates are discursive and thus non-natural (i.e. not modally robust) properties. Further, as predicates figure in assertions, and assertions are discursive moves, predicative differences and their contrastive determinacy are negotiated discursively: correct and incorrect moves are coupled to differences between predicates, where differences between predicates can only be manifested in moves that depend essentially on their authorisation.

The arbitrariness of signs therefore encroaches upon the order of concepts. There is no clear-cut ontological distinction between words and concepts, between signs and their meaning. Suppose the English expression 'table' referred both to everything that is a *table* in my language and to everything that is an *asphodelus* in my language. Perhaps I have never had occasion to remark upon this fact simply because I have never had any reason to talk about asphodeli; I only know of them from reading Homer and know little more than that they are a kind of flower. Perhaps there are properties that *tables* and *asphodeli* have in common, which make it sensible to designate both with a single expression. This is a problem with which the language of lyric poetry continually confronts us, since it generates semantic dimensions that were previously hidden to us. It creates expressive worlds precisely by bringing semantic nuances into unsuspected connections, thereby yielding *unexpected harmonies*.[71] Indeed, all understanding continually suppresses the possibility of semantic nihilism by creating unexpected harmonies, as every expression is utterly new and deals with utterly new ontic circumstances. Things are never quite the same when we repeat the same expression. Hence, every expression transcends the unsurveyable plurality of sensibly available information by relating it to a *focus imaginarius*, to a concept.[72] The difference between the given and the thought, which is the signum of our epistemic finitude, presupposes our ability 'to dissolve an image into a concept'.[73] Nietzsche is thus correct when he says that 'every concept comes into being by making equivalent that which is non-equivalent.'[74] Nevertheless, our capacity for conceptual complexity reduction is not bound exclusively to the imagination of the isolated individual; instead it is discursively regulated. This regulation occurs first via language acquisition and then through participation in the game of giving and asking for reasons.

Although contextualism does not have to be spelled out as a form of pragmatism, it clearly unsettles the idea that truth is a relation between what in the best case is a purely receptive (mirroring) mode of registration *alias* mind (consciousness, thought, language, etc.) and the totality of facts (*alias* world, being, etc.). There are no 'facts' for us unless we can determine what they are. Even when we take into consideration that we neither know nor will ever know most facts – an assumption shared by everyone who grasps the concept of a fact – this does not mean that there are facts that lack determinacy. There cannot be undetermined facts: if there were, they would be determined through their being distinguishable from determinate facts. Determining what determinate and indeterminate facts are involves applying a mode of registration, where this generates presuppositions given not by the facts it can register but by its contingent 'tuning'.

Modes of registration, that is, need to operate on a particular setting, which conditions what can be registered. If we can understand discourses as modes of registration that have the general property of generating meta-pragmatic presuppositions, the assumption of a pure reception of facts comes under impossible pressure, and with it the idea of absolute objectivity. For the idea of absolute objectivity is nothing less than the idea of the world in the sense of the totality of all facts. And if there can be no infinite mode of registration, no mode that can register not only all (for it) objective facts but also all facts about itself, then the world in the sense of a totality, of an immediate unified horizon, no longer plays a role in our epistemic economy.[75]

With this discussion of modes of registration, I want to emphasise two points. First, the assumption of a totality of fixed facts starts to crumble when we see how different facts become available depending upon the setting or tuning of a given mode of registration. Second, even if we choose to understand it as a horizon or in a regulative sense, the thought of such a totality in fact becomes obsolete for the following reason: in order to enjoy the status of being a fact, any assumption of a totality must itself be available for examination in a discourse. Yet the totality cannot be an object of a mode of registration, since any candidate mode would have to be able to record all the facts about its own functioning. But this is impossible in principle: no mode of registration can actively exclude all sceptical alternatives. Even the kind of reflection on totality we find in classical metaphysical thinking can never exclude the possibility that it finds itself, qua cognitive activity of a finite individual, in a state of deception of a hitherto undetected kind.

We should therefore see the idea that the world is everything that is the case as a highly questionable assumption generated by the metatheory. Against this background, the Wittgenstein of the *Tractatus* had to entertain a mode of registration, the solipsistic ego, which is itself no longer a part, but only the boundary, of the world.[76] He thus introduces an idealised knower, someone in the impossible condition of surveying all there is without being an addendum to reality. It follows that there is nothing to say about this ego that could possibly be either true or false. The solipsistic ego is thus an absolutely propertyless pure mode of registration.

'Here it can be seen that solipsism, when its implications are followed out strictly, coincides with pure realism. The self of solipsism shrinks to a point without extension, and there remains the reality co-ordinated with it.'[77] The later Wittgenstein quite rightly renounced this idea, as it still has too much to say about that whereof one cannot speak. Besides, he had since discovered the problem that arises for the concept of totality once we appreciate how all facts must be determinable and that determinacy is not factual, but normative.

The contingent determinacy of discourse, its respective *tuning*, makes it impossible to give a philosophical (metatheoretical) confirmation of the idea of absolute objectivity or of a world that exists in itself while being thoroughgoingly determined. Instead, our discursive nature seems to imply that such a concept of the world is fundamentally misconceived. We cannot attach any sense to the idea of an absolute world, the states of which are determinate independently of the application of specific modes of registration. In what follows, we will find further corroboration that the notion of an absolute world as a thing in itself is a senseless assumption. Specifically, we will consider an argument for renouncing a certain conception of objectivity that goes together with a dualism of mind and world, facts and discourses, matter and form, and so on. This will allow us to see the motivation behind those varieties of anti-representationalism that explicitly appeal to Wittgenstein's private language argument.[78] At the same time, the concept of the world that we defended in Part I will begin to unravel. Only at the end of this study will we be in a position to try to recover the presupposition of a world, Habermas's 'formal presupposition of an objective . . . world'.[79]

9

Private Language and Assertoric Content

In his *Philosophical Investigations*, Wittgenstein famously set out a range of arguments aimed at undermining the foundations of solipsism. Among these, the most significant are his reflections on the problems of rule-following and the possibility of a private language. Both form components of his elaborate refutation of solipsism.[1] The kind of solipsism that Wittgenstein has in his sights is the sceptical result of the modern phenomenalism he had learnt about from Schopenhauer and Kant.[2] Although his overall engagement with solipsism is in no way restricted to epistemology or semantics, I will be focusing on a specific argumentative core of his approach. To be sure, I want to suggest neither that the existential dimension of solipsism plays no role for Wittgenstein, nor that the role it does play is somehow of lesser philosophical importance. But a thematic restriction of solipsism to a *sceptical* problem suits our current project of sketching a dialectical, or meta-epistemological, analysis of epistemology.

I will begin by concentrating on Wittgenstein's private language argument, considering it primarily as an attempted refutation of sceptical solipsism. In my view, this was his central aim in these passages. *Sceptical solipsism* is the assumption that the way the world appears to a conscious thinker is no different from how it would appear to them were they metaphysically isolated, alone with their representations of the world – that is, were there no other conscious subjects to whom the world appeared in some way or other. Sceptical solipsism is therefore *not* the position that there are good reasons to assume that the advocate of solipsism is the sole existing subject, while their representation of a world and the other subjects it contains is metaphysically empty. This absurd position – which, arguably, can be triggered by sceptical solipsism – can be labelled *metaphysical solipsism*. But the kind of sceptical (or methodological) solipsism that forms the target of Wittgenstein's deconstruction asserts merely the *possibility* of metaphysical solipsism, not its *actuality*. For the sake of simplicity, my discussion in what follows will be restricted to this variety of solipsism, which is, after all, the solipsism that has assumed a methodological function in epistemology from Descartes onwards.

Sceptical solipsism grounds an epistemic asymmetry. It makes it seem plausible that the assumption of a *represented* world and the subjects related to it (cognitively anchored within it) is secondary to the *representations* that a given subject might form of the world and the subjects related to it. Sceptical solipsism is thus the thesis that our representations of the world are epistemically primary vis-à-vis the representable world. If we know anything about the representable world at all, we know it only via our representations.

Solipsism arises from a methodological exercise based on two operations: *firstly*, it distinguishes the world in itself from the represented world by deploying the contrast of objectivity. This leads to the concept of a world of appearances. Appearances here are truth-evaluable entities – i.e. representations that either do or do not represent what is the case. If all representations were false, a pure world of appearances (Schopenhauer's 'world as representation') would nonetheless remain in place as a totality of intentional correlates. *Secondly*, solipsism presupposes a particular metaphysics of intentionality, according to which a subject can relate to something without other subjects having to be in the picture; other subjects need play no constitutive role in establishing relations to objects. For, on this view, the social world too is demoted to a system of representations: all the persons with whom we share that world are, qua intentional correlates, just so many more appearances.

Solipsism is thus based on an epistemological operation (a theory-level transition) that underlies such highly diverse positions as Locke's classical empiricism, certain variants of transcendental philosophy, and Berkeley's subjective idealism, to name but a few examples. If we want to dislodge solipsism, we therefore have to discover a blind spot lurking in all those positions for which solipsism plays a methodologically essential role – and therein lies the real impetus behind the private language argument.[3] Whether or not the argument also delivers a positive case for a form of semantic social externalism is something we will have to consider in what follows.

Phenomenalism is the philosophical thesis that we stand in no direct contact with the world of objects – the world we paradigmatically refer to with singular expressions such as 'house', 'cat' and 'chair' – but that our reference to the world is instead mediated by our reference to our phenomenal states (representations).[4] The position thus concedes to Cartesian scepticism that we find ourselves in a private inner space in which it is quite possible that no *esse* obtains independently of its *percipi*. But phenomenalism does not see this as damaging; rather, it identifies it as the true condition of grounding an epistemological foundationalism that holds out the prospect of being genuinely scientific. Ultimately, it introduces a class of entities with which (a) we stand in direct contact and to which (b) we are supposed to be able to make infallible reference by means of a privileged class of sentences (such as 'protocol sentences'). These entities are indubitably given sense data or sense contents. Whatever the world in itself might be like, it remains the case for the phenomenalist that, *for us*, it cannot be anything other than a logical construction on the basis of what is immediately given to us. If protocol sentences, on this picture, can be understood as reports that record the immediately given, it then seems a promising strategy to develop a scientific language that allows us to construct a systematic world picture on the basis of the protocol language. Epistemology would then be the science that decides how protocol sentences are to be translated into a scientific language. A complete description of the world would thus be a complete catalogue of all protocol sentences, with epistemology assigned the job of establishing the principles for translating the immediately given into protocol sentences. This model obviously does without the assumption that building a world picture requires a subject to have peeked out from behind the veil of her representational world and compared it with a world in itself; and so it seemingly avoids the dilemma that drives modern epistemology, namely, of bridging an ontological and epistemological chasm between cognitive subject and worldly object. For, on the phenomenological conception, the best description of the world would contain nothing other than the systematic catalogue of all protocol sentences, such that there could be no more talk of a trench between cognition and object.[5]

Epistemological foundationalism attempts to establish a hierarchical system for distributing certainty: its varieties each distinguish a class of indubitable and thus absolutely certain entities, so-called sense data, alias *impressions*, *ideas of sensation*, *mental images*, etc., which in each case are located somewhere on the spectrum of representations in general.[6] The problem is that any conceptual division of labour according to which there is an overall genus of representations 'in our mind' threatens to transform into a metaphysical scepticism. Systematic philosophy has to take precautionary measures against this danger. For Kant, this meant putting an end to the 'scandal of philosophy',[7] the idea that we cannot know whether metaphysical solipsism is false. To the extent to which philosophy begins from sceptical solipsism, it tries to show either that metaphysical solipsism is false (see Kant) or that it is meaningless (see Carnap). In this way, substantial philosophy is deployed to ensure that methodological scepticism does not grow into metaphysical scepticism.

According to the foundational idea of phenomenalism, protocol sentences are necessarily true because they record indubitable entities. In the case of sense data, there is no separating being and appearance: a sense datum *is* precisely as it *appears* to a given subject. Following Anton Friedrich Koch, we can call such putative atomic items 'primitive states of affairs' [*Ursachverhalte*].[8] When I find myself in the phenomenal state of having a red-sensation, for example, it is immediately certain that I see red, although it is by no means immediately certain that I see something red. That I see red is beyond all rational doubt. If it is possible to establish a system of assertions which (a) has protocol sentences as its foundation (which, because they indicate the presence of items that cannot possibly conceal anything, are self-intimating) and (b) contains assertions that are logically dependent on the protocol sentences, one can construct a world picture that does without theoretical reference to a given world of consciousness-independent objects. And if we can secure such a picture, Cartesian scepticism will look quite uninteresting, a mere expression of metaphysical humbug (which was of course one of logical positivism's iconoclastic ambitions).

It is obvious enough that phenomenalism, at some point or other, leads us astray. We need only reflect on how we would react were someone to declare that, from her point of view, for all she knows, we are nothing but constructions out of sense data. Needless to say, persons and other public objects are not commonly understood as constructions out of sense data; if they were, the phenomenalist would need a global error theory for our pre-theoretical object talk: all sentences about public objects would literally be sentences about our representations. Wittgenstein was especially conscious of how phenomenalism generates a particular *problem of other minds and bodies*, since it treats others as appearances, behind which there might quite possibly be no mentally endowed corporeal beings.

For our immediate purposes, we need not delve through the details of modern phenomenalism as it has been developed by its various avatars. The important point to bear in mind is that the key phenomenalistic move consists in isolating a particular class of expressions that are meant to be necessarily true because, in their case, it is supposedly senseless to distinguish between true and false.[9] Where there is no difference between being and appearance, the idea goes, complete transparency must reign and all error is excluded. To be sure, this is a confusion: if there is a class of sentences that seem to be eligible for truth-or-falsity but, on closer inspection, turn out to be immune to falsity as such, they cannot really be necessarily true in the desired sense. This is one of the reasons why the early Wittgenstein thought that contingency is a logical hallmark of empirical content. On his account, protocol sentences must either have the logical form of tautologies, which would deprive them of their privileged status, or they cannot play the role of maximally secure foundations.

Descartes himself combated Cartesian scepticism by committing to the existence of entities with (at least) two crucial properties: they are (1) not distinct from ourselves and (2) can only be as they appear. What I experience in my private inner space, my pain for example, is more familiar to me (*notior*) than all events in the sensibly intuited world. 'For what can be more intimate than pain?'[10] The *res cogitans* that each of us is, Descartes believes, is more epistemically transparent to us than the *res extensa* to which we have only indirect access. Access to *res extensae* is thus insurmountably mediated by self-intimations of *res cogitans*. Given this set-up, the immediacy of our self-relation seems to promise an advantage in terms of intimacy and certainty. But this advantage vanishes on closer inspection. The putative insight into the alleged coincidence of being and seeming on this side of the facts cannot itself be a case of the coincidence of being and seeming; to enjoy the kind of immediacy to which it appeals, it would have somehow to turn against discursivity from *within* discursive space. The alleged self-transparency is only a seeming transcendence and merely indicates a single point in the infinite mediation of logical space. We introduce it in order to get a foothold in something that we believe to be a pure experience of truth where no distinction between being true and taking to be true can be drawn.

Descartes and the logical positivists follow the common anti-sceptical strategy of tracking down a foundation for our knowledge that can vouch for its own truth. Such a foundation has to be so constituted that (1) it represents a case where being and seeming coincide and that (2) we can know that there has to be such a foundation a priori – i.e. through philosophical reflection alone. The foundation of our knowledge must be such that it cannot elude us in principle, else we fall victim to our methodological scepticism – the kind of scepticism to which we are methodologically committed by deploying the concept of representation.[11]

The motivating theory driving the concept of representation contains an answer to the question of how sensory illusion is possible. It deals with the problem of whether it is possible to find a criterion of truth that guarantees the difference between true and false (contentful and empty) representations a priori.[12] Hence Descartes' own famous attempt to argue that all clear and distinct ideas are contentful, an attempt which echoes the argumentative strategy pursued by the Stoic theory of cataleptic representation (καταληπτικὴ φαντασία).[13] The combination of clarity and distinctness is his candidate for a self-transparent criterion of truth. Yet only representations (ideas) can be clear and distinct, meaning that the search for a criterion of truth lands us with a commitment to assigning a central methodological function to the concept of representation. This is what lays the cornerstone of solipsism, which thus stems from a prior sceptical operation. It is important not to invert the true order of explanation here: it is not as though the concept of representation alone implies representationalism, which then in turn implies scepticism. Rather, the concept of representation *already* supposes a sceptical reflection, a theory of error, that first introduces the concept in order to explain the fallibility of objective knowledge.

Descartes and the logical positivists also share the further assumption that the foundation of our knowledge cannot be public: there can be no differences of opinion as to what it is. For whatever is public can be contested by methodological scepticism, and this immediately opens up the space for a renewed conflict between sceptics and dogmatists. But where there is a genuine conflict of opinion, there is also a difference between being and appearance; to at least one party, the object has to appear to be other than it really is. And to avoid this possibility, the foundation of our knowledge needs to be sought in a strictly private inner space.

Since he does not want his own animosity to phenomenalism to lead to any acquiescence with scepticism, Wittgenstein famously deploys a series of arguments to show that the idea of a private language is incompatible with the *use* of our language. According to Wittgenstein, linguistic beings cannot possibly be locked into a private inner space, else their language would fail to function. Among these arguments, the much discussed *private language argument* is of particular relevance. One way of understanding the intention behind the argument is that it is supposed to rule out the possibility of a language with which we might talk about an inner private space 'if we construe the grammar of the expression of sensation on the model of "object and designation"'. Yet, if one does not, 'the object drops out of consideration as irrelevant',[14] as there is simply no longer any object (the sensation) since objects can be designated – i.e. tagged with a label.[15]

Wittgenstein's private language argument takes aim at someone who claims to be able to record with absolute certainty what occurs within her private inner space (consciousness), while being able to talk about what occurs in the public world with only relative certainty. The argument attempts to convict solipsism of a semantic inconsistency by showing how the would-be private linguist is forced to talk about something that cannot really be talked about.[16] Wittgenstein goes as far as to assert that what one cannot speak about with *others* is not something one can *speak* about with oneself either, meaning that solipsism loses any possible justification.[17] If we can show that every language has to be public, the phantom of private language disappears. The idea of a private, purely monological inner space, in which I can speak with absolute certainty about the private episodes that occupy it (e.g. my representations of the world), turns out to be inconsistent. By the time we are through with the argument, the notion of such a space stands revealed as based on a fundamental misunderstanding of how language functions.[18]

Wittgenstein himself explains that the aim of his philosophy is 'to shew the fly the way out of the fly-bottle'.[19] We find an example of what he means in a remark from the 'Notes for lectures on "private experience" and "sense data"': '(The solipsist flutters and flutters in the flyglass, strikes against the walls, flutters further. How can he be brought to rest?)'.[20] The fly that Wittgenstein wants to lead to freedom is the solipsist, who bumps up against the walls of her private inner space and thinks she has somehow to break through to the world beyond her representations. Wittgenstein's way out of the fly bottle is not to show the solipsist how she can logically work her way out of her sense data; he does not help her locate the property of representations that would supposedly guarantee the objective reality of a class of representations sufficiently large to achieve a satisfying mediation of world and representation. Rather, the way out of the fly bottle is 'the diametrical opposite of solipsism'.[21]

On my reading, Wittgenstein does not add to the canon of transcendental arguments that aim to derive metaphysical theses from the structure of our understanding. Instead, he attempts to reduce any form of phenomenalism to absurdity by demonstrating solipsism's constitutive commitment to a form of nonsense. And he does so by articulating a position that counts as its diametrical opposite. The reason his argument should not be classed as transcendental is that transcendental arguments introduce a set of reflections on the nature of our understanding without transcending the conditions of an individual's understanding. They represent a course of reflection undertaken by the isolated subject and, as such, they still belong within the Cartesian sphere of methodological solipsism. Consequently, they already insinuate a certain metaphysics of intentionality, according to which *a* subject can refer to something without there being other subjects in the picture who guarantee, in one way or another, that the reference succeeds or fails. Wittgenstein attacks just this presupposition; lacking a sufficient reconstruction of how practical being-in-the-world is constitutive of subjectivity, it too leads to solipsism. Hence the private language argument has to be interpreted as an argument for solipsism's 'diametrical opposite' (see chapter 10).

As our discussion of the phenomenalist strategy has indicated, the success of Wittgenstein's argument depends on whether or not it can deprive solipsism of its logical foundation. This foundation, as we have seen, consists of a class of statements possessing the following properties: (1) they are necessarily true; (2) their truth cannot really be in doubt, because their contents cannot *be* other than they *seem*. The complete transparency of their content means that they are indubitable. Indeed, it is meant to be *senseless* to doubt them: one cannot doubt anything that cannot even *appear* to be other than it is.

Any reconstruction of the private language argument must avoid sharing any solipsistic premises. In light of our discussion of contextualism, it is clearly of particular relevance that Wittgenstein's 'diametrical opposite' of solipsism (which is usually understood as *social externalism*) implies an indispensable commitment to the contextualism of language games.[22] According to Wittgenstein, the determinacy of a statement, and thus its assertoric content, is a function not of the correspondence between language and world but of language itself. It is only in language that we can establish a distinction between correct and incorrect, and thus secure the determinacy of a content.[23] Accordingly, the world can be everything that can be the case *for us*; and, once we have grasped this insight, we can see that the assumption of a world in itself, a world consisting of the totality of all mind- and language-independent facts, is without specific content. For there can be nothing determinate for us independently of what can or cannot be the case – i.e. of what can be affirmed or negated. For us, talk of a world in itself, in which everything is the case anyhow, is metaphysically empty. That is, there is no world for us in which all the facts already lie arranged, because facts always have to be something determinate. And, as we cannot understand how there can be any determinacy in the absence of an assertoric discourse that determines what is to count as correct and what as incorrect, it cannot make sense *to speak* of a world determined in and of itself, let alone to count it among the truth

conditions of our statements. *As we cannot speak about indeterminate items,*
and since all determinacy for us is discursive, it is senseless to speak of a world
determined in and of itself. If the world is everything that is the case, and if that
which is the case can only ever be something for a discourse that determines what
can be the case for it, then there is no longer any reason to understand the world
as the totality of all modally robust facts, where such facts always already fix what
is objectively true and false independently of our discursive practices, even when
it might escape our grasp.[24] In other words: the world as the totality of all
facts may well be something we talk about, but, in determining it as an
object of language, it is *ipso facto* a determinate object of a discourse and
ceases to be the world in itself. *The world-in-itself is therefore always already*
the world-in-itself-for-us – it does not follow that the world in itself does not exist,
merely that it is determinate for us only provided it can be something *for us.*

The concept of the world as the totality of all facts is thus incompatible
with Wittgenstein's approach in his later philosophy, where he instead
tries to show that assertoric determinacy is a function of a normative game.
This does not mean that facts are a social construct and that it is therefore
not true, say, that there were mountains before there were competent users
of the concept 'mountain'. Rather, it belongs to the conditions of possessing the concept 'mountain' that every competent user of the concept is
able to understand that the existence of mountains precedes the existence
of the concept of mountains, just as our own existence precedes our self-
understanding. Yet it is no absolute fact that, for example, the Himalayas
exist, if by 'absolute fact' we understand a fact to which we would have
optimal access if we could model our concepts according to specifications
laid out by the world alone. We might transpose ourselves hypotheti-
cally into the world of absolute facts and try to determine whether the
Himalayas exist; but this will hardly get us very far. For, in the hypotheti-
cally absolute world, it is far from clear that there is any kind of boundary
at all between mountains and valleys. Moreover, from another cosmic
perspective, one might possibly see mountains as valleys and valleys as
mountains. Mountains and valleys are relative to our spatial orientation
on earth and, more particularly, to our interests in determining states of
affairs as thus and so. It is only given such factors that we fix what should
count as a mountain and what as a valley. Competent use of the relational
concepts 'valley' and 'mountain' thus presupposes that their conditions of
use have been normatively established, such that deviant semantic behaviour can be sanctioned accordingly. Whoever designates the mountain as a
valley is not simply objectively in error but is trying to shift the boundary
of the language game – i.e. to alter its grammar in Wittgenstein's sense. The
assumption of a world that is thoroughgoingly determined in itself, that is
just as the totality of all true judgements would represent it, is senseless for
Wittgenstein: there can be no totality of all true judgements without there
being discursive practices whose grammar is contingent, even if in all (or
at least most) cases it is not replaceable.[25]

But if we ask whether it is an absolute fact that the Himalayas would be located where they are *here and now* even if nobody had a concept of a mountain, the answer is surely 'yes and no': 'yes' insofar as it belongs to the concept of a mountain that it exists independently of our will and discretion; 'no', insofar as we lose any reference to the world when we strive after a view from nowhere. Concepts are clearly normative insofar as one can use them correctly or incorrectly within the context of a language game and its grammar. This normativity has to be inscribed in every concept, as Wittgenstein's thought experiment of a private sensation language is meant to show. But it follows from the thoroughgoing normativity of all concepts that, while it belongs to the concept of a mountain that it exists independently of our holding-true, this does not mean that it exists as a mountain *in rerum natura*, as it were, independently of our practice of distinguishing it from a valley.

Now, with the help of Wittgenstein's analysis we can show that an adequate understanding of rule-following already includes a rejection of solipsism and, at the same time, of a private language. In §258 of *Philosophical Investigations*, Wittgenstein develops the famous thought experiment in which someone (call her A) tries to establish a private sensation language by writing an entry in a sensation diary, whereby only she can understand whether she has a particular sensation S. Since only A has access to her sensations, nobody besides A can say whether A has really had the sensation S that she records in her diary on a particular day. Other subjects can at best guess what is really going on with A, while A knows with unshakable certainty whether and when she has or has had S and what kind of feeling S is.

Yet how can A know that her sign 'S' really means S? How can she so much as connect her as yet nameless sensation with a sign, such that she correctly uses the sign in the case of every S-event? How can A know that she in fact currently has S and not S^2? It is obviously not sufficient for A to point to a further sensation, say one which always accompanies S, that allows her to say with absolute certainty that she currently has S and not S^2. If the sensation S^3, which helps to distinguish between *S and* S^2, is once again purely private, immediate, and transparent and incorrigible only for A, the supposed expedient of S^3 is of no help; it too fails to ensure that S^3 is not S^4. A lands herself in a vicious infinite regress if she bases her absolute certainty that S today does not designate S^2 on her having a further sensation (e.g. an infallible or inner intuition) that is once again accessible to her alone, and so on and so on.[26]

The problem is thus that A has 'no criterion of correctness'[27] for her assertion that she is currently having a sensation of S and not S^2.[28] It follows from this, however, that there is no difference between the presence of S (*being*) and the impression (*seeming*) that S, and not S^2. By hypothesis, the difference between being and seeming is suspended for the private inner space. This means, however, 'whatever is going to seem right to me is right. And that only means that here we can't talk about "right".'[29] Since there can be no difference between the *correct* application of a rule – i.e. of the expression 'S' – and the *apparently correct* application of this rule in the private inner realm, every impression of following a rule is already *ipso facto* following a rule. But if there is to be a difference between a general rule and individual cases of its application, there also has to be room for a false application of the rule; not everything can be a case of application of a particular rule.[30] The rule therefore distinguishes between correct and incorrect but does not decide as to its application. We cannot exclude incorrect usage.

The putative epistemological advantage of private language is that it is meant to contain only true statements. It is certainly this feature which the phenomenalist intends to exploit. Yet a language that contains only true statements cannot contain any rule book, for every deviation from a rule in the language must also represent a true statement. But this just means that private language is responsible to nobody and nothing, not even to the sensations it records. It is simply without rules. The result is total semantic anarchy in the use of its concept words; their use can never go awry. It is therefore just as correct to classify a present sensation as S as to classify it as S^2 – *anything goes*. Privacy's supposed epistemic advantage thus transforms into total assertoric arbitrariness.

The advantage of a private sensation language over against public speech thus turns out to be the mere semblance of an advantage; it cannot even be publicly verified as *existing* semblance without public speech already having determined it as its other. We are meant to be dealing with a class of representations, sensation concepts, for which being and seeming coincide. Any application of these concepts, simply in being an application of these concepts, will be a truthful application; for any contravention of the rules of their application is unthinkable. But since such a language lets us pass off any random claim as knowledge, we cannot really use it to formulate knowledge claims at all. As a language, private language is self-undermining.

A private sensation language does not even allow us to *refer* to anything: as long as there is no difference between truth and holding true, we are free to take ourselves to be referring to anything whatsoever and to be doing so entirely correctly. With the resources of private language alone, that is, it is impossible to mark any difference between something and something else (S and S^2), because anything, at any time, can be understood as S or as S^2. The private language user can therefore not even say that S is 'something', as 'something' already belongs to 'our common language'.[31] If the private language user assures us that she really is picking out something to which she makes error-immune reference, to which nobody besides herself can have any cognitive access, and which she chooses to designate as S, she already finds herself in the catchment area of public language. She assumes that she is onto something she can identify insofar as she distinguishes it, for example, from everything that everyone else can also identify. But the conditions of possible identificatory (and therefore conceptual) reference are not fulfilled if *any* registered item whatsoever fulfils them. Likewise, the hungry person who sees everything as food can never be satisfied (but can certainly be ill): even the animalistic reference structure of hunger presupposes discriminatory capacities.[32]

For Wittgenstein, the notion of a conceptually indistinguishable and, in this sense, fully private sensation fails on account of the social universality of language, a feature that he goes on to interpret as a function of language's essential normativity. Yet the normativity of language implies that we must be able to distinguish the contravention of rules from their correct application – the very ability that the private linguist cannot display. Precisely because of the advantages it claims to enjoy on account of its greater intimacy, private language contravenes the conditions of the possibility of any observable difference between *S* and something else, meaning that *S* is not even a something, albeit not a nothing either, as Wittgenstein puts it.[33] 'So in the end when one is doing philosophy one gets to the point where one would like just to emit an inarticulate sound. – But such a sound is an expression only as it occurs in a particular language-game, which should now be described.'[34]

Wittgenstein, it should be emphasised, does not dispute that we can entertain 'private' thoughts about our sensations, in the sense that we simply happen not to share them with others. We can speak with ourselves, soliloquise. He merely asserts that this presupposes a prior initiation into a universal, public language. The private language argument does not make the nihilistic (not to mention absurd) claim that there are no private episodes. Rather, it sets out to show that our private episodes form parts of a public drama, because our own relation to our private episodes is linguistically mediated (we use sensation words, for example). *Because linguistic mediation would be impossible under the conditions of an exclusively private language,* our relation to our sensations always already stands in relation to our relations to others. Since there can be no language 'governed' by rules whose contravention is impossible in principle (in which every application of a rule would be permitted because no formulation of the rule could be excluded), the language we use to talk about our sensations cannot be private. This means, however, that the private inner space from which the solipsist, like the fly in the fly bottle, seeks an escape becomes a *private* inner space in the first place only once it has been cordoned off *as* such a space within the medium of a universal language.

If left to the resources of private language alone, the private linguist could not even understand the difference between her statements about her sensations and her statements about public objects; her sensations would be so private, so to speak, that she could not claim to know of them that they were not public. In short, the difference between private and public objects is itself public. In this chapter, we have been concerned primarily with attempts to exploit this difference in the service of a foundationalist project: it is supposed to provide our beliefs with a foundation via recourse to a supposed epistemological asymmetry between the private and public use of signs. But this distinction must itself be publicly comprehensible. It is senseless to insist that an individual speaker standing on one side of the distinction is debarred from saying anything that could possibly be comprehensible to another speaker.

Since the publication of Kripke's influential interpretation, there has been some consensus that the private language argument is an application of Wittgenstein's general reflections on the problem of rule-following, which he develops primarily in §§143–243 of the *Philosophical Investigations*, the paragraphs that immediately precede the private language considerations. Read in this light, the private language argument can be interpreted as an argument against the possibility of a rule that cannot be contravened. Kripke argued that Wittgenstein first formulates and then tries to dissolve the general paradox according to which every application of every rule could be arbitrary. The result of such arbitrariness would of course be the implosion of the very concept of a rule. It speaks in favour of Kripke's reading that Wittgenstein himself expressly talks about a paradox:

> This was our paradox: no course of action could be determined by a rule, because every course of action can be made out to accord with the rule. The answer was: if everything can be made out to accord with the rule, then it can also be made out to conflict with it. And so there would be neither accord nor conflict here.[35]

We can see what Kripke's Wittgenstein is after by varying one of the latter's examples. Suppose we wanted to determine which rule a person S follows in constructing the series 2, 4, 6, 8, 10. She promises to continue the series as soon as we have discovered which series she is following. A good hypothesis would be that S is following the rule +2. Yet nothing speaks against the hypothesis that S is following the rule +2 *until 10,000 and then +4*, so that after 10,000 she would continue with 10,004, not with 10,002. There seems to be no reason to exclude this possibility.[36] Yet what if S tells us she is following the rule '+2' and still proceeds to write 10,004 after 10,000? How can we know that by 'the rule +2' she does not mean *the rule +2**, which says '+2 until 10,000 and then +4'? S could tell us that she does not mean '+2*', but how can *she* know that when she has never continued the series to 10,000? How can she determine in advance that she will write 10,002 after 10,004? Besides, how can we be sure that she does not understand every numerical expression from 10,000 onwards differently to us, so that by '10,004' she understands just what we do by '10,002'?

Suppose S is alone and conducts an inner monologue. She determines to mean +2 by '+2', and not +2*. The problem now is that S cannot know what she will mean by '+2' when she reaches 10,000, as she has never counted that high. She does not know the 'whole use'[37] of her rule, even if she knows how one adds 2 to a given number. Her honest intention to apply the rule '+2' cannot by itself determine that she will really apply +2. In other words, the correctness of her application of the rule, its agreement with the rule, does not depend on her intention alone. If it did, she would end up entangled within a private language, and everything that seemed correct in her eyes simply would be correct. For algebra, of course, this can hardly be the case, meaning we need another explanation of rule-following besides an appeal to intentions.

Nor does it get us any further if we appeal to the essence of the rule itself. For even if there were a supersensible realm in which all rules were stored for all eternity, S, relying purely on her own mental resources, could not be sure which rule she had 'downloaded' from that world; as an isolated judging subject, she can make no distinction between its correct and incorrect application. How can she know, that is, what she will mean by '+2' in the future or what she meant by it in the past, when her meaning what she does is an exclusively private experience, just like the private application of *S*? Ultimately, S cannot 'appeal . . . to something independent'[38] from her own resources, since she could once again end up interpreting her judgement in a completely arbitrary manner.

The Platonic assumption, that we grasp rules in an independent realm through acts of mental apprehension (intuition), is of no help. Since the act of grasping Platonic ideas has to be performed by finite subjects, the sceptical game just plays itself out all over again, and it remains unclear *which* idea exactly the finite subject has grasped. This is something that has to be communicated discursively.[39] For how can one know that one has grasped the idea of the rule +2 and not rather the idea of the rule +2*? Even if the ideas interpret themselves, and grasping the idea '+2' implied that the idea is really +2 and not +2*, *we* could hardly put this information to use: the mere grasping of an idea does not tell us anything about what we will do as soon as we, say, reach 10,000. For a finite mind, grasping the idea +2 implies grasping the idea *22,222* just as little as grasping the idea *table* means grasping the idea *table with three legs*. Grasping an idea cannot possibly imply having an overview of its entire application, and it is therefore no accident that Plato himself downgrades the world of rule-application to the domain of unknowable seeming, of *doxa*. Grasping an idea can determine in advance neither how we as finite thinkers will proceed at a determinate point in our conceptual history, nor what we will think at such a point about what we have done in our conceptual past. Insofar as the idea is in my mind, it is a finite content that will immediately be followed by another, a point that Kripke saw clearly: 'For Wittgenstein, Platonism is largely an unhelpful evasion of the problem of how our finite minds can give rules that are supposed to apply to an infinity of cases. Platonic objects may be self-interpreting, or rather, they may need no interpretation; but ultimately there must be some mental entity involved that raises the sceptical problem.'[40] Wittgenstein does not so much give us an argument against the existence of Platonic ideas as bring us to see how postulating them makes no real contribution to solving the problem of rule-following. For, ultimately, we have to *apply* ideas, and the notion of intuitive apprehension does not help us understand how we do so. We cannot grasp rules *uno intuito*, as they are not independent of the potential infinity of their application. The universality of the rule is determined through individual cases, and which rule one follows is something one knows only by deciding to judge or act in such and such a way in a given situation.

The rule that S is alleged to grasp privately (through the intellectual intuition of an idea, for example) cannot possibly show her all its applications. Since the cases to which the rule applies are potentially infinite, and no finite mind can survey or anticipate such an infinity of cases, it is unwise to make possession of such an ability a condition of ascribing to ourselves, say, the capacity to perform addition. An eidetic manifestation in grasping a rule cannot possibly present a finite subject with the totality of its applications, as the rule cannot somehow determine its complete range of applications in advance for a finite mind. In order to decide what one is dealing with in a given situation, and how one should go on, it is not enough to resort to a pre-formulated rule: whatever the formulation, it cannot determine whether or not one is actually dealing with one of its applications.

Our use of rules is therefore necessarily underdetermined. At any given time, we are confronted with entirely new constellations – i.e. with instances of rules that are not anticipated by the rules themselves. Therefore, even in those cases where a canon of rules is established by an authorised group of experts or a commission, we cannot always shirk the task of having to alter ready-formulated rules or of subjecting them to innovative interpretations. The practice of applying case law, for example, is hardly thinkable without adequate corrective mechanisms, which come into play whenever a certain case brings to light an unforeseeable property of a pre-formulated rule. The same goes for mathematics: on occasion, an extended inferential practice can reveal inconsistencies, and there must be room for the formation of corrective mechanisms that work towards their removal. There can therefore be no iron-clad rules (and thus no 'infinitely long rails',[41] as Wittgenstein says) exempt from any form of correction; our stock of information can change at any moment, compelling us to make partial revisions to our systems of rules or our practices.[42] The impossibility of an iron-clad canon of rules to orient us in our dealings with the world follows from the essential normativity of rules. Given this normativity, the existence of rules presupposes a binary code which distinguishes between correct and incorrect applications. And, because of our finitude, the norms that determine the code's realisation are always norms-in-context: there is no escaping to some matrix of absolute norms.[43]

To explain rule-following, we might appeal to a capacity such as Kant's 'power of judgement'. But this only presents us with yet another dead end. Famously, the function of this 'power' is either to *determine* which rule should be applied in a given case or to *reflect* on which rule has been applied in a given case.[44] But assuming a general rule under which particular cases are subsumed on the model of *modus ponens* already triggers the regress of rules, and invoking the power of judgement merely cuts this off ad hoc. Kant himself is certainly aware of the problem: a passage in the first *Critique* explicitly formulates the regress argument in order to then introduce a special talent, the power of judgement, as a means of evading its consequences. Because of the particular relevance of this passage, it is worth quoting it at length:

> If the understanding in general is explained as the faculty of rules, then the power of judgment is the faculty of **subsuming** under rules, i.e., of determining whether something stands under a given rule (casus datae legis) or not. General logic contains no precepts at all for the power of judgment, and moreover cannot contain them. For **since it abstracts from all content of cognition,** nothing remains to it but the business of analytically dividing the mere form of cognition into concepts, judgments, and inferences, and thereby achieving formal rules for all use of the understanding. Now if it wanted to show generally how one ought to subsume under these rules, i.e., distinguish whether something stands under them or not, this could not happen except once again through a rule. But just because this is a rule, it would demand another instruction for the power of judgment, and so it becomes clear that although the understanding is certainly capable of being instructed and equipped through rules, the power of judgment is a special talent that cannot be taught but only practiced.[45]

Kant thus introduces a faculty, the power of judgement, in order to avoid the infinite regress which looms as soon as we understand rule-following as subsumption. The *subsumption model of rule-following* is based on the problematic assumption that all rule-following functions like a *modus ponens* inference: a rule implies all its applications, such that every application of a rule presupposes a simple conditional of the form: P (rule) → Q (application): if the rule obtains, all instances of the rule are already determined as such, because there are truth-apt judgements about what is an instance of the rule when the instance is subsumed under the rule. All applications of a rule are, accordingly, implied by the rule, as the particular is implied by the universal. Yet each cognition presupposes that something can be grasped *as* a case falling under the rule, which is why Kant sees thinking as judging – i.e. as the connection of individual (subject) and universal (predicate). Judgements are rules, however, meaning that, for Kant, all cognition is the subsumption of a given object under rules.[46]

According to the subsumption model of rule-following, we can analyse a rule as a set of conditions, such that we have a case that falls under the rule if and only if all the conditions that an analysis of the rule brings to light are fulfilled. The power of judgement thereby has the task of bringing together the universal and the particular by recognising some fact as a case that falls under the rule. If all conditions are fulfilled (P), we can infer by *modus ponens* that we are dealing with a case that commits us to applying the rule (Q).

Now, Kant's problem is how it is possible to identify the right conditions (P), and thus the rule. Doing so in turn requires rules to specify which meta-rules have to be fulfilled in order to identify the rules that have to be fulfilled for us to be entitled to assert P, and thus to be entitled to the *modus ponens* of rule-following. To establish the conditional that serves as the first premise for the *modus ponens* inference, the conditional thus has to be made available *modo ponente*, whereby the foundational conditional has the form P* (meta-rule) → [P (rule) → Q (application)]. By hypothesis, the same goes for this conditional, because the meta-rule too is subject to the conditions of its own applicability, and so on *ad infinitum*.

We thus face a regress if we assume that an identification of a case as falling under a rule should be understood as an insight into the inferential connection of the universal and the particular. In order to avoid the regress, Kant introduces the power of judgement. This power serves the function of identifying circumstances as cases which fall under a rule without conceptual mediation. The power of judgement thus pre-discursively identifies circumstances that have to obtain for us to be dealing with a case that instances a certain rule. But if the power of judgement is supposed to recognise cases without judgement – i.e. without any specification of meta-rules for its own exercise – Kant owes us an explanation of how this power can immediately recognise a case *as* such without judging. Without one, the assumption of a power of judgement seems ad hoc, at least if it is invoked to put a stop to the regress of rules. The problem is that Kant insists we can only determine something in judgement. But if everything is determinable only in judgement, the same goes for the truth conditions of judgement, which are connected to the conditions of the judgement's elements – in the simplest case, its subject and predicate – obtaining or not obtaining. These conditions can for their part only be determined in the judgement, necessitating a judgement about the truth conditions of the first judgement, and so on *ad infinitum*. In order to prevent the regress, Kant assumes an immediate mode of registration of the general conditions of a concept, of the individual instances to be subsumed under it. The mode of registration, the power of judgement, cannot itself judge – at pain of triggering the regress – but must grasp something as something without judging. But, if we are supposed to trace all assertoric determinacy back to judgements, this is simply ruled out.

To be sure, if taken in isolation, Kant's model possesses considerable plausibility and does justice to a familiar phenomenon. Think, for example, of someone with a talent for mathematics. One way of measuring the extent of someone's mathematical talent is to see whether they can just grasp the solution to a problem – and thus a rule – immediately, in an instant, without needing to grasp the rule in terms of further rules. This is why mathematical talent is also the only tool we have at our disposal for successfully discovering previously unknown mathematical terrain.

Similarly, in the jargon of chess, one speaks of a player having *seen* a move through what people in chess circles often call *intuition*. A grand master stands out because of his ability to use his intuition to break established rules and to institutionalise new ones in the process.[47] This is how progress occurs in chess theory. The introduction of a new variant of a certain opening usually comes about thanks to spontaneous 'inspiration' which only retrospectively solidifies into a rule. In all such cases, a specific local intelligence is at work, which can only be taught to a limited extent. The creative foray into new possibilities, into the not-yet-established, cannot be a rule-guided process, which suggests that we need to presume a faculty that can capture these forays in the net of articulated rules. Just because creative energies do not themselves flow along paths determined by established rules does not mean that their manifestations cannot be captured retrospectively in a rational form.[48] Insofar as every application of a rule is a projection into the not-yet (since every situation is new for us), all rule-following, for Kant, takes place in this manner, meaning it is always explicable only *post festum*. Yet Kant assumes that all inferential connections are fixed independently of our grasping them – that is, that rules are concepts that imply their instances (the particular). While the activity of the power of judgement is not itself guided by explicit rules, it operates by intuitively discovering inferential connections.

Returning to the rule-following problem more generally, Kant's solution appears to be the introduction of a specific capacity. Because he understands concepts as rules, he sees himself confronted with this problem just as much as Wittgenstein.[49] Wittgenstein compares strategies such as Kant's with a use of language 'in which people say: "Mr. Unknown did it" instead of: "It isn't known who did this" – so that they don't have to say there is something they don't know.'[50] It therefore seems as though Kant first introduces the problematic subsumption model and then goes on to postulate a capacity in order to resist the vicious regress that the model invites.

Yet, regardless of the incoherence of the subsumption model, Kant is entitled to his postulation of faculties thanks to phenomena familiar from the context of heuristics. The problem here is that Kant tends to overgeneralise a local insight and inflate it into a maximally general account of human rule-following (a theory of rationality). And the weakness of this strategy stems from its adoption of the subsumption model of rule-following in the first place, from understanding all rule-following as subsumption (or, to put it in more Kantian terms, understanding all thinking as judgement). Elementary instances of rule-following, such as the use of colour words, cannot be understood on this model. Which conditions have to be fulfilled before we can rightly judge that a colour patch is green? What relation obtains between some general rule governing the use of the predicate __ *is green* and the stated greenness of a given colour patch? That a given colour patch is green does not follow from any general rule; we cannot confirm its greenness via a rule-governed procedure that involves locating it within the inferentially articulated total context of all predicates.

To be sure, we need to avoid the converse error, of atomising the use of colour words and other simple predicates: if someone is entitled to assert that a given colour patch is green, they are thereby entitled to assert that it is not red, that colours exist, that forms exist, etc. If someone is a competent speaker, they always already inhabit a holistic context within which they exercise an ability to mark a variety of distinctions. If you know how to apply some predicate, you are *ipso facto* able to apply other predicates.[51] If, by 'the universal', we understand a set of concepts determinable by their reciprocal relations of inclusion and exclusion, we might then understand Kant's power of judgement as the capacity to locate a given empirical episode within a larger conceptual context, a capacity of which we make use at every moment of our conscious lives. The power of judgement makes the individual into the particular by determining it as a case that falls under a rule. The raw data that we take up in receptivity do not reveal anything universal, and thus nothing determinate, without our assistance; in themselves, they have no informational value. So, at every moment, we have, for example, to count on the objects of our perception being more than their facing surfaces or on their continuing to exist when we are not paying them any attention. No empirical test can justify this universality retrospectively, even though we would be in no position whatsoever to orient ourselves in a world – i.e. in the public domain – without it. Objects are always projected beyond their current *percipi* into a virtual space and can potentially present us with indefinitely many aspects.

Kant's philosophy operates in the mode of an analytic of finitude; it investigates how we can refer to a common world of which we are only ever confronted with individual glimpses. Essentially, such reference is possible because we can register particular episodes that determine individuals as particular instances. Our finitude, for Kant, consists precisely in our needing to have transcended each individual given in order to be able to register it *as something* at all. Without our conceptual intervention, there would simply be no stable world for us.[52] In this picture, the power of judgement plays the role of mediating, so to speak, between particular episodes and the universal drama in which they take place. It thus enables us to have knowledge of *worldly scenes*, by first establishing a context in which particular episodes have to be located.[53]

Rule-following is not identical with registering something as something; in other words, *rule-following is not judging*. A judging that is meant to help us determine something as something has to make use of determinations that we cannot in turn determine as something. There must therefore be 'a way of grasping a rule which is *not* an *interpretation*, but which is exhibited in what we call "obeying the rule" and "going against it" in actual cases. Hence there is an inclination to say: every action according to the rule is an interpretation. But we ought to restrict the term "interpretation" to the substitution of one expression of the rule for another.'[54] Wittgenstein's point is that rule-following is not always interpretation and therefore cannot consist in judging. If we judge that we have followed this or that rule, we follow further rules, and, while we could interpret these in turn, we do not always follow them by interpreting them. At some point or other we have to stop conceiving our rule-following as judging. But this means that our orientation within the world is not thoroughgoingly discursive but always relies on a non- or pre-discursive dimension. This dimension, however, is something we cannot grasp, since grasping it would necessarily involve determining it under the conditions of our finite discourse.

Wittgenstein therefore looks for an alternative, non-Kantian solution to the problem. As he is aware, the puzzle first becomes urgent when one presents it in the form of a paradox. For paradoxes only rarely have ad hoc solutions, and, as we saw when analysing Cartesian scepticism in chapter 6, they can be solved by substantial philosophy (if at all) in at best a qualified sense.[55] And as Kant's theory of the power of judgement, though, is a piece of substantial philosophy, we cannot without further ado reconstruct it as an adequate (dis)solution to the rule-following paradox.

The central difference between Kant's and Wittgenstein's solution to the rule-following problem is that Kant conceives rules as something general under which particular instances have to be subsumed. As we have seen, the rule is thus determined in advance for Kant, such that the determining power of judgement merely has to determine a given case as falling under the rule. Even the reflecting power of judgement, which, conversely, searches for a rule instanced by the particular case, *finds* the universal, but does not *invent* it. For Kant, therefore, the universal is already fixed, and variability resides solely on the side of the instances that have to be brought under the concept. But, to understand why Kant works with this general conception of rules, it is vital to see how the introduction of the power of judgement makes sense only within the context of the *Critique of Pure Reason*'s global project: namely, of drawing the boundaries of reason with the help of reason itself. For Kant, these boundaries are necessary and universal.[56] But this just means that Kant acquiesces with a subsumption model of rule-following from the outset. And, as a result, he is inevitably faced with a version of the rule-following problem that he can resolve only by stipulating a special faculty. For, according to Kant, there are transcendental conditions of discursivity as such: these stand fixed in advance and are discovered, rather than first produced, in transcendental reflection. Our categorial equipment cannot change – it is a priori.

Wittgenstein reverses this order of explanation, understanding the explication of rules as a secondary matter in relation to rule-following; he can put a stop to the regress of rules by casting suspicion over the idea that rules require explication rather than over the phenomenon of rule-following itself. The universal is generated by the individual, the rule by the manner in which it is followed. In other words: the multiplicity of appearances grounds the unity of their sense.

Wittgenstein draws an important distinction between *following a rule* and *knowledge about the rule one is following*. This distinction is constitutive for our ability to engage in discursive practices: it cannot be a legitimate requirement on the validity of a practice that its rules have to be made explicit in advance. Practices are information-processing systems that can never fully retrieve their meta-pragmatic presuppositions without collapsing under the resulting burden of information. This means that any attempt to discover an absolute network of rules, rules that organise and precede *all* practices as a condition of their very functioning, represents a highly problematic endeavour.[57] Contextualism is thus incompatible with a transcendental philosophy of finitude as long as the latter, *firstly*, is committed to a subsumption model of rule-following and, *secondly*, tries to solve the resultant problem with the discovery of a conceptual framework that is supposed to be constitutive of subjectivity as such.

Wittgenstein's distinction between implicit and explicit knowledge, or between knowledge as an ability (knowing how) and knowledge as a transparent cognitive state (knowing that), also enables him to dissolve the so-called *paradox of analysis*. This paradox lies behind Augustine's famous difficulty that he knew what time was as long as nobody asked him.[58] We can formulate the paradox as follows: how can the task of finding the correct definition or analysis of a concept X present philosophy with such great difficulties, when one already has to know what X is in order to raise the analytical question to begin with? That is, if one did not somehow already know what X was, how could one ask what it is? One could hardly pose the question without knowing *what* exactly was in question. To formulate the paradox somewhat more formally:

(1) Either S knows what X is or S does not know what X is.
(2) If S knows what X is, why does S have difficulties stating what X is? If someone knows something, they can surely state what it is that they know.
(3) If S does not know what X is, then S cannot be certain that their question 'What is X?' has any content whatsoever.
(4) Therefore, S already knows what X is when S asks what X is.

If X is a predicate (e.g. __ *is a shadow*), knowing what X is means knowing its meaning. But this cannot be a question of always already possessing a definition or analysis of X, else one could not refer to X without being able to state explicitly what X is. And this would undermine the possibility of any cognitive progress; we can acquire knowledge about states of affairs or objects only when we do not already know what they are. The paradox can be resolved quite easily as soon as we take into account that we can have *implicit* knowledge of what something is, including the meaning of a predicate. Knowing the meaning of a predicate merely means having the ability to apply it competently. But, given the regress problem, it cannot be a requirement of having this ability that one also be able to grasp hold of a universal in order to then subordinate individuals to it as particulars. In order to be a competent user of a predicate, that is, one need not be in a position to give it an explicit definition or to replace it with other, potentially simpler or more fundamental predicates by means of logical analysis. Rather, the regress argument shows how the assumption that we need to know the rules we follow in order to follow them represents an incoherent ideal. The description of following a particular rule is not itself an act of rule-following in every case.

If, like Kant, we want to say that all observation (thought) consists in following rules (judgement), then explicit definitions of applied rules, by contrast, would amount to second-order observations, and thus observations of observations (the applications of rules). That is, they would be interpretations in Wittgenstein's sense. These higher-order observations would of course themselves be instances of rule-following and, as such, they could not be self-confirming but would require confirmation at the level of a higher-order observation (via a theory-level transition). It falls to the respectively higher-order observation to describe the system of rules mastered by its competent users. But, following this logic, the attainment of an absolute standpoint can be ruled out as impossible in principle: one always has to follow rules in order to perform a given operation, without thereby being in a position to specify the rules *in ipso actu operandi*.

Rule-following is therefore a practical accomplishment and not a disinterested thought process. Theoretical analysis of a concept can only make explicit what is already implicit in our practice, which is not to say that the process of explication cannot lead to modifications at the practical level. For theory is itself a discursive practice that establishes rules, demarcates authorizing criteria, and so on. Without this possibility, there could be no scientific progress in the minimal sense of making discoveries about the world that were not already implicit in our practice. Before a certain point in time, nobody knew that water was identical with H_2O, even though there were plenty of competent users of the expression 'water'. The theoretical explication of a concept, paired with appropriate scientific activities of investigation, led to our discovery that what we refer to with the term 'water' is H_2O. Competent users of an expression do not, therefore, need to have attained a complete overview of the meaning of the expression. Moreover, they cannot, which is in any case not a merely *de facto* impossibility; if everything had to be explicated, we would be so occupied with making rules explicit that we would never get around to applying them.

We must therefore possess implicit, pre-discursive knowledge. Every theory of rule-following has to make room for the distinction between following a rule on the one hand and possessing knowledge of the rule one is following on the other. One upshot of this distinction is, as we have seen, that there can be no ultimate explication of the rules that anyone and everyone has to follow in order to be able to follow any rules at all. For every attempt to carry out such an explication in turn presupposes a set of rules – and we cannot make *these* explicit in order to undertake the first explication. This problem exposes an opening for scepticism hidden in the architectonic of every epistemology that insists on finding an absolute foundation or ultimate explication of the fundamental rules of all rule-following. Accordingly, the necessary finitude of objective knowledge also affects the theoretical structure of transcendental philosophy. Since it tries to thematise the categorial equipment of anonymous subjectivity as such, it subjects itself to the conditions of explicating rules. But because all understanding (even at the level of supposedly transcendental rules) is finite, this process is essentially open-ended. *A vital insight gained through our engagement with scepticism is thus that finite epistemic beings do not even transcend their finitude in explaining their finitude.* This insight does not represent a sceptical problem: it merely teaches us to give up on an exaggerated ideal that otherwise leads to scepticism. Appealing to the need to make rules explicit, one might insist that epistemic finitude has to be overcome or externally grounded. But then the sceptic will have been in the right all along; we could no longer understand how we are able to understand anything at all. Radical translation really would begin at home, as Quine suggested, and we could no longer be sure whether our words ever had any meaning. Semantic nihilism would have won and solidified into a positive thesis.

Yet our constitutive finitude protects us from this result: were semantic nihilism true, we could not even really suspect it to be the case. We would simply be unable to entertain any of the rational considerations that have the power to convince us it was true. Semantic nihilism is at best a transcendent threat, and it is no accident that it was a common topic of discussion in the onto-theological tradition, specifically in reference to God's unknowable will, which, not coincidentally, is a spectre that looms large in Descartes' discussion of scepticism.

Besides the divergences between Kant's and Wittgenstein's solutions to the problem of rule-following that we have already mentioned, it is of course important to emphasise that Kant's theory operates within the framework of a methodological solipsism that Wittgenstein wants to reject outright: his theory develops the problem of rule-following, or rather of the application of rules, within the context of a theory of representational subjectivity.[59] Kant principally investigates the anonymous, isolated, judging subject. Unlike Wittgenstein, he is concerned with the systematic question of how it is possible for us to refer to a world by means of our representations without thereby representing this world itself, which always exceeds what any of our representations can represent.[60]

Kant, of course, expresses this idea by saying that the world (or, indeed, any of the other regulative ideas) cannot be given in any individual intuition, where intuitions are empirical representations that represent determinate states of the world, but never the world qua *omnitudio realitatis* (see chapters 3 and 4 above). Specifically, Kant investigates the synthetic mechanisms that govern the transition from one representation to the next in the pure intuition of time. These cannot be psychological laws of any sort (laws tied to our contingent make-up), else we would fall victim to a Humean scepticism for which the connections between our representations are contingent products of entirely natural habitual processes. Kant investigates not the empirical, psychologically individuated subject but, rather, anonymous transcendental subjectivity, which – according to one of Kant's most important theses – extends into the moral dimension of the ought – that is, into the dimension of normativity. We could thus integrate intersubjectivity into Kant's concept of representation if we could show that morality in the Kantian sense implies intersubjectivity. The prospects for countering the objection that Kant's methodological solipsism fails in light of the rule-following problem might therefore be at least somewhat better than we were initially led to expect.[61]

We can give the problem of rule-following the following summary formulation. A rule obtains only where we can mark a difference between correct and incorrect. Where this difference cannot obtain in principle, there can be no rules. But a private language does not satisfy this minimal requirement; it permits any move whatsoever. If we want to explain how it is possible for S to follow a rule, our explanation must not contain any premises that imply the possibility of a private language. This means, however, that we cannot conceive of rule-following as the triadic relation between a private inner realm (consciousness, mind, soul), an abstract entity (rule, idea, essence) and some factual constellation or other (a case falling under the rule). If, that is, we do not add from the outset any further parameters that turn rule-following into a public activity, we will sooner or later be forced to admit the possibility of a private language. And, in that case, it is left entirely to S to determine, in her private inner realm, whether or not she is confronted with a situation that should be determined as instancing a rule.

10

The Diametrical Opposite of Solipsism

Wittgenstein's own solution to the problem of rule-following is based on the insight that, because they presuppose social norms, rules are always ingredients in a practice requiring a plurality of actually participating subjects. Since this condition is not fulfilled in the case of a private language, such a language cannot constitute a practice. If we manage to show that there can be no rule-following without practices, we will also have dislodged methodological solipsism; for this aims to articulate the rules of (a) subjectivity as such. Ultimately, if there are no rules without practices, there simply cannot be any for a subject stuck in a state of metaphysical isolation. And, if we take this point on board, we will no longer have to worry about how an isolated judging subject might go about making a belated return to the world. The result, for Wittgenstein, is the diametrical opposite of solipsism: such a position amounts to the idea that all private rule-following (which, as I have already emphasised, should not be confused with the following of private rules!) takes place within the context of a practice and thus under the conditions of an essentially public mode of being-in-the-world. Solipsism therefore has to be reconstructed as a particular social pathology; it manifests as a borderline case of the social, not as an insight into its metaphysical or epistemic foundation.

We can reconstruct Wittgenstein's dissolution of the rule-following problem as an application of a plausible confirmation theorem:

> **Minimal Verificationism**: *If we know that a given mode of registration cannot register any refutation of a certain assumption, then the assumption cannot be confirmed by the results of any test carried out by means of that particular mode of registration.*[1]

The following example illustrates the theorem's application to the rule-following problem. Suppose S wants to test the reliability of her colour perception. S regards her colour perception as a solipsistic mode of registration that processes an input it has not itself produced. The test consists in S holding up a series of differently coloured cards; for each card, she asks herself introspectively which colour the card seems to have. In this manner, S compiles the doxastic report: 'Card 1 is red and seems to me to be red; card 2 is green and seems to me to be green. . . .' From this report, S makes the inductive inference that her colour perception is reliable, as each card appears to her to be exactly as it really is.

Clearly, S's experiment is highly successful at delivering true results and, moreover, even lends the assumption that her colour perception is reliable seem to be infallible. Equally clear, however, is that the procedure has no heuristic value. Nobody will grant that S possesses an infallible mode of colour-registration and that her experiment has demonstrated as much. A phenomenalist who wants to ground all beliefs on an infallible mode of registration must therefore reject minimal verificationism. She will then be just like the isolated judging subject in the colour experiment. Roger White draws the correct conclusion from this 'experiment': it is impossible to discover that appearances correspond to reality if our only route to reality is appearances themselves.[2] It follows, however, that the difference between reality and appearance cannot be extrapolated from a private confrontation with appearances: such a confrontation precludes the formation of any corrective mechanisms, and without such mechanisms a candidate condition of objectivity would lack any point of reference. The difference between being and seeming is not something that we can read off from seeming alone. Any would-be attempt to mediate our relation to the world through an infallible foundation of sense data (thus through potential seeming) is on a par with S's test of the reliability of her capacity for colour-registration. It is doomed to failure, because it is incapable of delivering any information with objective content (and so can deliver nothing determinate).

We obtain a decidedly different situation, however, if we supplement the experiment with a further parameter: *another person*, T, shows S the colour cards. Whenever T points at a card, he utters a corresponding colour name. Let us suppose that S has good reasons to believe that T does not wish to deceive her and sincerely designates each card using the colour expression that fits his colour impressions. Since S is a normal speaker – i.e. is already initiated into the competent use of colour names – she will have to correct her beliefs if, for each card to which T points with the accompanying exclamation 'red', she makes a mental note that the card is green and seems to her to be green. This extension of the original experiment now enables the tested mode of registration to record both correct and incorrect results.

The introduction of another subject can therefore help us evade the aporia of a private language insofar as the other evinces potentially different reactions to the displayed colour cards. This variation is a condition of disagreement, which is in turn the condition of the possibility of forming corrective mechanisms.[3] But, with the formation of such mechanisms, we have instituted norms-in-context and thus the difference between correct and incorrect. The possibility of contradiction (of a number of people disagreeing about something publicly available to their modes of registration) is a decisive engine driving the evolution of discourse.[4] Without the possibility of contradiction, there would be no objectivity. In short, objectivity presupposes potential disagreement: there would be no objectivity if all subjects initially found themselves in a position where, in order to get in touch with how things are, they first had to transcend their private impressions.

The difference between holding-true and truth, and so the very possibility of error, first becomes intelligible through encountering the disagreement of others. The 'discourse of the other', as Cornelius Castoriadis named this phenomenon, is a condition of the possibility of objectivity.[5] In this sense, differences of opinion are a condition of the possibility of grasping the difference between holding-true and truth. In other words, *disagreement is a condition of the intelligibility of the concept of objectivity.* And this means that objectivity commits us not so much to an always already (i.e. ontically) thoroughgoingly determined world, populated predominantly by mindless entities, as to an ongoing engagement with others; for their dissent is an indication of objectivity. We would have no access whatsoever to objectivity were we unable to contemplate the possibility of another subject's contradicting us. Consequently, objectivity exists only within discourses, where these institute norms-in-context that cannot themselves be fully objectified.

To be sure, objectivity cannot be reduced to the following idea: we would have a complete picture of objectivity if and only if we could catalogue all the correct assertoric moves permitted by a given community. Truth cannot be restricted to its members' usage of rules, at pain of simply transferring the error of private language onto the community as a whole, whose dispositions would then be just as infallible as those of the private linguist.[6] Where precisely to locate the distinction between truth and holding-true is another question. What is certain, however, is that we could not draw the distinction from the first-person standpoint if we were immune to correction. Our representations alone cannot correct us, because they are *our* representations. Thus, the 'I think' cannot be the ground of objectivity; nor does it help to turn it into an 'I that is We' or a 'We that is I'.[7]

There must be something public, something we recognise as a concomitant of our recognising the difference between truth and holding-true. This does not mean that someone who *already* enjoys a capacity to form beliefs about the world does not thereby already possess the capacity to correct their beliefs about it on their own; they can quite clearly do this without needing another subject in the picture to exercise an active influence over their various operations of information-processing. If someone believes that she can run through walls, she will sooner or later have to correct her belief if it motivates her to action, regardless of whether anyone is around to point out the error of her ways. The private language argument, in short, asks not whether soliloquising is possible – a question which can be answered only in the affirmative – but, rather, whether someone could really acquire beliefs about the world were no data available to her besides private sensations. But walls already take us beyond private sensations. And the private linguist cannot recognise that she bashes into a wall; at best she can register a pain event. It is impossible to acquire beliefs about walls in the way the private linguist envisages, as her beliefs about her private sensations would be deprived of assertoric content; they cannot be true or false for her independently of whether she holds them to be true. And where there is no possibility of criticism, of potentially showing that something held to be true is in fact untrue, there is simply no possibility of truth either.[8]

There can be no contravention of rules in a private language, because its rules have no objective use. Since, by hypothesis, it is impossible to commit an error, every rule can be applied to every case; everything is just what it presents itself to be. But the contrast of being and seeming is a condition of the possibility of a discourse whose statements can claim successful epistemic access to the world. Statements that make a claim to truth are assertions insofar as it is a mere platitude that to assert that p implies presenting p as true.[9] So, a practice where this contrast does not obtain cannot have any assertoric content.

Crispin Wright has formulated a condition of objectivity to the effect that there can be assertoric content only where it is empirically – and not analytically or a priori – permissible to make an inference from

> (a) X believes what is expressed by 'p' (holding true)

to

> (b) What 'p' expresses is true (truth).[10]

We thus cannot say that a subject X stands in a cognitive relation to facts where it is guaranteed a priori that, for a class of statements whose members can be values of 'p', we can make an inference from every instance of p in (a) to (b). If we formulate the objectivity condition in this way, it is quite clear why the private linguist cannot retreat to the idea that her language has a distinctive advantage, namely, that, in all of its sentences, (a) and (b) coincide. The private linguist, that is, accepts the condition of objectivity but asserts that there are values for X and p that result in the constitutive coincidence of (a) and (b) and so fulfil the objectivity condition in an epistemically privileged manner. This means, however, that the private linguist must assert that X has a propositional attitude to p, viz. 'belief' or 'holding-true'. Given (b), this *must* fulfil truth conditions, but this of course presupposes the contrast of (a) and (b), which the private linguist thus undermines. In short, if statements of the private language can be values of p, then p can have no truth conditions, because truth conditions can never be such that they are *necessarily* fulfilled. If (a) and (b) coincide, (b) no longer plays any role – but then, trivially enough, (a) and (b) cannot coincide. 'That is to say: if we construe the grammar of the expression of sensation on the model of "object and designation" the object drops out of consideration as irrelevant.'[11]

The upshot of this line of argument is that the private linguist cannot establish any propositional attitude towards her sensations. There is thus no prospect of her interpreting them as *objects* she might designate via arbitrary rules, even rules that she has to withhold from her fellow inhabitants of the world. Since these other subjects would have no epistemic access to her private information, they would be precluded from scrutinising the assertoric content of her statements. In the case of private language, therefore, the trouble is not only that the condition of objectivity would, *per impossibile*, have to be fulfilled *necessarily*, but that it in fact lacks application altogether. With this insight, the case for the supposed epistemic advantage of a private language is finally and decisively undermined.[12]

Borrowing a distinction from Kant (who was, moreover, certainly aware of the sociality of belief formation), we might say that the private linguist has no *beliefs* [Überzeugungen], only *convictions* [Überredungen] that are in principle incommunicable. According to Kant, the possibility of (a) expressing a potentially true belief (holding-true), therefore (b), rests on the possibility of communicating judgements: 'the judgments of each and all understanding, if true, must therefore be in agreement with each other.'[13] Hence Kant's remark that '[c]onviction may, therefore, be distinguished, from an external point of view, from persuasion', because 'in this case the presumption, at least, arises that the agreement of all judgments with each other, in spite of the different characters of individuals, rests upon the common ground of the agreement of each with the object, and thus the correctness of the judgment is established.'[14] Without the possibility of having an 'effect on the reason of others'[15] – i.e. without an other – we would have 'only *private* validity of the judgment'.[16] So, according to Kant, too, there can be no truth-apt reasons in the absence of other rational subjects, because without them we could never guarantee a contrast between (a) and (b) for a given class of statements. But, without such a contrast, there can be no objectivity at all; a class of statements for which the coincidence of (a) and (b) is a priori cannot claim any objective reality. It is disagreement which manifests the potential divergence of truth and holding-true. There can be objectivity only where there is potential dissent.

It is important to hold on to the idea that the principle of minimal verificationism – and thus the minimal condition of discursive objectivity – brings sociality into play. At a minimum, it points us to a form of I–you sociality, but in most cases to a form of I–we sociality. The social, and thus the other as a scrutinising authority, is indispensable for the institution of rules – rules whose conditions of application cannot be fulfilled by a private subject alone. Other subjects are therefore necessary for our access to the *concept* of objectivity and thus for our epistemic access to the world.

Our epistemic access to the world is characterised not merely by the fact that we happen to know this, that and the other but also by the fact that we raise knowledge claims and, in so doing, bring justificatory conditions into play.

Our epistemological access to the concept of an objective world, a dimension of objects and events that transcends any individual episode of awareness, depends upon others taking a different view. Sociality and objectivity are thus sense-dependent concepts, a form of dependence which, as we have seen, Brandom carefully distinguishes from reference dependence.[17]

Sociality is not an ontic condition of the existence of objects but an ontological presupposition of our epistemic access to the objective world. Wittgenstein's thesis of the sociality of objectivity is therefore no variety of reference dependence idealism: it is not a thesis asserting that there would be no worldly determinacy were there no beings around to determine worldly states. Rather, he is merely trying to pose the question of *how* we can establish a mode of epistemic access to the world – a mode of access that we all clearly possess but which tends to be distorted by the solipsistic asymmetry between the first and third person.

Crispin Wright has objected against verificationist readings of the private language argument that they fail to consider how, given that rules are not self-interpreting, we cannot neglect the social dimension of rule-following.[18] In fact, Wittgenstein sees rule-following as a practice requiring a kind of stability that is not ontologically given at all – the stability needed is essentially normative, not natural, and has to be traced back to an ought, not an is. Practices do not bring about the facts they register; rather, they depend on the *de facto* distinctions that obtain between certain objects and others. And even if it were the case that practices first brought facts into being, it would have to be possible for the practices to register the facts, meaning they still enjoy a degree of independence from the modes of registration peculiar to the practices in question. So much is contained in the grammar of a 'mode of registration'. For facts, as the content registered, would still obtain independently of whether or not they were being registered *hic et nunc*.

Accordingly, it is the normative stability of practices that first makes possible our epistemic access to facts. In this respect, facts are always only facts *for* a practice or discourse; we need to reduce the world's potentially infinite structural complexity to restricted patterns we are capable of registering, else there would be no world *for us*. This does not mean that we produce the facts we register: it would be absurd to maintain that, if we reduce the world's complexity by, for example, designating certain living beings as mammals, mammals then exist simply because we have taxonomised the world in such a way that we are in a position to register them.

If there are to be registerable items, we have to factor in a difference between holding-true and truth, bearing in mind that the possibility of this distinction does not imply that the rules that facilitate our cognitive access to the world (and so our practices) are themselves independent of rules (and thus of our practices). That would be an equally absurd assumption. Our practices are dependent on their respective rules because they constitute them *as* one set of distinct practices among others.

Conversely, our rules are dependent on our practices because they cannot be said to exist independently of their applications. This is what distinguishes rules from natural entities such as mountains: there are undoubtedly certain objects that exist only if practices exist – most trivially, practices and their rules. Yet the rules that govern practices are independent of those practices insofar as we can make true and false judgements about the rules from within the practice itself.

Which rules constitute a context – i.e. a practice – is something that its participants have to negotiate intra-discursively. At the same time, they are fallible regarding the question of *which* rules they are following, as can be seen easily enough in the case of law: ignorance of the law is no defence. If you are caught on the tram without a valid ticket, you will have to pay the penalty, regardless of whether you can prove you had no knowledge of the rules followed by your fellow, unpenalized, passengers. Explicit knowledge of rules is not constitutive of their validity.

The validity of a rule presupposes neither its being known nor its merely being recognised; both still represent explicit attitudes towards something (unless it is legitimate to speak of implicit recognition). This is why contextualism does not assert that rules are independent of our practices, merely that it is only through our practices that we can enjoy a cognitive relation to a world of objects and events. For we can have no intentionality, and so no mental reference to something *as* something, without normative stability. This is a position that surely merits the label *the diametrical opposite of solipsism.*

The question of which rules we follow also depends on which rules we take ourselves to follow. Yet the discourse thematising the rules that constitute a practice is a further discourse; and this further discourse is occupied with the validity of rules that cannot necessarily be verified within the discourse it thematises. Which norms-in-context constitute a context and whether the norms-in-context themselves are truth-apt is something that has to be discerned within a further context, a context we attain with the help of a theory-level transition. This condition applies, at any rate, for all discourses that are not exclusively self-referential – that is, for all discourses that do not consist merely in the reconstruction of their own norms-in-context and thus in an exploration of their latent conditions of operation.

Our discourses grant us the ability to describe and classify the world's properties. This is what a zoologist does, for example, when she divides up the animal world according to the rules of her taxonomical practice. Such an activity involves a range of conventions and patterns of behaviour that allow the zoologist to refer to the animal world. But the classification of animals is not arbitrary. It corresponds to what is the case. To be sure, the division of the animal world into amphibians, mammals, fish, etc., can be carried out only by beings who have formed practices with a suitable normative stability. Yet it would be nonsense to assume that the classifications embodied in the animal world are ontically (e.g. causally) dependent on these practices. If this were the case, the discourse itself would be of no service to those involved.

Semantic space therefore contains normative restrictions. These, however, should not be conflated with ontic conditions on objects. Instead, they serve to open up paths of cognitive access to the world – which is only ever a world for us – while we have to determine where we direct our attention. The concept of a world is tied to our search engines. This does not mean that all objects under investigation are somehow produced or 'constituted' by our search engines. The facts that are facts for us are facts for us only insofar as we know that they are true independently of our holding them true.[19] It is therefore part of the competent use of the concept 'mountain', for example, that one knows that mountains exist independently of the fact that we deploy the concept 'mountain' in order to talk about mountains. The same goes for 'lion', 'moon', and so on.[20]

A familiar idealist approach is the attempt, by thinking of objectivity as a hidden subjectivity, to capture the conditions of objectivity in terms of holding-true. Such a strategy, though, faces the equally familiar problem that our information-processing cannot, on the whole, produce its own contents. Which entities we encounter in the world depend only to a limited extent on our own discretion. We are receptive, and so finite, epistemic beings, even if it turns out that we can derive the *concept* of objectivity from that of a normatively stable subjectivity, namely as one of its necessary ingredients. Of course, the distinction between subject and object is bound to the presence of subjects. But, again, this does not mean that the objects subjects discover in their proximate or distal environment depend upon these subjects' existence.[21]

Wittgenstein's solution to the rule-following problem is to introduce a decisive parameter – a parameter that should render the phenomenon comprehensible without having any part in the ineliminable weaknesses of solipsism. He argues that the independent authority or criterion of correctness needed to establish the difference between correct and incorrect is the (actual or expected) *agreement* of a community over whether someone has followed a rule. '"So you are saying that human agreement decides what is true and what is false?" – It is what human beings *say* that is true and false; and they agree in the *language* they use. That is not agreement in opinions but in form of life.'[22] Without agreement in forms of life, it would be impossible to establish any rule that can so much as be contravened, because agreement or its absence fixes a difference between the correct and the incorrect in the first place. Being correct is being subject to universal agreement.[23]

It is only this minimal practice of confirmation or refutation (or of reward and punishment) that enables modes of registration to function.

It is not, however, a practice that is facilitated through the introduction of *explicit* rules: rather, because it is the practice which secures the stability of rules, the former cannot be grounded on the latter. Wittgenstein introduces 'forms of life' not as part of a substantial philosophical doctrine but as a contribution to his dissolution of the rule-following problem, and we need to bear this in mind when we come to weigh up the concept's genuine explanatory yield. It is also important to keep in mind how in the course of Wittgenstein's reflections it is the rule-following problem which first opens up the phenomenal inventory of the 'natural history of mankind' and its 'forms of life'.[24] Were it to turn out that his solution to the problem boiled down to a dogmatic appeal to natural history, his reflections would end up at an obvious explanatory disadvantage (see chapter 14 below). His solution would then be no better off than Kant's invocation of the power of judgement: both would stand revealed as measures introduced merely ad hoc to stop the looming regress.

On my reading, Wittgenstein's solution to the problem of rule-following is therefore most definitely a variety of a *community view*: rule-following is a communal activity or custom that cannot be generated by an isolated judging subject. By providing an explanation of how a normative practice can be established, as a practice that rewards correct moves and punishes incorrect moves, the so-called community view is supposed to explain how we can register error, and so truth. The most important objection to this view, which is advocated most prominently by Kripke and Wright, amounts to the claim that it cannot explain how a community could possibly err as a collective. Put simply: if the ultimate criterion of truth were the agreement of a community, then everything it decided to do or think would be correct.[25] The community could observe the contrast of objectivity between holding-true and truth just as much (or as little) as the isolated solipsistic subject. It is easy to imagine the kind of consequences this thesis might entail should the global community, with few exceptions, agree to the introduction of any kind of abominable practice. There would no longer be anything to object to a *1984*-style dystopia, fully equipped with its peculiar linguistic usages, legislated autocratically and enjoying communitarian ratification. We can imagine still worse scenarios in which moral atrocities are legally prescribed and endorsed by all members of the community (which, to be sure, would have to establish the existence of another community, another tribe, to be subjected to the relevant atrocity).

To be sure, it is unclear how exactly one should delineate the boundaries of the ultimately decisive 'community'. If it should transpire that the majority of linguistic beings in the universe, the absolute global community of discursive beings, cultivate the practice of sacrificing 50 per cent of their newborn offspring in some gruesome religious rite, this could hardly be taken as a reason to infer an obligation to do the same. We clearly need to draw a distinction between an empirically general statement about what most humans *do* and a normative statement of what they *ought to do.*[26] The community view is ultimately introduced in order to do justice to this distinction (in Kripke's terminology: the distinction between dispositions and norms).

Every theory of truth has to make logical space for the distinction between the *truth of a judgement* and the *agreement of a community about whether a judgement is true.* Otherwise the idea of objectivity would be self-undermining, having the disagreeable consequence that everything a given community held true would be true in virtue of their holding-true if only they all agreed. This result would be not only empirically objectionable but inconsistent; for the community-establishing distinction between correct and incorrect, without which there could be no normativity, must be applicable to the judgemental practice settled upon by the community itself.

This means that members of the community must be able to engage in incorrect moves. But if all members of the community must be able to go astray, we have the possibility of global error disseminated within a given community: the community can be unclear about its own norms and their implications, such that their explicit knowledge might be incompatible with their implicit norms-in-context. We reckon *de facto* with the possibility that communities can err; that they do so is not only obvious in moral cases but is presupposed by even the most restricted notion of scientific progress. If ever an actual community were firmly convinced that the earth is flat and built their physical theory on this assumption, it would be difficult to defend the assertion that the community and their physics were not in error, however much its members might be unanimous in their judgement. And even the most radical relativist inhabiting an affluent twenty-first-century society will prefer her own dentist to the dentist available to Aristotle.[27]

That does not mean that objectivity has to be understood as a binary relation of *discovery*, such that a given world was always already as we find it presented in our best theoretical accounts. Objectivity does not have to be understood *from without* but can equally be understood *from within*: we come to an awareness of the concept of objectivity as a necessary element of genuine discourses. By establishing the contrast of objectivity between truth and holding-true, we incur ontological commitments to a determinate concept of the world, and which commitments we incur depends on the discourse at issue. A discourse projects an overall structure onto the domain of its investigation and thereby potentially constructs a worldview in order to create a space for future information-processing in the near and distant future.

Wittgenstein's thesis that the mode of registration *truth* implies a relation to a community does not exclude the possibility that we might correct our beliefs by working outwards from within. The agreement of which he speaks does not imply agreement in *all* judgements. In fact, the explanation runs in the other direction: he introduces the community in order to explain how it is possible for us to *distinguish* between correct and incorrect applications of a rule. Accordingly, his introduction of the community neither presupposes any absolute harmony between all judgements nor aims at any consensus as the telos of discourse; rather, it presents a *condition of disagreement*.[28] The community acts as a guarantor of objectivity only insofar as it is a site of potential disagreement. Its sanctions are discussed *within* the community, creating a space for possible deviations and thus allowing for possible transformations at the level of the community itself. In short, the private language argument does not shift infallibility from the individual to the community – *pace* a frequent objection to Kripke's version of rule communitarianism – but, rather, explains the conditions of the possibility of a discourse through the possibility of genuine conflicts of belief within a community.

Wittgenstein wants his argument to move us beyond the idea of a ready-made, given world whose states determine truth and falsity in and of themselves. In other words, he turns against a positivism about facts by showing how facts cannot determine of their own accord which rule, or indeed whether any rule at all, has been applied in a given case. *Facts cannot determine how they are registered (which evidently does not entail that there are not any facts about rules).* Because truth has to be determined linguistically, and since language is a normative, rule-governed practice, we have to introduce normativity into our concept of truth, albeit without threatening the idea of an objectivity that is constitutively independent of individual or communal holding-true. Wittgenstein therefore attempts to explain how discourses can generate criticism from within, without invoking a view from nowhere that would somehow grant us an overview of the totality of all facts.[29]

No such overview can help us determine what we *should* do. No possible registration of the facts can alter the normativity of our practices without those practices themselves already having determined what may and may not effect modifications within them – that is, without their already having determined what constitutes a fact for a given practice. Discursive practices determine their own boundaries by marking a distinction between themselves and everything else, a distinction fixed by their norms-in-context, their hinges. They fix certain entry conditions, which facts cannot fulfil by themselves. And, for this reason, discourses can register only those facts that are compatible with their modes of registration.

If, therefore, we can restrict Wittgenstein's communitarian criterion so that it demands only a minimal publicity, the community view need no longer commit us to an absurd communal solipsism. The 'community' is then no longer an actual social group, merely the dimension of alterity within which every conversation unfolds. Imposing this restriction, however, does not itself suffice to reintroduce the possibility of genuine criticism: in the Wittgensteinian picture, this possibility is endangered especially by how the community not only operates as a touchstone of correctness but is also responsible for first *training* its members to follow particular behavioural patterns: by reacting to their behaviour with positive or negative sanctions, the community works to transform mere behaviour (events) into templates of action.

According to Wittgenstein, what one *should* do is ultimately grounded in what others *in fact* do. No putative independent authority, regardless of its ontological status, can play any role here, because it cannot *determine* what one *ought* to do. But, by pursuing this line of thought, we invite the danger that our picture might become so 'fraught with ought' that being, the 'is', drops out completely.[30]

Wittgenstein's rule-following considerations do indeed imply a radical anti-realism about rules. The private language argument implies that the truth or falsity of assertions cannot be reduced to a relation between mind and world. For 'truth' functions as a normative concept and cannot be traced back to any natural property of sentences. When we recognise S as applying the rule +2, this is not because S grasps some entity, however conceived, but simply because he would be excluded from the community of adders were he to declare that he was applying the rule +2 while stubbornly insisting on following 10,000 with 10,004. 'That it is false that 10,004 is the successor of 10,000 in the series $2 + 2 + 2$, etc.,' is therefore not a statement of ontology but a statement about what those whom we may class as competent adders take to be true. The 'facts' here cannot provide us with any place of refuge, somewhere we might retreat to in order to find our epistemic bearings: '*Don't always think that you read off what you say from the facts; that you portray these in words according to rules. For even so you would have to apply the rule in the particular case without guidance.*'[31]

Whatever ontological structure the world might ultimately possess, every attempt to determine something about it in the form of an assertion presupposes that the assertion could be false. And in order for an assertion to be true or false, it must be a possible candidate for evaluation. Yet the ability to evaluate an assertion is not one that an individual can acquire privately: every isolated, private exercise of the relevant capacity already stands in relation to its universal, public exercise. Where the minimal conditions for evaluating a statement are not met, we can no longer speak of a statement at all. Since a private language in Wittgenstein's sense does not fulfil these conditions, it cannot contain any statements and is simply devoid of assertoric content. Although its original motivation was to deliver solid epistemological foundations, it cannot even contain any true sentences.

Another reason for the impossibility of a private language is simply that the private linguist can go about constructing her private language only by taking as a starting point the public language into which she has already been initiated. For whatever steps she makes in establishing her private language, however she might try to use it to mark various distinctions, she always retains her relation to the language she absorbed prior to embarking upon her experiment. Once a subject belongs to a linguistic community, she can never fully liberate herself from its grip – a fact taught us as much by experience as by the private language argument. Once someone has the ability to speak, attaining the supposed intimacy of private language is out of the question.[32]

But say someone wanted to establish a private language *ab initio*? In that case, it is hard to see how she could so much as hit upon the idea of compiling a purely private dictionary for her sensations. Why should she oppose her private episodes to the public world when, on this hypothesis, she is yet to speak to anyone else and so has no knowledge of the public as such? Even if a child raised in the jungle by wild animals attempted to capture her experiences in language, it would not be as though she wanted to create a private language. The project of a private language, that is, makes sense only under the conditions of an already established public language – for example, as an epistemological project designed to provide the transparency of the *cogito* as an anti-sceptical grounding. The idea of a private language is in no sense 'natural' but, rather, an artificial product of a quite specific set of epistemological considerations. Dismissing the idea, therefore, is by no means to dismiss a universally shared intuition.

11

McDowell's Disjunctivism as an Anti-Sceptical Strategy

As we have seen, any satisfactory solution to the problem of rule-following will have to steer clear of solipsistic assumptions. In this chapter I argue that we will thus make no progress if we follow McDowell in supposing that the mind is *immediately* open to the world.[1] McDowell suggests that we can leave Cartesian scepticism behind once we have grasped how it sets in only under particular philosophical conditions – namely, when we assume a *highest common factor* between *mere* appearances as if *p* and veridical appearances (representations) that *p*. According to McDowell, only a theory of appearances with the associated debilitating assumption of such a common factor paves the way for Cartesian scepticism.[2] The highest common factor theory reckons with the possibility that *all* appearances might be empty provided it is true that some appearances are in fact empty, however much they appear to refer to something in virtue of their content. This (for McDowell, philosophical) assumption leads to the familiar representationalist picture of a world of representations, on which any given representation with which we are presented possibly fails to re*present*. The common factor theory thereby ends up eliminating the possibility that the content of an appearance could be a state of the world beyond appearances.[3] The theory thus locates content 'in the mind' – a dubious move.

McDowell rejects the common factor theory. And, by doing so, he intends to establish a form of direct realism as the starting point for all coherent theories about the relation between mind and world. If we want to test whether McDowell's attempt to counter Cartesian scepticism with a direct realism is a viable option – that is, if we want to circumvent the common factor theory that motivates the general paradox of Cartesian scepticism in the first place – we will simply need to recall the considerations that originally lent Cartesian scepticism its *prima facie* plausibility.[4]

McDowell's disjunctivism represents a therapeutic project of an avowedly Wittgensteinian inspiration. The Achilles' heel of Cartesian scepticism, according to McDowell, is the classical concept of representation insofar as it plays a vital theoretical role in motivating mental representationalism. By *mental representationalism*, I understand the fundamental thesis that finite, intentional beings have access to the world only as a *represented* world.[5] On this view, representational access to the world is mediated by a set of success conditions that have to be fulfilled if we, as intentional beings, are so much as to refer to anything whatsoever *as if* it were independent of the fact *that* we refer to it. Every instance of veridical perception – i.e. of enjoying mental access to the world – first requires *representational purport*, which does not guarantee representational *success*. If it could, we would be able to exclude illusions a priori. An important characteristic of the theory of mental representations, however, is its invocation of the primacy of representational purport over representational success.[6] This theoretical attitude clearly stands in need of justification; it is hardly self-evident either that the world we experience is always only the world as representation, or that we can access the world only when certain representational conditions are fulfilled on the side of the subject.

It is precisely at this point that McDowell's disjunctivism steps in. In contrast to the classical concept of representation, McDowell contests whether there are in fact neutral presentations of things, i.e. representations, which appear to us exactly as they would if they had no ontological correlates. In other words, McDowell denies the validity of the principle of aparallaxia (see p. 100 above). He describes the position he attacks as the theory of the highest common factor. We find such a theory in Kant's famous 'progression' [*Stufenleiter*] of 'species of representation' in the *Critique of Pure Reason*:

> The genus is **representation** in general (*repraesentatio*). Under it stands the representation with consciousness (*perceptio*). A **perception** that refers to the subject as a modification of its state is a **sensation** (*sensatio*); an objective perception is a **cognition** (*cognitio*). The latter is either an **intuition** or a **concept** (*intuitus vel conceptus*). The former is immediately related to the object and is singular; the latter is mediate, by means of a mark, which can be common to several things.[7]

According to the highest common factor theory, there is an intentional state or act common to both veridical perception and hallucination or illusion, such that it is always legitimate to ask whether our intentional acts are epistemic successes or failures. The theory thus assumes a difference between intentional and ontological correlates and asserts that we can refer to the latter only via the former. McDowell, however, disputes the idea that there are mental representations in this sense in the first place. The concept of representation is fully motivated only once Cartesian scepticism has already done its work by reminding us of our fallibility. This reminder leads indirectly to the view that all our representations could ultimately lack ontological correlates, or that they could have quite other ontological correlates than we might suspect, even when putatively ideal epistemic and discursive conditions are fulfilled on the part of the subject. This is why the theory of the common factor is committed to the assumption that all appearances might be metaphysically empty provided it is true that some representations are metaphysically empty, despite their seeming to be fully contentful.

The upshot is the by now familiar representationalist picture of a world of representations. On this picture, every individual representation with which we find ourselves presented might not *re*present anything at all. And hence we confront the famous gulf between the *logical space of nature*, in which there are merely causes and effects, and the *logical space of reasons*, in which we find the knowledge claims and their candidate justifications that comprise the game of giving and asking for reasons. Nature and normativity threaten to come apart.

McDowell argues that we should leave Cartesian scepticism behind precisely by demonstrating its dependence on the postulation of a *common factor* between *mere* appearances and veridical appearances *that* p. Only a theory of appearances committed to a common factor, he thinks, produces Cartesian scepticism:[8]

> [S]uppose we say – not at all unnaturally – that an appearance that such-and-such is the case can be either a mere appearance or the fact that such-and-such is the case making itself perceptually manifest to someone. As before, the object of experience in the deceptive cases is a mere appearance. But we are not to accept that in the non-deceptive cases too the object of experience is a mere appearance, and hence something that falls short of the fact itself.[9]

On this alternative picture, our thoughts stop nowhere short of the worldly facts, as McDowell – like Wittgenstein – repeatedly insists.[10] Rather, with our perceptual judgements we refer to the world in itself, not to our representations of the world. We are not trapped behind a veil of perception separating us from the world itself. In Wittgenstein's words: 'When we say, and *mean*, that such-and-such is the case, we – and our meaning – do not stop anywhere short of the fact; but we mean: *this-is-so*.'[11]

According to McDowell, then, if the world is open to us at all, it is *ipso facto* open to us immediately – indeed, the world is simply open to us in all true judgements about it. For, when we argue about how things are, the world must surely be immediately open to us at some point or other, else we would continually entangle ourselves in infinite regresses.[12] At the very least, the world as representation would have to be immediately open to us: there cannot be intentional correlates inserted between our intentional correlates and our representational intentions, at pain of requiring another intentional correlate, and so on *ad infinitum*. Following this line of thought, the sceptical assumption of phenomenally indistinguishable states seems to disappear – that is, of states whose truth values supposedly remain beyond our reach because we have no access to the totality of all those propositions that are incompatible with representational success.

McDowell thus offers his *disjunctive conception of appearances* as an alternative to what he considers the foundational weakness of the Cartesian paradox, the theory of a common factor.[13] The disjunctive conception distinguishes two meanings of 'appears', which McDowell illustrates with reference to linguistic usage in ancient Greek. The verb φαίνεσθαι, meaning 'to appear, present/manifest', can be constructed either with an attributive participle or with an infinitive. The latter construction serves to convey that someone or something merely *seems* to be thus and so. Thus, φαίνεται σοφὸς εἶναι means 'he seems to be wise'. The participle construction, by contrast, shows that something presents or manifests in such and such a way. So, φαίνεται σοφὸς ὤν means 'he is manifestly wise'.[14] This latter meaning underlies Aristotle's demand 'to account for the appearances' (ἀποδοῦναι τὰ φαινόμενα)[15] – i.e. not to distort the manifest through theoretical constructions, the cue from which Husserlian phenomenology famously took its concept of appearance.[16] According to McDowell, the disjunction of mere appearance and manifestation of the world means that not all appearances can be *mere* appearances. Rather, most appearances are appearances in the sense of the manifest. And that the world is manifest to us means that we should completely discard such suspiciously metaphysical concepts as 'external things' or 'things in themselves', so that we can instead work with the idea that the world is immediately present to our conceptuality. In other words, we can do without the mediation of representations.[17]

McDowell consequently expounds disjunctivism as a form of *realist immediatism*, which advocates the 'idea of an unmediated openness of the experiencing subject to "external" reality'.[18] In this way, disjunctivism tries to undermine the sceptical premise that our acquisition of perceptual entitlement for our beliefs (about the external worlds, other minds, etc.) is mediated by appearances.

Prima facie, this would seem to be an effective strategy against the sceptic for whom *looks-talk* is epistemically prior to *is-talk*. On the representational model of modern epistemology, thoughts such as 'my present conscious state seems to be in all respects that p' underlie all thoughts of the form 'I see, hear, etc., as though p'. But if we can now show that having at least some representations *that* p is a condition of asserting that we have representations *as though* p, then we seem to have circumvented the sceptical reduction of being to seeming and its concomitant sceptical paradoxes.[19] This is precisely McDowell's claim, and disjunctivism's success or failure stands or falls with it.

McDowell's attempt to oppose Cartesian scepticism to a form of direct realism, however, does not adequately face up to a fundamental sceptical problem. To see how, we need to take any old sceptical argument that culminates in instances of the paradox formulated in chapters 5 and 6. Recall that the fundamental sceptical thought relevant for Cartesian scepticism does not depend upon the depiction of *specific* scenarios that eliminate the external world; it can be formulated on a much more general level. In any case, there is (if there are any) in fact only *one* sceptical scenario that does without the external world in any sense: namely, the solipsism of the moment. On this scenario, the world would consist of exactly one thinking subject inhabiting but a single moment; and in this moment, while it lasts, the subject has the empty impression of having a past and future, a memory – quite simply – of existing. The point of Cartesian scepticism, therefore, has nothing to do either with the problem of the external world in the narrow sense or with the question of whether life is a dream, or but the shadow of a dream. The dream argument represents merely *one* instance of a sceptical scenario, and, as Crispin Wright in particular has urged, it is just this point that McDowell misses.[20]

Clearly, we can think of a *perfect hallucination* that is *perfect* to the extent that what it presents us with is something that, although unreal, from our perspective is indistinguishable from something (a) that is real and (b) to which we could enjoy normal perceptual access. We need only think of a *fata Morgana*, say, or mirages on hot asphalt on a summer's day, and then abstract from the conditions that allow us to see through such illusions. Imagine that parts of King's Cross station consisted of holograms, but that we were always at such a distance from them that it would never occur to us to check whether they were holograms. To say that there could be at least some perfect hallucinations is not to say that we could not discover that they were hallucinations. But whether or not we can discover *all* perfect hallucinations is an *empirical* question. So, we cannot exclude a priori that there are perfect hallucinations that we could never actually discover.

In his critique of McDowell, Timothy Williamson invokes a certain kind of perfect hallucination that he calls 'elusive objects'. These hallucinations are so constituted that they alter as soon as we turn our attention to them, making them impossible to register.[21] Perfect hallucinations have the general property that we cannot possibly have any direct access to what they present us with – because what they present us with does not exist. Where we think we see the reflective surface of a pool of water in the desert, there simply is no water.

Now, there is nothing (1) to which we have any direct access and (2) that indicates a criterial difference between a perfect hallucination and a veridical perception.[22] McDowell himself must assume that a veridical perception shows itself not to be a perfect illusion. Yet how does this not undermine our fallibility? Our fallibility surely also implies that we can think we are hallucinating when we are in fact enjoying a veridical experience. Even if, seen from a metaphysical perspective, veridical perceptions are criteria to which we have direct access, it by no means follows that there is never something that remains concealed from us due to *contingent*, non-metaphysical parameters. It is not the case that we have veridical perceptions only when we simultaneously know that we do. At best, McDowell shows that under idealised conditions we can know of each veridical perception that it is a veridical perception insofar as there is no intervening veil of perception. But if one has no direct access to a fact that indicates a criterial difference between hallucination and perception, and if one has no access to anything that is presented in a hallucination, it follows that one has no direct access to facts presented in a veridical perception.[23] The question of whether we have direct or indirect access to what one might call the disjunctive fact that, say, we are currently having either a veridical perception or a hallucination does not depend essentially upon whether there is a veil of perception. The sceptic questions the immediacy of our access to the world on the basis of considerations pertaining to our fallibility; she points to how, even in cases of veridical perception, we can be misled by factors that are neutralised only under extremely idealised conditions (which, in any case, do not apply in cases of standard empirical knowledge acquisition). Considerations of this kind are the real ground of the theory of the common factor, since it merely asserts that there is a type of neutral phenomenal state common to both a hallucination and a veridical perception. This does not mean that perception can be traced back to this phenomenal state *cum aliquo*. The Cartesian sceptic does not draw on a metaphysical picture of the mind, such that there is a highest common factor, which in the good case latches onto reality and in the bad case does not. Rather, it assumes, much more modestly, that there is no second-order guarantee that any given knowledge claim amounts to knowledge, because the concept of a knowledge claim and the concept of knowledge have to come apart. Otherwise, we could not account for knowledge acquisition, and this would amount to a serious epistemological shortcoming.

We understand what it means to say that the way the world appears to us is also a way it could appear in a perfect hallucination; a veridical perception and a hallucination must still have in common that they both present us with something or other. But this presentation is just the common factor McDowell wants to eliminate. If his sole aim was to register a protest against the reification of this common factor into some kind of a mental entity, that would leave Cartesian scepticism untouched: the sceptic is merely after a conceptual common factor that makes room for the possibility of a perfect hallucination, without necessarily having to formulate a theory of mental entities. Positing a common factor simply consists in accepting that we have evidence for the fact that we cannot always distinguish a veridical perception from a perfect hallucination *in ipso actu operandi*. The basis of this indistinguishability is simply that, in any case where a subject is entitled to say that p, she is, in virtue of that fact alone, also entitled to say that her present state of consciousness seems, in all respects, to be as though p. The point, therefore, is that, while it may well be true that either we perceive some object or we hallucinate it, the real problem consists in our inability to decide whether we are perceiving or hallucinating on a case-by-case basis. We thus have to accept that, while something or other is always presented to us, we can never infer which member of the disjunction is fulfilled without treating a given common factor as falling on one side or the other of the alleged radical disjunction. And so, despite McDowell's detour, the common factor ultimately returns to haunt disjunctivism.

David Macarthur has raised a similar objection to disjunctivism insofar as the doctrine claims to function as a successful anti-sceptical strategy. Macarthur points out that, in order to motivate Cartesian scepticism, it suffices to introduce a minimal *causal model of experience* that comprises the following two aspects:

(1) an inner component (subjective experience), where this cannot imply any particular metaphysics of what counts as an intentional correlate of subjective experience; otherwise, we could make an inference merely from the givenness of an intentional correlate to its ontological correlate, meaning *per impossibile* that there would be neither hallucinations nor illusions;

(2) a relevant, identifiable efficient cause that brings about the subjective experience, however we choose to specify the causal relation.[24]

Since (1) in no way commits us to assuming sense data or other mental entities but merely accounts for the fact both that there are hallucinations and sensory illusions, and that there could be perfect hallucinations, adopting the causal model as a minimal assumption is not yet to advocate a substantial or problematic theory of mind. Rather, the minimal causal model of experience is an entirely natural idea (for which we happen to have psychological evidence from the natural sciences). Furthermore, the insight that an inference from an effect (subjective experience) to a cause is always problematic is just as natural; every effect can be elicited by various causes, making any unequivocal, infallible attribution impossible.

The causal model of experience therefore leads directly into Cartesian scepticism: (1) is logically independent of (2), such that, for every mental state that is a candidate for being a perception, it is an empirical question whether we have (1) and (2) – i.e. a perception – or *only* (1) – e.g. a perfect hallucination. Moreover, the causal model of experience is compatible with a direct realism because the direct realist must concede that our sensory experiences of existing objects have to be causally elicited. One can see a glass, for example, because the glass is the cause of one's seeing it, even though one can certainly hallucinate a glass without the 'glass' thereby being anything other than an intentional correlate. Now, a veridical perception is, by hypothesis, phenomenally indistinguishable from a perfect hallucination, as (1) and (2) are logically independent; a veridical perception certainly presupposes that (2) is fulfilled, which does not change anything as to (1). For this reason, no analysis of the phenomena can justify us in assuming that the claim that large parts of our presumed waking life are really hallucinatory must be false.

It is of no help to disjunctivism to appeal at this stage to how we can make statements of the form (a) 'My present state of consciousness seems to be in all respects as though p' in the game of giving and asking for reasons only if we have already learnt to make statements of the form (b) 'I see, hear, etc., that p'. Scepticism confronts us not with a *quid facti* question but with a *quid juris* question. The task is not to show that doubt is phylogenetically or ontogenetically prior to certainty but to ask whether and how we can escape doubt once it has arisen. And, once it has arisen, sceptical doubt cannot be allayed through ad hoc measures, for example, by recommending direct realism as a form of therapy.[25] McDowell's conception of the logical space of reasons with no outer boundary as the space in which we always already conduct our cognitive lives does not so much dissolve the sceptical paradox as attempt to circumvent it – as is typical of McDowell's general anti-sceptical strategy.[26] As he explicitly tells us: 'The aim here is not to answer sceptical questions, but to begin to see how it might be intellectually respectable to ignore them, to treat them as unreal, in the way that common sense has always wanted to.'[27]

Insofar as McDowell's strategy of suppressing the sceptical question insinuates that common sense always treats sceptical questions as 'unreal', it involves a questionable presupposition. How can common sense even come to know about sceptical questions if, by hypothesis, it cannot understand such questions without ceasing to be common sense? How can it ignore sceptical questions without entering into some kind of relation to them? And even if it does ignore them, to whom are sceptical questions supposed to be directed if not to the subject whose naïvety they have corroded – the subject who sets out as an exemplar of common sense only to return *post festum* as a sceptic? The recourse to common sense is thus not only a category mistake, invoking a fact where we wanted a justification: there is also nothing determinate *to which* one might have recourse if 'common sense' in the eminent singular simply does not exist.

On closer inspection, to invoke common sense is to recommend a merely theory-*internal* escape route, an attempt to avoid the difficulties of the theory itself with reference to a supposedly stable *external* anchor. However, this means that 'common sense' is not a reality to which we can easily retreat as soon as disjunctivism makes itself available as the therapeutic alternative to scepticism. Rather, it turns out that 'common sense' (just like the 'natural attitude' of phenomenology) is a theoretical posit designed to circumvent the sceptical problem.

Moreover, sceptical questions operate exclusively with assumptions derivable from such foundational epistemic concepts as 'knowledge', 'reason', 'justification', and so on; they appeal to no presuppositions that so-called common sense cannot take on board in good faith. Otherwise, the paradoxes and antinomies lurking within our concepts would not have their (quite evident) power to unsettle us (see chapter 14 below).

Even if, for all its considerable difficulties, we still want to retain disjunctivism as an effective strategy against Cartesian scepticism, it is unlikely that it can solve an additional problem: however welcome we might find McDowell's return to the unity of thought and being, it cannot help us banish the rule-following problem. McDowell understands Wittgenstein's notion that there is a case of following a rule that is not an interpretation[28] in terms of a 'meeting of minds', in which the rule-following subject sees what the other intends with her words without any diversion via an explicit formulation of the rule (or a translation manual) being required.[29] Accordingly, McDowell supposes that the transparency of communal practice underwrites the transparency of the world itself. He follows the hermeneutic tradition in conceiving initiation into practices in terms of 'Bildung';[30] far from being an appeal to the supernatural, such processes of initiation merely actualise the second-nature capacities of the adult rational animal.

Be that as it may, we are still faced with the aspect of the rule-following problem that concerns how we can *evaluate* statements about facts. And, to deal with this, it is not sufficient to accept McDowell's proposal that our concepts immediately reach out to the world, particularly if one adds in the contention that the world is everything that is the case.[31] Even if, as McDowell assumes, everything that is the case is conceptual in some sense or other, these purely factual concepts cannot exercise any restriction on our use of rules, unless we supplement this account with a story of our initiation into discursive practices. McDowell's *naturalised Platonism*[32] – in essence: his Aristotelianism – is therefore open to the general objection to Platonism that derives from Wittgenstein's later philosophy.[33]

The best way of solving this problem in fact seems to be to appeal to a new conception of facts, one which would allow facts to be determined through the roles they are assigned within the essentially social game of giving and asking for reasons. This is the alternative path taken by Brandom.[34] However, deciding to pursue this strategy means no longer starting off with consciousness and ascribing it an immediate relation to the world, a relation that is coeval with consciousness and thus already present whenever a conscious subject asks itself how it relates to the world. Yet this is precisely how McDowell intends to upset the foundations of Cartesian scepticism. He tries to show how what the sceptic puts into question is something that conscious subjects must always presuppose: an epistemic being's certainty of being in the world. This starting point, however, remains wholly within the framework of the modern image of representations, according to which an isolated judging subject can successfully refer to the world.

The rule-following problem thus reappears for McDowell's metaphysics of intentionality: insofar as he does not build the social dimension of rule-following into his disjunctive conception of appearance, he cannot solve the Kripkean problem that arises both for Platonism and for every form of realism or idealism built on the assumption that we have to bring *facts* under rules. In order to explain the possibility of error and thus guarantee the validity of norms, we cannot ignore their social dimension.

'In order to make a mistake, a man must already judge in conformity with mankind.'[35]

'Error' can designate a binary relation between a thinker and a fact judged by a thinker just as little as 'truth' can. It is hard to find a way around Wittgenstein's insight that we are never alone with the world, because intentionality is only possible given an ability to refer to determinate items. Intentionality qua conceptually distinct structure is always already social. Determinacy, and so assertoric content, does not come about independently of norms, else it would be impossible to guarantee that the use of rules (the application of concepts to facts) is not utterly arbitrary and so always 'true' – that is, neither true nor false. The determinacy of assertoric content is thus due to the normativity of concepts, which in turn requires a social parameter. Such a parameter, however, plays no theoretically grounding role in McDowell's metaphysics of intentionality.[36] In the formation of the human mind, '*Bildung*' comes too late for us to be in touch with facts, because we have to be in touch with the world in order to be initiated into a community.

Facts are not norms – although which norms define a community is evidently a matter of fact. If it is correct that concepts are rules, it follows that they are norms; for, by distinguishing the correct from the incorrect, a norm constitutes a general difference between compliance and contravention. A norm therefore says what *ought* to happen but does not predict which applications it will have. To do so, it would require an infinite formulation, but at the price of having any determinate content. It is for this reason that a norm is no 'superlative fact'[37] that fixes permissible and impermissible applications for an infinite range of cases in advance. Instead, a new decision is required as to what should be allowed and what proscribed for each case where a rule is to be applied.[38] The next statement (action, assertion, question, etc.) in a system of assertions – or, more generally, the next move in a practice – always presupposes an act of decision-making, because what should occupy a given position in a system of assertions is not something the rule can determine in advance. 'The rule does not do work, for whatever happens according to the rule is an interpretation of the rule.'[39]

Wittgenstein operates with, on the one hand, a contrast between an eminent intellectual achievement, an 'as it were, non-discursive grasp of grammar'[40] that promises us immediate cognitive contact with 'superlative facts' (absolute facts, Platonic ideas, Fregean thoughts) and, on the other hand, an ultimately groundless decision borne by nothing beyond human practice. As a consequence of the fact that our rules at any one time contain a necessarily finite number of applications, the contrast between *intuition* and *decision* helps illuminate the finitude of our understanding. Wittgenstein therefore identifies the weakness of appeals to intuition as the fundamental problem of solipsism. Whatever intuition revealed would be necessarily true: appearance (presentation) and being would coincide in a pure disclosive vision, which always sees more than it can articulate. But this would mean that intuition's supposed insight is blind: wherever you believe you can see everything you can really see nothing at all.[41]

If it were simply in the hands of the isolated judging subject to decide which statement counts as a valid successor move in some system, every interpretation could be brought into conformity with the rule and every statement would count as permissible. But, in any case where it is possible to apply the rule correctly, it must also be possible to apply it incorrectly, and nobody can guarantee this *privately*, however much they might be isolated *physically*. We therefore have to distinguish between *private rule-following* and *following a private rule*.[42] While there is, quite trivially, private rule-following (soliloquising, reading, wandering alone in the forest, etc.), following a private rule, by contrast, cannot really be rule-following given the impossibility of establishing a correct/incorrect distinction for the latter. Consequently, we should not understand Wittgenstein's private language argument as a theory of the factual genesis of language within the context of a communal practice. Rather, it is a penetrating argument against the idea that solipsism can provide us with secure epistemological foundations.

12

Stage-Setting and Discourse: The Community in Context

The notion of following a private rule that comes under attack in Wittgenstein is a purely conceptual construct. We find it invoked wherever a theory operates, be it explicitly or implicitly, with the picture of a subject who begins trapped in an internal world and has to struggle to imbue her representations with objective reality. Instead of trying to work outwards from within, Wittgenstein reverses solipsism's order of explanation, explaining the internal as a function of the external. Even our private inner lives, the existence of which Wittgenstein by no means disputes, are occupants of a public context insofar as we are members of a linguistic community. Our representations bear the stamp of that context. A thinker is able to distinguish competently between S and S* (say, between a stomach ache and a headache) because she is able, under suitable circumstances, to state which sensations she experiences. For Wittgenstein, therefore, being in pain under normal circumstances does not mean perceiving a logically private object or having an intellectual intuition; rather, it means being able to communicate that one is in pain to another subject. If A is aware that she has S, this does not mean that she is in a position correctly to identify some private object along the lines of a word-object model (that she can pin the right label on it); rather, it means that she can exhibit tokens of pain behaviour that others can understand as an indicator of sensed pain; the tokens could, for example, enable a doctor to make a correct diagnosis of some illness or internal injury.

The concept of 'circumstances' or of a 'situation' performs a vital role in Wittgenstein's solution to the rule-following paradox, a role neglected by Kripke in his one-sided focus on the concepts of a community and its agreement. Yet, for Wittgenstein, it is not merely a community which determines whether A, in a given case, has uttered a valid statement; for, in order for a community to ascribe a determinate assertoric content to A's behaviour, it has to assign it a position within a certain context (language game). Whether or not A correctly applies a rule is a function not only of the agreement that reigns within a sufficiently large social unit but also of the circumstances surrounding the respective instance of putative rule-application. Wittgenstein is especially clear about this when discussing the problem of education or, in his jargon, of *training*. As he puts it in a passage in his *Remarks on the Foundations of Mathematics*:

> But how then does the teacher interpret the rule for the pupil? (For he is certainly supposed to give it a particular interpretation.) – Well, how but by means of words and training?
> And if the pupil reacts to it thus and thus; he possesses the rule inwardly.
> But this is important, namely that this reaction, which is our guarantee of understanding, presupposes as a surrounding particular circumstances, particular forms of life and speech. (As there is no such thing as a facial expression without a face.)
> (This is an important movement of thought.)[1]

Wittgenstein makes repeated references to the practice of linguistic training, and it is crucial to keep in mind that he introduces the ideas of circumstance and context in this connection. Meredith Williams has given a spirited defence of the thesis that Wittgenstein's contextualism is inseparably linked with his theory of language acquisition or linguistic training.[2] She has shown that a certain 'stage-setting', which she also designates as 'the right kind of context', is indispensable for setting limits to both the teacher's and the pupil's horizon of expectations: '[T]he classificatory work of language cannot take place without stage setting, without the right kind of context. One can't name an object or property without providing the logical space for individuating that which is to be named.'[3] Without this restriction we could not explain why a child, despite the infinitely many ways it might understand the teacher's expressions and actions (i.e. despite the infinite possible errors he might commit), selects only a restricted few, such that the teacher can generally tell when the child fails to follow the rule as the teacher intends – i.e. makes a mistake.

Unfortunately, a problem arises here, which speaks in favour of Chomsky's adoption of a restricted innatism (of a language of thought/ an innate grammar): if circumstances contribute to the individuation of an expression's meaning, we have to presuppose that the child is able to make competent distinctions between particular circumstances. But, on the present hypothesis, the child should be able to acquire this discriminatory capacity only thanks to prior initiation into a linguistic community: making distinctions is a matter of rule-following, and rule-following is normative, and thus social. The child cannot be a *tabula rasa*. But, be that as it may, it will not get us any further if we simply decide to join Chomsky's camp and suppose that the child comes equipped with a biological – and thus natural – capacity, because nature, by definition, cannot be normative.[4] Nature will not do the trick as long as we do not charge it with normativity. Williams's solution consists in drawing a distinction between behaviour and rule-following (action), whereby rule-following is norm-governed behaviour. Instances of mere behaviour also involve access to a discrete world, but are disciplined and structured given the exposure to normative constraints, and thus rules, that takes place through initiation into a linguistic community. Without assuming a natural behavioural basis for rule-following – i.e. without invoking a qualified naturalism – contextualism would leave us without any solid ground beneath our feet: we would be unable to explain how the stable logical space of reasons we inhabit as competent users of a language could so much as emerge. Without qualified naturalism, the problem of rule-following pushes us towards a groundless semantic scepticism, which renders both language acquisition and its natural (biological) foundation utterly unintelligible.[5]

The problem of rule-following therefore leads to a liberal naturalism, to the idea of the 'natural history of human beings',[6] which simply cannot be identical with the meaningless nature entertained by physicalism. In this way, pursuing the central Wittgensteinian theme of normativity helps to facilitate a self-knowledge of human nature, so to speak, that is incompatible with the metaphysics of physicalism. The hope that we might trace meaning back to physicalistically describable events fails, and 'nature' becomes a phenomenon revealed to us by a particular argumentative strategy, namely, that of pursuing the problem of rule-following and tracing out the logical space of its possible solutions. The kind of naturalism that emerges from pursuing this strategy does not understand 'nature' as the totality of the given (that is, as the world), as whatever supplies us with the information that we, as finite epistemic beings, have to build up into a whole, into a world picture. Rather, 'nature' here functions as a name for the whole within which we attain self-knowledge and to whose emergence we make our own distinctive contribution as normative beings. 'Nature' is reeled into the domain of normativity, into the domain of the social.

On this picture, as human (second) nature itself belongs to (first) nature, we should regard our practices neither as transcendent nor as mere illusions. For the social world is not extramundane. It is not somehow incompatible with its own biological pre-history. Yet our practices would be transcendent if nature were nothing other than a causally closed universe of particles with no place for cognitive beings. Such beings would somehow have to reach beyond nature – a model that Wittgenstein seems to recommend in the *Tractatus*.[7] Indeed, if we could in fact successfully carry out the project of reducing our practices to evolutionary strategies of self-preservation and of reducing these, in turn, to elements in the causally closed universe, such beings would be mere illusions.

We can regard the idea of a second, human nature (the most sophisticated recent defence of which has been offered by McDowell) as a consequence of scepticism. It functions, that is, as an anti-sceptical strategy against Cartesian scepticism, which it seeks to interpret as a harmless reminder of our epistemic finitude (rather than as an epistemological threat). As we have seen, the problem of rule-following arises as soon as we understand discursive practices as systems individuated by their respective norms-in-context, and, since it leads to the danger of rule-scepticism, it confronts us with the threat of semantic nihilism. Now, the idea goes, we can resist this nihilism only by taking account of our normative nature, which, in spite of the arbitrariness of grammar, is historically invariable. Yet, crucially, it must be possible to assert the resulting *liberal naturalism of second nature* under the sceptical conditions to which contextualism originally commits us. For, after all, it was only thanks to contextualism that we discovered the necessity of invoking second nature (at least if we want to prevent our practices from assuming a transcendent character). But then a certain problem comes into view: we can, *ex hypothesi*, develop no theory of second nature that contains context-free assertions, and second nature therefore becomes a mere assumption introduced in order to prevent the groundlessness of rules from collapsing into semantic nihilism.[8] We then help ourselves to the concept of a first nature in order to anchor second nature in something that can serve as the stable ground of the instability of human practice.

In the context of language acquisition, we can see how initiation into the use of elementary expressions already presupposes a *stable practice of agreement*, a usage or custom. Following Wittgenstein's insight, the association of sign and word cannot itself already constitute a complex linguistic process, as is suggested by the Augustinian theory of language acquisition cited at the very beginning of the *Philosophical Investigations*. For linguistic initiation cannot presuppose that the child already brings with it a kind of wordless language of thought which it then translates into adult language.[9] Wittgenstein therefore consciously employs the crude expression 'training' in order to underscore how a speaker's first linguistic steps cannot be a matter of suddenly gaining an insight into particular reasons; reasons become available only once an entire network of concepts has been established.[10] Initiation into the language community, and thus into the game of giving and asking for reasons, cannot itself appeal to reasons. The first acquisition of a language cannot take place via an explicit process of instructing participants *in statu nascendi* how to do things with words. Before a participant is able to decide both how and how not to act, her natural behaviour must be subject to a course of training that first establishes the possibility of deviant behaviour, and thus of action. Sanctions precede the grasp of an existing rule. We cannot first present an infant with a set of rules and then induct her into language, because the presentation of the rules would, of course, already presuppose the relevant *fait accompli*. Quite trivially, the child cannot learn her first language by being taught its rules in that very language. Linguistic initiation therefore essentially begins from bodily training (how to pronounce sounds that are recognisable by others as moves in their game).

When it comes to settling which rule someone is following, the agreement of a group of experts about the truth of a statement is not sufficient. Determining the assertoric content of a statement also requires a set of circumstances, stage-setting, that determines which reactions of the putative rule-follower *ought* to count as indicative of intelligent – i.e. rule-governed – behaviour.[11] Stage-setting sets boundaries to the community's horizon of expectations. In order for a statement to have assertoric content, only a selection from an infinite set of its possible contents can be ascribed to it in assessing its validity. And which contents are or are not considered (selected) depends upon the circumstances of the statement's expression.

Mutatis mutandis, the same is true not only for all assertions but for all and any moves (gestures, actions, etc.) within a practice that can count as successor moves in a contextually delimited series. Therefore, the assertoric content of a statement cannot be evaluated without reference to (1) its minimal conformity and (2) a context. But, without further specification, the idea of context threatens to lapse into triviality; it has to amount to more than a reminder that in order to make determinate statements we have to be confronted with a determinate configuration of objects (or facts). For, in any case, under the conditions of the rule-following problem facts or objects cannot immediately form a context in and of themselves; they first need to be assigned to a larger system that for its part supplies an operating system, a normative software, as it were. The minimal condition for having a context, that is, is the validity of the norms that distinguish between correct and incorrect performances, and these norms enjoy no determinacy whatsoever without recourse to a practice. The point is not that practices are utterly worldless (transcendent): the present requirement on determinacy merely implies that practices place their participants in a relation to the world, and that we could not specify this relation without the mediation of norms – if we take norms out of consideration, we are left without any sort of determinable relation to determinate items. It is only once there are fixed contextual parameters determining which contents can come into question in the first place that the particularities of the world can play a role in determining a statement's assertoric content. What the context maintains is thus not its relation to a stable actuality or world but the uninterrupted, disagreement-generating conversation between participants in a corresponding discourse. The context thereby allows for a kind of holism: it creates a system within which it first becomes possible to evaluate statements.

We do not, however, need to impose the tools of systems theory on Wittgenstein, as he already deploys his own concept of a system:

> All testing, all confirmation and disconfirmation of a hypothesis takes place already within a system. And this system is not a more or less arbitrary and doubtful point of departure for all our arguments: no, it belongs to the essence of what we call an argument. The system is not so much the point of departure, as the element in which arguments have their life.[12]

Arguments – i.e. reasons – are elements of a system and their lifeblood. They move in the 'stream of life'[13] – i.e. in the continuous creation of discourses, which generate their own conditions *post factum* without ever being able to make them fully explicit.

Wittgenstein's reflections on rule-following thus suggest an answer to the question of how normativity, meaning and objectivity hang together. A weighty objection to his entire line of thought could appeal to how it tries to make do without appealing to propositions, even though doing so seems, quite trivially, to be unavoidable if we want to explain the content of propositional attitudes. For belief reports of the form 'S believes that p' to be comprehensible, we have to ascribe to S an attitude towards a proposition where this has at least the following properties:

1 *Conceptual identity*: A proposition is what makes all translations of a sentence into another language (or into another grammatical voice, etc.) possess the same meaning. 'He is tall', 'Er ist groß', 'É alto', etc., have the same meaning because they express the same proposition. The same goes for translations of a sentence within a language, such as when we replace 'Peter loves Petra' with 'Petra is loved by Peter'.

2 *Ontological quality*: Propositions are true or false independently of whether we hold them to be true or false.

3 *Univocity*: Propositions necessarily always have the same truth conditions, and this is what distinguishes them from sentences. The proposition *that he is tall* is true if and only if he is tall, while the sentence 'he is tall' can be true or false only once it is established which proposition it expresses. For the series of signs 'he is tall' can have infinitely many meanings, depending on the language and context in which it is expressed.

4 *Absoluteness*: Propositions, unlike sentences, are absolute in the sense that they do not possess the truth values they do in virtue of the context in which they are expressed.[14]

Wittgenstein's considerations show, however, that propositions understood in this sense do not perform any meaningful function in explaining the assertoric content of sentences in the context of the rule-following problem. Wittgenstein's reflections, that is, aim to show not that there are no propositions but, rather, that it is superfluous to assume them. The game of judgement functions only on the condition that assertoric content is assigned to discursive moves, such that it makes no sense to abstract from the embedding of assertoric content in discursive practices.

This is why the Wittgensteinian tradition tends to regard propositions as the secular successors of Platonic ideas. One of the most significant reasons for Plato's postulation of ideas was that they allowed him to explain the assertoric content of statements, which he explained in the *Sophist* as a relation (λόγος) between ideas. On this conception, ideas have (inter alia) the same properties as propositions.[15] Following established usage, we can label the assumption that propositions exist as *Platonism*, without, however, wanting to suggest that Platonism in its various modern forms (e.g. Frege's philosophy of mathematics) shares all the assumptions of *Platonic* Platonism.

Wittgenstein's contextualism is notoriously anti-Platonic and can be placed within the philosophical programme of inverting Platonism initiated by Nietzsche. While Plato conceived appearances – i.e. individual cases (the individual) – as a simulacrum of the universal – the concept – Nietzsche reversed this order by thinking of the universal as a simulacrum of the individual: individual instances determine the universal and not the other way around. Therefore, our orientation to particulars cannot be secured via recourse to our orientation to the universal. The private language argument shows how the assumption of an intuitive relation between the mind and a mental object (idea, proposition, sense-datum, etc.) cannot explain how the distinction between correct and incorrect can so much as arise, let alone play a meaningful role within the continuous re-creation of a practice. But, in order for a statement to have determinate content in the first place, it has to be capable of being correct or incorrect. Suppose our sentences could possess assertoric content only by expressing a proposition and, since every verbalisation already represents a step into the sensible world (whereas propositions are ultimately meant to be purely mental entities), that we would have to grasp this proposition intuitively; our sentences would then have their foundations in a private language. As isolated judging subjects, we would be occupied first and foremost with our representations, which we would merely exchange in communication with others. We might call this the *transportation model of understanding*: 'The paradox disappears only if we make a radical break with the idea that language always functions in one way, always serves the same purpose: to convey thoughts – which may be about houses, pains, good and evil, or anything else you please.'[16]

The point of the private language argument comes to the claim that, semantically speaking, we simply cannot be all alone with our representations. The cost of such isolation is the elimination of objectivity. This is why assuming the existence of propositions is of little use when it comes to solving the paradox of rule-following: even supposing propositions exist, we could never even close in on them without our language. For the actual function of our language is incompatible with the conceptual identity, ontological quality, univocity and absoluteness of propositions. According to Wittgenstein, there is no objectivity without sociality, whereby the latter is a necessary, but not a sufficient, condition of the former. Were it sufficient, we would lose the contrast of objectivity, which is why contextual parameters have to be built into our 'game of judging'.[17] These fix the discourse within which a fact counts as a fact. This means leaving behind not objectivity, *tout court*, but, rather, the idea of a world that consists of absolute facts, of facts that are always already determinate in and of themselves, independently of all and any discourses.[18]

To this extent, we should not grant Davidson our unqualified agreement when he describes his idea of semantic triangulation as a Wittgensteinian insight. Davidson's concern is not to bring into question the idea of an utterly independent world of absolute facts but to show that we can have access to such a world only given our cultivation of the necessary notion of objectivity in and through communication.[19] Wittgenstein, by contrast, opposes the idea that our attitudes to the world are realised in expressions that have propositions as their contents, items that are true or false regardless of our discursive practices. Rather, he sets out to fundamentally contest the idea that the world reveals itself to us in the shape of pure thoughts that either grasp what is the case, and are thus true, or fail to do so, and are therefore false. Since, given Wittgenstein's insight, meaning presupposes the normative stability of a practice, we have to abandon the *Tractatus*'s idea of a Schopenhauerean *'pure cognitive subject'*, which, as a 'clear eye of the world', enjoys a purely spiritual apprehension of reality.[20] For this reason, Wittgenstein can think of his proposal as *the diametrical opposite of solipsism.*

Wittgenstein does not want to advocate any kind of negative dogmatism that would cast doubt on the existence of propositions (or of abstract entities in general). Instead, he recommends agnosticism: on account of our linguistic nature, we cannot know anything about propositions. But then there must be an alternative explanation of the assertoric content of our statements, one which exploits nothing more than the resources placed at our disposal in judgements. For Wittgenstein, then, the question of the existence of propositions is both undecidable and irrelevant. Objectivity neither can nor need be grounded on the cognitive subject's private intentional access to propositions that are eternally true or false independently of any subject's holding-true.

To be sure, Wittgenstein's anti-realism about rules is a response to exposure to extreme sceptical conditions. It is no accident that the generation of a sceptical paradox plays a central role in grounding his account of rule-following. The paradox drives us to the insight that understanding a rule need not be an interpretation. Insisting otherwise inevitably invites an infinite regress. 'Interpretation comes to an end',[21] and the end of interpretation is thus an action, an ultimately groundless decision, and every attempt to seek out a justification for the specific action (the deed) in which interpretation culminates must fail. 'If I have exhausted the justifications I have reached bedrock, and my spade is turned. Then I am inclined to say: "This is simply what I do."'[22] If the deed contradicts the community's customs, the doer will be sanctioned, without the community having to be able to cite reasons for why it cultivates the particular customs it does. This does not mean that the outcast is cast out from the truth, however, as he can begin (in time-honoured fashion) to form a new faction.

Both Wittgenstein's formulation of the rule-following problem and his solution are thus based on the following plausible premises:

(1) Every concept is a rule.

(2) Where there is a rule, there is a difference between its correct and its incorrect applications.

(3) Facts, propositions, beings, essences or ideas cannot state without further ado whether somebody has applied a rule correctly or incorrectly. They cannot state *which* rule has to be brought into consideration in order to determine whether somebody has applied a rule correctly or incorrectly. The world (everything that is the case) does not speak. Therefore, strictly speaking, the facts carry no normative force.[23]

(4) Concepts have to be deployed in order to determine what someone intends or thinks – that is, for ascriptions of attitudes with assertoric content to be possible. Since concepts are rules, and mere facts cannot determine whether someone has applied a rule, facts cannot determine what someone intends or thinks either.

(5) In order to determine what someone intends or thinks, it is therefore of no help to posit a private relation between their consciousness and the world. For such a private relation cannot guarantee any distinction between correct and incorrect.

(6) Strictly speaking, there cannot be any kind of relation between consciousness and world if the world cannot be determined from within consciousness. A relation between consciousness and nothing determinate, or between consciousness and the ineffable, is no relevant kind of relation.[24]

(7) In order to assess whether a rule has been applied, there needs to be a community that decides which rule has been applied and whether it has been applied correctly. Behaviour that is deviant in principle (a private language) is possible only at the price of a total loss of normative determinacy.[25]

(8) The community that decides which rule has been followed, and with what degree of success, inculcates a range of behavioural patterns into its members. These allow them to apply a rule in any given case so they can go on in the right way. That is, it *trains* its members. This does not mean that the community always has to be present at each rule-application as a kind of adjudicatory panel.[26] Grasping a concept is rather a matter of having non-propositional knowhow such that, other things being equal, applying it successfully does not require any explicit reflection.

(9) The application of rules (the deed) takes place not in a void but always under specific circumstances. The circumstances restrict the selection of rules (the space of possible actions) of the members of the community. In other words, the circumstances determine the relevant alternatives available to a member of

the community at any given time in order to fix which rules can play a role in determining the situation.

Contextualism is a form of relativism. It states that we have to introduce a further parameter into the merely seemingly dyadic relation between mind (language, consciousness, soul, subject . . .) and world (nature, being, totality, object . . .), so that we have at the very least a triadic relation. The third parameter is the context of assessment,[27] which can of course be specified in a number of different ways. Contextualism thus contrasts with representationalism insofar as the latter understands our grasp of truth as a dyadic relation that requires no assessment relative to a third parameter.

It seems, of course, to be a mere realist platitude (R) that 'propositional truth' designates a relation between mind and world. We might express this platitude with the following equivalence:

(R) p is true $\leftrightarrow$ things (the world) are as p says.

This statement of (R) does not yet say anything about what the world is or in what sense it obtains 'outside of' a discursive system. (R) is, in fact, *prima facie* metaphysically neutral. Yet it is easy to feel a temptation to interpret (R) to mean that 'truth' is a dyadic relation between the world and a doxastic system whose relation to the world is fixed by the former relatum: whenever there is a dyadic relation to the world, a state of the doxastic system is either true or false – i.e. propositional. But the formulation of (R) presupposes a dyadic relation to the world, a presupposition to which contextualism adds a third parameter.

If we think of truth as a dyadic relation from the outset, we run the danger of inflating the platitude (R) into a metaphysical thesis. (R) can then seem to presuppose the concept of a thoroughgoingly determined world, where this world consists of facts that *always already* precede their discursive determination.[28] It is just this picture which comes under attack in later Wittgenstein. According to Wittgenstein, the world (qua thoroughgoingly determined *omnitudio realitatis*) plays no role in the assessment of our statements. If we understand the world as everything that is the case – that is, as the totality of all true propositions – we fail to recognise the problem of rule-following: the problem was supposed to show that propositions can make no relevant contribution to our epistemic economy, because this economy is normative without remainder. The idea of a world in itself – understood as an atemporal, complete structure of all true propositions, to which we gain access under favourable cognitive conditions – runs into serious difficulties once we introduce the conditions imposed upon us by the rule-following considerations.

Wittgenstein's premises are motivated provided our everyday justificatory practices have, for one reason or another, come under sceptical pressure. And his reflections on rule-following owe their plausibility to a specific picture of those justificatory practices. This picture, he thinks, holds philosophy captive.[29] It consists in opposing a private inner realm to a public world, raising the question of how it is possible to transcend the inner or, conversely, how the public world could possibly reach into the inner. Wittgenstein's corrective to the picture shows that it is only within the public and social medium of language, and so within the public world, that we can oppose the private inner to the public outer realm in the first place. In other words, the distinction between private and public is itself public and not private. It is not the isolated judging subject who, from within, carves out a realm of objects distinct from herself. Rather, the converse is true: the private subject (as the privative expression already indicates) can be determined only against and in terms of the public community of rule-followers.

13

Solipsism's Representations and Cartesian Scepticism

It is important to bear in mind how Descartes' anti-sceptical strategy is meant to function. Descartes intends it as a protective mechanism against the solipsism implicit in the motivation of his own project, its methodological scepticism. The oft-criticised mental representationalism of post-Cartesian empiricism is a *consequence* of Descartes' philosophy, not its *presupposition*. It is a result of the Cartesian methodological scepticism that came into play once philosophers no longer accepted Descartes' anti-sceptical strategy, with its notorious appeal to the idea of a benevolent God who secures the existence of an external world and the certainty of mathematical truths. Against the background of this rejection, Cartesian scepticism can seem to necessitate an acquiescence in solipsism.

Wittgenstein is therefore right to attack Cartesian scepticism at its roots. He identifies the problematic link that leads from methodological scepticism to the possibility of scepticism: namely, the link between doubts about the existence – and thus the concept – of an external world, on the one hand, and, on the other, the idea that, while we have epistemically privileged information about our private episodes (sense data, sensations, intentionality, etc.), we can disclose the causes of these episodes only through subjecting them to analysis. The idea that we are endowed with epistemically privileged mental states is a theory construction designed to keep methodological scepticism at bay.

In this context, Wittgenstein contests the idea of an epistemic asymmetry between mind and world. He attacks the notion, constitutive for mental representationalism in general, that our modes of epistemic access to *res cogitans* and *res extensa* respectively are of radically different kinds. If we remove representationalism as a target, Wittgenstein's rule-following problem loses its principal focus; for he clearly addresses his reflections on rule-following to the very solipsism that presented him with a standing theoretical and existential temptation.[1]

In Descartes, methodological scepticism draws on the concept of representation in general or as such. This is supposed to pick out intentional correlates of mental states that are neutral as to their truth value.[2] It would be a mistake to think that the concept of representation and the entire idiom of intentionality that, in the wake of Descartes, developed into the language of the philosophy of consciousness somehow represents an arbitrary or accidental philosophical invention. Rather, it arose as the result of a specific line of sceptical thought. As soon as we think of ourselves as subjects endowed with mental intentionality, as subjects who can access the world only insofar as it is mediated by our representations, Cartesian scepticism has already done its work.[3] The subject/object split is a philosophical *artefact*, not a *discovery* about the ontological structure of a world that consists of minds (subjects) on the one hand and the world/nature (objects) on the other. Wittgenstein's line of argument does not itself presuppose methodological scepticism as a motivating factor but tries to surpass this form of scepticism with a new, potentially more radical form, which emerges in the course of the rule-following considerations.[4] This new form of scepticism exposes the solipsistic foundation of the inherited concept of representation, revealing its commitment to the possibility of a private language, which, Wittgenstein wants to show, founders on the idea that there might be no public facts about meaning. The argument – or rather paradox – underlying this scepticism begins to dissipate once we realise that the community sanctions its members not at the level of a merely linguistic exchange, as it were, but by providing them with real-world friction, and that this grounds the validity of their judgements. The normativity of judgements resides neither in the solipsistically conceived mind nor in some naturalistic bedrock 'out there'.

A brief survey of the history of scepticism shows up varieties of scepticism that aim to spread confusion within one, several, or even all *particular* philosophical disciplines (philosophical scepticism). But it also reveals the persistent presence of varieties of scepticism that turn against the practice of philosophy itself (anti-philosophical scepticism).[5] In the modern period, Descartes provides an example of a philosopher who implements a form of philosophical scepticism by building the problem of scepticism into the sophisticated methodological construction of his own theory. Hume, by contrast, went on to advocate a form of anti-philosophical scepticism insofar as he tried to make out a contradiction between our everyday practices of successful knowledge ascription, on the one hand, and our philosophical attitude towards these ascriptions and their justification, on the other. Hume's famous 'sceptical solution' to the sceptical problem consists in a reliance on *nature*. It is the demands of 'nature' that, sooner or later, will force us away from philosophical reflection and towards the objects and occupations of everyday life. If we allow ourselves to be puzzled by philosophy and its paradoxes only on certain occasions, there need be no danger of suffering any kind of lasting intellectual damage (see chapter 14 below). And, nearer to our own time, Wittgenstein proposes a similar anti-sceptical strategy, seeking to naturalise the contribution of the community to our awareness of normative friction.

If we turn to antiquity, we can find a form of philosophical scepticism in

Plato. Famously, the founding text of epistemology, the *Theaetetus*, gives a particularly clear presentation of the dream argument.[6] In addition, Plato's confrontation with the sceptical positions of the Sophists informs every dimension of his philosophy's overall justificatory programme, and his epistemology stems to a substantial extent from his engagement with scepticism (the Sophists, Heracliteans, Eleatics) – so much is clearly in evidence in the *Theaetetus*, for example. Moreover, he would likely not have developed his theory of justice in the *Republic* without having the social 'Darwinism' of a Thrasymachus to exploit as a foil.

To a certain extent, therefore, we can see Plato too as incorporating sceptical arguments into his own position, especially when he wants to highlight the epistemological indispensability of pure thought at the expense of sensibility. Plato, that is, established an epistemological and ontological asymmetry between true being (the intelligible) and simulacra (the sensible), which was ultimately subjected to a genuine reversal in modern philosophy, particularly in Heidegger's history of being and Wittgenstein's rule-following considerations. Given this reversal, we can understand conceptual unities (the intelligible) as generated retrospectively from their instances through our regulation and interpretation of our own behaviour. Such interpretation does not represent what was simply the case before it came on the scene but retrospectively posits the conditions of the order we want to accept.[7] The fact that our behaviour acquires the logical form of action subject to normative assessment is a consequence of regulations that classify certain behavioural episodes in ways that the original, uninitiated agent could not have anticipated.

The classical opponent of Plato's philosophical scepticism is *Pyrrhonian scepticism*. The latter turns against philosophy quite generally insofar as philosophy represents an attempt to make life (βίος) the *object* of a theory.[8] The Academic sceptics had already argued tirelessly against the possibility that we might fix upon any criterion that could guarantee that a given representation is sufficiently clear and distinct for us to infer the presence (ὑπάρχειν) of an extra-mental object from its intentional correlate. Yet, for Sextus in particular, Pyrrhonian scepticism goes further: it not only destroys the solipsism of the Stoics' representationalism but also abandons any project whatsoever that assigns epistemic primacy to philosophical theorising. Sextus' anti-philosophical scepticism thereby sets in motion a course of reflection that ultimately leads to Wittgensteinian acquiescence in 'customs', 'mores' and 'institutions' – i.e. in the νόμοι. 'To follow a rule, to make a report, to give an order, to play a game of chess, are customs (usages, institutions).'[9]

Sextus and Wittgenstein, that is, both advocate a direct negation of the Platonic project whose guiding intentions receive condensed expression in the allegory of the cave. In the allegory, the customs and institutions that unite human beings resemble the chains that bind together the members of the cave-dwelling community as they go about their common project of inductively mastering the shadowy scene that plays out across

the cave walls. The philosopher has to tear herself free from the community and pierce through its world of appearances in order to see the
essence of the cave for what it really is. For Plato, therefore, philosophy
is the paradigmatically *extra*ordinary because it allows theoretical insight
to step in and take the place of our ordinary ways of life, our habits.[10]
From a theoretical perspective, the hermitage of the philosopher is an
unwanted consequence of his insight that we have to grasp the assertoric
content of language as propositional content. Indeed, it was in terms of
this insight that Plato introduced the notion of ideas: in part, this notion
functions as a theory of conceptuality, which explains how statements can
express a propositional content even though that content is true or false
independently of whether it is asserted here and now. The notion of ideas
is therefore based (like all theoretical philosophy) on a semantics, on a
theory of conceptual content.

By contrast, Wittgenstein objects that the illusion is not in fact to be found
in the cave: rather, illusion is generated precisely through our attempts to
transcend the conditions of the cave. There is no theory-level transition
that does not for its part generate its own conditions, whereby the resultant theory cannot completely retrieve these conditions without effecting
a further theory-level transition. Insofar as Wittgenstein offers an alternative analysis of assertoric content, it is that he wants to liberate us from
the (representationalist) picture that has so far held us captive.[11] Against
Plato, he maintains that we have no need to leave the cave in order to
secure stable assertoric content for our statements. Rather, he says, it
suffices to give a correct analysis of the relations that the cave-dwellers
maintain both to one another and to the shadows cast upon the cave walls.
And, once we have this analysis, we will see that we *cannot* transcend
the conditions of the cave.[12] Wittgenstein argues that positing Platonic
ideas (and their ontologically reduced successors such as essences, sense
data, facts, and so on) does not lead to any explanatory progress when
it comes to the all-important question of how it is possible to establish
rule-governed contact with both the world and others. We thus need to
deprive the Platonic 'flight' (φυγή)[13] from finitude of its semantic foundation. If our everyday practices are already in order, if they do not stand
in need of justification from an external view adopted from no particular
standpoint (the cave's sunlit forecourt), then it is quite absurd to want to
abandon those practices. If we try to turn away from them, we will be left
with nowhere to aim. This is just what the rule-following problem teaches
us. It binds us inseparably to a community, which is neither a figment
of our imagination nor a projection of an internally felt presence of the
radically other.

Once we realise that linguistic meaning hangs together with rule-
following, we can begin to appreciate that it is the attempt to leave
finitude behind which throws us into the ultimate confusion: we seem to
be manoeuvred into a position where we no longer know what we mean
by our words. Rule scepticism follows on the heels of making a certain

assumption, namely that the ability to follow a rule requires having an overview of the totality of its possible applications, even though it remains impossible in principle for us to attain such an overview. Against Plato, Wittgenstein thus alleges that there could be no intuition without rule-following – that is, no non-discursive grasp of propositional content (ideas) that was not discursively determined. Whenever we claim to have grasped an idea, we raise a fallible knowledge *claim*, and we have to be able to convey this discursively because the determinacy of the expressions we use in such linguistic communication is normatively governed by communal custom. Or, in other words, since any moves we make have to be intra-discursively identifiable, and thus presuppose discursive hinges, we cannot step outside of the linguistic community in order to rehearse the alleged primeval scene of setting up the conditions for a social contract. It is only within a discourse that we can mark a distinction between an intuition (an *actual* apprehension of an idea) and error (the *apparent* apprehension of an idea). The criterion of someone's having genuinely grasped an idea is not her impression of having done so – that would just lead us back to private language – but, rather, her ability to convey what she has apprehended in discursive form. It is the discourse which decides what does and does not get to count as apprehension, meaning that intuitions too can be determined only discursively. In short, it makes no sense to assume that there is non-assertable propositional content: because propositions feature in discourse as assertions, all propositional content is bound to the condition that it must allow of being cast in assertoric form. And this is possible only in the apologetic dimension of knowledge.[14] So, even if we really could apprehend ideas in an intuitive mode, this apprehension would be quite idle were we unable, in a given case, to muster discursive evidence showing that we did not merely *think* we apprehended an idea. Whenever we say that we have grasped some idea or other, we are already making moves within the realm of the communicable.

While the later Wittgenstein restricts himself to attacking the semantic foundation of Platonism/Cartesianism, Sextus goes further: he wants to furnish a proof that the Platonic–Aristotelian striving for knowledge leads not to eudaimonia but to restlessness and dissatisfaction. In order to do so, he has to show that, in the very place where Plato and Aristotle sought absolute unity – i.e. in pure theoretical thought – a dispute inevitably arises as to how precisely this should be characterised. Sextus therefore attacks Platonism not merely as a semantic or epistemological position but as a form of life that purports to offer a theoretically sophisticated recipe for happiness. Confounding the foundational theoretical operations of contemplative philosophy has, he thinks, the unexpected effect that the striving for knowledge disappears.

With his pragma-centrism, we can see Wittgenstein applying the same operation against the Cartesian 'project of pure enquiry'[15] into our theoretical attitude towards the world. To be sure, after the *Tractatus*

Wittgenstein avoided building this *ethical* dimension of his thought into the construction of his arguments.[16] His attempt to replace 'essence' and 'intuition' with 'rules' and 'rule-following' – in other words, with practice – thus hangs together with his arguments for the impossibility of grounding our knowledge on a philosophical foundation. The ground we hit upon when we drive the philosophical question to its outermost boundary is thus, according to Wittgenstein, not an absolute unity that we grasp through intuition but human action, and this is always part of a tradition, a form of life. 'Giving grounds, however, justifying the evidence, comes to an end; – but the end is not certain propositions' striking us immediately as true, i.e. it is not a kind of seeing on our part; it is our acting, which lies at the bottom of the language-game.'[17]

Wittgenstein's project can be regarded as, in essence, a perpetuation of the Pyrrhonian sceptical tradition. The latter does not doubt that we 'know' anything in the everyday sense of the word or that we have justified beliefs. Rather, it tries to show that neither human knowledge nor our justifications depend upon a philosophical grounding.[18] But this means that both Sextus and Wittgenstein owe us an explanation of how substantial, constructive philosophy – i.e. theory – could have arisen to begin with under the conditions of everyday practice.

Pyrrhonian scepticism allows us to give a clear formulation of the *basic problem of quietism*, for it arises as soon as this particular form of therapy has (supposedly) finally enabled philosophy to find peace.[19] The problem is not so much that quietism would like to stave off the temptations of solipsism through argumentative therapy. Rather, the key question concerns the aetiology of the illness that the sceptic promises to cure through her self-conscious silence – where does 'philosophy' in fact come from? If the temptation to philosophise is rooted in our everyday discursive practices, then any simple return to these practices can only perpetuate the problem. It is not enough, therefore, for quietism to act as a cure for philosophy; it must also strive to purge the everyday of its tendency to engage in philosophical reflection. Yet, if it then tries to offer some kind of systematic account of precisely which elements of the everyday stand in need of therapy, that would amount to offering its own philosophical theory, a theory of the everyday. And it would then contravene its own guiding concern to avoid giving any *philosophical* justification of the everyday, to avoid all ideals. As long as she pursues this route, therefore, the quietist's promise of salvation founders on its failure to assume anything other than an ultimately theoretical form. The fulfilment of its promise remains an ideal, and the retreat to practice leads, whether the sceptic likes it or not, to a reformation of our customs and practices. This process must therefore strictly avoid attaining the status of 'theory'. And, as a result, it can be in no position to state how we *should* live if we are to fulfil its aims. Sextus therefore simply retreats to this 'conformity with traditional customs' (τὰ πάτρια ἔθη),[20] while Wittgenstein attempts to bring his therapeutic understanding of philosophy together with an existential insight that does justice to the actual plurality of forms of life.

As is well known, Sextus discusses a foundational problem of empiricism that can be formulated as follows:[21] since we, frequently enough, encounter differences of opinion over the objects of our five senses, we have to assume that our contact with these objects cannot be immediate. If we all stood in immediate contact with the objects of the senses, no conflicts of opinions could arise; there would be no potential or actual difference between the *being* of the thing itself and how it is presented to us – i.e. its *appearance*. In order to guarantee the possibility of deception and thus of genuinely conflicting opinions about sensorily present objects, we have to assume that there can be two parties (subjects) so constituted that the same thing can appear, or be presented, differently to each party.

Representations are postulated in order to make sense of the relevant deviation of appearance from being and are inserted between the two parties and the presented objects. Sextus labels these using the classic expression πάθη (affection/impression) or φαντασίαι (representations).[22] In contrast, Sextus calls that which causes our affections and thus exists outside of them (τὸ ἐκτὸς καὶ τοῦ πάθους ποιητικόν)[23] 'the externally existing thing [i.e. to our affections]'. Famously, given empirical presuppositions, we face the sceptical problem of having to guarantee that not *all* representations can be objectively empty (Sextus calls this being 'affected vacuously' (κενο-παθεῖν),[24] and this triggers a search for a property of representations as such that can rule out the possibility that all representations might lack objective content. Borrowing from Stoic epistemology, Sextus calls such a property a 'criterion of truth' (κριτήριον τῆς ἀληθίας).[25] The epistemological function of the criterion of truth is, on the one hand, to guarantee that there is at least one contentful representation and, on the other hand, to distinguish contentful from non-contentful representations as such. The Stoics' official criterion of truth is the so-called apprehending or cataleptic impression (καταληπτικὴ φαντασία). By definition, this criterion has to be distinguished from the acataleptic impression (ἀκατάληπτος φαντασία) by being a *factive* mental state. From S's having a cataleptic impression that p, we can infer that p. Zenon's famous definition of a cataleptic impression therefore insists that whoever has one is always in a position to know that he has one, on the basis that it arises through a causal process, the cause of which can only be the thing itself.[26] This means that a cataleptic impression has to be intrinsically distinguishable from an acataleptic impression. However, since there is no *logical* connection between representations and worldly states, such that we can make out a priori which of our experiences are in fact cataleptic and which are not, the Stoics do not state any further material criterion of truth to distinguish between cataleptic and acataleptic impressions a priori. They simply insist that we know with absolute certainty whether or not we have a cataleptic impression. Antiochus therefore made a comparison between light, which illuminates both itself and the objects it shines upon, and cataleptic impressions, which point both to themselves and to their causes.[27]

These considerations, however, are vulnerable to Cartesian scepticism. Roughly speaking, there are two ways of avoiding the aporia that results from the concept of representation and lead us to the principle of aparallaxia. The first, *anti-realist* strategy, which can be found most prominently in post-Kantian idealism, consists in doing away with the assumption of a potentially unknowable world in itself that comes to be represented in our representations.[28] The second, *realist*, strategy attempts to naturalise representations by showing that there can be meaning, and so language and thought, only thanks to presuppositions that are furnished not by thought alone but by the natural world as described in our best available scientific theories.[29] The anti-realist strategy grounds the represented in representation, while the realistic strategy grounds representation in the representable. This basic opposition plays out in multiple variants of the contemporary debate between internalism and externalism. But it was already subject to intense discussion in the wake of early sceptical critiques of Kant's transcendental philosophy, with anti-realism bearing the label *criticism* and realism the label *dogmatism*.[30]

Before we can get these debates adequately in view, it is vital to have a proper appreciation of their sceptical origin, else our attempts to resolve the problem of representation might lack a sufficient motivation. If it should turn out, that is, that the only possible motivation for introducing the concept of representation is a form of scepticism, then it may well be that the task of deciding how best to deal with the concept is not a question of finding the right anti-sceptical strategy – be it one that assigns explanatory priority to representation or one that assigns explanatory priority to the representable. Instead, we need to engage with whatever theory motivates *scepticism* to begin with. If we can show, that is, that a sceptical paradox is responsible for the concept of representation, rather than the converse, it makes sense to take a step back (and behind) the grand anti-sceptical theories of the philosophical tradition and to look more closely at the concept's original motivation.[31]

The concept of representation owes its *prima facie* plausibility to a familiar requirement: we have to make theoretical room for the possibility that there can be alternative modes of presentation of the same object. This means, however, that there can be no logical connection between representations and determinate facts, where such a connection rests on a principle that distinguishes a priori between objectively contentful and contentless representations. Even if it really is necessary to use the concept of representation to explain the possibility of alternative modes of presentation, it still needs to be shown that there are least some representations that actually represent something. Adopting Stoic terminology: it needs to be shown that there have to be at least some cataleptic impressions (καταλήψεις). Without such a demonstration, the door to Cartesian scepticism and its paradoxes is wide open. For, as we have seen, these are motivated by the principle of aparallaxia, which states that we always find ourselves in a mental state that is phenomenally indistinguishable from another state that does not meet some relevant epistemic goal (in the context of justified belief acquisition: truth). According to this principle, firmly believing that a given mental state is a case of our being in the good case is of no help, as the problem just reiterates for the second-order mental state of firmly believing that a given mental state is an example of the good case. Expressed in a simple formula, the principle maintains that no mental state one can be in is such that one can know which state one is in simply by being in that very state.

On closer inspection, therefore, mental representationalism turns out to be inconsistent, because it implies the general Cartesian paradox. Following the general rules of engagement for attacking a paradox, we have no hope of dissolving a paradox if we mistake it for an argument whose conclusion we have to accept as true *faute de mieux* – i.e. because we think the argument consists of true premises which jointly imply its conclusion (see chapter 6 above). If one becomes convinced by Zeno's paradoxes that there is no movement but only eternally inert monistic being, this is no indication that one has attained some special insight. It merely suggests that there is as yet no sufficient solution to the paradox in view. Likewise, a legitimate demand to place on any epistemology is that it should avoid letting Cartesian scepticism turn into an argument to the effect that we are entitled to no substantial assumptions that go beyond mere experiential reports.

From the time of the Academic sceptic Carneades at the very latest, the Sceptics' favoured argumentative strategy against the Stoics consisted in deriving a variety of Cartesian scepticism from Stoic premises. In pursuing this strategy, Carneades too made use of the classical problem of alternative representations, which had plagued ancient theories of perception from the start.[32] Carneades' argument operates with the idea that, for every contentful representation with a relevant causal origin, we can always come up with an alternative empty representation that is phenomenally indistinguishable from its contentful counterpart. This is, as we have seen, just the meaning of the principle of aparallaxia. Every contentful perception could also, for example, be simulated through a perfect hallucination. It follows, however, that there could be a perfect hallucination that would be indistinguishable from cataleptic impressions. And this in turn shows that the cataleptic impression is unsuitable as a criterion of truth. It does not achieve what it purports to, namely, enabling us to decide between empty and contentful representations 'from within'.[33]

Because Sextus rejects all dogmatic claims, he has to show that there is ultimately no satisfactory criterion of truth. This does not mean he has to show that there *cannot* be a satisfactory criterion in principle; that would just amount to another instance of negative dogmatism, which Sextus of course cannot advocate without ceasing to be on a distinctly *sceptical* search for knowledge (ἐπιμονὴ ζητήσεως),[34] a search that can never terminate in a positive result. To be sure, this does not mean that Sextus has to refrain from putting forward arguments against specific versions of a criterion of truth. It merely means that he can offer no universal destructive argument, one that would be applicable to all and any versions whatsoever of a criterion of truth. This is why he is always careful to adapt the structure of his arguments to his respective opponent, which has the effect, to be sure, that the strength or weakness of Pyrrhonian arguments tends to depend upon which opponent is being targeted in any given case.[35]

The range of arguments that Sextus constructed against representationalism has since become canonical, and, in one form or another, they pervade the post-Cartesian literature on representationalism. In forming his arguments, he quite clearly exploits the external world problem that is thrown up by empiricist mental representationalism. As we have already discussed, this inserts a mediating world of representations, impressions or ideas between consciousness and the world. Thus, contrary to a common prejudice, this conception is no modern invention but can already be found in antiquity.[36] Consider, for example, the following passage from Sextus' discussion of the concept of representation, which merits being quoted at length:

> Next, even if we grant that appearances are apprehended, objects [τὰ πράγματα] cannot be judged in virtue of them; for the intellect, as they [the stoics – M. G.] say, sets itself upon external objects [τὰ ἐκτὸς ὑποκείμενα] and receives appearances not through itself but through the senses, and the senses do not apprehend external existing objects, but only – if anything – their own feelings [τὰ ἑαυτῶν πάθη]. An appearance, then, will actually be of the feeling of a sense – and that is different from an external existing object. For honey is not the same thing as my being affected sweetly, nor wormwood as my being affected bitterly: they are different.[37]

The major representationalist premise has it that representations mediate between us and objects in such a way that we can never in fact make judgements about objects that are not ultimately about our representations of objects. Typically, the representationalist regards this as harmless, given their subterfuge of positing a relation of resemblance (ὁμοίωσις) between representations and objects. However, that manoeuvre is blocked.[38] For if, by hypothesis, the isolated judging subject cannot step outside of her representations in order to compare them with the objects they supposedly represent, how is she supposed to know that such a relation really obtains?[39]

One possible way out of this predicament might be to *postulate* a resemblance relation on the model of an inference to the best explanation. Wilfrid Sellars called this attempt to explain how representations can so much as be representations *of anything* 'hypothetico-deductive realism'.[40] The basic problem with hypothetico-deductive realism is that it takes the *assumption* of an external world-in-itself of causally interacting *res extensae* and transforms it into a *hypothesis*. It is then easy enough to counter this hypothesis with a sceptical alternative, so as to draw attention to how no inference to the best explanation can possibly do justice to the natural certainty that was the original motivation for the inference.[41] Moreover, the best explanation *for us* is not necessarily the best explanation *in itself*, especially if we first introduced it as a falsifiable hypothesis. Even if the best explanation available to us were indeed to suppose a causally active world of objects, which bring about our representations qua affections of our sensibility, this does not necessarily entail that it delivers a description of what is really the case. What is more, it is not as though everybody will think it the best explanation, especially not those who, maybe out of religious conviction (think of certain brands of Hinduism), believe that the 'external' world is an elaborate simulacrum. It is simply not true that 'common sense' presupposes the existence of an external world so that we can, as it were, outsource justification to the *consensus gentium* of humanity as such. There is no overall metaphysical agreement on these issues. And, even if there were, how exactly would someone who defends the view that literally everybody believes that there is an external world affecting our sensory system know that literally everybody believes this? Clearly, we are not dealing with something like a highly general sociological hypothesis.

Suppose, though, that the 'external world' were a name for a hypothesis. Its plausibility could then be weakened or strengthened by arguments based on the supposition that only an inference to the best explanation (from appearances to reality) lets us justify the hypothesis to begin with. But this just means that we have made our allegedly naïve belief in the existence of an external world, the world to which our judgements refer, directly hostage to the Cartesian sceptic.

Furthermore, there is a simple probabilistic argument against hypothetico-deductive realism: this form of realism accepts that the probability of the external world hypothesis (EWH) increases through the accumulation of phenomenal data (i.e. through experience). Yet, unfortunately, the accumulation of phenomenal data increases the probability not only of EWH but of *every* sceptical hypothesis.

A simple example illustrates the point. Say that Gilles leaves his Parisian apartment one morning and ascertains that the ground is wet. With the help of an inference to the best explanation, he formulates the hypothesis that it rained during the night – after all, there are visible clouds in the sky, frequent rainfalls are to be expected at this time of year, and so on and so forth. Yet the same phenomenal situation is equally compatible with the hypothesis that the moisture on the ground is not the result of any natural phenomenon but, say, of a romantic comedy having being filmed on Gilles' street, which involved the creation of a suitably rainy backdrop. Since the objective probability of *both* hypotheses increases in light of the phenomenal data, those data do not grant Gilles an entitlement to assume that it rained and, therefore, that no artificial rainy scene has been shot in front of his house. Now, if our epistemic attitude to the world were comparable to Gilles' attitude towards the phenomenal data, together with his background knowledge of the overcast sky and the seasonal weather, etc., the Cartesian sceptic could place us in a very awkward situation indeed: everything that speaks in favour of assuming an extra-mental objective world (with respect to some background assumptions) equally speaks against it (with respect to some other background assumptions). So, if we opt for the strategy of hypothetico-deductive realism, we only land ourselves with a sceptical aporia: we let the 'natural' assumption that our representations represent an objective world shrink down to a mere hypothesis, to which it then takes only the slightest imaginative effort to concoct an untold number of alternatives. In short, we place ourselves wholly at the mercy of Cartesian scepticism.

At this stage, it is also important to point out that the seemingly natural attempt to distinguish *normal* hypotheses from *sceptical* hypotheses also fails. It is perfectly possible to formulate Cartesian scepticism deploying hypotheses of the 'normal' variety. There are, that is, normal sceptical hypotheses.[42] While it might well be conducive to psychological hygiene to grade the threat-levels posed by different sceptical hypotheses, it is epistemologically irrelevant. Once again, *The Truman Show* gives us an example. The protagonist of the film seems to live in small-town America and to lead a perfectly normal life. Yet, unbeknown to him, his entire life has been staged as part of a television programme. All the people he encounters are actors who move in and out of his world as the scene demands. He and he alone takes that world to be real. And, because everyone he meets is an actor, Truman too unwittingly becomes an actor, playing the roles he is continually assigned by those around him. Truman himself – whose name, of course, indicates that the film portrays the human condition, that of the true man, who always lives within given constraints – remains trapped within his illusion as the whole production coaxes him into believing that there is no reason to escape the confines of his limited world. After all, he would only need to travel to a neighbouring town in order to discover that that there actually is no neighbouring town in his narrowly circumscribed studio-reality. Yet, because the world Truman inhabits provides him with everything he could wish for, and because his wishes have been psychologically conditioned by the production team, who feed him all the information he possesses and could ever wish to possess, he does not escape from it of his own accord.

Of course, if somebody continually asked themselves whether they were really in a *Truman situation*, we would likely diagnose them with a severe form of paranoia. And somebody who, say, seriously wondered whether everyone around them was not in fact a cleverly disguised alien working for an extra-terrestrial TV channel would surely be suffering from some kind of psychological pathology. We should therefore see *The Truman Show* as a sceptical hypothesis, operating with common sceptical tools; it is weakly contingently evidence-transcendent, rather than evidence-transcendent in principle.[43] All the information that, in Truman's eyes, confirms his first-order theories about the world follows from the intrinsically best explanation that Truman lives in *The Truman Show* – though this explanation is the best explanation *for him* just as little as the assumption that we are brains in vats is the best explanation for us of our own informational state. As long as we have no access to any *objective* probability distinct from our *subjective* calculations of probability, invoking the probability of the external world hypothesis does not get us any further.

Part of the power of Cartesian sceptical scenarios lies precisely in how they put us in situations where we have to appeal to the distinction between subjective and objective probability but cannot do so without begging the question. Because we can never be in a position to exclude ordinary sceptical scenarios a priori, scenarios in which most or all of our beliefs would be false, the distinction is simply not available to be exploited in any non-question begging (and so minimally successful) anti-sceptical strategy. At the same time, Cartesian scepticism also teaches us that we have no good reasons for taking any old sceptical scenario to be true. If we take *one* sceptical scenario to be true without specifying any reason for our choice, we then have to take *all* sceptical scenarios to be true (see chapter 6 above). But, since some are mutually incompatible, we cannot in fact endorse all sceptical hypotheses at once. So, if Cartesian scepticism convinces us that the 'external world' is really the name of a hypothesis, we merely beg the question if we then try to escape from scepticism by arguing that the external world hypothesis is in better shape than all other hypotheses. We have to measure the quality of a hypothesis against the information-processing tools at our disposal, and, in light of scepticism, we cannot simply take these to be reliable without further ado.

By contrast, Sellars himself attempts to develop a scientific realism that forces us to accept the existence of an external world. On his theory, our sensibility stands in non-inferential – i.e. non-theoretical – contact with the world. Our conceptuality first comes into play when we *talk* about our sensibility. Accordingly, our causal contact to the world belongs to the natural order, which admits of causal-nomological description. Yet for us, in our descriptions of this order, it can only ever be thematised within the logical space of reasons.[44] What we describe thus diverges from our descriptions such that, according to Sellars, we find, on the one hand, a causally affected sensibility, which makes causal, non-inferential contact with the external world, while, on the other, we find ourselves within the space of reasons, a realm of inferences that form the objects of our normative commitments.

By pursuing this strategy, Sellars extends the difference between *causes* and *reasons* to a dualism of nature and mind. But he thereby faces the following problem: he has to explain how we can *know* about a nature that presents a purely natural order, a realm of 'is' rather than 'ought', even though our knowledge of this order qua knowledge already brings normativity into play and so presupposes its own fallibility. For, according to Sellars, our knowledge of the existence and operations of the natural order cannot be a priori; it can be acquired and extended only in and through the natural sciences.

One of the ways in which Sellars's metaphysics should be distinguished from German idealist ventures in *Naturphilosophie* is that the former does not understand the natural order as a necessary function of the logical space of reasons; it does not ascribe nature an explanatory role within a broader programme of rendering explicit the mind's theoretical self-awareness. Simply put, both Schelling and Hegel assume that nature is the other of the mind. But it exhibits a natural teleology towards mind in that it has to become transparent to itself in our awareness of the role it plays in explanations of the natural order.[45] The other of mind is thought by mind as *its* other; it therefore stands in a relation to mind, which in turn has to suppose such a relation in order to do justice to anything like its epistemic contact to the natural order. But *this* assumption is not itself natural. It is not something that nature can explicitly suggest to us. By definition, nature can produce only causes and effects and cannot give us any reasons – and so it cannot a fortiori give us any reasons why it cannot give us any reasons. The 'objective idealist' postulation of a nature that comes to grasp itself in the mental realm need not strike us as some piece of implausible speculation once we acknowledge that, as thinking beings, our access to sense is inferentially, and thus normatively, mediated. But this does not mean we have to infer that there is an external world 'out there', ready to be discovered.

Let us state a simple principle of intelligibility: our epistemology (in the case at hand: our self-awareness as potential knowers of elements in the natural order) has to be compatible with the fact that we can get reality right. In light of this principle, we can see that reductive naturalism about the natural order is itself a theory, not something thrust upon us by nature. If naturalism were, so to speak, a natural phenomenon, it could not have the right kind of justification. Therefore, it has to vindicate its status as a theory. Yet, insofar as it is a theory, it relies on the idea that nature does not reveal itself in the form of theorising. Hence theorising has (to say the least) a problematic status in the worldview of naturalism. Our epistemological access to nature is always theoretical, not natural. In other words, the distinction between nature and mind (theory) occurs within the medium of human mindedness. If this medium is essentially characterised by the game of giving and asking for reasons, the distinction between a natural in-itself and a mental for-itself is itself a fallible assumption, an assumption which presupposes a discursive operation that comes with its own contingent hinges. Since naturalism is a theoretically grounded assumption, not a natural kind, or any kind of entity that stands awaiting our discovery, the concept of nature is sense-dependent on normative concepts (such as truth and objectivity). As we have seen, this does not entail that the natural (natural objects) is reference-dependent on our beliefs about it. But we should nevertheless avoid representing nature as a closed totality – that is, as the 'world'. Naturalism should not be a *world*view, else we will end up identifying nature with our concept of nature.

If we seek out philosophical reasons for why scientific realism can triumph over Cartesian scepticism, we do so at the expense of our naïve orientation to the world. Formulated in good old dialectical jargon: we have to insist that immediacy is not itself immediate, but mediated. This insight corresponds to the common observation that the concept of the given is not itself given. Rather, the given is a theoretical construction, a postulate. For example, if we explain the given in terms of sense data, we face the familiar dilemma that either we have to be able to discover sense data through infallible introspection, or we have to argue that they can be given even though they are themselves theoretical constructions.[46] Likewise, reductive naturalism is not itself a natural event but a product of reflection and, as such, should be rendered theoretically transparent. The alternative is the threat of a 'non-transparent objectivism',[47] which hypostasises its own reflective operation and thus puts the ontological fiction of a totality of purely causal objects in the place of its totalising abstraction. Reductive naturalism typically mistakes itself for reality and, therefore, has the ontological status of a fiction gone wild.

Another of the putative escape routes that Sextus attacks extensively attempts instead to enrich the concept of representation. Specifically, it argues that representations can be interpreted as reliable indicative signs (ἐνδεικτικὰ σημεῖα) of an object-world.[48] Yet the very *raison d'être* of the concept of representation is to allow room for the possibility of deception and thus for the possibility of genuine differences of opinion. This means, in turn, that not all representations can possess objective reality. We have to find a way to distinguish between *representational success* on the one hand and *representational purport* on the other.[49] But since the concept of representation would lose its purpose if *all* representations were successful, there must be both correct and incorrect representations, and we have to be able to make a principled distinction between these two classes if we are not to make ourselves vulnerable to Cartesian scepticism all over again. Yet how can we make the distinction between contentful and empty representations without stepping outside of our representations and comparing them with their purported objects? How can we be justified in asserting that representations can be indicators of things in themselves if, by hypothesis, there can be no immediate access to things in themselves?

Sextus gives this problem the following structure:[50] if the representation is really an indication of the represented, and the represented is supposed to obtain independently of the representation ('in itself'), we confront the aporia of having to assume either (1) that we can know from the indicative sign alone that it indicates something real, or (2) that we have to be able to apprehend the indicative sign together with the indicated object, or (3) that we can apprehend the indicative sign only after we apprehend the indicated object. Now, 'indication' is a relational concept; an indicative sign is always an indicator of that which it indicates. There cannot be an indication that does not indicate anything. Therefore: (1) if we can know from the indicative sign alone that it indicates something, we can then grasp the indicator independently of or prior to the indicated in order to infer the latter from the former. But this is impossible: we can apprehend the indicative sign as an indicator only if at the same time we apprehend what it indicates. (2) If we grasp the indicative sign and the indicated at the same time, it is of no use relying on the indicator to *find* a route of access to the indicated. And (3) is in any case absurd: we do not want to grasp the indicative sign through the indicated. In this way, Sextus shows how it is senseless to conceive of the world of representation as an indication of a representable world, at least without ascribing to ourselves the capacity to be in epistemic contact with the representable world regardless of any specific indicative sign. If we are able to mentally 'indicate' the world, the world in itself already has to be apprehended, and this was the very possibility that was supposed to be excluded. Indeed, the original reason for introducing representations was to maintain a divergence between representation and representable so as to explain the possibility of error. But such an explanation of the possibility of error presupposes that the theorist has sidestepped the problem and gained error-free access to the representable world as such.

If it is supposed to be possible, without having recourse to some particular representation, to draw a distinction between objectively empty and objectively contentful representations, it should be possible to talk about things in themselves without mediating representations at all. And this contradicts the original representationalist assumption. But if we decide instead to take a particular, supposedly contentful representation and use it as a measure, we face the following dilemma: either we presuppose that the selected representation is contentful, in which case we simply beg the question, or again we have to evaluate the supposedly paradigmatic representation in advance, without recourse to representations, and so are still no closer to reaching firm epistemic ground. It thus becomes increasingly hard to avoid the obvious conclusion: it is impossible to find our way out of the realm of representations with the help of representations alone.

We might try to exploit the resources of rational reflection in order, for example, to demonstrate that there have to be at least some contentful representations in order for there to be representations at all. But the resulting options are equally unsatisfying. One is to presuppose that rational thought has access to things in themselves from which sensibility is debarred. Alternatively, one might aim for a representationalist theory that tries to establish a priori arguments for the desired conclusion. Taking this route would once again reduce our perfectly functional, everyday notion of representation to a *theory* of representation, to which it would again require little invention to come up with sceptical alternatives. In short, the supposed immediacy of sense certainty dissolves either into the quite different certainty characteristic of rational thought or into a theory of representation that is not only vulnerable to Cartesian scepticism but has already implicitly succumbed to it in the very process of articulating itself as a theory.

To prove that there can be representations at all only provided at least some, or even most, are contentful, there remains of course the option of constructing transcendental arguments. This is the route Kant took in his Refutation of Idealism in the *Critique of Pure Reason* and its governing analysis of the conditions of objectivity of our representations (see chapters 1–4 above). Here, Kant investigates not merely how our representations are *de facto* contentful but how they can be contentful at all.[51] Unlike Descartes, Kant is concerned not with the truth of representations but with something more fundamental: their truth-*aptness*. His *primary* concern is thus no longer the question of how we can guarantee a priori that a sufficiently large set of our beliefs about the world are *de facto true*. Rather, he addresses himself first and foremost to the question of how we might guarantee that our beliefs as such are *de jure* truth-*apt*, in the sense that they can so much as refer to objects *as if* they were independent of acts of reference. The Kantian problematic therefore investigates the conditions of the truth-*aptness* of our representations, how representations, and so beliefs quite generally, can be directed at something potentially independent of a given representation or belief.

The notion that, as a thinking being, he can refer to himself as a thinking being is not one that seems to present Descartes with any kind of difficulty. According to the *cogito*, the self-reference of thought even guarantees its truth. This operation presupposes that there is an epistemic asymmetry between beliefs about the world and beliefs about our mental states. If I cannot know without further ado whether the representation of an object – a table, say – is really the representation of the object it presents to me, I can nevertheless be quite certain that I have a representation that *presents* me with a table, where this presentation does not guarantee that it is a *re*-presentation. Yet how do things stand with the representation of the *thinker*? If the thinker is a substance, as Descartes assumes, how can I be so sure that I refer to a thinking substance whenever I intend to do so? For, as far as its existence is concerned, this thinking substance can quite obviously depend just as little on anybody's referring to it *here and now* as extended substance, the table for example, can depend in any innocent sense on somebody's referring to it. If everything that thinks is a substance, then our reference to everything that thinks, ourselves included, is just as fallible as our reference to any other object. Kant brings out this very problem when he supposes that our beliefs about ourselves as thinking substances refer to appearances and not things in themselves. For, qua intentional correlate of an act of reference, we are not given to ourselves in a way that somehow differs from epistemically and metaphysically less suspicious objects, such as tables, trees and rivers.[52]

In this way, Kant problematises both the unity of the representing subject and the unity of an intentional correlate, of a stable mental representation as such. This makes him the first to conjure the spectre of semantic nihilism, of the possible impossibility of meaning and thus of 'relation to the object'.[53] *Cartesian scepticism* merely asks whether there are *ontological* correlates independently of there being intentional correlates. It asks how we can know whether so much is the case, whether we are entitled to make such an assumption. It thus lays out a dialectical terrain that lies within the ambit of the question: are there representable objects in the external world that exist independently of our representing them? *Kantian scepticism*, by contrast, problematises the assumption implicit in the Cartesian question: namely, that, while there are certainly doubts we should take seriously, we can in any case be certain of having a stable sematic relation to our own representations – that is, to stable *intentional* correlates. Kant, however, quite rightly notes that epistemic reference to objects of the internal world, to states of the subject, is no more or less problematic than epistemic reference to external objects.

Kant's radicalised sceptical problem therefore highlights the issue of how we can ensure that the representations we think we have are, as such, '*my* representations' at all.[54] In other words, how can I ensure (contrary to Hume's bundle theory) that I do not fall victim to a kind of semantic schizophrenia and would not have 'as multicolored, diverse a self as I have representations of which I am conscious'?[55] We cannot engage in intentional reference to ourselves as thinking entities without thereby establishing a fallible mode of access to the targets of that reference. If, as Descartes supposes, the unity of the thinking self were substantial (that is, the unity of an object with a distinct epistemological and ontological character), our representations would then together 'belong to no experience, and would consequently be without an object, and would be nothing but a blind play of representations, i.e., *less than a dream*.'[56] Kant therefore takes the epistemic boundary that Descartes had drawn on the basis of a supposed mind–world asymmetry and internalises it. For the asymmetry in fact follows from a broadly fallibilist account of our epistemic intentions rather than from anything intrinsic to the mind–world relation. Insofar as we refer to an intentional correlate by way of an epistemic intention, we have no truth-guaranteeing reasons to suppose a corresponding *ontological* correlate, where this is a substance that acts as a truth-maker for the intention, which is in turn fixed by its semantics. And since, by hypothesis, the same considerations apply equally to all projects in the realm of self-knowledge, the upshot of this line of thought is that, by assuming a thinking substance, we undermine the supposed self-certainty of thinking. Kant summarises this problem of self-reflection in a famous passage:

> Through this I, or He, or It (the thing), which thinks, nothing further is represented than a transcendental subject of thoughts = x, which is recognized only through the thoughts that are its predicates, and about which, in abstraction, we can never have even the least concept; because of which we therefore turn in a constant circle, since we must always already avail ourselves of the representation of it at all times in order to judge anything about it.[57]

We are here in the eye of the Kantian storm. Kant turns the Cartesian problematic against Descartes and applies it to the supposedly infallible self-reference of thinking substance. Recognising that Cartesian scepticism functions differently from how Descartes himself envisaged, he contradicts Descartes' own theoretical diagnosis of the Cartesian problematic by applying the epistemic asymmetry between mind and world to the mind, all the while drawing our attention to how the mind, as long as it can refer to itself, surely has to belong to the world. Cartesian dualism will not solve the problem, because it merely insists that the world consists of both thinking and extended substance. But the problem of Cartesian scepticism is how we can guarantee that we in fact refer to the world in the first place. If the subject – or whatever he, she or it that refers to the world really is – itself belongs to the world qua substance, the epistemic asymmetry leads into the cul-de-sac of semantic nihilism. We can no longer be sure that there is any reference to any object whatsoever: *reference to objects itself becomes the object of a knowledge claim that, being a knowledge* claim, *cannot guarantee its own truth* a priori.

Kant develops a theory of self-consciousness according to which self-consciousness as synthetic unity always presupposes a difference between what is *given* and what is *thought*.[58] The multiplicity of analytic unities is encompassed by a synthetic unity, whereby the former could be nothing at all without the latter. On this basis, Kant goes on to infer that self-consciousness is possible only under the presupposition of an external world. The fact that our reference to individuals must, in principle, be truth-apt guarantees the truth of sufficiently many true judgements about the world.

In the same spirit, but without getting entangled in fully transcendental structures, one might deploy Davidson's critique of (Kantian) form–content dualism in order to develop an argument that rules out the possibility that all or most of our representations are empty. Davidson's aim is to articulate an account of truth and meaning that makes representationalism largely superfluous. Yet one of his basic presuppositions is that there is a causal relation between the world and (some of) our beliefs; he too faces up to the Cartesian sceptical problem and asks how it is possible to ensure that most of our beliefs are true, even though we cannot acquire guarantees of their truth by stepping outside of them and comparing them with the world. However, instead of this leading him to a version of representationalism, Davidson instead develops a coherence theory of truth and knowledge.[59]

Davidson wants to overcome Cartesian scepticism on the basis of an argument that our best attempts to translate a completely foreign language into our own cannot fail entirely. He intends his argument to rule out the picture of a pure, uninterpreted world on the one side of a sheer 'boundary' [*schlechthin scheidende Grenze*], with a series of conceptual interpretive efforts on the other, where these have the job of first bringing structure to the bare worldly matter. Davidson begins with the consideration that, if we presuppose any such *form–content dualism*, we have to concede that two languages might be, in principle, mutually untranslatable. According to a thesis prominently advocated by Benjamin Lee Whorf, languages present us with conceptual patterns that serve to structure purely given material into a world.[60] Since, on the Whorfian thesis of *linguistic relativism*, the world appears utterly different to speakers of widely varying languages, it is quite possible that they could not understand one another at all; none of the speakers of one language could bring the words of speakers of another into any meaningful connection with their world. Suppose that worldly structures were only projections of different conceptual patterns and that, in an extreme case, two languages really varied so greatly that they provided utterly different conceptual patterns; the danger would arise that speakers could find no way whatsoever of translating one language into another; no expression of one language would refer to an object in the other, because the two languages presumably shared no expressions.

Davidson's argument operates with two parameters: (1) form–content dualism and (2) the resulting situation of radical translation; (2) follows from (1) because form–content dualism in principle allows for the possibility of utterly divergent forms. Because a content will be presented completely differently depending upon which of the forms is imposed on it, a translation from beliefs developed on the presupposition of form F into beliefs developed on the presupposition of form F* cannot rely on the assumption that belief systems F and F* refer to the same objects. Hence the translation of F-beliefs into F*-beliefs is radical; one cannot be sure that F-beliefs and F*-beliefs have anything in common.

However, Davidson remarks, in order to find a practicable strategy for establishing mutual understanding between F-beliefs and F*-beliefs, every competent speaker of F* has to assume that most F-beliefs are true. Otherwise, it would be impossible to formulate any workable hypothesis as to what somebody to whom we ascribe F-beliefs means by her words, gestures and actions (i.e. by her expressions). 'Charity is forced on us; whether we like it or not, if we want to understand others, we must count them right in most matters.'[61] Suppose a translator T finds herself in a situation in which she had to translate the expressions of a speaker S. S produces a sound sequence that, to the best of T's knowledge, expresses the concepts X, Y and Z. If S uses X, Y and Z in order to express beliefs completely different to those that could be expressed according to a relevant dictionary, it would be quite impossible for T to understand S's utterances. T has to work on the assumption that S is a sufficiently competent speaker of her language and possesses a sufficiently large set of true beliefs which, moreover, she is able to articulate in linguistically well-formed expressions. Otherwise, T would have to formulate hypotheses of the form that, with her expression 'XYZ', S could be expressing X^*YZ or XY^*Z or XYZ^* or X^*Y^*Z, and so on *in indefinitum*, instead of just XYZ. Therefore, to begin with, the expression 'XYZ' would have no recognisable assertoric content at all. It would be incomprehensible since, in essence, it could mean everything and nothing. In order to reduce the indefinitely large set of interpretive possibilities to a manageable selection, T would have to suppose that, when S offers an explanatory expression of the form 'By X I understand P, by Y Q, and by Z R', she does not use P, Q or R falsely or in a radically different manner; and T could only explain this possibility by assuming that she has ascribed false beliefs to S, once again necessitating a further reduction of interpretive possibilities to a plausible set of candidates, etc. At some point, T has to ascribe enough true beliefs to S if she is to have any hope of understanding her.[62]

The same considerations apply to an even greater degree under the conditions of radical interpretation. Famously, the Quinean foreigner could be responding to rabbit ghosts when she utters 'gavagai' – entities that do not even exist according to the belief system of the translator's own community. Who knows what the native speaker really sees when she points in the direction of an event that we, in virtue of the form of our beliefs, interpret as a rabbit hopping by?[63] If understanding is to be possible at all, we have to assume at some point or other that the person to be understood possesses true beliefs. This by no means rules out that we can understand someone who expresses false beliefs, as long as both parties refer to a common world. In Wittgenstein's words: 'In order to make a mistake, a man must already judge in conformity with mankind.'[64]

Transferring Davidson's argument to our own problematic, one might say that the representations of other subjects (though Davidson admittedly speaks of beliefs instead of representations in the problematic sense of mental states) must be contentful. If we want to interpret their actions, we have to adopt the same principle of charity and assume that they do not continually act on the basis of hallucinations, illusions or completely false beliefs. Indeed, if we are to take them seriously as agents, we have to assume that most of their representations are veridical. Lacking any form of immediate access to the world, everyone acts according to their representations. Every hypothesis about why someone acted as they did is therefore at the same time a hypothesis about their representations and their relation to the world. In brief, in order to understand another subject as a being that has representations and acts on the basis of them, we have to assume that some of their representations are contentful.

Davidson accepts that we fall victim to scepticism as soon as we assume that the only way we can test the truth of our beliefs is by comparing them with the world in itself, where the world in itself is located outside the totality of our beliefs. His anti-sceptical strategy thus consists in showing how the coherence of our system of beliefs implies that most of our beliefs are true.[65] In other words, Davidson attempts to construct a *transcendental argument* with the quite classical intention of showing that we could have no beliefs at all unless some or even most of them were true. 'Truth' must be so understood that no belief could be true if we found ourselves in a sceptical scenario. Translated back into the terms of our discussion, this means that at least some of our representations must be contentful if there are to be representations at all. However distant Davidson may be from Kant, the two men share the general anti-sceptical strategy of transcendental arguments, arguments that are supposed to show that we do in fact know a great deal, even if we grant the assumption that we cannot step outside of our beliefs.

In his discussion of the Stoic concept of representation, Sextus does not explicitly rule out arguments of this variety. But this is simply because the Stoics' radical empiricism prevented them from choosing this particular argumentative route. Hence Sextus did not have to meet them on transcendental terrain. Besides, the Stoics do not advocate merely an empirical realism of the Kantian variety, which would be compatible with a transcendental idealism; they embrace a form of metaphysical realism – that is, a realistic ontology according to which there really are things in themselves, with which we stand in causal interaction. The Stoics do not assume that 'things in themselves' have to be mere limiting concepts, ineliminable parameters in explanations of the objective reality of our representations. If one combines empiricism with a realist ontology – i.e. with a metaphysical realism – it is not enough simply to count the world as a necessary presupposition of thought: there must be a causal relation that obtains between things in themselves and our representations, and this relation cannot itself be merely represented. The causal relation between representation and things in themselves should not be degraded to the status of a mere hypothesis, at pain, as we have seen, of becoming entangled in radical Cartesian scepticism (and ultimately in semantic nihilism).

Yet transcendental arguments cannot hold the danger of Cartesian scepticism at bay as long as they concede to the sceptic that the world in itself could, in principle, be out of reach – however much such arguments might be at pains to show how this need really entail no epistemological drawback. Davidson is essentially in agreement with Kant that there is something that produces representations in us by causally affecting our sensibility, where the resultant representations cannot be identical with what they represent via those causal connections. The representation of a tree is the effect of a tree in combination with corresponding environmental factors on the object side and corresponding discriminatory abilities (i.e. conceptual capacities) on the subject side. And since the representation of a tree is not itself a tree, there has to be something that is causally independent of the representation. Were we not in causal contact with our environment, we would lack many of our empirical concepts, for their content frequently depends on what they refer to and on what is causally responsible for our possessing them in the first place. If we appreciate this fact, a more self-conscious investigation of the world can lead us to an acknowledgement of how we by no means always enjoy a full understanding of our own concepts: their content depends on how the world is, and how it is can very often remain concealed from us over long periods of time indeed. Famous examples in discussion of semantic externalism are natural kinds such as 'water', the chemical structure of which (according to Putnam at least) belongs to their concept, even though we can be competent users of the concept 'water' without always already knowing what that structure is.

However, we could deploy this semantic consideration as part of an anti-sceptical strategy only if it were incompatible with the possibility that we could find ourselves in a sceptical scenario. Anti-sceptical strategies that operate with transcendental arguments always come with a general shortcoming: at best, they show that it is necessary to *assume* the truth of a certain belief or class of beliefs – what Barry Stroud calls the 'privileged class'.[66] This falls short of proving that some candidate p for a relevant belief or class of beliefs is actually true. It does follow from such arguments that we are entitled to assume that p is true and, consequently, that we are entitled to assume that p. But, however good our justification for p, there is always room for the sceptic to construct scenarios in which the assumption that p would still be necessary for us, even though p would be false.[67] As is so often the case, the sceptic here makes use of a candidate member of the privileged class herself – here, the belief that holding-true and truth must potentially diverge in every case in which there can be anything like a claim to objectivity (what we have been calling the contrast of objectivity). The sceptic thus appeals to this potential divergence, the contrast without which there cannot be any holding-*true*, and applies it to transcendental arguments.

In other words, the sceptic fights transcendental arguments with their own weapons: after all, showing that we can take something to be true only if we understand what it means for something to be true is itself an element in a transcendental argument. To understand what it means for something to be true entails understanding that we can hold it to be true, and that we can hold something to be true that is not true, else truth and holding-true would not in general be (potentially) divergent. Faced with transcendental arguments, then, the sceptic will succeed in her destructive enterprise simply by appealing to the contrast of objectivity. That is, she will succeed as long as she can continue to invoke sceptical scenarios that are quite compatible with the possibility of our forming transcendental arguments to demonstrate that we have a privileged class of beliefs that we have to hold true, without it necessarily following that they are true. If there is to be knowledge, and thus cases where truth and holding-true coincide, truth and holding-true must at least potentially diverge. Otherwise, nothing true could be held to be so. However the structure of our understanding might be constituted, nothing *more* can ever follow from that structure than an assurance that the conditions of our understanding are indeed fulfilled. But it does not necessarily follow from this assurance that the objects we understand are constituted as we suppose. So much would follow given a prior acceptance of reference dependence, but transcendental arguments need not – and usually do not mean to – entertain any such commitment.[68]

Thus, even if a causal relation between our representations and a world in itself is a necessary assumption – indeed, an assumption we can justify without recourse to experience – the Cartesian sceptic can still respond that this necessary assumption is thoroughly compatible with the possibility that we are, say, brains in a vat. This represents an empirical possibility that cannot be excluded by any a priori argument. Brains in a vat could be the kinds of beings who can have coherent beliefs only because they have to presuppose a causal relation between their beliefs and the world. Besides, beings like us could be hooked up with each other in such a way that they could communicate, or at least seem to communicate: the events that play out in the representation world of brain A could, say, be attuned to the events in the representational world of brain B in such a way that, whenever A has the representation of communicating with B, B always has a representation of A's communicating with him.[69] Such a Leibnizian version of a 'brain in a vat' scenario meets the transcendental structure required by Kantian and Davidsonian principles of communication and interpretation and yet clearly amounts to a sceptical hypothesis. Ultimately, transcendental arguments are anodyne in sceptical contexts.

Philosophical analysis, in the form of a self-conscious thematisation of the conditions of possibility of communication, might well demonstrate the necessity of *assuming* a common objective world. Yet it does not follow, at least without begging the question against the sceptic, that there is a common objective world that is in any sense external either to communication or to our implicit or explicit assumptions about communication and its possibility. From the fact that, as Habermas puts it, language users have to 'formally presuppose one and the same world',[70] it does not necessarily follow that the world is as it is according to our communicative suppositions. Thus, semantic externalism either simply presupposes the negation of sceptical scenarios or, to the extent to which it reckons with a potential gulf between internal and external worlds, invites us to construct new sceptical scenarios against our honest anti-sceptical intentions. Davidson's analysis of the triangulation between speaker A, objective world, and speaker B does not therefore offer any immediate clues for developing a successful anti-sceptical strategy. Indeed, his thesis that intersubjectivity is the source of objectivity even facilitates the construction of sceptical scenarios: it raises the prospect that the phenomenology of communication is fully compatible with the complete absence of an actual world beyond the necessary communication-theoretical *assumption* of an actual world.[71]

It should hardly be surprising that we can construct sceptical scenarios in which communication is perfectly possible. Famously, Leibniz even used his *clock analogy* to recommend such a model as the best answer to Cartesian substance dualism, all the while developing a variant of Cartesian scepticism that he regarded as perfectly tenable. On his model, all representational worlds (monads) are synchronised with one another like clocks whose strokes are programmed by their inner mechanism. Leibniz called this *pre-established harmony*.[72] When I perceive a speaker A, there is no external object (speaker A) that affects my sensibility, merely a further representation in the overall series of my representations. Now, the representations of all representers (all monads) are so programmed that each represents both that about which they are communicating and the representer with whom they take themselves to be communicating. A conversation between two people about a blue cube, for example, is no public course of events in a public world; rather, it consists of two utterly separate courses of events, whereby the representation of a blue cube, of a corresponding situation, and of another speaker all arise within the series of representations of each speaker. In the entire scenario there is no real influence either between the speakers or between the speakers and a world in itself. Since monads have no windows, they cannot process any information communicated externally (be it from the world or from other monads).[73] Monads themselves produce the information they process, and they do so in such a way that, under normal operating conditions, they are unaware *that* they produce it.

My aim is hardly to proselytise on behalf of the monadological hypothesis of pre-established harmony; I simply want to point out how it can be (mis)used as a sceptical scenario in order to expose the weakness of transcendental arguments within anti-sceptical strategies. If, that is, the causal relation between our beliefs and the world were only a further belief (albeit one necessarily shared by everyone else), we could never in fact escape from the web of our beliefs. The sceptic could confront us with a devastatingly large set of sceptical scenarios that are evidence-transcendent in principle, delivering us yet again entirely to the mercy of Cartesian scepticism. Transcendental arguments against Cartesian scepticism are thus dangerously close to the situation in which the balance on which impressions are weighed is merely the impression of a balance.[74] Their aim is to show that the idea of the world's having a causal influence on our representations is a necessary assumption, which, for its part, has to be a representation – for, by hypothesis, we cannot climb out of our representations. But this does not help us evade further mutations of Cartesian scepticism, such as Leibnizian monadology.

Of course, a form of Berkeleyan idealism always remains an option. This entails combining empiricism instead with an *idealist* ontology, for which there are no *objects* that affect our sensibility, but only God, where God may not be understood as an 'object' in any ordinary sense. Yet this ultimately sceptical position can seem to be a plausible theory of representation in the first place only if we have given up on the original philosophical problem. The position avoids explaining how, on the one hand, as finite epistemic beings we are fated to have to process information that, on the other hand, is given by a world in itself with which we enter into causal relations. Yet, if we do decide to avoid the problem of the relation between mind and nature by adverting to an alternative information source, we clearly incur a quite formidable explanatory burden – though it remains to be seen whether such a project can be carried out.[75]

If, by contrast, we introduce Cartesian scepticism as a *paradox*, and not as an *argument* for motivating revisionary beliefs (as I have recommended in chapter 6), a different possibility comes into view. We can come to see that a *sceptical* epistemology, in the sense of a theory of epistemology, does not constitute a serious alternative. We might compare such an epistemology with Zeno's answer to his own paradox, when he recommended eliminating the word 'movement' from ontology and accepting an ultimate homogeneous reality, without change and difference, in which Achilles really cannot overtake the tortoise. Modern subjective idealism's assertion that there is no *res extensa* can be compared with Zeno's assertion that there is no movement. Both result from taking a paradox for an argument.

Wittgenstein's diametrical opposite of solipsism – i.e. his contextualism – points to a way out of the problems of a sceptical theory of representation: it reconstructs conceptual (propositional) content as assertoric content and shows how the latter depends on actually existing assertability conditions. But assertability conditions presuppose the stability of a discourse, and such stability can be established and maintained only when participants within a discourse make *particular*, *determinate* moves. These moves are always already public and, as such, are made in an interpersonally shared, common world. We do not, therefore, need to step outside of our representations and beliefs. Nor need we answer the question whether we, as individuals, are stranded in isolation with our mental states. Our mental interior is defined through its contrast with the community: *the private/public distinction is public, not private; and it is not drawn by representing subjects but is a matter of communal negotiation.* Yet, if we want to avoid once again letting the community slip from our grasp, we cannot simply allow truth to dissolve into justification and admit an incommensurable plurality of discourses. We must surely avoid a situation, that is, in which we cannot be certain whether our apparently shared meanings do in fact have so much as a shared foundation – in other words, whether there actually is public reference to the world. It is to secure such reference that Wittgenstein introduces *second nature*. Under the conditions of contextualism, however, this ploy leads to theoretical difficulties that Wittgenstein did not expressly thematise. It is to these that we must now turn.

14

The Failure of
Liberal Naturalism's Metatheory

Throughout the course of the second part of this study, it should have become increasingly clear that, if contextualism cannot ensure that the normativity of discourse – and thus all discursively communicable knowledge – is in a position to register facts, it loses any worldly anchorage. The heart of the difficulty lies in the attempt to formulate the sense dependence of objectivity and subjectivity in such a way that we do not slide into a thesis positing the reference dependence of objects on subjects. Wittgenstein is occasionally accused of endorsing a version of linguistic idealism. The allegation is that the world fully disappears from his picture of discursive practices (forms of life), with these practices threatening to reduce to what McDowell famously calls a 'frictionless spinning in the void'.[1] We find statements pointing in this direction especially in the *Philosophical Grammar*, where 'language remains self-contained and autonomous'.[2] Wittgenstein is very much aware of the danger of solipsism, and he tries to avert it by demonstrating how discourse is socially anchored. All discourses presuppose communal action, which would not exist were there no *persons* (that is, at the very least, thinking and acting subjects in space and time) external to the supposedly solipsistic I. Yet, as we have seen, in confronting solipsism with this kind of deterrent, he runs the risk of establishing a *solipsism of the 'we'* insofar as he absolutises the social-semantic dimension of discourse. The worry is that truth then ultimately reduces to *communal* holdings-true.[3] Just like Sextus, Wittgenstein 'solves' this problem via a recourse to 'human nature'.[4] Human nature reveals itself in how human beings can achieve mutual understanding even under the conditions of radical interpretation; there are 'very general facts of nature'[5] which make such communication possible.

Yet from the metatheoretical standpoint, this retreat to nature is problematic. Nature itself is only a theoretical construct of a contextualism that seeks a foundation for its plurality of contexts in a unifying principle – nature – in order to avert the danger of their incommensurability. The natural foundation of all discourses is meant to guarantee language's relation to the world because language is itself a natural product: 'I want to regard man here as an animal; as a primitive being to which one grants instinct but not ratiocination. As a creature in a primitive state. Any logic good enough for a primitive means of communication needs no apology from us. Language did not emerge from some kind of ratiocination.'[6] So as not to drift into a discourse-theoretical relativism, Wittgenstein and Sextus, just like Hume, think that one can place one's trust in nature, which blindly, without reflection, takes care that everything runs its usual course regardless of any metatheoretical uncertainty. In Hume's famous words:

> Nature, by an absolute and uncontrollable necessity has determin'd us to judge as well as to breathe and feel, nor can we any more forbear viewing certain objects in a stronger and fuller light, upon account of their customary connexion with a present impression, than we can hinder ourselves from thinking as long as we are awake, or seeing the surrounding bodies, when we turn our eyes to them in broad sunshine.[7]

Wittgenstein quite clearly avoids developing a *theory* of nature and life. The need to renounce theory is a result of his theory construction, which *shows* that the 'stream of life'[8] cannot be brought to rest through explicit rules. For Wittgenstein, too, the finitude of discourse – the fact that its relative stability presupposes historically unstable (i.e. contingent) hinges generated purely via operations of selection – occurs within the given framework of nature – indeed, within a 'natural history of mankind'.[9] This natural history is not something that any discourse could investigate through theoretically untainted observation. Nature is and remains the blind spot of all observation, the ultimate unifying horizon that Luhmann calls simply 'world'.[10] Wittgenstein expresses this idea by saying that '[i]t is always by favour of Nature that one knows something.'[11] That is to say: a language game, and thus any discourse in which we can raise knowledge claims, is possible only 'if one trusts something',[12] which Wittgenstein distinguishes *expressis verbis* from the certainty of *being able* to 'trust something'.[13] What the language game relies upon is nothing upon which one might demonstrably rely: the threat of a regress[14] means that we have no complete access to the presuppositions of the language game, not without stepping outside of it and generating a new language game with its own presuppositions, and so on *ad infinitum*.

Wittgenstein (unlike Luhmann) does not reflect on the theory conditions of *this* observation in turn. Doing so would lead him to suppose a further blind spot, which, by definition, he cannot observe within the context of his theory. The liberal naturalism that introduces nature as an unknowable yet stability-guaranteeing ground of unity pushes against the boundaries of its own theory. It claims to know more than it really can. And this accounts for the highly cautious expressions with which Wittgenstein speaks about life and nature and explains why he avoids placing his hidden naturalism at the centre of his theory construction.

Liberal naturalism allows for a second nature that finds articulation in the form of a natural history of mankind. On account of its motivation, marked as it is by its path through contextualism, it cannot have any *direct* access to nature – that is, in the sense of a first-order theory. Liberal naturalism is not a piece of natural-scientific, first-hand empirical knowledge. Nature, the habitual, the everyday and second nature – liberal naturalism's favourite defence mechanisms against scepticism – show up only *ex negativo* as in themselves unknowable guarantees of discursive stability. There is no possibility of acquitting contextualism from the charge of relativism without postulating a unity for all contexts: nature or the world. Yet this unity exceeds our theoretical reach since, by hypothesis, we could thematise it only *within* a context. The theme of unity must be bound to the conditions of *a* context, conditions which are not absolute, because they themselves generate a blind spot, namely, their own specific presuppositional structure. Reconstructing nature or the world is a discourse-internal affair. As a result, given the contextualist motivations in play, nature shrinks to an assumption, to a regulative idea of the metatheory.[15] This operation explains liberal naturalism's apparent advantage over its more metaphysical cousins. But, at the same time, it significantly weakens its case.

One result of this line of thought is the elimination of any strict separation between first-order observations and their metatheory. First-order theories turn out to be constructions of the metatheory insofar as they operate under suitably determinate conditions within a stage-setting they cannot fully thematise. The discourse that thematises first-order theories – i.e. the metatheory – is itself governed by operating conditions. As such, it can only ever state what appears to first-order discourses in a way that is itself subject to the qualification of revisability. *The metatheory is itself finite.* There is, of course, a multiplicity of metatheories, but all share this same fate.

The supposedly secure distinction between the world and our access to it therefore disappears, for the sense dependence of objectivity and subjectivity is itself relative to a context and no longer simply a given fact. The concept of sense dependence turns out to be reference-dependent on the metatheory, and so too, therefore, does the insight into the independence of the world in itself, the world we describe in all true judgements. And insofar as the metatheory grasps its own finitude – having at its disposal no theoretical tool that would grant it an exemption from the finite conditions of discourse – it transpires that the world is reference-dependent on the metatheory. The insight into the world's mere sense dependence is valid *for* the metatheory, which thus describes the operating conditions of all first-order theories that have the world as their object. But there is therefore no way to exclude the possibility that the world is reference-dependent on subjectivity, where this now means: relative to a context – and so, in this case, relative to the context of a specific metaphysics, the metaphysics of naturalism. Nature, the world, and even life – all seem to vanish into the theory.

This result, however ironically, is a consequence of the theory's motivating contextualism. And it now seems that the absolute idealism we have thus far been seeking to avoid suddenly threatens to find a promising point of entry. Surprisingly, then, metaphysical naturalism and absolute idealism converge at this deeper motivational level, in that they both draw on the reference dependence of the world as a totality within the metatheory. However, this can only be bad news for metaphysical naturalism, which at this point of the dialectic is well advised to retreat to the weaker standpoint of liberal naturalism if it wants to avoid issuing in substantial metaphysical knowledge claims about reality as a whole.

Contextualism originally seems to follow from the justification conditions of knowledge. This is not something we can posit absolutely, however, as truth must be potentially distinct from justification; we do not want contextualism to define truth as communal holding-true, at pain of reviving the private language problem at the communal level. In order to avoid a solipsism of the 'we', truth and discourse must remain distinct, a realisation that moves liberal naturalism to place truth in nature: it determines the social-semantic dimension within which truth and justification are distinguished as a configuration of nature and life. Yet, as Hogrebe notes, there is a category error at work here. In place of a reflective consideration of the as yet categorially indeterminate 'dimension of distinctions', we have a determination of that very dimension: liberal naturalism wants to make it available as nature in order to capture the potential instability of different discursive presuppositional structures within a unifying theory.[16]

The conjunction of contextualism and naturalism is untenable. Talk of human nature, the 'stream of life', and so on, cannot be cashed out under contextualist conditions. Their invocation turns out to be itself another context-relative observation, which cannot claim to transcend conceptual relativity and reach out to the world's ultimate unity. Unlike Wittgenstein, however, Sextus is fully aware of this, which is why he too refrains from *asserting* anything about nature, preferring to see his naturalism as subject to revision and as adaptable to altered dialectical circumstances. Accordingly, while Sextus does not go beyond finitude, Wittgenstein seems continually to seek to address the absolute, that which contrasts with our finitude, under the headings of 'nature' and 'life', in order to ensure that our discourses ultimately remain commensurable and translatable. In this way he determines the unity of discourses as nature.

The self-conscious naïvety aimed at by Wittgenstein's therapeutic philosophy therefore comes up against its own theoretical motivation – i.e. its underlying contextualism. Contextualism is incompatible with the dogmatic assertion of a determinate absolute (immediacy), be it nature, life, or even God. What remains is a paradoxical insight into our finitude, an insight based simply on the fact that, qua discursive beings, we refer to determinate items. The determinacy of our reference cannot be guaranteed without the stable background of a discursive practice; for, without such a background, it would collapse into Quinean indeterminacy. Our words have to mean something or other, and this presupposes that they are always used in a distinct context. But we can determine how contexts differ from one another only within a further context, which, for its part, has to be conditioned in some way or other. An absolute retrieval of the totality of all conditions is therefore impossible. This does not imply any fragmentation of knowledge in the notorious sense of the 'postmodern condition': the instability of the conditions of discourse at the same time acts as a guarantor of its stable functioning.[17] We cannot expect more of knowledge than that it is something we *claim* to have, without being able to ensure on any given occasion that we have thereby grasped the truth. Knowledge claims are subject to revision because we cannot have any true beliefs without holding something determinate to be true. But what counts as something determinate for us presupposes the stability of a discursive practice, and this is the basis of the finitude of objective knowledge.[18]

From the standpoint of the metatheory we are concerned only with objectivity. Because this is not itself an object, we here lose our access to objects. For this reason, we must also resist saying that, thanks to the grace of nature, the frictionless course of our everyday justificatory practices continues to function in spite of the challenges presented by epistemological paradoxes. This strategy would require nature to be the object of our metatheory; but the metatheory has no objects, and it does not refer to the world as it *is* but how it *appears* to discourses under certain conditions. The general Cartesian paradox, which first led us towards contextualism, therefore ends up putting the everyday under threat by relegating our *concept* of the everyday to a mere assumption. Whatever the everyday might be or whatever everyday knowledge ascriptions really are is not something we can know independently of metatheoretical presuppositions. As a result, modernity's project of pursuing epistemology as *prima philosophia* comes under serious threat: epistemology comes to sublate its object domain (all first-order discourses) within itself insofar as it recognises its objects as constructions – that is, as reference-dependent entities. Of course, the objects thematised by the metatheory's object discourses are not creations of the metatheory. But the same cannot be said of the object discourses themselves: these are not modally robust facts but observations of the metatheory.

Nature does not offer a refuge to philosophical reflection, a place where it can escape into immediacy. We have no absolute knowledge with the specific content that nature is the unifying horizon of all contexts, and the act of claiming such knowledge must also be subject to the contextualist conditions of finitude. Nevertheless, if it is not to undermine itself utterly, epistemology must plough ahead in its investigations of the nature of knowledge. The insight into finitude implies the further insight into the finitude of epistemological discourse. This does not mean, however, that it is impossible to carry that discourse forward. On the contrary, just as with any other discourse, its finitude functions as a guarantee of its ongoing execution. Truth functions as a regulative idea, which we have quite possibly already attained in a number of true judgements. Only we cannot know what we do independently of all holding-true, and thus independently of our finitude. We may well know a considerable amount, and I believe that we in fact do (indeed, I know that I know many more or less mundane things). But we can determine what we know only within particular contexts, and, because these are finite, our knowledge claims are finite too – the present claim included. No actual knowledge is identical with a survey of probabilities, even if probabilistic reasoning and statistical evidence can play the role of justification in suitable contexts (including natural-scientific knowledge acquisition).

The assumptions of liberal naturalism overstep the boundary of finitude drawn within meta-epistemological discourse. It asserts an absolute, nature, which we cannot access. In epistemological paradoxes we touch upon an absolute *ex negativo*, but an absolute we cannot determine. This does not represent any shortcoming on the part of our cognitive capacities but belongs to the conditions of possibility of the search for knowledge. The heuristic conditions of knowledge acquisition indicate an absolute because they teach us a lesson about our finitude by distinguishing it from the infinite – in the case at hand, from an impossible absolute knowledge.[19] Insofar as we explain the impossibility of absolute knowledge within our meta-epistemological discourse, we also learn that an absolute world, a world described by all true judgements, is a necessary assumption. Without it, we would not know anything about our finitude, which consists in the fact that we cannot engage in any context-free determination of which judgements are true. But this, of course, is already to say too much . . .

In Part I, one of the principal starting points of our discussion was the idea that there is a difference between everyday knowledge ascriptions and their philosophical thematisation – i.e. epistemology. As a consequence, we have been distinguishing throughout our enquiry between first-order theories and their epistemological metatheory: while first-order theories quantify over what is the case, and thus refer to the world, the metatheory reflects on the conditions of first-order theorising. At one stage, we designated the metatheoretical stance as 'dialectic', since the task of the metatheory is to test first-order theories for dialectical inconsistency. In Part II, we have considered the motivation for contextualism and shown that our justificatory practices do not allow us any immediate access to the world, even though they do not exclude our knowing the world in itself. We have now arrived at a crucial result of this discussion: the boundary between everyday knowledge claims and their epistemological thematisation can itself be drawn only within epistemological discourse. In other words, what now comes into view is that everyday knowledge claims are elements of epistemological theory. Accordingly, we have to see them against the background of the two governing tendencies of epistemology we identified earlier. These tendencies[20] stem from how, on the one hand, epistemology has to guarantee everyday knowledge claims and ascriptions (these being the objects of its explanations) and from how, on the other hand, these claims and ascriptions inevitably come under pressure because scepticism is integral to epistemology's very motivation. The everyday is deployed as a particular move within the dialectical game of epistemology. It is through making this move, and so through distinguishing the everyday from the context of epistemology, that the everyday is generated *as* the everyday. We saw the importance of this move for 'common-sense' approaches to scepticism when discussing Moore's naïve ontology of individuals.[21]

The conjunction of contextualism and naturalism is thus at the very least susceptible to paradoxes if nature qua unifying horizon (and thus qua concept of the world) is relative to the context of contextualism and, as such, not immediately observable. It also follows that we cannot conceive of our finitude as our *nature*, even if it appears necessary to do so within the context of theoretical reflection. With the operation of self-refutation, or 'turning the tables', Pyrrhonian scepticism, the real driver of epistemology, applies the insight into finitude to the metatheory itself. We must then see how our own position is inherently open to revision and concede that a 'picture' has indeed held us captive. We can never completely capture the elements of the mythology that lie behind our theory-building and make them fully explicit – this is the insight of Pyrrhonian scepticism, which, with Stanley Cavell, we might call the 'truth of scepticism'. The heart of this insight is that our attitude towards the world and to knowledge as a whole cannot itself be one of (propositional, assertorically determined) knowledge.[22] The ultimate unified whole of world and knowledge – i.e. totality – is constitutively elusive because we cannot determine anything unless the conditions of discursive rationality are in play. We can only ever reach out to the whole via negation and exclusion; our epistemic strivings generate hinges, which select what does and what does not count as a valid move. In this way, alternatives are edited out of the picture, alternatives of which we cannot possibly be aware from within the discourse itself; the discourse can register only what it constitutively permits as a potential element. Everything else disappears into the background. If we attempt to overstep the boundaries of discourse, we simply land in another discourse. As Thomas Nagel has convincingly shown, we cannot adopt a view from nowhere because, as long as we do not stand anywhere in particular, there will be nothing for us to see.[23]

Yet this insight into finitude itself belongs to a discourse, namely that of the metatheory. And part of the metatheory's motivation is Pyrrhonian scepticism. Without the theory-level transition from first-order knowledge (of the world) to knowledge of knowledge of the world, a transition that aims to thematise all first-order knowledge as such, we would never attain the insight into the discursive relativity of justification. We owe the sceptical (paradox-prone) insight that everything (on the level of first-order thought) is relative (to the metatheory) to what Heidegger calls our transcendence.[24] This relativity does not entail that we could not know anything under conditions that differ from our own local epistemic situation; it is just that we cannot know whether we know anything under the conditions of the theory of reflection. We do not know in the individual case *whether* we know something. In order to find out what we know, we have to investigate the world and adopt specific justificatory practices. Whether (and which of) these practices lead to an accumulation of true judgements and thus to knowledge can be decided only in given circumstances. It does not lie at the discretion of epistemology.

In his seminal *Versuch über Wahrheit und Zeit* [Essay on truth and time], Anton Friedrich Koch has elaborated the 'antinomic nature of discourse'[25] by demonstrating that the combination of self-reference and finitude, and so every negative self-relation (finitude), generates an antinomy. We see this in explicit form in the antinomy of the liar, for example, but it plays a role in all antinomies. For Koch, we obtain the general formulation of the antinomy from the concept of a self-referential negation. Were there a self-referential negation (following Koch, we can call it v), it would, qua negation of itself, be so defined that: $v \leftrightarrow_{\text{def.}} {\sim}v$. Since the expression v reappears on the right-hand side of the equation, the self-application of the definition entails $v \leftrightarrow {\sim}({\sim}v)$, which in turn, given the same application, entails $v \leftrightarrow {\sim}({\sim}({\sim}v))$, and so on *ad infinitum*. Self-referential negation therefore generates the paradigm of all antinomies, even though we cannot understand it without formulating a particular antinomy such as the liar.

Brandom shows us how we can formulate another version of the same antinomy, although his own aim is in fact to dissolve it.[26] Hegel is famous for his introduction of a Spinozistic foundational axiom of determination, according to which *omnis determinatio est negatio*.[27] According to this axiom, everything is what it is in virtue of not being everything it is not. Brandom designates this position as 'strong semantic individuational holism'.[28] Suppose, now, that there was a world consisting of two elements, A and B. Since the axiom of determination is valid for this world (as it is for all worlds), A would stand to B in a relation of exclusion. Were this not the case, there would be no world: there could not be anything at all were there only one 'element'.[29] For, *ex hypothesi*, every *one* must differ from *another*. But, if they are relata of a relation of exclusion, we need to ask whether the relation for its part is a determinate relation (something rather than nothing). This question naturally demands a positive answer, else we could not exclude the relation of exclusion being one of inclusion – and our barely created world could once again implode under the pressure of indeterminacy. The relation between A and B must therefore itself be something determinate. But, if it is determinate, we are entitled to ask what it is distinct from. In our minimal world, it cannot be distinct from the relation of inclusion, because this relation does not even feature. So it has to be distinguished from its relata. Accordingly, we have at least two relations: the meta-relation (R_2) of the relation between (R_1) and A and the meta-relation (R_3) between (R_1) and B. Since everything is exclusively determined by the relation to its other, (R_1), (R_2) and (R_3) have to be distinct; each stands in relation to something respectively different and is thus differently determined. But this set-up results in infinitely many relations, as the three relations we have now stand, for their part, in determining relations to one another, and so on *ad infinitum*. One cannot keep the antinomy of the axiom of determination at bay by saying that all these relations are the same in virtue of being relations of exclusion, because this relation too features in an excluding relation thanks to which it is determined vis-à-vis its other. In its purity, then, strong individuational holism represents a negative self-relation and becomes antinomic.

Finally, we can formulate a third version of the antinomy on the basis of the axiom of determination. We need only introduce a simple world containing two items, P and Q. If P is so defined that it is not Q, and Q is defined as not being P, we thus have the following definitions:

(1) $P \leftrightarrow_{\text{def.}} \sim Q$
(2) $Q \leftrightarrow_{\text{def.}} \sim P$

It is easy to see that the combination of (1) and (2) entails the following:

(3) $P \leftrightarrow_{\text{def}} \sim(\sim P)$ [since Q and $\sim$P are equivalent]

Unfortunately, because P is equivalent to $\sim$Q, this is no proof of the validity of the elimination rule for double negation. Bearing that equivalence in mind, it is clear that (1) and (2) commit us to understanding (3) as follows:

(4) $P \leftrightarrow_{\text{def.}} \sim\sim(\sim Q)$

Since we can make infinitely many applications of these equivalences on either side of definitions (1) and (2), sanctioned as they are by the definitions themselves, all solid ground slips from beneath our feet. We have no reason to stop at any specific point in the expression of determinate content. At this point, it might seem sensible to try to avoid this last version of the antinomy by insisting that P is first of all P, and then, in addition, distinct from Q. But this means asserting that something or other can be what it is simply by being what it is. Such an in-itself, the idea of which underlies the classical distinction between substance (= in-itself) and accident (= relation), can itself be determinate only if, qua substance, it is distinguished from accidental relations. Accordingly, in the logical space of the distinction between substance (S) and accident (A), the substance is itself an element that behaves like P in relation to Q in the P–Q world. This means that there is a logical space, the substance–accidents world, which engenders the very problem of the P–Q world at a logically higher order. As we can make respective identifying reference to A, S, P and Q only if we are able to draw distinctions, differential relations have to be in play, and these perpetuate the antinomy at every logical level. The assumption of simple elements (Wittgenstein's 'objects' in the *Tractatus*, Platonic ideas or Aristotelian ἁπλᾶ, Russellian sense data, etc.) – in other words, the myth of the given in its purest form – founders on the antinomy. The antinomy continually recurs because, as discursive beings, we cannot have an identificatory apprehension of anything whatsoever without distinguishing it from another something within the medium of differentiating mediation.

If every negative self-relation is a case of the universally antinomic nature of discourse that Koch and Brandom have shown us how to formulate, it is not surprising that the same goes for the self-referential finitude where we have now arrived in our investigation. The entire course of our reflection thus generates an antinomy, which we have made explicit, little by little, through the successive stages of our theory construction. Pyrrhonian scepticism's operation of 'turning the tables', of an ultimate self-application, is thus completed. At the boundary of discourse, everything collapses beneath us. But, if we are not to end up on the sceptical note sounded by self-referential finitude, it is worth joining Brandom in undertaking a final attempt to recover the world – even if Rorty insisted some decades ago that it is 'well lost'.[30]

15

A Final Attempt
to Recover the World:
Brandom with Hegel

Rorty famously characterised Robert Brandom's philosophical project as an attempt to lead analytic philosophy – or, to be more precise, *semantics* – from its Kantian to its Hegelian phase. Yet his execution of this project betrays a constitutive blind spot when it comes to the concept of totality, of the world. At the centre of Hegel's own attempt to construct an absolute idealism we find an endeavour to remove this very blind spot. Brandom, to be sure, mentions the 'world' or totality only in passing and determines it purely *ex negativo*. For his avowed aim is not to establish an ontology in the sense of a first-order theory of what there is (of what the world is like) but to *dissolve* a question that is notoriously susceptible to paradoxes: how can we have mental, and thus semantically mediated, access to the world, where the world is what is prior to our conceptual efforts. According to Brandom, what we can learn from Hegel is that access conditions to an objective world ought to be explicated within the framework of an 'objective idealism'. Under this label, Brandom does not understand any kind of ontology claiming something of the form that, for example, being is really 'mind' or 'spirit'. Rather, 'objective idealism' is the thesis that, for us, the concept of an objective world is an implication of our concepts of error and belief revision. Our epistemic processes of trial and error, which Brandom identifies with Hegel's notion in the *Phenomenology of Spirit* of 'experience',[1] are so constituted that they refer to a world in itself, a world independent of our semantic self-explications. Idealism 'at its best' does not make any claims of reference dependence, abjuring theories that assert that something – in the present case, the world – would not exist if something else – in this case, semantically competent beings – did not exist.[2] Hegel, Brandom assures us, does not want to assert that the concept 'world' would not pertain to anything if the concept 'cognition of the world' did not pertain to anything. Objective idealism is the considerably more innocuous, but nonetheless interesting assertion that our game of giving and asking for reasons is constitutively geared towards discovering what is always already the case in an intersubjectively communicable manner. The objective world is thus assigned an irreplaceable function in the constitution of the social-semantic dimension within which we can register and test claims to objectivity, to knowledge of what is the case anyhow. On this account, the objective world is nothing but what is the case independently of its featuring in any relation to the social-semantic dimension.[3] This is its concept.

According to Brandom, only the social-semantic dimension can be articulated inferentially: every assertion involves semantic commitments, and these can be made explicit in the various processes through which we become aware of what really follows from what.[4] Our discursive rationality as a whole thus consists in nothing other than a relentless, ongoing process of semantic explication, governed by a reciprocal control of discursive commitments. The authors of these commitments, the inhabitants of the social-semantic dimension, engage with the world in a manner that, unlike parrots and thermometers, is not tied to any mere stimulus-response schema. For, as sapient subjects, they can determine what it is that affects them in a given case and, crucially, what they are committing themselves to when they determine it as being such and so. But to determine what something is means assigning it a predicate within a proposition, whereby the sum of all predicates together form a totality, the Kantian *omnitudio realitatis*. Within this totality, each predicate is the predicate it is via the exclusion, and thus negation, of all the predicates with which it is incompatible. Brandom thinks that the idea of every-thing hanging together with everything else within these predicatively explicable relations of inclusion and exclusion finds expression in Hegel's doctrine of determinate negation. He thus reduces this doctrine to Hegel's principle of determination, thereby robbing it of its true anti-sceptical thrust in the *Phenomenology of Spirit*.[5] The much quoted *omnis determinatio negatio est* is not a semantic (let alone an ontic) principle, according to which each element in a semantic network is related to each other element via inferential relations that confer meaning upon it. Rather, the very notion of determinate negation is a description of the theory-building process of the *Phenomenology of Spirit*. A so-called shape of consciousness is a way of drawing an overall distinction between objects, insofar as they are supposed to be 'out there' [*Gegenstand*], on the one hand, and our access conditions to them on the other hand [*Begriff*]. Each succes-sor of a given shape of consciousness is defined through its attempt to make minimal repairs to the conceptual architecture that precedes it in the hierarchy of such shapes. 'Determinate negation' belongs to the dialectical toolbox of the Hegelian system of ways of thinking about the relationship between mind and world. And therefore it should not be misconstrued as a principle governing the ultimate theory of semantic content; indeed, Hegel precisely avoids operating within a mind–world framework of any kind.

For Brandom, semantic holism – the theory that all predicates belong to an inferentially articulable totality – is *assertable* only under a certain presupposition: namely, we have to assume that the world is thoroughgoingly determined and *objectively* so – i.e. its thoroughgoing determination is reference-independent from its relation to semantically competent beings. If we are capable of revising our beliefs upon realising that they simultaneously commit us to ascribing two incompatible predicates to the same item, we are *ipso facto* capable of understanding the concept of an objective world. For an objective world is nothing other than a domain in which nothing *can* possess incompatible properties, while the subjective world, the social-semantic dimension, is a domain in which nobody *ought* to have incompatible beliefs – which does not exclude, but rather includes, the possibility that they *can* have them.[6] Marking this *deontological difference* between subjective and objective incompatibilities is at the same time to place them in a relation of reciprocal determination: only someone who understands the nature of this difference understands what it means to revise one's beliefs in order to aim at truth. The concept of an objective world is therefore sense-dependent on our semantic self-consciousness, whereby, it is important to note, this reciprocal conceptual or semantic determination should be located not in the world as a causal process but merely within our semantic self-consciousness. By mapping out the terrain in this way, Brandom hopes to define the concept of an objective idealism without hypostatising a world-positing subject or an absolute subjectivity.

Clearly, Brandom wants to free Hegel from any suspicion of a vulgar *esse est percipi*, for which there are, say, mountains only if there are semantically competent beings who can correctly apply the singular term 'mountain'. Yet he believes that the alternative to this absurd kind of idealism (which, in this minimal form, not even Berkeley would take seriously) is the view that the world is always already there, without any necessary relation to its becoming known. 'The *thought* [my emphasis, M. G.] that that world is always already there anyway, regardless of the activities, if any, of knowing and acting subjects, has always stood as the most fundamental objection to any sort of idealism.'[7] The negation of idealism so understood thus comes down to the thesis that, for any given worldly fact, if it is an object of knowledge, it is only contingently so. Everything that is the case in the objective world would also have been the case in a modally robust sense even if there had never been anybody around to note that it was the case. We can therefore identify a semantic echo of the world in a set of modally robust concepts, concepts that carve out a domain of thought and action we come to regard as 'always already there anyway' on account of its semantic property of repelling incompatibilities.

In this way, Brandom introduces the world as an *access condition* to the concept of objectivity, and thus as an element of his theory. He invokes the concept of the world only as an element in a semantic triangulation between disputing subjects or contradictory beliefs, on the one hand, and the objective world, on the other. Since the latter cannot contain incompatible states, it is tasked with repelling all contradictions. The important point here is that the world hardly enters the theory as a simple matter of course, as something perfectly self-evident. Rather, the theory presupposes the world as its other, as something to which our discursive access needs to be guaranteed a priori.

Among traditional readers of Hegel, this construction may well raise the suspicion that Brandom's concept of the world betrays a 'tenderness for things': 'The ordinary tenderness for things, the overriding worry of which is that they do not contradict themselves, forgets instead, here as elsewhere, that contradiction is not thereby dissolved but is rather shoved elsewhere, into subjective or external reflection.'[8] This protective attitude clearly finds expression in Brandom's deontological distinction. And, just as obviously, Hegel's low estimation of such 'tenderness' hardly has a merely external, polemical bearing on Brandom's concept of the world: for Hegel ultimately maintains that contradiction is an *ontological* structure. Within the grand systematic framework of his absolute idealism, he wants to show how the single adequate 'definition of the absolute'[9] can be yielded within a theory – indeed, within a 'system of totality'.[10] However, a system of totality would clearly be incomplete if it were restricted to an investigation of the social-semantic dimension to which actual totality, the thoroughgoingly determined objective world, remains external. Such a world would be characterisable only *ex negativo*. And, in the final analysis, this kind of approach always leads to an unknowable thing in itself, to something ultimately characterised by nothing more than its absolute descriptive emptiness; we are brought right back to the pure 'being' that opens the *Logic*.

Brandom himself makes only desultory reference to the idea of totality that is so central to Hegel's project. At one point, he distinguishes a 'world of facts' from Hegel's 'infinity', understanding by the latter nothing more than a holistic relational structure.[11] According to Brandom, however, this requires anchoring in immediacy, else it would implode into a relation without relata.[12] Therefore, everything must first of all just be what it is, so it can then be determined vis-à-vis everything else. This means that the holistic structure with which Brandom identifies Hegel's *concept* (*the* concept) consists of objects to which we refer with singular expressions. If everything is determined only because, in principle, it can be distinguished from everything it is not, then everything must first and foremost simply be what it is: something that *can*, but does not have to, feature in relations of inclusion and exclusion.

Yet Hegel himself famously wants us to take seriously the contradiction of a free-floating relation, the notorious 'movement from nothing to nothing and thereby back to itself',[13] so that this might go (or return) 'to ground' [*zugrunde gehen*] – i.e. to its ground [*zum Grunde*]. Without passing through the constitutively labile categories of the logic of reflection, we have no chance of reaching the concept. Admittedly, Hegel introduces the concept by explaining how universal, particular and individual are moments of its totality. Yet, for Hegel, it is precisely not the individual – i.e. the functional position of singular terms – that is the sublated immediacy of being but, rather, the universal. This is also this sense in which he argues against 'sense certainty' that its attempt to relate to singular items in fact always already transforms them into universals. Hegel's concept of the 'universal' can be translated as the dimension of distinctions (to borrow once again from Hogrebe): the universal is the logical space within which distinctions can be drawn as such. Accordingly, being is the universal because it is simply the name for the as yet undetermined dimension of distinctions, the universality of the concept.

Brandom, by contrast, seems to think that Hegel joins him in advocating an ontology of individuals on the basis of a semantic argument. On this argument, the world is the totality of all objects or individuals to which we can make individuating reference with singular terms. The use of singular terms presupposes that each respective object of reference is a substance in the Aristotelian sense – i.e. an underlying substrate bearing determinate properties – which we can go on to lend predicative articulation and thus deploy inferentially in the game of giving and asking for reasons. While we have only a conceptual and holistic access to these objects (via inferential semantics), this does not sublate the immediacy of the world. The world is what appears within the total mediation of the social-semantic dimension as 'brute thereness',[14] as the always-already that underlies our conceptual activities as their ontic ground. Revealingly, Brandom explicitly identifies this 'brute thereness' with Hegelian immediacy.

Unlike Hegel, Brandom sees immediacy ('being' in the 'Logic of Being') not as a concept but as the given *sensu strictu* – i.e. as the sheer fact of the world. We semantic beings simply find ourselves placed in this world without knowing how and why. Yet this concept of the world or being is precisely that which Hegel, that 'great foe of immediacy',[15] as Sellars labelled him, set out to dissolve through his absolute idealism. This world is not an unmediated something that preceeds our concept of the world, because, as Brandom himself acknowledges in the passage cited above (p. 251), this assumption is itself a *thought*. This does not mean that the world is *only* a thought (a patently absurd thesis), merely that the concept of the world has to be motivated within a theory, and so motivated in its proper context. And this in turn simply means that any theory of *totality* that takes the world as the always-already, as a presupposition of the concept, is always already a *theory* of totality. In this sense, Hegel argues in the 'Logic of essence' that being, in his particular terminological sense, is a *presupposition* of essence.[16] Brandom also makes use of this idea, but, in striking contrast to his treatment of many of the other foundational concepts and presuppositions of his theory, he does not raise it to semantic self-consciousness and examine it from a suitably critical distance.

We thus find ourselves face to face with the unthematised blind spot of Brandom's theory. Its concept of the world reveals a residual naturalism,[17] which, in a more recent essay, leads him to formulate an adaption theory of experience – i.e. of empirical concepts. Indeed, he even intends to attribute this theory to Hegel.[18] Brandom maintains that the world has to be understood as the always-already that we aim to grasp with our concepts, even though it is constitutively inexhaustible. The world thus plays a dual role. On the one hand, it remains that which we can never fully rein in with our concepts. On the other hand, it fulfils a function in our negotiation of discursive contradictions, since this requires an inference to an objective world understood as that which repels incompatibilities. Without the world's assuming both these tasks at the same time, we could not continue to weave the ever more finely grained conceptual web in which we hope to capture it.

In the 'Logic of essence', especially in its theory of 'reflection', Hegel develops a theory of *presupposition*, according to which being is the presupposition of essence. Presupposition has a dual meaning. On the one hand, being is a *pre*-supposition or *pre*-positing [*Voraus*setzung] of essence and thus of reflection in the sense employed by Brandom. Reflection can only be exercised on being, which consequently appears to reflection as its constitutive other. Being is thus an ontic *pre*-supposition of reflection: whoever or whatever reflects already finds itself confronted with a world that he, she or it cannot regard as its own product. On the other hand, being is also an ontological pre-*supposition* or pre-*positing* [Voraus*setzung*] of essence – i.e. of essence itself, which reflects itself in itself and thereby generates its own point of departure. Insofar as essence is 'the movement of nothing to nothing and thereby back to itself',[19] and therefore absolute negativity, it is at the same time itself. It is identity and difference in one. This sameness that essence maintains with itself in its difference consists merely in how it sublates its positing that posits nothing as itself from the outset. Yet insofar as it posits nothing as itself, it sublates its positing, the positing that originally aims to discover something that is independent of its being posited (a *pre*-supposed). This, in brief, is the logical structure that Hegel calls 'presupposition', which he explicitly determines as 'positing the sublating of positing'.[20] But what is all this supposed to mean?

I suggest that we concretise Hegel's logical matrix with the help of the concept of the world. Doing so can open up a path towards transforming Brandom's objective idealism (*malgré lui*) into an absolute idealism. To begin with, we need only remind ourselves that propositional knowledge is a factive intentional attitude. If we are confronted with a case of knowledge that p, then it is at least the case that p, and, further, it is likewise the case that someone holds it to be true that p. A propositional content must therefore be something for someone in such a way that they can refer to it *as if* it exists independently of their referring to it. This assumption, as we have been emphasising throughout, is necessary to guarantee the contrast of objectivity between knowledge and holding-true.[21] The concept of knowing thus presupposes at a minimum that someone can make use of a conceptually determinate content *as if* it were independent of their referring use. For this is just what it means to hold something true with epistemic intention. In other words, this means that someone must posit something – i.e. a conceptual content – such that the content itself is freed from the referential relation thus established; the content (p) is supposed to be the case independently of its featuring in any relation to an instance of knowledge. The facticity or objectivity of knowledge therefore presupposes that there is something that can be known, but that need not feature in any relation to knowledge. The problem is that the same thing, namely p, is both known and the case when we know it to be the case, which makes it hard to distinguish between the semantic content of knowledge and what is the case. This builds a boundary concept of objectivity into the concept of knowledge, which Kant designated as the 'noumenon in the negative sense'[22] and appears in Brandom as the 'immediacy' or 'brute thereness' to which we orient our conceptual efforts without ever being able to fully capture it. Yet since this immediacy is meant to be thought as the totality of thoroughgoing objective determinacy, and not as the indeterminate immediate, there is always the inherent possibility of hypostatising it into an objective world (and thus into a positive noumenon). The world therefore appears to a thinker as the objectively existing source of information, somehow or other transformed into semantic content, and this raises the problem that there now seems to be a gulf in the inferential order between something that assumes and something that resists conceptual shape.

In Hegelian terms, the objection to Brandom would thus be that he considers only the first sense of presupposition and neglects the second. Put in our own terms, the result is that he fails to provide a sufficient account of his own theory construction at the metatheoretical level. His theorising, that is, presupposes that semantics assumes an objective world that repels contradictions. This presupposition of an objective world, which Habermas calls a 'formal presupposition', is not something we can justify by raising a potentially revisable knowledge claim within the already established game of giving and asking for reasons: the objective world is what enables these claims and, as such, cannot appear among them. The world becomes a presupposition of the theory *within* the theory and thus an a priori of worldliness as such, a designation of the immediacy of reflection itself in the pure negativity of total semantic mediation. Brandom's concept of immediacy therefore remains trapped in the aporia of the 'Logic of essence', which, in a deliberate echo of Fichte, conceptualises a paradoxical *'absolute* internal *counter-repelling'* in which nothing more is posited than positing in the mode of presupposing.[23]

Throughout this study, we have seen the antinomy of essence recur time and again. It consists in positing something as not posited – and thus as immediate or given – which can only occur *within* a theory tasked with determining the relation of mind and world or of ought and is. In Brandom, however, this process is presented as though the given or immediate were itself given or immediate. His *pragmatist adaptionism* is thus visibly at pains to edit out Hegel's idealist claim to present the self-explication of the whole in a philosophical theory of totality. He therefore consistently reduces Hegel's concept of experience to a naturalised adaptation strategy that the social animal 'human being' pursues in the face of the mercilessly univocal world, in the face of 'brute thereness'.

Hegel himself, of course, does not remain trapped within the antinomy of pure negativity but takes a further decisive step in the 'Logic of the Concept'. It is here that the true nature of his project first becomes clear. This consists in providing an 'evolutionary theory of logical space',[24] as Anton Friedrich Koch has labelled it. In the course of this project – i.e. in the development of being and essence into the concept – it transpires that the real is in fact an objective logical space that not only bears an affinity to our thought but is the objectivity of its fundamental structure of self-relation. The self-relation of thought thus finds its primary expression in the insight that all first-order, being-logical theories fail on account of how they pass off the whole as a given, as though it might be grasped in a theory of totality without always already being related to it. The seeming independence of being, codified in Brandom's concept of the world, turns out to be the negation of negation – i.e. a kind of thinking that presupposes being as its other. This observation, to be sure, takes place from the standpoint of a second-order theory of totality, what Hegel calls a series of definitions of the absolute. Everything that counts as being for a first-order theory of totality appears as a presupposition of that theory from the point of view of Hegel's metatheory, which itself consists in nothing more than a genealogical reconstruction of its own status as a theory.

To be sure, Hegel's final word on being is that it is the universality of the concept.[25] A tentative translation of this would be that being is the very fact that logical space obtains. Being is the ur-state of affairs that there could possibly be states of affairs, some of which are the case, and thus facts.[26] Which states of affairs there are – i.e. which possible determinations and so relations of inclusion and exclusion are the case – is not for a *Science of Logic* to investigate. Empirical investigation can *intentione recta* already rely on logical space's obtaining, which appears to it as its other – an other that can never be fully cognised because the universality of the concept qua logical space cannot be empirically exhausted. Everything that is the case, that is, is a subset of the possible. That the set of all states of affairs is larger than the set of all facts is what allows us to assume that, of any two incompatible beliefs directed at states of affairs, only one can be true (actually obtain). Yet this fact is not itself given as a further worldly fact. In other words, the presence of logical space is not a fact among others, and this means it cannot be contrasted with anything else, including the social-semantic dimension whose structure, if we follow Brandom, at best guarantees access conditions to an independently available objective world.

Logical space can particularise itself only provided something is the case without itself being logical space. Yet everything particular qua particularisation of logical space can only be a case of its internal differentiation, meaning there is no need for logical space to reach beyond itself. This is just what Hegel, in his capacity as the radical thinker of immanence, objected against Schelling and any other conception of the world/ totality as something transcending our conceptual apparatus.[27] So while the concept of the given (being) plays an important role in the constitution of logical space, the given as such, as we learn in the 'Logic of essence', is not itself given but a presupposition of reflection. This presupposition of reflection cannot be mastered by essence, not without 'going to ground' in the contradiction of presupposition. To a certain extent, we might summarise Hegel's *Science of Logic* as an attempt to articulate the fact that the concept of the given is not itself given. The conceptual framework within which we become aware of the structure of concepts cannot be found in the world by, as it were, simply directing our gaze at worldly affairs. Among other things, this has the consequence that the world is not an element in the world order. The world is not an object related to anything in the world. Hence, the world cannot be the object of a subject, the target of a factive mental state with specifiable reference conditions to what there is. But this just means that there cannot be a specific mind–world problem. And, for this reason, we ought not to puzzle over how we might access the world: the very idea of mental conditions of access to what there is ultimately needs to be dropped, for the simple reason that the mind, if anything, clearly always already exists. It therefore pre-dates, so to speak, any more specific attempt to give an account of its epistemic success.

Brandom conceives logical space as an inferentially articulable social-semantic dimension and bases his semantics on the insight that discursive communicability is a condition of the determinacy of knowledge (in line with minimal verificationism).[28] He thus assumes that we cannot think through an absolute relationality – i.e. the independent existence of the social-semantic dimension – without doing away with the necessary independence of relata. Without the independence of relata, no relation could be thought as determinate without for its part standing in a relation to a relation, and without this meta-relation in turn standing in a relation to a relation, and so on *ad infinitum*. An individuational holism thus understood would collapse into a 'movement from nothing to nothing and thus back to itself'. Absolute relationality requires anchoring, a stable point of reference. Brandom, however, determines the anchor of reflection as the objective world and thereby reifies it into a given – this is where I see his relapse into the 'Logic of Being'. We can avoid this difficulty, however, if we explain the given as an element of semantic theory that is not for its part something merely given: such a theory qua metatheory always already reconstructs its own conditions of possibility, and in the process of doing so it explains the supposedly given as a presupposition of the social-semantic dimension. If we make room for this kind of explanation, and so elevate the world from the thing in itself to a moment of logical space, Brandom's residual naturalism should no longer have the appearance of a default presupposition. Indeed, it should come to seem highly questionable. Why should we still assume that the 'objective' world to which semantically competent beings adapt themselves is always already simply how it is, without thereby *always already* being geared towards self-knowledge and normativity? The possibility of a true reconciliation of mind and world beyond naturalism – that is, in Rorty's slogan 'The world well lost' – can therefore come into view once the metatheory comes to recognise that it was always already at work in every first-order theory. This would then open the way to a genuine realisation of 'being with oneself in the other'. Of course, this by no means amounts to the absurd thesis that each of us, in our capacity as semantically competent beings, comes into the world equipped with the magical energy required to bring forth objects *ex nihilo*.

And with this prospect in sight, Pyrrhonian scepticism is brought to completion: we have finally seen how it might be transformed into a philosophical *method*. A metatheory of discursive formations faces the infinite task of testing given theories for dialectical consistency. Whether explicitly or implicitly, contemporary philosophy too practises this method insofar as we investigate the fundamental concepts of given discourses, be they discourses of natural science, of the so-called humanities, or of everyday life. Practising this method amounts to laying the foundations for the systematic project of a methodology of philosophy, a project that sets out not to resolve supposedly 'serious' problems but merely to define the dialectical topography of possible solutions, so that we might better evaluate their prospects for success. Given that discourse does not come to an end, there is no reason to believe that the self-reference of finite thinking will ever come to a final standstill. We remain with Hegel's Dionysian insight: 'The True is thus the Bacchanalian revel in which no member is not drunk; yet because each member collapses as soon as he drops out, the revel is just as much transparent and simple repose.'[29]

Notes

Introduction

1 Williams, *Descartes: The Project of Pure Enquiry*, p. 65. The idea of a world as the 'object of any representation which is knowledge' (ibid.), and thus the absolute concept of the world, seems to follow seamlessly from the reflection that, 'if knowledge is what it claims to be, then it is knowledge of a reality which exists independently of that knowledge, and indeed (except for the special case where the reality known happens itself to be some psychological item) independently of any thought or experience. Knowledge is of what is there anyway' (ibid., p. 64).

2 On this theme, see Cassam, *The Possibility of Knowledge*.

3 See, for example, Schaffer, 'From contextualism to contrastivism in epistemology'; 'Contrastive knowledge'; and 'Skepticism, contextualism, and discrimination'.

4 Schaffer himself would in fact rather avoid this consequence, since he understands the respective opposition of knowledge class (p) and contrast class (q) as 'local' ('From contextualism to contrastivism', pp. 91ff.). He attempts in this way to restrict the validity of the principle of closure. For a contrary view, see above, pp. 94f.

5 For an extensive account, see Gabriel, *Antike und moderne Skepsis: Zur Einführung*.

6 See Brandom, *Tales of the Mighty Dead: Historical Essays in the Metaphysics of Intentionality*, p. 50: 'Concept P is *sense dependent* on concept Q just in case one cannot count as having grasped P unless one counts as having grasped Q. Concept P is *reference dependent* on concept Q just in case P cannot apply to something unless Q applies to something.'

7 One might also conceive the difference as one between ontological (= sense-dependent) and ontic (= reference-dependent) idealism. See my account in Gabriel, 'Endlichkeit und absolutes Ich – Heideggers Fichtekritik'.

8 See, for example, Williams, *Unnatural Doubts: Epistemological Realism and the Basis of Scepticism*, p. 37. On this topic, see above, pp. 83f. With his theoretical diagnosis, Williams ultimately intends to contest the idea that Cartesian scepti-

cism presents us with a genuine paradox. He argues that the assumptions informing the premises are in no way natural but, rather, are substantial epistemological positions which he seeks to disavow.

9 PI, §309.
10 PI, II, p. 578.
11 OC, §505.
12 On this point, see Jay Bernstein's sketch in 'Hegel's ladder: the ethical presuppositions of absolute knowing.'
13 On the relation of scepticism to metaphysics in light of Hegel's and Schelling's concepts of infinity, see my sketch in *Transcendental Ontology*, pp. 2–34; 104–19. For my most extensive treatment to date, see *Sinn und Existenz: Eine realistische Ontologie*.

Chapter 1 Negative Dogmatism and Methodological Scepticism

1 On both tendencies of epistemology, *conservatism* and *scepticism*, see above pp. 77ff.
2 The famous formula 'in reality' was already used prominently by Democritus, who opposed the common-sense/manifest image (νόμος) and true actuality/scientific image (ἐτεή). See D16 in Taylor, *The Atomists: Leucippus and Democritus*, 9: 'By convention sweet and by convention bitter, by convention hot, by convention cold, by convention colour; but in reality atoms and void.' (νόμῳ πλυκύ, νόμῳ πικρόν, νόμῳ θερμόν, νόμῳ ψυχρόν, νόμῳ χροιή, ἐτεῇ δὲ ἄτομα καὶ κενόν.) Sextus Empiricus paraphrases this statement as follows: 'perceptible things are thought – that is, held by opinion – to be, but it is not these things that truthfully are, but only atoms and void.' (AL VII 135: νομίζεται δὲ εἶναι καὶ δοξάζεται τὰ αἰσθητά, οὐκ ἔστι δὲ κατ'ἀλήθειαν ταῦτα, ἀλλὰ τὰ ἄτομα μόνον καὶ τὸ κενόν.) Of course, this idea goes together with Democritus' negative dogmatism, according to which the human being is cut off from true actuality through his senses. The senses bring about representations within him, the reality of which he can never prove. See especially D 16-21. Democritus is naturally only one voice in the colourful canon of pre-Socratic negative dogmatism.
3 CPR, AVIII.
4 See Rorty's distinction between 'constructive' and 'reactive' philosophy in *Philosophy and the Mirror of Nature*, pp. 366–79.
5 OS, 1.8.
6 PI, II, p. 226.
7 See Heidemann, *Der Begriff des Skeptizismus: Seine systematischen Formen, die pyrrhonische Skepsis und Hegels Herausforderung*.
8 Robert Fogelin develops a similar concept of Cartesian (in contrast to Pyrrhonian) scepticism in 'The skeptics are coming! The skeptics are coming!', p. 165.
9 The strategy of such an integrative anti-scepticism has recently been pursued by Kern in *Sources of Knowledge: On the Concept of a Rational Capacity for Knowledge*.

10 See Burnyeat, 'The sceptic in his place and time.'

11 See also Grundmann and Stüber, *Philosophie der Skepsis*, p. 10. Grundmann and Stüber even go as far as to understand all epistemology as the 'philosophy of scepticism' (ibid.).

12 The term stems from the literature on Pyrrhonian scepticism. Sextus Empiricus himself distinguishes three different kinds of attitude towards the search for knowledge: (1) dogmatism, (2) academic scepticism (negative dogmatism) and (3) (Pyrrhonian) scepticism. The dogmatist claims to have acquired knowledge (εὕρεσις), while the negative dogmatist claims to know that the knowledge the dogmatist claims to have acquired is in fact impossible to acquire (ἄρνησις εὑρέσεως / ἀκαταληψίας ὁμολογία). The true (Pyrrhonian) sceptic, by contrast, simply prolongs the search indefinitely (ἐπιμονὴ ζητήσεως) by entangling any given (apparent) cognition in a series of aporia. These force the would-be knower to proceed to a further cognition, which is in turn enmeshed in aporia (see OS, 1.1–4). The Pyrrhonian sceptic does not thereby claim to know that we cannot know some specific thing or even that we cannot know anything at all (and is to this extent undogmatic), but he achieves his goal through relentlessly repeating the procedure of putting dogmatic (substantial) philosophical claims into question.

13 See Kersting, 'Plädoyer für einen nüchternen Universalismus', pp. 8f.

14 The *locus classicus* for Hume's naturalism is his *Treatise of Human Nature*, esp. Part 4, sect. 1. A more recent exponent of the thesis that an unnatural doubt underlies every form of scepticism, and that this is scepticism's weakness, is Michael Williams (see in particular *Unnatural Doubts*). Whether we ought in fact to see this as a strength or a weakness of scepticism cannot be decided here. See too chapter 14 below.

15 See, for example, Kersting, 'Plädoyer für einen nüchternen Universalismus', p. 8. See James Conant's distinction between the 'hard-headed customer' and the 'sceptic' in 'Varieties of scepticism', esp. p. 132.

16 See, for example, OS, 1.20, 177, 186, 212 *et al.*

17 See Jaspers, *General Psychopathology*. I was made aware of the link to Jaspers by Cohen, 'Sextus Empiricus: skepticism as a therapy', pp. 405f.

18 Scepticism 'has for its object the contingency with regard to the content; as soon as it is presented with the subject matter or the content, scepticism demonstrates that, inwardly, the content is what is negative.' Hegel, *Lectures on the History of Philosophy 1825–6*, Vol. 2: *Greek Philosophy*, p. 303.

19 To be sure, the history of philosophy contains not only dogmatism and scepticism, alias negative dogmatism, but also Pyrrhonian scepticism. Pyrrhonian scepticism propagates a certain form of life which is not exhausted by the formulation of any particular epistemological problem. For an overview of this topic, see Gabriel, *Antike und moderne Skepsis* and *Skeptizismus und Idealismus in der Antike*.

20 Hegel, *Phenomenology of Spirit*, §205.

21 Andrea Kern aptly describes these strategies as 'positions of moderation', since they make concessions to methodological scepticism. Kern, *Sources of Knowledge*, pp. 89f., 109ff and *passim*.

22 CPR, B132.

23 CPR, §16.

24 See CPR, B133: 'Therefore it is only because I can combine a manifold of given representations *in one consciousness* that it is possible for me to represent the *identity of the consciousness in these representations* itself, i.e., the *analytical* unity of apperception is only possible under the presupposition of some *synthetic* one.'

25 It is one of the implications of Wittgenstein's private language argument that a private sensation language cannot contain any assertions precisely because one cannot distinguish between correct and incorrect assertions within it. If everything is correct, nothing is correct (see PI, §258). Without the distinction between permitted and proscribed moves – i.e. without normativity – no system of assertions can be established. For a detailed discussion, see chapter 9 below.

26 The term 'error theory', central to the contemporary discussion of relativism and contextualism, was introduced by J. L. Mackie. Mackie advocates a local error theory, according to which all moral judgements are false insofar as they seem to be judgements about something, objective values, although it is impossible (for Mackie at least) to think of a world that has these moral values built into its fabric such that we could grasp them in moral judgements. '[T]he denial of objective values will have to be put forward not as the result of an analytic approach, but as an "error-theory", a theory that although most people in making moral judgments implicitly claim, among other things, to be pointing to something objectively prescriptive, these claims are all false' (Mackie, *Ethics: Inventing Right and Wrong*, p. 35). In the contemporary debate, the term 'error theory' is somewhat slippery: some philosophers understand it as the *ontological* thesis that such and such an object thematised by such and such system of assertions does not exist. Others understand it as the *semantic* thesis that a certain system of assertions misleads us, in virtue of its surface grammar, into reckoning with a class of monadic objects, when there is in truth only a class of polyadic objects. An example for the semantic thesis would be the judgement 'the sun moves', which misleads us into looking for a movement property that pertains to some objects and not to others. Closer inspection, however, shows that the judgement 'the sun moves' expresses the proposition 'that the sun moves relative to a parameter P, which fixes what does not move.' Whenever I use the expression 'error theory' in what follows, I intend to designate any theory that claims some system of assertions to rest upon an error about its subject matter, whether this is spelled out as an ontological or as a semantic theory.

27 A relativist could here entertain the sceptical thought that we cannot know whether there might be grounds for assuming 55 unmoved movers in the future or for higher intelligences, grounds unavailable to us in light of the information currently at our disposal. This does not mean, however, that we ought to shy away from asserting that there are not 55 unmoved movers. It is likely that some future will look back at our present as naïve. They may do so for a host of factors of which we are unable to form any concrete idea. Yet

the fact that such a future is merely thinkable poses no threat to the present. Our doxastic system can only be restructured from within, meaning that whoever appeals to paradigm shifts and the like in order to justify scepticism can hardly convince anyone who does not, out of fear of knowledge, shy away from asserting that they know that there are neither witches nor 55 unmoved movers.

Chapter 2 Kant's Negative Dogmatism

1 Fichte had already interpreted Kant's system as 'negatively dogmatic' in his 'Review of *Aenesidemus*', p. 71. Fichte thereby distinguished Hume's scepticism from Kant's negative dogmatism in arguing that, whereas Hume asserted the unknowability of the thing in itself that affects us, he followed Kant in trying to show 'that the thought of a thing possessing existence and specific properties in itself and apart from any faculty of representation is a piece of whimsy, a pipe dream, a nonthought. And to this extent the Humean system is skeptical and the Critical system is dogmatic – and indeed negatively so' (ibid.).
2 CPR, B451.
3 On the sceptical method of the antonomies and Kant's implicit connection to antique scepticism, see Engelhard, *Das Einfache und die Materie: Untersuchungen zu Kants Antinomie der Teilung*, pp. 136–42. See also Odo Marquard's classical work *Skeptische Methode mit Blick auf Kant*.
4 CPR, B274-79.
5 See Conant's exposition in 'Varieties of scepticism'.
6 As Conant makes clear, this presupposition is more problematic than it initially seems. See ibid., p. 107.
7 'Concept P is *sense dependent* on concept Q just in case one cannot count as having grasped P unless one counts as having grasped Q' (Brandom, *Tales of the Mighty Dead*, p. 50).
8 Quine, *Word and Object*, p. 22.
9 For this view, see also Williams, *Groundless Belief*, p. 2: '[I]f sceptical arguments did not exist, I do not think that any content would be given to the idea of showing that knowledge is possible.'
10 For this distinction, see Schelling, 'Philosophical letters on dogmatism and criticism'.
11 Luhmann, *Die Wissenschaft der Gesellschaft*, p. 127 (translation A. E.).
12 Further evidence of this inevitability has recently been provided by Crispin Wright's attempt to reformulate Kant's refutation of idealism via a precise analysis of Humean scepticism's logical structure. See Wright, 'Warrant for nothing (and foundations for free)?' esp. pp. 201–3.
13 See McDowell, 'Having the world in view: Sellars, Kant, and intentionality', p. 435: 'the intentionality, the objective purport, of perceptual experience in general – whether potentially knowledge yielding or not – depends . . . on having the world in view, in a sense that goes beyond glimpses of the here and

now. It would not be intelligible that the relevant episodes present themselves as glimpses of the here and now apart from their being related to a wider world view.'

14 Were they also practically replaceable, Hume would have to fear that his writings could lead to the collapse of human civilisation as we know it: this could hardly function as it does without the habit of thinking intrinsic connections between events. The distinction between logical and practical replaceability corresponds to Hume's distinction between philosophy and nature. Though we cannot *logically* avoid regarding certain assumptions as replaceable, we are unable to replace them *in practice*.

15 CPR, BXXX.

16 See the oft-cited opening of the *Critique of Pure Reason*: 'Human reason has the peculiar fate in one species of its cognitions that it is burdened with questions which it cannot dismiss, since they are given to it as problems by the nature of reason itself, but which it also cannot answer, since they transcend every capacity of human reason' (CPR AVII). According to Kant, rational beings incline to metaphysics in virtue of their very rationality. They believe, falsely, that they can ultimately satisfy this inclination with knowledge (i.e. with *answers* to their questions).

17 I say *potentially* diverge because the point is not that we are trapped in our representations and simply have no access to the representable, to the world in itself. In what follows, I shall be arguing that true beliefs connect us directly with the world. Only false beliefs seal us off into the empty realm of mere holding-true. Hume, of course, sees things otherwise.

18 McDowell calls the image of a world outside of the mind, which is to be compared with the world within the mind, a sideways-on picture. He rejects this together with Kant. See McDowell, *Mind and World*, pp. 34ff.

19 See McDowell, 'Having the world in view', esp. pp. 445, 490.

20 See Davidson, 'A coherence theory of truth and knowledge', p. 144: '[O]f course we can't get outside our skins to find out what is causing the internal happening of which we are aware. Introducing intermediate steps or entities into the causal chain, like sensations or observations, serves only to make the epistemological problem more obvious.'

21 CPR, B93.

22 Sellars, *Empiricism and the Philosophy of Mind*, p. 54.

23 For the refutation of representationalism in antiquity, see my account in 'Zum Außenweltproblem in der Antike: Sextus' Dekonstruktion des mentalen Repräsentationalismus und die skeptische Begründung des Idealismus bei Plotin'.

24 Hegel, *Phenomenology of Spirit*, §73.

25 Andrea Kern revives this Kantian insight into epistemic finitude in a similar way in *Sources of Knowledge*, esp. pp. 31–51. Kern introduces the category of truth-guaranteeing reasons which undermine an absolutely dividing boundary between mind and world. She does not, however, distinguish between a *formal* and a *material* criterion of truth, meaning that it is occasionally unclear whether she wants to show that we know whether we know something, since

truth-guaranteeing reasons are reflexive, or whether she simply wants to say that we know at least that we possess truth-guaranteeing reasons if we know anything at all.

26 For a more extensive discussion of this point, see Gabriel, *Das Absolute und die Welt in Schellings Freiheitsschrift*.

27 CPR, B133.

28 The analytical unity of consciousness pertains to all common concepts as such, e.g., if I think of **red** in general, I thereby represent to myself a feature that (as a mark) can be encountered in anything, or that can be combined with other representations; therefore only by means of antecedently conceived possible synthetic unity can I represent to myself the analytical unity. A representation that is to be thought of as common to **several** must be regarded as belonging to those that in addition to it also have something **different** in themselves; consequently they must antecedently be conceived in synthetic unity with other (even if only possible representations) before I can think of the analytical unity of consciousness in it that makes it into a *conceptus communis*. And thus the synthetic unity of apperception is the highest point to which one must affix all use of the understanding, even the whole of logic and, after it, transcendental philosophy; indeed this faculty is the understanding itself. (CPR, B133–4)

29 Fumerton therefore in fact describes a Kantian position precisely when he takes himself to be arguing against the supposedly Kantian idea that we impress a form onto a wholly unstructured world-material (the manifold of sensation).

But despite the periodic popularity of extreme nominalism and rampant antirealism, it is surely absurd to suppose that it is even in principle possible for a mind to force a structure on a *literally* unstructured world. There are indefinitely many ways to sort the books in a library and some are just as useful as others, but there would be no way to begin sorting books were books undifferentiated. Indeed, it comes to us with far too many differences for us to be bothered noticing all of them. And it is in this sense that the mind *does* impose order on chaos. (*Metaepistemology and Skepticism*, p. 78)

Compare Castoriadis, 'The logic of magmas and the question of autonomy', p. 306: 'This is the old problem of Kantian criticism, which one could never glide over. All organizational forms immanent to the transcendental consciousness . . . cannot provide anything if the "material" they are to "form" does not already include in itself the "minimal form" of being form*able*. Let it be noted in passing that the idea of an *absolutely* disordered universe is for us unthinkable.' See also his book *The Imaginary Institution of Society*, pp. 12ff.

30 See Luhmann's interpretation of 'order from noise' theories in Luhmann, *Social Systems*, p. 172.

31 Following Kant, Habermas speaks in this connection of a 'formal presupposition of the world' (*Truth and Justification*, p. 98; see too pp. 77, 16, 27, 61). He

sees this in the necessary 'presupposition of a single objective world existing independently of us' (p. 20).

32 Schelling's and Hegel's respective ways of thinking about the unconditioned connect up with this point. On this topic, see Gabriel, *Transcendetnal Ontology*, especially pp. 2–34.

33 OC §131.

34 CPR, B534.

35 CPR, B300.

36 See Cavell, *The Claim of Reason: Wittgenstein, Skepticism, Morality, and Tragedy*, p. 62: 'Experience must, *sub specie humanitatis*, make sense. "A freak of nature" is one explanation which makes sense of experience; but it is . . . a specific explanation, competent only under certain conditions. And the field of sense, over which explanations range from "I just don't know" to "It's a freak of nature", is broader than any a priori bargain knows. Science, history, magic, myth, superstition, religion, are all in that field. There is no short-cut across it.'

37 This conception is of course extremely important for the phenomenological tradition's concept of the world, as Husserl continually affirms. See, for example, Husserl, *The Crisis of European Sciences and Transcendental Phenomenology*, p.142: 'The world is pre-given to us, the waking, the always somehow practically interested subjects, not occasionally but always and necessarily as the universal field of all actual and possible praxis, as horizon. To live is always to live-in-certainty-of-the-world.' On the anti-sceptical reinterpretation of the concept of the world in Kant and post-Kantian idealism, see Gabriel, *Transcendental Ontology*, pp. 2–34.

38 'We have sufficiently proved in the Transcendental Aesthetic that everything intuited in space or in time, hence all objects of an experience possible for us, are nothing but appearances, i.e., mere representations, which, as they are represented, as extended beings or series of alterations, have outside our thoughts no existence grounded in itself' (CPR, A490/B518f). The only thing which Kant believes rescues him from an *esse-est-percipi* idealism is the assumption of the thing in itself – i.e. the *assumption* that something exists independently of our representations. Kant therefore opposes his *formal* to a *material* idealism, which 'itself doubts or denies the existence of external things' (CPR, B519). He advocates what Marcus Willaschek designates as a 'minimal', as opposed to a 'qualitative', realism (see Willaschek, *Der mentale Zugang zur Welt: Realismus, Skeptizismus und Intentionalität*, pp. 13f.). To be sure, we must assume that the existence of 'external things' is independent of our representations (else we could not explain why we could not simply represent whatever we liked). Yet how they appear to us (their qualities) depends upon our apprehension of things.

39 Compare Kant's only superficially contradictory statements: 'I freely admit that the remembrance of David Hume was the very thing that many years ago first interrupted my dogmatic slumber and gave a completely different direction to my researches in the field of speculative philosophy' (P 4:260). On 21 September 1798, Kant wrote to Christian Garve that the antinomy in the concept of the world 'first aroused me from my dogmatic slumber and

drove me to the critique of pure reason itself, in order to resolve the scandal of ostensible contradiction of reason with itself' (Kant, *Correspondence*, p. 552).

40 CPR, B451f.

41 For Kant's engagement with different varieties of scepticism, see Forster, *Kant and Skepticism*.

42 CPR, A369ff.

43 A good overview of Putnam's various conceptions of realism can be found in Heidemann, 'Metaphysik und Realismus in der Erkenntnistheorie'.

Chapter 3 Metaphysical Realism and the Naïve Ontology of Individuals

1 Williams, *Descartes: The Project of Pure Enquiry*, pp. 64f.

2 See Moore, 'Proof of an external world'.

3 Ibid., p. 128.

4 Ibid., p. 130. Kant does in fact define *'empirically outer* objects' without further ado as things 'that are to be encountered in space' (CPR, A374).

5 Kant does not of course intend to demonstrate the existence of the external world as it is invoked by mental representationalism. Mental representationalism ultimately reduces it to a possible hypothesis to explain our feeling of being passively affected. Kant's own presuppositions, his concept of the world in particular, enter into his refutation, which thus has a very different aim to Moore's. Moore, it must be said, does not address any strictly exegetical question but, rather, asks whether Kant's Refutation of Idealism and its presuppositions actually provide an adequate description of the problem of the external world.

6 CPR, B207.

7 CPR, B272.

8 'Mode of registration' translates the German *Registratur*. *Registratur* is a technical term used throughout the text to designate any means for registering and presenting information in a determinate manner according to an in-principle specifiable process or procedure. The term is deliberately unspecific as to the kinds of information in question, the kinds of output the *Registratur* produces, the medium that realises the registering activity, how the *Registratur*'s principles of selection function, how the *Registratur* processes information (if at all), and whether the information registered is generated by the *Registratur* itself or given to it externally. As such, 'mode of registration' encompasses not only such physical products as measuring devices or computational tools, and not only natural processes such as perceptual systems, but also consciousness and discourses themselves. See chapter 8 for a discussion of discourses as modes of registration.

9 Moore, 'Proof of an external world', p. 132.

10 CPR, B278.

11 Ibid.

12 Moore, 'Proof of an external world', p. 130.

13 See Moore, 'A defence of common sense', p. 46: 'In the case of the term "physical fact", I can only explain how I am using it by giving examples. I mean by "physical fact", facts *like* the following: "That mantelpiece is at present nearer to this body than the bookcase is", "The earth has existed for many years past". . . . But, when I say "facts *like* these", I mean, of course, facts like them *in a certain respect*; and what this respect is I cannot define.'

14 Sellars calls this picture *the manifest image*, which he distinguishes from *the scientific image* with which it stands in conflict. See Sellars, 'Philosophy and the scientific image of man'.

15 A practising Hindu will believe, for example, that his life is entangled in interconnected destinies which form part of an encompassing unity, transcending space and time. What she experiences is, for her, a kind of dream inspired by a God. The doctrine of the Maya, the illusion in which we live, has hardly gone unknown in the West and was widespread, for example, in the Romantic period (it was especially important for Schopenhauer in light of his reading of Kant). Were India representative of humanity as a whole, the prospects for the everyday realism of *common sense* would look dim. Common sense is clearly not a static concept, especially as it is unclear how one might begin to make a survey of which peoples and groups do and do not consider themselves inhabitants of Moore's world of public physical objects.

16 With Jay Bernstein, we might define modernity precisely as a loss of the *sensus communis*. It can still be experienced in aesthetic experience, but then only momentarily and in the mode of absence. Bernstein understands modern art as the work of mourning which grieves the loss of a common sense. See Bernstein, *The Fate of Art: Aesthetic Alienation from Kant to Derrida and Adorno*.

17 CPR, B883: 'The **naturalist** of pure reason takes as his principle that through common understanding without science (which he calls "healthy reason" [Common Sense!, M. G.]) more may be accomplished with regard to the most sublime questions that constitute the task of metaphysics than through speculation.'

18 Luhmann, *Die Wissenschaft der Gesellschaft*, p. 653. The effects of science are not coincidentally related to scepticism, as Luhmann also remarks. 'Science makes us aware of invisible threats, of radioactivity, of holes in the ozone layer, of the unconscious. It removes the foothold we previously thought we had in the world. It reduces the normal to an extremely unlikely contingency. It relativises, historicises, and exceptionalises the familiar conditions of human life, without replacing their familiarity with a functional equivalent' (ibid., p. 654).

19 Anton Koch's monumental *Versuch über Wahrheit und Zeit* represents an important exception. Koch attempts to combine an ontology of individuals with the thesis that all cognitive projects are necessarily incomplete. His position is far removed from the ontology of individuals that I want to bring into question here, insofar as he aims to show that there can be a system of individuals at all only when subjectivity as an individual – i.e. subjectivity in space and time – also features within such a system. Koch calls this the 'subjectivity thesis'. This thesis goes far beyond a naïve ontology of individuals, since it makes individuals and subjectivity mutually dependent.

20 Heidegger, in *Being and Time*, famously turns against the naïve ontology of individuals, which he sees as the origin of the very scepticism that it goes on to combat as its supposed other. The naïve ontology of individuals results, in his view, from a generalisation of a certain concept of being suggested by the natural attitude to the world. A complex philosophical position follows from this thesis, which Heidegger, following Fichte, characterises as dogmatism in his 1929 Freiburg lecture 'Der deutsche Idealismus (Fichte, Schelling, Hegel) und die philosophische Problemlage der Gegenwart', p. 127.

21 See Habermas, 'Actions, speech acts, linguistically mediated interactions and the lifeworld', p. 70.

Chapter 4 Conceptual Relativity and the World

1 On this, see Zimmermann, *Der 'Skandal der Philosophie' und die Semantik: Kritische und systematische Untersuchungen zur analytischen Ontologie und Erfahrungstheorie.*

2 CPR, B534.

3 As in Goodman, *Ways of Worldmaking.*

4 If the idealist fails to account for this divergence, she becomes a subjectivist who identifies truth with the private holding-true of some individual judger. If two parties then argue about subjectivism, it would be true for one and false for the other, leaving no room to exclude subjectivism's being at once true and false. The truth that subjectivism can be true for one party and false for another would in turn be true for one party and false for another, and so on *ad infinitum.*

5 On this topic, see Gabriel, 'Kunst und Metaphysik bei Malewitsch – Das schwarze Quadrat als Kritik der platonischen Metaphysik der Kunst'.

6 Novalis, 'When numbers and figures', p. 325.

7 One of the strengths of Goodman's position surely lies in how he attempts to do justice to art without reducing it epistemologically. On the basis of an aesthetic of the non-propositional, Wolfgang Hogrebe's entire philosophical approach opposes the assumption of a unified standard discourse modelled on a purely objective cognition of the world. See Hogrebe, *Die Wirklichkeit des Denkens.* On Hogrebe's aesthetics of the non-propositional, see Gabriel, 'On Wolfram Hogrebe's philosophical approach', esp. pp. 209ff.

8 See Davidson's arguments against linguistic relativism in 'On the very idea of a conceptual scheme'. We cannot consistently leave the concept of the world behind if we want to be able to take account of a plurality of conceptual decisions or contexts. An example of an attempt to replace talk of the world with talk of different versions of the world is again Goodman's *Ways of Worldmaking.* Goodman's argument for his irrealism appeals to the impossibility of saying what the world is without having already fixed a frame of reference, which represents the world in a certain fashion. The question of what the world is independently of all frames of reference is then either senseless or itself defines a new frame of reference (a frame of reference without a frame of reference):

'We are confined to ways of describing whatever is described. Our universe, so to speak, consists of these ways rather than of a world or of worlds' (ibid., p. 3). Nevertheless, it should be noted that in the cited passage, Goodman simply replaces the expression 'world' with 'our universe' and so speaks as though all versions do make reference to something that we commonly call the world, but which he simply renames 'our universe'. Goodman, therefore, does not truly get rid of the world as the unified background against which we can distinguish different perspectives.

9 Kant himself, of course, operates not with a plurality of conceptual frameworks but with a finite and knowable set of concepts (categories and ideas). On his account, all appearances must be structured by just these concepts if they are to be something for us, something to which predicates can be applied in judgements of experience. The conceptual decisions that determine what constitutes an appearance as such are therefore neither variable nor optional.

10 From the very beginning, Kant's dualism of form and content has invited a number of philosophers (including of course, in recent times, Quine, Goodman, Putnam, Rorty) to assume a pluralism of transcendental forms which grant access to an objective reality. If one accepts the possibility of a plurality of frames of reference (of transcendental forms) and understands 'appearances' as contents that come about only in virtue of their conceptual organisation (be these a priori in Kant's sense or not), then it still makes sense to assume a thing in itself. In this case, it is a matter of empirical, and so revisable, conceptual decisions which allow us to see what there is in respectively different ways. In one respect, the same thing can differ; it might be, say, the object of a fetish for one person and a physical object for another. In the respect in which it is and remains the same thing, however, it is no longer available to a conceptual decision and is, to that extent, a thing in itself. This is not to say that the concepts Kant takes as fundamental (categories, ideas, etc.) are optional and so replaceable. Kant looks for a set of concepts which provide for the possibility of taking various conceptual decisions in the first place. I am here extracting his distinction between the thing in itself and appearance from the narrower context of his transcendental philosophy, in order to show how we can substitute the thesis of conceptual relativity for the naïve ontology of individuals without advocating a relativism that is liable to succumb to paradoxes.

11 See Hogrebe, *Echo des Nichtwissens*, pp. 317–30, here pp. 317f. Hogrebe calls the 'space that is split up by every distinction which we draw' the 'space of possible distinctions, which we can also designate as the dimension of distinctions. Each introduction of basal distinctions makes use of this dimension and, as such, it can no longer be distinguished from other spaces. Indeed, though it cannot be designated positively we cannot do without it, as we would otherwise be unable to use our distinctions to generate a universe. It is the fully diaphanous semantic background of all semantic contrasts, the transcendental condition of their possibility.'

12 CPR, B310f.

13 Luhmann, *Die Wissenschaft der Gesellschaft*, pp. 212f. (translation A. E.).

14 See CPR, A250f.:

All our representations are in fact related to some object through the understanding, and, since appearances are nothing but representations, the understanding thus relates them to a **something**, as the object of sensible intuition: but this something is to that extent only the transcendental object. This signifies, however, a something = X, of which we know nothing at all nor can know anything in general (in accordance with the current constitution of our understanding). . . . This transcendental object cannot even be separated from the sensible *data*, for then nothing would remain through which it would be thought. It is therefore no object of cognition in itself, but only the representation of appearances under the concept of an object in general, which is determinable through the manifold of those appearances.

15 Hogrebe, *Prädikation und Genesis: Fundamentalheuristik im Ausgang von Schellings 'Die Weltalter'*, p. 49.

16 Crispin Wright has pursued a similar strategy in his 'Warrant for nothing', pp. 201–3.

17 CPR, B275.

18 CPR, B278.

19 CPR, BXXXIVf.

20 This is one of the central theses of Prauss, *Kant und das Problem der Dinge an sich*.

21 For the distinction between sense dependence and reference dependence, see Brandom, *Tales of the Mighty Dead*, pp. 50f.

22 A monumental attempt to spell out the reference dependence of subjectivity and objectivity can be found in Anton Friedrich Koch's *Versuch über Wahrheit und Zeit*. A generalised form of what is often known as 'Trendelenburg's gap' lurks behind the question of the extent to which subjectivity and objectivity are sense- or reference-dependent. The question then becomes whether any analysis of intentionality – that is, of our mental access to the world – allows an inference to the structure of the world itself. See Trendelenburg, 'Über eine Lücke in Kants Beweis von der ausschließlichen Subjectivität des Raumes und der Zeit'.

23 'Theory-level transition' translates the German *Metabase*, from the Greek μεταβαίνειν, meaning 'to transcend'. Here it indicates transitioning or passing over to another categorial level.

24 In a famous letter to Garve from 21 September 1798, Kant states explicitly that it was the cosmological question which, in the form of the antinomies, had awoken him 'from my dogmatic slumber and drove me to the critique of reason itself, in order to resolve the scandal of ostensible contradiction of reason with itself.' See Kant, *Correspondence*, p. 552. Kant thus explicitly recognises two problems that led him from his dogmatic slumbers: Humean scepticism and the world problem.

25 CPR, B311.

26 CPR, B312.

27 The unknown something underlying all objects, which can be thematised conceptually without ever becoming an object itself, is significant not only

in a narrowly philosophical sense but also within aesthetics. I am here once again thinking of Kaspar Malevich's *Black Square* (1915), which instigated objectless art. Suprematism sets out from the idea that art, science and religion (various conceptual frameworks) all relate to some object that cannot be grasped independently of conceptual decisions. It is the radical objectlessness that is nevertheless objectified in all objects. This is why Malevich expresses it as a geometrical form without any content: he ultimately intends the image to capture the primordial intentionality that is directed to something without already having grasped anything through concepts. All conceptual frameworks are inherently directed at grasping something that cannot be grasped conceptually. We can see that Kant's thing in itself does not designate any existing beyond by observing how he integrates it into the construction of his theory of freedom, and thus into his concept of the *mundus intelligibilis* (in the context of his practical philosophy).

28 CPR, BXXXIXfn.
29 AL, 7.393: εἰ δὲ πάντ᾽ ἔσται πρόδηλα, οὐδὲν ἔσται τὸ ζητεῖν καὶ ἀπορεῖν περὶ τινος. ζητεῖ γάρ τις καὶ ἀπορεῖ περὶ τοῦ ἀδηλουμένου αὐτῷ πράγματος, ἀλλ᾽ οὐχὶ περὶ τοῦ φανεροῦ. ἄτοπον δέ γέ ἐστι τὸ ζήτησιν καὶ ἀπορίαν ἀναιρεῖν.
30 Moore, 'Proof of an external world', pp. 138f.
31 The *omnitudio realitatis* is 'the idea of an All of reality' (CPR, B603f). Since every determinate something or other is distinguished from everything it is not and is discursively determinable through a specifiable series of distinctions, we must, Kant says, assume an All or a 'sum total of all possibility' (CPR, B601). 'All true negations are then nothing but **limits**, which they could not be called unless they were grounded in the unlimited (the All)' (CPR, B604).
32 Kant's oft-cited admission: 'I freely admit that the remembrance of David Hume was the very thing that many years ago first interrupted my dogmatic slumber and gave a completely new direction to my researches in the field of speculative philosophy.' See P 4:260.
33 CPR, B75.
34 Strawson takes this thought, spelled out in the Analogies of Experience, to be constitutive for the Refutation of Idealism. See Strawson, *The Bounds of Sense: An Essay on Immanuel Kant's Critique of Pure Reason*, pp. 125–40. Strawson encapsulates Kant's argument in the fundamental insight that 'the idea of a subjective experiential route through an objective world depends on the idea of the identity of that world through and in spite of the changes in our experience; and this idea in turn depends on our perceiving objects as having permanence independent of our perceptions of them, and hence being able to identify objects as numerically the same in different perceptual situations.'
35 See Koch, *Versuch über Wahrheit und Zeit*, § 5.
36 CPR, B537. See too B611, 647.
37 For an extensive account of this idea, see Gabriel, *Der Mensch im Mythos: Untersuchungen über Ontotheologie, Anthropologie und Selbstbewußtseinsgeschichte in Schellings 'Philosophie der Mythologie'*, §5.
38 A critique of pure reason can 'sever the very root of **materialism, fatalism,**

atheism, of freethinking **unbelief,** of **enthusiasm** and **superstition,** which can become generally injurious, and finally also of **idealism** and **scepticism,** which are more dangerous to the schools and can hardly be transmitted to the public' (CPR, BXXXIV).

39 Andrea Kern uses the phrase 'paradoxical reinterpretation of sceptical doubt' in order to emphasise an aspect of Wittgenstein's engagement with scepticism. A paradoxical reinterpretation accepts one or several sceptical premises but doubts whether they result in any sort of epistemic disadvantage. What is conceded to the sceptic is, rather, that she has uncovered an essential move of our justificatory praxis in some domain. See Kern, 'Understanding scepticism: Wittgenstein's paradoxical reinterpretation of sceptical doubt'.

40 For Kant, metaphysical enthusiasm [*Schwärmerei*] is '**a delusion of being able to *see* something beyond all bounds of sensibility,** i.e., to dream in accordance with principles (to rave with reason).' See Kant, CJ, A124.

41 CPR, B274.

42 See Conant, 'Varieties of scepticism', p. 98:

> the term 'scepticism' (and its variants, such as 'Cartesian scepticism' or 'Kantian scepticism') therefore refers not just to one particular sort of philosophical *position* (i.e. held by one or another sort of sceptic) but rather to the wider *dialectical space* within which philosophers occupying a range of apparently opposed philosophical positions (such as 'realism', 'idealism', 'coherentism', etc.) engage one another, while seeking a stable way to answer the sceptic's question in the affirmative rather than (as the sceptic himself does) in the negative.

43 A prominent exception is Peter Unger. See Unger, *Ignorance: A Case for Scepticism.*

Chapter 5 Direct and Indirect Sceptical Arguments

1 Following Robert Fumerton, one can correlate the distinction between logical and dialectical analysis with the distinction between normative epistemology and meta-epistemology. While *normative epistemology* presupposes certain foundational epistemological concepts and tries to determine what we know or believe, *meta-epistemology* investigates the fundamental concepts of epistemological discourse itself. See Fumerton, *Metaepistemology and Skepticism*, pp. 1f. Like Fumerton, in what follows I attempt to argue for the thesis that a dialectical analysis of epistemology (that is, meta-epistemology) enables us to clarify the relation between epistemology and scepticism that ultimately eludes enquiry at the level of strictly logical analysis of sceptical arguments (i.e. at the level of normative epistemology).

2 That epistemology has a tendency to emphasise securing knowledge at the expense of seeking knowledge is Wolfram Hogrebe's diagnosis. It receives an especially clear formulation in Hogrebe, *Prädikation und Genesis*, pp. 47f.

3 Robert Nozick makes a similar observation regarding 'How is X possible?' questions. In order to ask, e.g., how freedom is possible, one must first entertain the possibility that freedom might be impossible. In other words, one has to introduce an alternative. In the case of the problem of freedom, this would be determinism. In the context of epistemology, the question of how knowledge is possible is, correspondingly, first enabled by sceptical hypotheses. See Nozick, *Philosophical Explanations*, pp. 8–11. See also Heidegger's thesis in §6 of *Being and Time*, that the problematisation of our access to the world presupposes a *'break'* and a 'deprivation of its worldhood' (Heidegger, *Being and Time*, pp. 105–6). The foundational epistemological question of what knowledge is also goes back to a *'disturbed assignment'* (ibid., p. 105). We could not pose it if we *sensu stricto* knew everything and so never crashed into any cognitive boundary. See Gabriel, 'Endlichkeit und absolutes Ich'.

4 PI, §219.

5 The famous citation reads 'When I obey a rule, I do not choose. I obey the rule blindly' (PI §219). The talk of blindly following a rule is misleading, however, insofar as, on Wittgensteinian premises, one can only see anything at all when one follows some rule or other *blindly*. It is only by refusing to be forced into a justificatory regress by citing reasons for interpreting rules in one way rather than another that we can exercise linguistic competence. In a different passage, Wittgenstein uses another of his favoured metaphors and says that we follow the rule *mechanically* (RFM, p. 422). The regress argument behind this idea and its sceptical presuppositions will be discussed extensively below in chapter 9.

6 Stroud, *The Significance of Philosophical Scepticism*; Williams, *Groundless Belief, Unnatural Doubts*, and *Problems of Knowledge: A Critical Introduction to Epistemology*. This thesis is widespread, and Stroud and Williams are by no means its sole ambassadors. Other prominent representatives of the thesis that, since epistemology is hopelessly Cartesian and therefore inevitably sceptical, we should leave the epistemological attitude behind are Rorty and Heidegger.

7 Heidemann comes to a similar conclusion in *Der Begriff des Skeptizismus*, where he sees scepticism as 'a condition of understanding epistemic claims' (p. 355). We take knowledge to require justification precisely because it comes under threat. 'We justify our epistemic claims because we see them threatened by scepticism. Epistemic justification is to a certain extent the appropriate reaction to threats to our knowledge posed by sceptical doubts' (ibid.).

8 David Lewis famously coined the term 'elusive knowledge' to designate the impression that knowledge dissolves into nothing when subjected to strict analytical scrutiny. See Lewis, 'Elusive knowledge'.

9 Strawson designates as 'naturalism' the anti-sceptical strategy that appeals to how we generally cannot avoid making assumptions that reveal themselves to be unjustified or unjustifiable under sceptical conditions. He uses the label 'naturalism' because the most prominent modern advocate of this strategy was Hume, who famously thought that *nature* compels us to make assumptions in our everyday lives that cannot be theoretically justified. See Strawson, *Skepticism and Naturalism: Some Varieties*. In chapter 14, we will see how important moves in Wittgenstein's anti-sceptical strategy are naturalistic.

Here, however, it suffices merely to point out, firstly, that naturalism itself presents a *sceptical* solution to a range of sceptical problems and, secondly, that it can be seen as one of the central results of Pyrrhonian scepticism. A closer look at Sextus' treatment of naturalism shows why, under sceptical conditions, we cannot see it as a justified assumption and so as a way out of the dilemma. Naturalism is itself a sceptical position which cannot be rationally justified according to the very standards accepted by the naturalist.

10 Heidegger follows Kant's dictum that the problem of the impossibility of proving the existence of a consciousness-independent world constitutes the 'scandal' of philosophy. 'The "scandal of philosophy" is not that this proof has yet to be given, but that *such proofs are expected and attempted again and again*' (*Being and Time*, p. 249). Heidegger sees the origin of this confusion in our employment of a naïve, indeed false, concept of the world in order to tackle the problem of the external world. The false concept of the world is always oriented 'with regard to entities within-the-world (Things and Objects)' (ibid., p. 247). Thus the world's actual way of being disappears from view.

11 In this sense, Robert Fogelin, a contemporary advocate of a (neo-)Pyrrhonian scepticism, speaks of 'epistemology's tendency to destroy its subject matter' (Fogelin, 'Contextualism and externalism: trading in one form of skepticism for another', p. 49). Michael Williams, another major neo-Pyrrhonian, describes the epistemologist's dilemma as follows: '[W]e can either accept scepticism, or make changes in our pre-theoretical thinking about knowledge that shrink the domain, or alter the status, of what we previously thought of as knowledge of objective fact' (*Unnatural Doubts*, p. 22). As will become clearer in our discussion of contextualism below, Fogelin's and Williams's diagnosis of the problem differs from that presented here. The most important difference is that I do not derive the dialectical tension between epistemology's basic tendencies from Cartesian scepticism alone.

12 A similar dialectical line of thought can be found in Thomas Nagel's *The View from Nowhere*. Nagel's entire book works with the tensions between the subjective standpoint of an observer of the world and her objective, uncentred concept of the world she wants to observe. According to Nagel, this tension is responsible for the fact that realism (the striving for objectivity) and scepticism (which systematically exploits our subjective inadequacies) always appear together. Nagel therefore sees the problem of epistemology in a constitutive 'inability to hold in one's mind simultaneously and in a consistent form the possibility of skepticism and the ordinary beliefs that life is full of' (ibid., p. 87).

13 Stephen Schiffer develops a topography of epistemology along these lines by reconstructing the foundational positions of contemporary epistemology as reactions to different respective premises of a sceptical argument. See Schiffer, 'Skepticism and the vagaries of justified belief'.

14 '[P]rudentiae est numquam illis plane confidere qui nos vel semel deceperunt' (AT VII, 8).

15 There is an important difference between the question of what knowledge actually is and the question of how knowledge is possible. In asking what knowledge is, we usually seek out a best or paradigmatic case of knowledge

and investigate which conditions have to be fulfilled in order for us to certify such a case as knowledge. This kind of analysis of the concept of knowledge is evident in its standard triadic analysis as justified true belief and is the target of those who try to immunise the standard analysis against Gettier cases. By contrast, asking how knowledge is possible involves investigating the conditions that have to be fulfilled for someone to refer to anything at all, something which can then be deployed in knowledge ascriptions.

16 The dream argument is already clearly formulated in Plato's *Theaetetus* (158b8ff.). Indeed, the *genius malignus* argument has a long theological pre-history, the relevance of which to the specifically Cartesian variant of external world scepticism has been explored by Dominik Perler. See 'Wie ist ein globaler Zweifel möglich? Zu den Voraussetzungen des frühneuzeitlichen Außenwelt-Skeptizismus'; also see the extensive discussion in Perler's *Zweifel und Gewissheit: Skeptische Debatten im Mittelalter*. Descartes himself is naturally aware that doubt about the senses' capacity to deliver cognition was already a topic in antiquity, a fact to which Hobbes notably refers in his first objection to the *Meditations*. Hobbes notes explicitly that the scepticism of the first meditation takes up an ancient problematic that was known as the problem of the criterion (κριτήριον). Hobbes even uses the Greek expression and refers specifically to Plato and 'other ancient philosophers' (*alii antiquorum Philosophorum*) who had already raised the problem of representations (*phantasma*) – that is, that whether anything independent of our representations corresponds to them is not something we can read off from our representations of the world. Descartes quite correctly replies that his scepticism is not supposed to be new. Rather, the first meditation clearly deploys it as a problem intended to distract the reader from the senses, so that she will turn her attention to purely mental objects (*ad res intellectuales*), objects distinct from everything corporeal that can be perceived through the senses. See AT VII, 171f. So Descartes himself concedes that the scepticism of the first meditation is no innovation, making it puzzling why Cartesian scepticism is so frequently regarded as a signum of modernity. In another passage (AT VII, 130) Descartes himself refers to the Academics and sceptics. As Gail Fine rightly emphasises, in her essay on Descartes and ancient scepticism, 'unlike many recent commentators . . . Descartes himself denies that his skepticism is more radical than ancient skepticism' (Fine, 'Descartes and ancient skepticism: reheated cabbage?', here p. 204).

17 Again, I am of course not claiming that Descartes himself advocated any kind of solipsism or scepticism. Descartes ultimately believes that a thorough examination of our thinking, triggered by the introduction of the possible impossibility of knowledge, will lead to a reclamation of knowledge via the certainty of our own and God's existence. Perler rightly emphasises this point against readings of Descartes that ascribe a form of scepticism to him on the basis of his representationalism. See Perler, *Repräsentation bei Descartes*, pp. 310–24. His representationalism belongs to his anti-sceptical strategy and not to his (methodological) scepticism.

18 See Wright, 'On Putnam's proof that we are not brains-in-a-vat', here pp. 235f.

19 Following Sextus Empiricus (OS, 2.97–103; AL, 8.145–58, 316–19), we can distinguish several forms of evidence transcendence (ἄδηλον): (1) strong contingent evidence transcendence (καθάπαξ ἄδηλον); (2) weak contingent evidence transcendence (πρὸς καιρὸν ἄδηλον); and (3) the in principle evidence-transcendent (φύσει ἄδηλον). Strong contingent evidence transcendence characterises, for example, attempts to answer the question of whether the number of stars existing at some randomly selected point in time is odd or even. (Sextus himself evidently contradicts himself here, since at one point he considers the number of stars to be a matter of strong contingent evidence transcendence [OS 2.97] and at another point considers it to be evidence-transcendent in principle [AL 8.317].) Since it is not a priori that we cannot determine the number of stars, and since there are nevertheless good reasons to assume that we will never succeed in doing so, we can speak in this case of strong contingent evidence transcendence. Weak contingent evidence transcendence pertains to cases where we are in no position to ascertain the truth value of a particular hypothesis, but where there are no good reasons why we could not introduce an appropriate decision procedure. For example: the precise number of all inhabitants of New York travelling from Times Square to Union Square within a given time frame is weakly contingently evidence-transcendent. Neither strong nor weak contingent evidence transcendence presents a sceptical problem, although it is possible to formulate sceptical arguments with scenarios possessing these levels of evidence transcendence. One need only think of Dretske's famous example of a visitor to a zoo in which, for some reason or other, all the zebras have been replaced by cunningly disguised mules. The same goes for Goodman's barn country, which suggests that the Cartesian sceptic can make do without scenarios that are evidence-transcendent in principle. Stewart Cohen distinguishes between 'restricted' and 'global sceptical alternatives' (Cohen, 'Contextualism and skepticism', here p. 103), which corresponds to the distinction between the contingently and the in principle evidence-transcendent. It may be that the global alternatives are stronger, although the sceptic would in certain circumstances be well advised to stick to the restricted ones. Genuine Cartesian sceptical scenarios are, by contrast, evidence-transcendent in principle, since it is a priori impossible to introduce any decision procedure to ascertain their truth value. According to Sextus, all metaphysical assumptions, the truth values of which can be ascertained only by means of interpretations of supposed indicative signs (ἐνδεικτικά), are *necessarily* evidence-transcendent. An example would be the metaphysical assumption (which Sextus loved to attack) of bodies existing outside of us, independently of our impressions (πάθη), which Sextus designates as 'external objects' (τὰ ἐκτὸς ὑποκείμενα) (see esp. OS, 2.72f.). If our impressions are merely indicative signs of external substances, we cannot simply infer the metaphysical constitution of external substances without further ado. His concept of indicative signs is related to the English concept of 'evidence', which plays an indispensable role in contemporary epistemology.

20 Moreover, no contextualist thus far has succeeded in setting out a theory of relevance that determines criteria that help to distinguish relevant from

irrelevant alternatives epistemically and not merely pragmatically. See Schaffer, 'From contextualism to contrastivism', pp. 87–90.

21 The following argument is a variant of Wright's argument against contextualism as an anti-sceptical strategy. See Wright, 'Contextualism and scepticism: even-handedness, factivity and surreptitiously raising standards', esp. pp. 242–5.

22 Brendel is of the view that we can even show the contextualist to be committed to the contradiction that $C_p(p)$ and that $\sim C_p(p)$. See Brendel, 'Was Kontextualisten nicht wissen'. Yet she misses the point that we never know that p in C_p. In C_C we know only that we know that p in C_E, from which it follows that we know in C_C that p. Now, if we know that p in C_C and that we do not know that p in C_p, this does not amount to a contradiction within a single context. Against Brendel's version of the anti-contextualist argument, one can object that contextualism operates with three contexts since it is *ex hypothesi* itself a context. It therefore results 'merely' in Moorean paradoxes of the form 'P and I don't know that P', but not in any logical contradiction. This is also Wright's point.

23 I here speak of having 'good reasons' for p. It is important to note the differences between having good reasons for p and having a warrant or entitlement for p. One might want to count someone as having a warrant for an assumption even though she might not be able to state good reasons for it. In certain argumentative contexts it can be highly significant that we are warranted in making assumptions about the external world, other minds or the past, even though we have undertaken no explicit justification. A dogmatist in James Pryor's sense, for example, averts the threat of Cartesian scepticism by pointing to how we are immediately entitled to assumptions seemingly threatened by Cartesian scepticism, even though we cannot cite any good reasons for our assumption. Pryor ('The skeptic and the dogmatist', p. 532) calls this 'immediate justification'. It is a characteristic of our everyday knowledge ascriptions that, when questioned, we have to be able to adduce good reasons for our knowledge, even though it is by no means necessary for us to believe that our knowledge rests on good reasons that have been negotiated *expressis verbis* in some decision procedure. In other words, it is a necessary condition of knowledge that the knower be in a position to produce good reasons for her knowledge and be able to defend them. Again, this does not imply that her knowledge acquisition is based on an explicit decision procedure, otherwise it would be impossible for anyone to claim observational knowledge, which is precisely characterised by its being a non-inferential mode of knowledge acquisition. See Robert Brandom's discussion of the concept of knowledge in *Making it Explicit: Reasoning, Representing, and Discursive Commitment*, pp. 199ff.

24 A perceptual reason is, for example, a perception that *p*. Say someone claims to know that her bicycle is in the car park: if challenged, she will usually, quite rightly, appeal to how she can see, or has just seen, that her bicycle is in the relevant location. She just provides a perceptual reason. Perceptions therefore belong to our game of giving and asking for reasons and are not pre-rational, purely sensorial events.

25 The internalist assumption of the *iterativity* of reasons confronts us with a familiar regress argument: we could never have any rationally justified belief if rational justification implied the iterativity of reasons, since we would then have to justify all reasons. The ensuing regress is obvious. Yet the same argument results from a form of externalism. Suppose, for example, an externalist asserts that we could have direct non-inferential knowledge of the external world without necessarily knowing that we have this knowledge. She could appeal to how a correct analysis of the causal influence of the world on our sense organs leads to the result that hallucinations and veridical perceptions are respectively caused by completely different processes, even though the two states are phenomenologically indistinguishable. Therefore, she reasons, we cannot know by introspection or through analysis of the phenomenological structure of perception whether we know anything about the external world. Yet such a variety of externalism faces two problems: (1) it commits a *petitio principi* against the sceptic insofar as it simply assumes the existence of an external world and that this assumption alone delivers a distinction between veridical perception and hallucination; (2) it opens the way to a second-order scepticism that, rather than asserting that we have no direct non-inferential knowledge of the external world, merely claims that we can have no good reasons for the assumption that we have direct non-inferential knowledge *that* we have direct non-inferential knowledge about the external world. As Fumerton argues: '[e]ven if we abandon strong access internalism, however, we might find skepticism that maintains that we have no justification for believing that we have a justified belief that *P* just as threatening as skepticism that concludes that we are unjustified in believing *P*' (*Metaepistemology and Skepticism*, p. 168).

26 See Grundmann and Stüber, *Philosophie der Skepsis*, pp. 44ff.

27 See also Kern, 'Warum kommen unsere Gründe an ein Ende? Zum Begriff endlichen Wissens', here p. 35: 'The regress of justifications hit upon by the sceptic is therefore a regress not only *of* justifications – the demand for reasons goes on indefinitely – but *about* justification itself, because it concerns a demand for reasons for reasons. It is a regress which arises precisely at that moment at which justification relates to itself and asks after its own credentials.' One possibility for refuting the indirect argument consists in looking for a counterargument that formulates an a priori justification for our trust in our everyday information-processing. This would mean demonstrating that there is 'immediate justification', where this implies extending the concept of 'justification' to such an extent that every explicit or implicit justification that *p* can already count as 'justification'. This strategy has been pursued by James Pryor, for example. See Pryor, 'The skeptic and the dogmatist' and 'There is immediate justification'. Pryor makes a distinction between 'justification' on the one hand and 'warrant' or 'entitlement' on the other. The concept of 'entitlement' is usually introduced in the sense of a non-inferential justification that we have to assume in order to avoid vicious circles, e.g. in epistemological justifications of logical axioms such as *modus ponens*. Accordingly, we are entitled to assume logical axioms if and only if they are indispensable for the operation of

our discursive rationality as such. In the theory of perception, one commonly speaks of 'perceptual entitlement' in this sense in order to show that we are entitled to knowledge claims on a basic perceptual level even when there is in principle no way to defend these against sceptical objections. Pryor's wide concept of 'justification' therefore seems to suggest that we are explicitly entitled simply to dismiss the sceptic, thus ultimately once again begging the question against him. Pryor's anti-sceptical strategy belongs to the rubric of externalist anti-sceptical strategies insofar as he introduces a broad concept of justification, on which it is no longer necessary to obtain a meta-justification for our perceptually based beliefs against the sceptic's objections. For this reason, Pryor designates his belief as 'dogmatism'. On the concept of 'entitlement', see Burge, 'Perceptual entitlement'; Dretske, 'Entitlement: epistemic rights without epistemic duties'; and Peacocke, *The Realm of Reason*, esp. chs 1–2.

28 By a 'theoretical diagnosis', Michael Williams understands: 'the strategy of attempting to uncover the sceptic's essential *epistemological* presuppositions. I shall never accuse the sceptic of incoherence. I shall not argue that his problems are pseudo-problems. On the contrary, I think that they are fully genuine, *but only given certain theoretical ideas about knowledge and justification*' (*Unnatural Doubts*, p. 37). Only once the motivation of a given form of scepticism has been made clear can we make any decisions about scepticism's coherence or incoherence. The same goes *mutatis mutandis* for every form of scepticism, not just Cartesian scepticism.

29 OC §383.

30 To be sure, Wittgenstein himself points to the possibility of a contingent match between dream and reality in another passage from *On Certainty*: 'Someone who, dreaming, says "I am dreaming", even if he speaks audibly in doing so, is no more right than if he said in his dream "it is raining", while it was in fact raining. Even if his dream were actually connected with the noise of the rain' (OC §676). It seems to me that, here, he wants to claim that the statement 'I am dreaming' can never be correct, meaning that Cartesian scepticism implies the possibility of a statement that can never be asserted. But this is no objection to Cartesian scepticism; in fact, it strengthens it. For the sceptical hypothesis asserts that nobody can ever be right if it is true. We can never be right when we are in a dream state if being right is a normative status implying assessability by others, something never given in the case of a dream in which we are solipsistic subjects. Wittgenstein's reflection thus strengthens the impetus of Cartesian scepticism. After all, what could possibly be more sceptical than the hypothesis that we might possibly never be right even though it seems to us as though we are? Thomas Nagel has raised a similar objection to Putnam's externalist anti-sceptical strategy in *The View from Nowhere*, pp. 71–3. Duncan Pritchard sees *On Certainty* §§383, 676, as an attempt to reject scepticism by excluding the possibility that it can be so much as comprehensible; these passages would thereby anticipate Wright's implosion argument. This interpretation is only partially correct, because 'being right', for Wittgenstein, is not merely a mental state, one brought about through competent thinking,

but an intersubjective state, which can be achieved only in a language spoken by several subjects. By definition, this is excluded in the case of the solipsistic dreaming subject. See Pritchard, 'Scepticism and dreaming', here p. 376. Wittgenstein himself frequently emphasises that entitlement and justification presuppose a form of life and, consequently, the existence of other subjects. See for example PI, §378; OC, §271.

31 This is the basis for those anti-sceptical strategies, discussed above, that attempt to distinguish relevant from irrelevant (sceptical) hypotheses. Sceptical hypotheses, that is, seem to be irrelevant because they do not present alternative explanations of our experiences of the world that need to be borne in mind in rational thought or action. The problem with this anti-sceptical strategy is not only that certain of its instances work with a possible worlds semantics, which is itself laden with philosophical presuppositions, but rather that it is impossible to contest the relevance of sceptical hypotheses per se. The sceptic can counter at any time that her hypotheses become relevant as soon as she expresses them. It is difficult to state a criterion for the relevance of alternatives that would a priori prevent the introduction of sceptical alternatives, as we can always construct sceptical hypotheses by bringing into consideration empirical possibilities that precisely cannot be excluded a priori. There cannot in principle be a philosophical argument to the effect that we are not in *The Truman Show*.

32 See Fogelin, 'The skeptics are coming! The skeptics are coming!', pp. 165f.:

> If that is right, then the skeptic's doubt – so the argument sometimes goes – undercuts the very expressability of his doubts. It is hard to see, however, how this threat of semantic (instead of epistemic) nihilism provides solace. Perhaps we just *are* brains in vats and so deeply fuddled semantically that no sense attaches to the sceptical scenarios we formulate – or to anything else either. Standard Cartesian doubt pales in comparison with the threat of semantic nihilism.

33 See my overview of the debate in Gabriel, 'Die Wiederkehr des Nichtwissens – Perspektiven der zeitgenössischen Skeptizismus-Debatte'.

Chapter 6 Crispin Wright's Implosion of Cartesian Scepticism and its Dialectic

1 Wright's anti-sceptical strategies can be sorted roughly into two categories. One kind of strategy confronts *Cartesian*, the other *Humean* scepticism. Characteristic of Humean scepticism, for Wright, is the problem of induction, which relegates the assumption of regularities in nature to a mere unjustifiable hypothesis. For his engagement with Cartesian scepticism, see Wright, 'Scepticism and dreaming: imploding the demon' and 'On Putnam's proof'. For his engagement with Humean scepticism, see Wright, '(Anti-)-sceptics simple and subtle: G. E. Moore and John McDowell', 'Wittgensteinian

certainties', 'Warrant for nothing' and 'Contextualism and scepticism'. The distinction between two forms of scepticism and the introduction of corresponding anti-sceptical strategies can already be found in Wright, 'Facts and certainty', though he has since made important modifications to his view.

2 David Macarthur observes that Cartesian scepticism rests on a reflection that leads into an equipollence of scepticism and anti-scepticism and which should therefore be seen as an instance of Pyrrhonian scepticism. See Macarthur, 'Naturalism and skepticism', pp. 114f.

3 See Schiffer, 'Skepticism and the vagaries of justified belief', pp. 161ff. Schiffer draws attention to how Cartesian scepticism cannot be motivated merely by introducing a logical possibility – else the logical possibility that I could have seventeen noses would also present a potential epistemological problem (how can I *know* that I could not have seventeen noses . . .). For this reason, we must first specify the epistemic relevance of Cartesian sceptical scenarios. It is not enough to generalise our everyday fallibility in light of the mere possibility of perpetual error, even though this generalisation is definitely a necessary moment of Cartesian scepticism.

4 A striking number of the surviving fragments from Heraclitus refer to the phenomenon of dreams: D21, 26, 73, 65, 88. Fragment D89 is especially worth mentioning: 'The world of the waking is one and shared, but the sleeping turn aside each into his private world' (τοῖς ἐγρηγορόσιν ἕνα καὶ κοινὸν κόσμον εἶναι, τῶν δὲ κοιμωμένων ἕκαστον εἰς ἴδιον ἀποστρέφεσθαι). The universal, though, is only open to thinking (D113). Heraclitus therefore already opposes the private and the public in order to distinguish between being awake and asleep. Here, I just want to point to how he explicitly deploys a method of self-exploration (D101, 116) in order to make his philosophical judgements, a method that was adopted much later by Descartes in order to introduce an analysis of representation. The combination of a methodological scepticism with a version of Cartesian scepticism is, to be sure, no mere idiosyncrasy of Descartes himself but can presumably be found in all philosophical traditions, at least in every epoch of Western and Indian thought. That self-exploration rather than absorption in the world is a philosophical command has in any case been a very widespread conception throughout the history of philosophy. For a thorough analysis of the sceptical arguments which underlie Heraclitus' gnomai and lead him to his thesis that, from an absolute perspective (God's perspective), all contradictions coincide in an encompassing unity, see Burnyeat, 'Conflicting appearances'.

5 Schopenhauer explains life as 'a *long* dream', which is distinguished from our brief (nocturnal) dreams through being organised by the principle of sufficient reason. See Schopenhauer, *The World as Will and Representation*, p. 38. The visible world that we inhabit is 'an insubstantial, intrinsically inessential semblance comparable to an optical illusion or a dream, a veil wrapped around human consciousness, something that can be said both to be and not to be with equal truth and equal falsity' (ibid., p. 446). According to Plotinus, it is literally due to the self-forgetfulness of spirit that we find ourselves seemingly confronted with a world that we believe we have not posited ourselves.

Spirit loses itself in the manifold of appearing objects by which it is practically intoxicated: ἔλαθεν ἑαυτὸν πολὺς γενόμενος, οἷον βεβαρημένος (*Enn.* III 8, 8, 33f.).

6 That there is a relation between sceptical hypotheses and art has clearly not gone unnoticed. Schopenhauer delights in citing Calderon's drama 'life is a dream'. Is it a relentlessly repeated credo of Greek religion and philosophy, found just as much in Homer, Pindar and Sophocles as in Plato, or later in Plotinus, that we are only shadows, or even but the dream of a shadow, as Pindar once wrote (σκιᾶς ὄναρ ἄνθρωπος (Pythian VIII 95 f.))? And, as Stanley Cavell has highlighted in his studies of Shakespeare and Cartesian scepticism, Shakespeare is also quite clear in this respect. See Cavell, *Disowning Knowledge in Six Plays of Shakespeare*. On the relation between scepticism and literature more generally, see Hüppauf and Vieweg, *Skepsis und literarische Imagination*. See too my own discussion in Gabriel, 'Der ästhetische Wert des Skeptizismus beim späten Wittgenstein'.

7 Euripides' tragedies frequently contain sceptical scenarios. The most famous can be found in *Heracles*. At the behest of his jealous mother-in-law Hera, Lyssa (madness) transports Heracles into a temporary frantic state. As a result, he is unable to recognise his own family and murders them. The gulf between our representations of the world and our relation to others and the gods is a general theme of (Greek) tragedy. Sextus also reports that the philosophers Anaxarchus and Monimos worked in the service of scepticism by advocating a form of Cartesian scepticism to the effect that all being is nothing more than a succession of images comparable to those we experience in dreams or delusional episodes: σκηνογραφίᾳ ἀπείκασαν τὰ ὄντα, τοῖς τε κατὰ ὕπνους ἢ μανίαν προσπίπτουσι ταῦτα ὡμοιῶσθαι ὑπέλαβον (AL, 7.88). On this, see Gabriel 'Zum Außenweltproblem in der Antike'.

8 The logical priority of appearance to being is the common denominator of phenomenalism and scepticism. For phenomenalism asserts that sentences about sense data or appearances are self-evident. The sentence 'The table seems to me to be red' cannot be false, whereas the sentence 'The table is red' is truth evaluable. This idea has led to the extremely implausible project of viewing the world as a logical construction out of sense data. Against this view, Sellars attempted to reverse the order of explanation and to trace 'looks-talk' back to 'is-talk'. See Sellars, *Empiricism and the Philosophy of Mind*. Anthony Palmer is incorrect to want to distinguish Pyrrhonian from Cartesian scepticism by claiming that, while the former rests upon a dualism of being and appearance, the latter rests on a dualism of inner and outer. Palmer, 'Scepticism and tragedy: crossing Shakespeare with Descartes', pp. 266–72. This is only a surface difference. Cartesian scepticism serves not only to distinguish inner and outer; as Brandom rightly emphasises, at the same time it distinguishes being from seeming by committing to a logical hierarchy of seems-talk and is-talk: 'Descartes and his tradition claimed that *looks-F* talk, with which it is possible to form a class of statements about which subjects are incorrigible, is a foundation of knowledge, and so must be prior in this sense to *is-F* talk, with which it is possible to express only corrigible, inferred beliefs. This view is the

essence of Descartes' foundationalism' (Brandom in Sellars, *Empiricism and the Philosophy of Mind*, p. 136).

9 See the second meditation, which bears the title 'De natura mentis humanae: quod ipsa sit notior quam corpus'. Descartes of course wants to recover being, and with God's help. But my aim here is not to provide an exegesis of Descartes' own philosophy, merely to investigate the logical structure of Cartesian scepticism.

10 See Descartes' programmatic explanation at the start of the *Meditations*: 'The moment has come, and so today I have discharged my mind from all its cares, and have carved out a space of untroubled leisure' (*Meditations on First Philosophy*, p. 13). The first step in understanding the *Meditations* is accordingly the mind's retreat into itself (*mens humana in se conversa* [AT VII, pp. 7f.]). Truth can be found only in the soul's private discourse with itself, not in public debate. It is therefore quite accurate to say that Descartes combines a methodological scepticism with a methodological solipsism, whereby there is the continual danger that these become an actual scepticism and an actual solipsism.

11 McDowell ('Knowledge and the internal', p. 404) calls this *'the interiorized conception of the space of reasons'*.

12 Perler encapsulates Descartes' strategy when he writes:

> In fact, the thinker is certain only of her own acts in the condition of doubt. The central point, however, is that this is not the starting point. Because of the minimal certainty of her own acts, the thinker can erect a new structure of knowledge step by step. The two keystones of this structure are, famously, the certainty of her own existence and of God's. It is decisive here that these two certainties can be won only by an examination of the acts and what they represent. . . . And as soon as the thinker has attained the certainty of God's existence, she also possesses a guarantee of the existence of external things. (Perler, *Repräsentation bei Descartes*, pp. 313f.)

13 Wright, 'Scepticism and dreaming', p. 91.

14 The iterativity of knowledge is not necessarily identical with the implausible internalist assumption that anyone who knows that p also knows that she knows that p. For this reason, it is important not to confuse iterativity with transparency or even infallibility. Rather, iterativity follows from the rational demand on knowledge that it be able to defend itself against objections.

15 The addition 'at least when they are confronted with a sceptical hypothesis' is of the utmost significance. For scepticism is not a natural problem that has an onset like some sort of illness. Rather, it is a product of reflection that presupposes a dialectical process of statement and contradiction. Scepticism is an eminently theoretical phenomenon. For this reason, I do not agree with James Pryor's attempt to dislodge sceptical concerns by appealing to the everyday justificatory structure of our perceptual beliefs. 'The skeptic makes claims about *all subjects*, even subjects who haven't heard his argument' (Pryor, 'What's wrong with Moore's argument?', p. 368.) The problem with this view

is that the dialectic of scepticism presupposes a prior confrontation with scepticism. The genesis of scepticism from our everyday trust in our cognitive capacities is a problem that will occupy us in chapter 14 below. In any event, it strikes me as problematic to let philosophy drift so far from the everyday that it no longer seems intelligible how philosophy might have arisen out of normal conditions.

16 We cannot know a proposition whose truth value is evidence-transcendent in principle, because there is no possibility of adopting an affirmative or negative cognitive attitude towards it. We can see this with the aid of a simple example. Suppose you are confronted with two cardboard boxes. One contains a cube, the other a ball of the same weight. The boxes both contain a mechanism with the effect that, as soon as you open one of them, its content evaporates. Any attempt to have a justified cognitive attitude either to the proposition (a) 'that the cube is in this box' or to the proposition (b) 'that the ball is in this box' necessarily fails.

17 Note, however, that this argument does not entail the thought that nobody can know that there is a table in front of them because it is possible that there is no table in front of them. This might follow from the *evil genius* argument, but not from the dream or the drug argument. Cartesian scepticism is not bound up with any ontological thesis about the essence of the external world. Therefore, it is also indifferent with respect to idealism and materialism if these are understood as versions of ontological monism. Cartesian scepticism is an exclusively epistemological problem. If it has relevant ontological implications, it does so only on the condition that ontology is a theory about our theories of the world, the justificatory mechanisms of which can be threatened by Cartesian scepticism. In modernity, Cartesian scepticism has therefore led from ontology to epistemology, a progression which is grounded in its logical structure. See Kant's emphatic rejection of ontology, which, he thinks, must give way to his 'modest' transcendental philosophy (CPR, B303).

18 The *ceteris paribus* clause is necessary in order to rule out cases in which somebody does not combine the propositions P and P → Q in the right way. The principle applies equally to 'justification'. If a subject S is justified in the assumption (1) that P, and if S is justified in the assumption (2) that P implies Q, then (*ceteris paribus*) S is *eo ipso* also justified in the assumption that Q. Cartesian scepticism does not, therefore, have to be understood as a problem specifically about knowledge; it can also be seen as a problem about justification, a fact that can bring far-reaching problems in its wake.

19 See Williamson, *Knowledge and its Limits*, p. 117, where he objects to Nozick's rejection of the principle of closure on the basis that it renders impossible any informative deduction. Dretske, who with his classic paper 'Epistemic operators' initiated the entire debate around the principle of closure, is of the view that his rejection of the principle is compatible with its restricted use in knowledge acquisition. Dretske believes he is able to reduce his rejection of the principle to sceptical Q, the negation of which is implied by everything that we believe, without us being able to have epistemic access to Q (or ~Q). See his more recent 'The case against closure', p. 17. As John Hawthorne ('The case

for closure', p. 38), rightly notes, Dretske's restriction of the principle seems ad hoc. The question is whether it is possible to recognise a logical principle within the scope of an epistemic operator while at the same time admitting that, in spite of its formal generality, it does not apply for a class of cases, which can be derived from it by *modus ponens*. Yet Dreske (even if he does not take this route himself) can still restrict the principle to non-sceptical Q: since every sceptical Q is evidence-transcendent, we always lose our entitlement to assume Q when our deduction arrives at Q in keeping with the principle of closure. But this undermines the conditional that we accept for P. Dretske could thus make an argument to the effect that sceptical Q undermines the deduction according to the principle of closure as soon as it is inserted in a conditional within the scope of the epistemic operator 'knows'.

20 Hawthorne, 'The case for closure', p. 29.

21 This is even Max Weber's view:

> It is not at all the case – as academic conceit would have us believe – that inspiration plays a greater role in science than in the solving of the problems of practical life by the modern entrepreneur. And on the other hand, people often fail to recognize that inspiration does not play a smaller part in science than in the realm of art. It is childish to imagine that a mathematician will arrive at any kind of valuable scientific discoveries by sitting at a desk with a ruler or other mechanical tools or calculators. The mathematical imagination of a Weierstrass is, of course, organized very differently both in its meaning and its consequences from that of an artist, and indeed, there is a fundamental difference in quality. But not in terms of the psychological process involved. Both are intoxication (in the sense of Plato's 'mania') and 'inspiration'. ('Science as a vocation', p. 9)

22 Wolfram Hogrebe has presented an ambitious theory of intimation or premonition, which investigates both the conditions of the possibility of the search for knowledge and its consequences for epistemology's attempts to underwrite our knowledge in formulating a theory of science. The concept of dialectical analysis that I have been suggesting follows Hogrebe's theory of the search for knowledge in several respects. On the problem of creativity and the unavoidable role of intimations and hunches, both in the sciences and in our more situated dealings with the world, see esp. Hogrebe, *Ahnung und Erkenntnis: Brouillon zu einer Theorie des natürlichen Erkennens*.

23 There are, to be sure, propositions that we hold true, and perhaps even take ourselves to know, even though it is in principle impossible *to know* them. Examples of such propositions are 'There is a world' or 'The world was not created five minutes ago *ex nihilo* together with traces of an extensive past', etc. Because we cannot produce any reasons for these propositions, which, following Wittgenstein, we can call 'hinge propositions', they cannot feature in knowledge ascriptions either, 'since an appropriate claim to know implies that one can offer relevant grounds in favour of that claim' (Pritchard, 'Wittgenstein's *On Certainty* and contemporary anti-scepticism', p. 198). It

also follows, though, as Pritchard notes, that hinge propositions can be called 'propositions', if at all, only in a highly improper sense.

24 This implies that a pure reliabilism is implausible. If someone could only ever know something in virtue of her being a reliable judge of states of affairs in the eyes of others, but where she cannot defend her knowledge when challenged, it would be at the very least counter-intuitive to count her as a knower. Similarly, we do not ascribe knowledge to a bird that consistently squawks 'red' whenever they are shown a red card.

25 In the *Theaetetus* (201c7–210b2) Plato famously rejects the definition of knowledge as true justified belief. But if we bear in mind that Plato first obtained the correct concept of λόγος only at the end of the *Sophist*, we can, following a familiar Platonic pattern, view the aporetic ending of the *Theaetetus* not simply as a putative refutation of the definition of knowledge as true justified belief but as a problem that needs to be resolved at a higher level (indeed, in this case, at a truly dialectical level).

26 On this, see Hogrebe, *Echo des Nichtwissens*, pp. 336f.

27 The iterative nature of knowledge (exploited by Cartesian scepticism) is by no means uncontroversial. We say of a child, for example, that she *knows* that she will get sweets when she follows a determinate behavioural pattern, even though we would hardly stipulate that the child has to be able to defend her knowledge against objections. Another objection argues that Cartesian scepticism becomes unavoidable once we accept the principle of iterativity. This is the strategy pursued by reliabilism, for example. My current aim, however, is hardly to defend the principle: we need to make its consequences broadly transparent before passing judgement on it, and to this end it suffices to lend it an initial intuitive plausibility.

28 Michael Williams formulates this as a *defence commitment* for knowledge: 'Knowledgeable beliefs must be defensible, but not necessarily derived from evidence' (*Problems of Knowledge*, p. 25). David Macarthur even goes as far as to base the difference between truth and holding-true on the possibility of taking doxastic responsibility in light of criticisms of our beliefs.

> Doxastic responsibility depends upon the fact that, if occasion arises, we are obliged to engage in rational reflection of our beliefs in order to determine whether we are entitled to continue to endorse them. Rational criticism plays a regulative role that we have some control over, helping to ensure that what we think is true is not mere guesswork or accident but genuinely tracks the truth. Our entitlement to regard our beliefs as true thus depends upon their openness to criticism and the way such criticism is conducted. (Macarthur, 'Naturalism and skepticism', p. 122)

29 See MacFarlane, 'Making sense of relative truth', pp. 334f. MacFarlane also sees an objection here to Brandom's model of the game of giving and asking for reasons, regarding it as an impermissible generalisation of philosophical discursive practice.

30 Luhmann, *Die Wissenschaft der Gesellschaft*, p. 274 (translation A. E.). It is for

this reason that science is capable of observing its own operations – that is, of formulating a methodology. Science is a matter not just of *what* can be observed but also, above all, of *how* best to go about making observations. Scepticism comes into question only in discourses for which this kind of switching between 'what' questions and 'how' questions is constitutive. Hence the paradigmatic role of philosophy, a discourse which has no content besides the examination of the 'how' of other discourses that already possess an independent content.

31 Fumerton labels this dialectical error 'epistemological commonsensism'. This position presupposes that epistemology has to put the case for common sense and so begs the question against the scepticism that forms part of epistemology's provisional method.

> We might call the view that rules out skepticism from the start and evaluates metaepistemological views in part by the way in which they allow one to avoid skepticism, epistemological commonsensism. . . . The most obvious question the skeptic will ask is *why* we should assume at the outset that the beliefs we take to be justified are justified. The answer that we must start somewhere will no doubt not please a skeptic who is disinclined to start a careful reexamination of all of our beliefs with the presupposition that most of those we take to be justified are justified. (Fumerton, *Metaepistemology and Skepticism*, p. 42)

32 As Macarthur explains, in 'Naturalism and skepticism', p. 123: 'The deep connection that exists between belief and reason-giving helps to account for the power of the skeptical problem. The skeptic demands a rational justification just where our reasons have given out.'

33 See Williamson, *Knowledge and its Limits*, pp. 23f. Using a similar example, Williamson aims to show that we are not always in a position to know whether we know something.

34 The iterativity used to motivate Cartesian scepticism corresponds to what Grundmann and Stüber call the *principle of the internalism of justification*. See Grundmann and Stüber, *Philosophie der Skepsis*, p. 29.

35 It is therefore not by chance that scepticism attacks the justification conditions, rather than the truth conditions, of knowledge. Sceptical arguments against justification have greater power because we cannot avoid them by formulating alternative conceptions of truth. They can only be avoided ad hoc, by removing the justification condition. This move, however, has untenable consequences. Ultimately, we deploy the concept of knowledge in such a way that it commits us to the possibility of having to defend our knowledge claims in the game of giving and asking for reasons.

36 In my formulation, the principle of closure in no way implies that someone who knows something also knows all the consequences of what he knows. This would be absurd given the implication that anyone who knows anything would *ipso facto* know all necessary truths, since all truths imply all necessary truths. If Thales, for example, knows that everything is ὕδωρ, then he does not

necessarily know that ὕδωϱ is (or will be) 'water' in English, or that it has the chemical structure H_2O. Moreover, he does not know all the necessary truths that logically follow from every proposition. Wright's own formulation of the principle differs from mine in that he works with the concept of *warrant*, which is neutral regarding the internal/external distinction. Wright's formulation of the principle states that: $(Wxt \{A, \ldots, A_n\}; \{A, \ldots, A_n\} \rightarrow B) \rightarrow WxtB$. That is: if someone is entitled to a series of assumptions and something follows from these assumptions, they are also entitled to what follows. Now, one can certainly be entitled to an assumption without being able to cite good reasons for it. For example, every non-philosopher is entitled to the assumption that there is a table in front of them when they see that there is a table in front of them, whereby they are entitled to the assumption that they are not merely dreaming that there is a table in front of them. But this does not mean that they must have (in every respect) good reasons for their assumption. Since my intention is to determine the relation between epistemology and scepticism, and since epistemology seeks explicit good reasons for our knowledge ascriptions, I am translating Wright's treatment of Cartesian scepticism into a theory of the philosophical justification of our beliefs. If, in the context of epistemology, it turned out that we were unable to justify any of our assumptions, the sceptic's programme would come into force, and appeals to our everyday entitlement to our beliefs would no longer be able to rescue us from the sceptic.

37 In order to explode the argument, one might doubt both the premises and the inference rules. But the question is then whether one is really doing justice to the paradoxical character of the argument, which consists precisely in how the premises and rules of inference do seem plausible at first glance. Either questioning the principle of closure or trying out an externalist strategy for avoiding iterativity probably already concedes too much to the sceptic, since it concedes that he cannot be defeated on his own turf. See too Cohen: 'To solve, or perhaps resolve the paradox, it is not enough to simply deny one of the propositions of the set. Such an approach leaves us wondering why, if the proposition is false, we find it so compelling. We are left with no explanation for how the paradox arises' ('Contextualism and unhappy-face solutions', pp. 190f.). Although refuting one of the premises of a paradox delivers a logically satisfying result, it is *dialectically* insufficient insofar as it understands the paradox as an argument that must be false, even though it is by no means clear which premise has to be false. One of the central tasks in dissolving a paradox, however, is to provide a dialectical diagnosis, which explains why the paradox can so much as seem to be a sound argument, despite the fact that we are convinced that something must have gone awry somewhere in its motivation. Paradoxes show us that one or more concepts (motion, knowledge, justification, truth, etc.) have some facet that we have not yet sufficiently understood, and which contrasts with another facet that is already transparent to us.

38 See Nagel's laconic remark 'The thought "I'm a professor at New York University, unless of course I'm a brain in a vat", is not one that can represent my general integrated state of mind' (Nagel, *The View from Nowhere*, p. 88, fn. 13).

39 It is important to note that my presentation here diverges considerably from Wright's. Nevertheless, I believe it is based on the same underlying consideration. Wright's presentation operates with a greater number of technical factors, most of which are bound up with the concept of 'warrant', a concept which in turn plays an indispensable role in Wright's own theory of truth. My concern here is not to do full exegetical justice to the complexities of Wright's approach, merely to uncover what I take to be the most important presuppositions that govern his implosion argument. I will have achieved my aims if I can show how these stumble into difficulties.

40 Regarding the motivation of this premise, we need only note that there are infinitely many empirical possibilities that entail our having to renounce an entire class of our knowledge claims, even though (thus far) we do not know or, for contingent reasons, could not know that corresponding empirical possibilities are in fact realised.

41 See Conant's analysis of the Cartesian problem of madness in 'The search for logically alien thought: Descartes, Kant, Frege, and the *Tractatus*', esp. pp. 148f. As Conant shows (against Frege), we have to admit the possibility that we can ask ourselves whether or not we are currently in full possession of our faculties, because it can be a perfectly sensible question to ask once we appreciate that our cognitive capacities are limited. Conant calls the structure of this question *the Cartesian predicament*: 'We want to frame a thought (about that which cannot be thought) but we run up against the problem that the thought we want to frame lies in its very nature beyond our grasp' (ibid., p. 121). This Cartesian difficulty sets in as soon as we attempt to draw any type of boundary between logically organised and illogical thought: 'The attempt to say that illogical thought is something that *cannot* be, to say that it involves a transgression of the limits of thought, requires that we be able to draw the limit. But this lands us back in the Cartesian predicament: it requires that we be able to sidle up to the limit of thought' (ibid., 150).

42 A similar objection to the implosion can be found in Tymoczko and Vogel, 'The exorcist's nightmare: a reply to Crispin Wright'. Tymoczko and Vogel do not see any contradiction in the LSD argument (Wright himself talks of daydreaming ('maundering')), but try to show that,

> if reasoning produces warranted belief, it does not produce warranted belief. The premises of the argument, including the claim that we have warrant for the belief that maundering precludes obtaining warrant by intellection, are embraced by the friends of reason, not by the intellectual skeptic [i.e. a skeptic who embraces the maundering argument, M. G.]. So, the maundering argument would make it impossible to maintain, even on its own terms, the view that reasoning produces warranted belief. There will be no comfort at this point in the observation that the argument can be continued so as to generate an explicit contradiction – not if that contradiction still follows from assumptions one is committed to by holding that intellection produces warranted belief. (Ibid., pp. 547f.).

43 Stack, 'Self-refuting arguments', pp. 332f.

44 See Fumerton, *Metaepistemology and Skepticism*, pp. 50f. The considerations which follow are a variation on Fumerton's example.

45 If we consider Cartesian scepticism as a classical sceptical paradox, then we have to agree with Wright when he censures Descartes' own eclecticism:

> Anyone encountering Cartesian scepticism for the first time is likely to feel that there is something dubiously eclectic about it – that, by comparison with his treatment of perception, Descartes goes suspiciously easy on the faculties essentially involved in his reflective project. One might naturally think that we merely stand to generalise the scope of the scepticism by pursuing the matter. But the fact is, on the contrary, that therein lies the key to the dissolution of the Dreaming Argument and all its ilk. ('Scepticism and dreaming', pp. 101f.)

46 Pritchard claims (in 'Scepticism and dreaming', p. 382) that Wright's introduction of a 'consistency constraint on epistemic rationality' is valid merely for the sceptic's opponent, not for Cartesian scepticism itself. But Wright works on the assumption that scepticism is an epistemological problem, not a natural one, meaning that he is within his rights to demand logical consistency.

47 In a handout to his seminar on sceptical arguments that was held in Heidelberg in 2004, after running through the implosion, Wright comments: 'Does that mark the collapse of Dreaming scepticism? It seems slightly shocking that it might.'

48 Two famous pop cultural examples are *The Matrix*, which was known to be inspired by Putnam, and Josef Rusnak's *The Thirteenth Floor*, which begins with Descartes' cogito and tries to show how a resulting sceptical scenario shakes the basis of our personal identity. David Cronenberg's *eXistenZ* falls into the same category. But the truly remarkable alternative to a Cartesian universe of private interior spaces is Lynch world. Both David Lynch's *Lost Highway* and *Mulholland Drive* speak a distinctly anti-Cartesian language. The uncanny in Lynch's films consists precisely in how they convey that we are not alone in our own house (in our minds). The famous Mystery Man in *Lost Highway* is (like the camera) at once always inside and outside. On the aesthetic dimension of scepticism, see Gabriel, 'Der ästhetische Wert der Skeptizismus beim späten Wittgenstein' and 'The art of skepticism and the skepticism of art', pp. 58–70. See too, of course, the work of Stanley Cavell, esp. *The Claim of Reason: Wittgenstein, Skepticism, Morality, and Tragedy* and *Disowning Knowledge in Six Plays of Shakespeare*.

49 This observation, which plays an especially prominent role in Cavell's work on Shakespeare, is central to my sketch of ancient scepticism in Gabriel, *Antike und moderne Skepsis*.

50 On the critical function of looks-talk under non-sceptical conditions, see McDowell, 'Knowledge and the internal'.

51 In *Truth and Objectivity*, Wright admittedly defends a standpoint that avoids the quietism that at least some interpretations ascribe to Wittgenstein. For

this position, no significant metaphysical debates are possible. See *Truth and Objectivity*, pp. 202ff. In making his defence, though, Wright himself operates under extremely sceptical conditions, which he accepts as a matter of methodology.

52 See Wright, 'Some reflections on the acquisition of warrant by inference'.

53 Wright has not, to my knowledge, repeated the implosion in any of his subsequent publications. Instead, he has suggested a 'unified strategy' in dealing with all sceptical paradoxes that integrates scepticism into theory construction in the sense I have been suggesting here. See esp. 'Warrant for nothing', 'Wittgensteinian certainties', and 'Hinge propositions and the serenity prayer'.

54 Andrea Kern has raised a similar objection to therapeutic programmes that attempt to demonstrate how the observational standpoint of epistemology is untenable. Such programmes are motivated by the observation that the project of a purely theoretical investigation of knowledge or knowledge acquisition seems to lead necessarily to sceptical paradoxes. Yet the therapeutic programme itself operates from an observational standpoint, which it strives to give up in favour of the supposedly normal processes of knowledge ascription. If we consider the normal processes of knowledge ascription, we do so from a philosophical standpoint. See Kern, 'Understanding scepticism'. The supposed therapeutic function of epistemology thus itself suffers from an alienated mode of reflection. On this topic, see my own discussion of Wittgenstein's therapeutic programme in Gabriel, 'Der ästhetische Wert des Skeptizismus'.

55 Anton Friedrich Koch has argued that discursive rationality as such has an antinomic constitution, such that we cannot escape the antinomy even in discourse's most external reflection on its own presuppositions. See Koch, *Versuch über Wahrheit und Zeit*, §§35–42. I intend to provide a more detailed engagement with his interesting reflections on another occasion. But see chapter 15 below.

Part II Contextualism and the Finitude of Discourse

1 OS, 2.128, 187ff. *et al.* A complete list of all passages can be found in Burnyeat, 'Protagoras and self-refutation in later Greek philosophy', p. 48.

2 A very good overview of *peritrope* arguments against relativism and scepticism in ancient philosophy can be found in Burnyeat, 'Protagoras and self-refutation in later Greek philosophy', and 'Protagoras and self-refutation in Plato's *Theaetetus*'.

3 Stephen Schiffer, in 'Skepticism and the vagaries of justified belief', shows how the fundamental theoretical options of contemporary epistemology can all be reconstructed as anti-sceptical strategies. See also my own discussion in Gabriel, 'Die Wiederkehr des Nichtwissens'.

4 For a more detailed presentation of this diagnosis, see Gabriel, 'Die Wiederkehr des Nichtwissens'.

5 I am in full agreement with Fogelin when he writes: 'Pyrrhonian skepticism, in its late form, uses self-refuting philosophical arguments, taking philosophy

as its target' (*Pyrrhonian Reflections on Knowledge and Justification*, p. 3). One of the passages in which Sextus discusses the *peritrope* comes in a discussion of the thesis that there are no proofs (οὐκ ἔστιν ἀπόδειξις). Sextus raises the objection that the thesis is justified by a proof and is therefore self-refuting. He answers his own objection by arguing that his statements might be compared with a purgative medicine that detoxifies the body while at the same time being expelled from the body together with the toxin. Accordingly, Pyrrhonian arguments should have the property that they negate themselves together with the possibility of a rational justification for our beliefs: δύνανται δὲ οἱ λόγοι καὶ καθάπερ τὰ καθαρτικὰ φάρμακα ταῖς ἐν τῷ σώματι ὑποκειμέναις ὕλαις ἑαυτὰ συνεξάγει, οὕτω καὶ αὐτοὶ τοῖς ἄλλοις λόγοις τοῖς ἀποδεικτικοῖς εἶναι λεγομένοις καὶ ἑαυτοὺς συμπεριγράφειν (OS, 1.188). This therapeutic comparison, designed to illuminate the liberating effect of sceptical arguments, is also ascribed to the Buddha in the Indian tradition. See Matilal, 'Scepticism and mysticism', p. 484.

Chapter 7 Pyrrhonian Scepticism as the Agent of Epistemology

1 The most important recent neo-Pyrrhonian work is Fogelin, *Pyrrhonian Reflections on Knowledge and Justification*. For a discussion of Fogelin's neo-Pyrrhonianism, see Sinnott-Armstrong, *Pyrrhonian Skepticism*. On Pyrrhonism in the context of an attempt to provide a conceptual analysis of scepticism, see Heidemann, *Der Begriff des Skeptizismus*.

2 Schelling, *Sämmtliche Werke*, X, 252; XIII, 247.

3 See Williams, 'Scepticism without theory'.

4 On this connection, see Sluga, 'Wittgenstein and Pyrrhonism'. See too Watson, 'Sextus and Wittgenstein'; Fogelin, 'Wittgenstein and classical scepticism'; Cohen, 'Sextus Empiricus: skepticism as a therapy', esp. pp. 417–21. See also Michael Williams's reflections in 'The Agrippan argument and two forms of skepticism', esp. pp. 138–44.

5 OS, 1.135.

6 The most important study of naturalism as an anti-sceptical strategy remains Strawson, *Skepticism and Naturalism: Some Varieties*.

7 AT VII, pp. 18f.

8 PI, II, p. 230.

9 OS, 1.23f.

10 See Strawson, *Skepticism and Naturalism*, pp. 14–21. According to Kripke, a sceptical solution to a sceptical problem begins 'by conceding that the sceptic's negative assertions are unanswerable. Nevertheless, our ordinary practice or belief is justified because – contrary appearances notwithstanding – it need not require the justification the sceptic has shown to be untenable' (*Wittgenstein on Rules and Private Language: An Elementary Exposition*, pp. 66f.). Kripke sees a parallel here between Hume and Wittgenstein (ibid., p. 68), in that neither looks for a straight solution to a sceptical problem – i.e. a refutation – but instead seeks a solution that is itself sceptical. Fogelin anticipated Kripke's Wittgenstein

interpretation in several respects. He describes both 'Kripkenstein's' sceptical paradox and the sceptical solution known in the literature as the *community view*. He also discusses the parallels with Hume. See the chapter 'Sceptical doubts and a sceptical solution to these doubts'.

11 The manifestly soteriological dimension of Pyrrhonian scepticism has spurred interpreters, from antiquity onwards, to seek out connections between Pyrrhonian scepticism and Asian philosophy. It has of course not gone unnoticed that there are remarkable parallels between antique Greek scepticism and the epistemological considerations that we can find most prominently in Indian philosophy. Such parallels have invited speculation about possible concrete lines of influence, especially since some of the anecdotes about Pyrrho mention that he travelled to India, where he 'associated with the Gymnosophists in India and with the Magi' (τοῖς γυμνοσοφίσταις ἐν Ἰνδίᾳ συμμῖξαι καὶ τοῖς Μάγοις) (Diogenes Laertius, *Lives of Eminent Philosophers*, 9.61). See Flintoff, 'Pyrrho and India'. Significantly, in Indian philosophy, mundane ignorance is usually deployed for speculative or mystical interests. We see this especially clearly in Nagarjuna, who explicitly asserts that he knows nothing and proves this with a version of the justificatory trilemma familiar from Pyrrhonism. See Matilal, 'Scepticism and mysticism' and Grentier, 'Sextus et Nagarjuna'. Some have also drawn parallels with *Chinese* philosophy, albeit without pointing to possible, let alone demonstrable, lines of influence. See Kjellberg, 'Skepticism, truth, and the good life: a comparison of Zhuangzi and Sextus Empiricus'. Kjellberg shows that the problem of the criterion and the structure of Agrippa's trilemma was also used by Zhuangzi.

12 OS, 1.28f.

13 See the famous penultimate proposition of the *Tractatus*: 'My propositions serve as elucidations in the following way: anyone who understands me eventually recognizes them as nonsensical, when he has used them – as steps – to climb up beyond them. (He must, so to speak, throw away the ladder after he has climbed up it.) He must transcend these propositions, and then he will see the world aright' (*Tractatus*, 6.54). Fogelin also draws this parallel between Pyrrhonianism's acquiescence in the *peritrope* and Wittgenstein's assertion (which, strictly speaking, cannot of course be an assertion) that the propositions of the *Tractatus* are senseless. See Fogelin, 'Wittgenstein and classical scepticism', esp. pp. 6–8.

14 Sluga (in 'Wittgenstein and Pyrrhonism') has shown that there might even plausibly have been a direct influence on Wittgenstein here, namely via the writings of Fritz Mauthner.

15 AL, 8.481.

16 As Wittgenstein himself clearly explains, 'What has to be accepted, the given, is – so one could say – *forms of life*' (PI, p. 226e). This kind of positivism of forms of life threatens to slide into a complete departure from critical philosophical activity. What could Wittgenstein, as a philosopher, say of a form of life that comes to take sadistic pleasure in exterminating a certain class or race of people (something that was hardly a distant historical prospect in Europe at the time)? Wittgenstein's problem is ensuring that we can hold on to some

kind of critical potential for distinguishing between better and worse forms of life.

17 We could say with Adorno, whose *metacritique of epistemology* clearly draws attention to this difficulty, that the 'nature' of naturalism plays the role of the non-identical. Nature plays the role of the 'nonidentity under the aspect of identity' (*Negative Dialectics*, p. 5) and thereby generates a contradiction. From within the theoretical attitude, it cannot be identified as the immediate underlying discursive mediation.

18 Maria Baghramian has given a clear account of this connection in her comprehensive study of forms of relativism:

> The point is that while allowing for the context-dependence of all assessments, we should not lose sight of both the commonalities in our interests and, more importantly, the one constant element in meeting these interests – the natural world which of course includes us. Our problem with this suggestion, the relativist will point out, is that the natural world is not available to us in a direct or unmediated form; rather, it presents itself to us through our concepts or conceptual frameworks. This is a serious objection . . .. But in our trial to accommodate the conceptual we must not lose sight of the natural. (*Relativism*, p. 204)

19 Cavell, *The Claim of Reason*, p. 47.

20 Gabriel, *Transcendental Ontology*, pp. 2–34, esp. pp. 10–17.

21 Williams is explicit about his appeal to Academic scepticism: 'But the Academics develop a fallibilist conception of sceptical assent. They think of sceptical assent as an alternative to knowledge. I think that they offer a glimpse of what we can see today as a better way to understand knowledge itself: contextualism' (*Problems of Knowledge*, p. 254). Robert Fogelin has also noted the analogy between Pyrrhonian scepticism and Wittgenstein's later philosophy and therefore describes the latter as an 'updated Pyrrhonism' (*Pyrrhonian Reflections on Knowledge and Justification*, p. 9). Fogelin sees Pyrrhonian scepticism as a project that attempts to draw boundaries in a way that anticipates Wittgenstein's restriction of meaning to moves within a practice. 'The point of Pyrrhonian skepticism is to reject all such moves that attempt to transcend – rather than to improve or perfect – our common justificatory procedures' (ibid., p. 89).

22 See Wittgenstein's programmatic statement in PI, §109: 'And we may not advance any kind of theory. There must not be anything hypothetical in our considerations. We must do away with all *explanation*, and description alone must take its place.'

Chapter 8 Contextualism, Normativity and the Possibility of Discursive Determinacy

1 Michael Williams calls this exaggerated demand on knowledge the 'Prior Grounding Requirement', see e.g. *Problems of Knowledge*, pp. 24f.

2 This anti-sceptical strategy has been pursued in particular by Michael Williams and Crispin Wright. See Williams, *Groundless Belief* and *Problems of Knowledge*; Wright: 'Wittgensteinian certainties', 'Hinge propositions and the serenity prayer' and 'Warrant for nothing'. Andrea Kern also argues against Cartesian scepticism by appealing to our necessary finitude, whose boundaries it seeks to overstep. See 'Warum kommen unsere Gründe an ein Ende? Zum Begriff endlichen Wissens'.

3 Michael Williams therefore exploits Cartesian scepticism only in order to demarcate our epistemic capacities. He ultimately uses it to justify a version of fallibilism: '[A]ll the skeptic's argument shows is that there are limits to our capacity to *give reasons* or *cite evidence*. This is a point about grounding. To get from what he argues to what he concludes, the skeptic must take it for granted that no belief is responsibly held unless it rests on adequate and citable evidence' (*Problems of Knowledge*, p. 148).

4 Andrea Kern speaks in this connection of 'positions of moderation' by which she understands all positions that 'regard the skeptical argument as valid but are nevertheless convinced they can make knowledge intelligible' (*Sources of Knowledge*, pp. 62, 79ff.).

5 It should be noted at this point that we here face the potential problem of how necessarily finite beings can have a concept of their finitude. The question is thus whether a subject who asserts their necessary finitude must not *eo ipso* already be beyond that finitude. This was, of course, Hegel's suspicion about Kant's epistemology, which, as we have described it above, is indeed a negative dogmatism insofar as it seeks to draw the boundaries of human reason with the help of reason itself, and thereby relies on the self-cognition of finitude. See chapter 15 below.

6 For a more detailed discussion of the point, see Gabriel, 'Endlichkeit und absolutes Ich'.

7 That the problem of self-application arises for Williams, too, can be seen in such general formulations as the following: '*all* justification takes place in an inferential and dialectical context' (*Problems of Knowledge*, p. 179; my emphasis).

8 Sextus explicitly compares his method with the establishment of a semantic paradox such as 'nothing is true' (οὐδέν ἐστιν ἀληθές) or 'I am saying nothing determinate' (οὐδεν ὁρίζω) – i.e. with a position that, when applied to itself, leads to its own cancellation (OS, 1.14f.). This is precisely what distinguishes the sceptic from the (positive and negative) dogmatist. While the latter asserts that what she asserts is the case, the sceptic constructs a position that potentially (δυνάμει) cancels itself out. Expressions such as 'nothing is true' have the property that they say something true (i.e. of all other expressions) as

long as they are not applied to themselves. This qualification is central, as Sextus would otherwise be unable to express anything at all. See OS, 1.15: εἰ ὁ δογματίζων τίθησιν ὡς ὑπάρχον τοῦτο ὃ δογματίζει, ὁ δὲ σκεπτικὸς τας φυνὰς αὐτοῦ προφέρεται ὡς δυνάμει ὑφ'ἑαυτῶν περιγράφεται ὀυκ ἀν ἐν τῇ προφορᾷ τούτων δογματίζειν λεχθείν. Fogelin rightly emphasises this aspect of Pyrrhonian scepticism when he says: 'Pyrrhonism admits of no direct justification. Pyrrhonism seems to have this peculiar feature: If true, it cannot be warrantedly asserted to be true' (*Pyrrhonian Reflections on Knowledge and Justification*, p. 10).

9 Following Foucault, one might say that statements are discursive functions. These functions can only be individuated given a discursive formation, where such a formation fixes the rules that constitute individual elements deemed worthy of attention in the eyes of participants. Thus, statements in logical discourse are propositions, sentences in grammatical discourse, family trees in genealogical discourse, symbols for elements, and laws for their configuration in chemical discourse, etc. There are thus criteria of individuation for statements as such. A statement can only be individuated as a statement against the background of a discursive formation. See Foucault, *Archeology of Knowedge*, pp. 79–106. According to Foucault, there are no statements without 'collateral spaces' (ibid., p. 97) – i.e. without the dispersion of other statements that it presupposes or by which it is presupposed. This relation of coexistence between statements is not purely logical – that is, not simply a matter of relations of inferential implication between propositions or of the concatenation of sentences but also a matter of the statement function in discursive practices.

10 Rorty connects precisely this holistic structure of all discursive practices with the hermeneutic circle:

> Our choice of elements will be dictated by our understanding of the practice, rather than the practice's being 'legitimated' by a 'rational reconstruction' out of elements. This holist line of argument says that we shall never be able to avoid the 'hermeneutic circle' – the fact that we cannot understand the parts of a strange culture, practice, theory, language, or whatever, unless we know something about how the whole thing works, whereas we cannot get a grasp on how the whole thing works until we have some understanding of its parts. (*Philosophy and the Mirror of Nature*, p. 319)

11 Luhmann, *Die Wissenschaft der Gesellschaft*, p. 25 (translation A. E.). Luhmann, of course, is concerned with the concept of understanding. But he understands this 'contextually', in just the sense with which we are occupied here. On the difference between system and environment as a condition of the possibility of observability, see Luhmann, *Social Systems*, pp. 176–210.

12 Both here and in my later discussion of the connection between private language and representationalism (see chapter 9 below), I largely follow Crispin Wright's concept of a discourse in *Truth and Objectivity*:

> Let us characterise as a *practice* any form of intentional, purposeful activity, and as a *move* any action performed within the practice, for its characteristic purposes. And now reflect on what is, or might appropriately be meant by the claim that a certain characteristic is *normative* of such a practice. Various proposals are no doubt possible, but we should recognise straight away a distinction between *descriptive* and *prescriptive* claims about normativity. A characteristic of moves in a particular practice is a descriptive norm if, as a matter of fact, participants in the practice are positively guided in their selection of moves by whether a proposed move possesses that characteristic. (*Truth and Objectivity*, p. 15)

13 Several advocates of this kind of contextualism deploy it as an argument for an anti-sceptical strategy. See especially Lewis, 'Elusive knowledge'; DeRose, 'Solving the skeptical problem' and 'The ordinary language basis for contextualism and the new invariantism'; Cohen, 'Contextualism and skepticism' and 'Knowledge, speaker and subject'. The work of Michael Williams does not belong to this class, because he argues for Pyrrhonian scepticism and not a variety of scepticism specific to the concept of knowledge.

14 Trivial contextualism is, to be sure, built into two-dimensional semantics, though this merely tries to introduce contextual parameters (time and place) into classical truth-conditional semantics. This represents a correction, but not a radical revision. On this, see MacFarlane, 'The assessment sensitivity of knowledge attributions' and 'Making sense of relative truth'. The contextualism we are concerned with, however, is incomparably more radical. It owes its modern formulation to late Wittgenstein and his abandonment of the concept of a totality of facts (the world), which sentences can picture correctly or incorrectly in virtue of how they express propositions. Early Wittgenstein had still assumed a totality of facts. The relation between sentence and world is accordingly binary. By contrast, late Wittgenstein no longer understands 'meaning' [*Bedeutung*] as essentially a relation between sentence and world; rather, he sees it as a normative concept upon which facts cannot exercise any immediate restriction. One might compare this shift within Wittgenstein's thought with the Pyrrhonian critique of the Greek ontological conception of truth: according to this conception, truth (ἀλήθεια), or the true (τὸ ἀληθές), is not an exclusively semantic quantity but instead designates that which is actual in and of itself, independently of our holding-true. Parmenides simply called this the existent, *tout court* (τὸ ἐόν, τὸ ὄν). Sextus attempts to show, through tireless argumentation, that there can be no truth in this sense, since contextual parameters (which he explicitly calls περιστάσεις – i.e. 'circumstances' or 'contexts') are built into our relation to the world, which makes it impossible to establish any binary relation between the world (the existent) and thought or language.

15 See the classical work by Kaplan, 'Demonstratives'; see too Stalnaker, *Context and Content*. A very good overview of two-dimensionalism can be found in Haas-Spohn, *Versteckte Indexikalität und subjektive Bedeutung*.

16 Nevertheless, as we shall consider in more detail in chapter 14, contextualism

leads to a variant of naturalism. The naturalism that combines with contextualism has to be strictly distinguished from the scientific naturalism or scientism that represents a widely accepted assumption in contemporary, especially anglophone, philosophy. Important discussions about contemporary scientific naturalism can be found in De Caro and Macarthur, *Naturalism in Question*.

17 Fogelin and Williams ground their contextualism starting from the concept of *justification*. Williams formulates contextualism as the thesis that 'all justification takes place in an informational and dialectical context' (*Problems of Knowledge*, p. 179). Both men are thus concerned with the conditions of possibility of investigation – i.e. with rationally controlled changes in informational state quite generally. In my view, however, the concept of verifiability is still more foundational than that of justification. Verifiability or assessability is the minimal condition for being able to classify something as correct or incorrect. Justification, by contrast, is merely the attempt to use reasons to show that something is correct. But, in order for there to be a distinction between correct and incorrect, there must be norms in place that allow one to assess something *as* something, which can be assessed as correct or incorrect relative to a normative frame of reference.

18 See Hogrebe, 'Erkenntnistheorie ohne Erkenntnis', p. 554, where he writes of Kant's as-if teleology:

> The power of judgement can only be successful in seeking out predicates if it supposes that given objects are embedded in contexts that do not elude our cognitive access in principle, and are thus purposively structured for our cognitive competency. This assumption cannot be justified *within* the functional circuit of our cognitive practice, and thus empirically in the strict sense (and certainly not logically). It is rather, in Kant's language, a transcendental principle or . . . a meta-pragmatic presupposition, which enables an intelligible exercise of the power of judgement.

In my view, Hogrebe's concept of a *meta-pragmatic* presupposition enjoys important advantages over its counterpart in Günter Abel's interpretationism. In a similar systematic context, Abel speaks of *interpretive presuppositions*. See Abel, *Interpretationswelten: Gegenwartsphilosophie jenseits von Essentialismus und Relativismus*, p. 129. But *interpretation* is a cognitive achievement, whereas meta-pragmatic presuppositions are, rather, presuppositions for there being cognitive achievements at all.

19 Crispin Wright sees contextualism as I am presenting it here as the positive lesson of Humean scepticism. He explains this lesson as follows:

> Wherever I get in a position to claim justification for a proposition, I do so courtesy of specific presuppositions – about my own powers, and the prevailing circumstances, and my understandings of the issues involved – for which I will have no specific, earned evidence. This is a necessary truth. I may, in any particular case, set about gathering such evidence in turn – and *that* investigation may go badly, defeating the presuppositions that I

originally made. But whether it does or doesn't go badly, it will have its own so far unfounded presuppositions. Again: whenever claimable cognitive achievement takes place, it does so in a context [!] of *specific* presuppositions which are not themselves an expression of any cognitive achievement to date. ('Warrant for nothing', p. 189)

20 That the concept of truth, insofar as it is used in epistemology, can first be introduced at the level of a second-order observation – i.e. at the level of a discourse theory – is shown extensively by Luhmann, *Die Wissenschaft der Gesellschaft*, pp. 167–270.

21 Luhmann, *Social Systems*, p. 115. Rorty too notes how the insight that all determinacy (reality) is always 'reality-under-a-certain-description' is gained by 'breaking the crust of convention' (*Philosophy and the Mirror of Nature*, p. 379).

22 On how neutralism fails in the case of moral relativism, see Dworkin, 'Objectivity and truth: you'd better believe it'.

23 Luhmann, *Die Wissenschaft der Gesellschaft*, p. 485 (translation A. E.).

24 See Castoriadis's model of an ontological genesis of social imaginaries in *The Imaginary Institution of Society*.

25 In the first of his Woodbridge Lectures of 2007 ('Animating ideas of idealism'), Robert Brandom rightly draws attention to how early modern philosophy saw a transition from resemblance to representational relations between mind and world. Cartesian analytical geometry represents geometrical forms in linear algebra. Yet their formulae bear no resemblance to the figures. One can see the foundational insight of early modern epistemology in the idea that we cannot directly infer the structure of the representable from the logical structure of our representations.

26 Hegel, *Phenomenology of Spirit*, §133.

27 Ibid., §206.

28 On this topic, see Heidemann, *Der Begriff des Skeptizismus*, as well as Forster, *Hegel and Skepticism*.

29 For an informative overview of the debates around sociology of science, which raged particularly fiercely in the 1970s and 1980s, see Meja and Stehr, *Der Streit um die Wissenssoziologie*.

30 See Luhmann, *Die Wissenschaft der Gesellschaft*, pp. 89ff.; see also *Social Systems*, pp. 55ff., 353ff.

31 The general rule, that nobody advocates a theory as absurd as their critics try to pin on them, applies here as well. Rorty, Kuhn and Feyerabend can all be found innocent of most of the philosophical crimes of which they are frequently accused. One often hears the simple objection levelled against them that a relativist cannot relativise their own position. Yet this objection is super-ficial, as we shall see. See the discussions of the antinomy of self-reference in chapters 14 and 15 below.

32 All observation is the use of a distinction to designate one side (and not the other). The distinction itself thereby functions unobserved; otherwise, in order to be observed, it would have to be a component for a distinction, which

for its part would then have to be deployed unobserved. Every observation is latent to itself in its dependence on distinction. But precisely this can be observed with the help of another distinction. What cannot be observed can be observed – even if only with the help of a schema transition, and thus with the help of time. Even if one does not only practise observations but inquires after the observer – i.e. after the system that can sequence and thereby differentiate observations – one carries out such a schema transition. See Luhmann, *Die Wissenschaft der Gesellschaft*, pp. 91f.

33 On this point, see Williams, *Unnatural Doubts*, pp. 22ff. Williams follows Stroud, according to whom the epistemological attitude to our knowledge as a whole always presupposes a form of 'detachment'. This attitude provisionally places all knowledge in suspension in order to undertake a neutral investigation of its validity.

34 The example of the signpost comes from Wittgenstein:

> A rule stands there like a sign-post. – Does the sign-post leave no doubt open about the way I have to go? Does it shew which direction I am to take when I have passed it; whether along the road or the footpath or cross-country? But where is it said which way I am to follow it; whether in the direction of its finger or (e.g.) in the opposite one? – And if there were not a single sign-post, but a chain of adjacent ones or of chalk-marks on the ground – is there only one way of interpreting them? (PI, §85)

35 An especially clear systematic reconstruction of Wittgenstein's regress argument can be found in Brandom's *Making it Explicit*, pp. 18–46. Brandom's elaboration goes beyond Wittgenstein's (and Kripke's) version of the problem in that he tries to show throughout the course of his *magnum opus* how all of the traditional problems associated with the concept of a concept can be reinterpreted with the help of a social externalism that takes its orientation from Wittgenstein. Brandom's treatment of the problem is also shaped by how it draws upon Kant and Sellars, whose theories of concepts, as Brandom shows, can also be interpreted as responses to the regress of rules argument.

36 PI, §201.

37 OC, §342.

38 See Wright's clear formulation of the regress:

> one cannot but take certain . . . things for granted. By that I don't mean that one could not investigate (at least some of) the presuppositions involved in a particular case. But in proceeding to such an investigation, one would then be forced to make further presuppositions of the same general kinds. Wherever one achieves warrant for a proposition, one's doing so is subject to specific preconditions – about one's own powers and understanding of the issues involved and about the prevailing circumstances – for whose satisfaction one will have no specific, earned warrant. This is a necessary truth. ('Hinge propositions and the serenity prayer', pp. 301f.)

However, Wright does not take into consideration that his 'necessary truth' *ex hypothesi* itself has ungrounded presuppositions, which could be false. See chapter 15 below.

39 See chapter 15 below for a more extensive discussion.

40 OC, § 341. Note Wittgenstein's wordplay here: *'certain* propositions' [gewisse *Sätze*] are, on the one hand, some propositions or other and, on the other hand, propositions of which we are certain.

41 I am here partly adopting an idea of Duncan Pritchard's, which, follow-ing Michael Williams, he formulates as follows: 'what defines a context is its hinges' ('Wittgenstein's *On Certainty* and contemporary anti-scepticism', p. 210). Pritchard thus connects Wittgenstein's anti-sceptical strategy with contextualism insofar as he shows that the concept of a context can be defined in terms of hinge propositions.

42 There are, of course, information-processing systems that produce the informa-tion that they go on to register. Conscious organisms are an example. Whoever notices pain registers an item of information produced by the very organism that, by means of another function, takes note of it. There are many autopoietic systems in this sense. We need think only of consciousness, which is capable of recalling memories, or of states, which assess the size of their self-incurred levels of debt, and so on. From the perspective of Luhmann's system theory, one would even have to say that all systems produce their own informa-tion (sense) insofar as they all draw specific boundaries between system and environment in order to determine what is to count for them as information. This model, however, is in danger of overlooking that autopoiesis is not authy-postasis – i.e. is not a matter of producing the environment in a causal sense – an absurd notion, against which Luhmann himself warns us: 'Autopoiesis does not mean that the system exists solely through itself, through its own power, without any contribution from the environment. Rather, the point is merely that the unity of the system, together with all the elements it consists of, are produced through the system itself. Of course, this is only possible on the basis of a continuum of materiality, which is given with physically constituted reality' (*Die Wissenschaft der Gesellschaft*, p. 30 (translation A. E.)).

43 See, for example, Castoriadis, *The Imaginary Institution of Society*, pp. 232–5.

44 The notion of a successful application of devices is thus itself normatively constituted.

> Physical laws can never exhaustively explain the function of measuring devices. The criterion of unimpeded functioning is thus normative. . . . In physics, for example, or, more specifically, in taking physical measurements, we find a prototype of the generalisable fact that results of empirical natural science do not suffice for a sufficient explanation of the cognitive methods deployed in observation, measurement and experiment. There remains a normative explanatory residue, which can only be attained from the auton-omous end-setting of the active researcher and the validity claims of the research community. (Janich, 'Szientismus und Naturalismus: Irrwege der Naturwissenschaft als philosophisches Programm', pp. 297f.)

45 In his discussion of the Quine–Duhem thesis, Paul Boghossian expresses this
point as follows:

> The theory of the telescope has been established by numerous terrestrial
> experiments and fits in with an enormous number of other things that we
> know about lenses, light and mirrors. It is simply not plausible that, in
> coming across an unexpected observation of the heavens, a rational response
> might be to revise what we know about telescopes; one can certainly imagine
> circumstances under which that is precisely what would be called for. The
> point is that not *every* circumstance in which something about telescopes
> is presupposed is a circumstance in which our theory of telescopes is being
> tested, and so the conclusion that rational considerations alone cannot decide
> how to respond to recalcitrant experience is blocked. (*Fear of Knowledge:
> Against Relativism and Constructivism*, p. 128)

46 Neither the realism nor the idealism mentioned here represents a well-
described philosophical position. Both would have to be elaborated in order
to determine exactly which assumptions they are respectively committed to.
I cite them here merely as examples of how we can pose the *'from where?'*
question regarding the information or data that require us to carry out alterations to our stock of information at every moment of our conscious lives. It is
important to see that neither idealism nor realism, nor yet any kind of scepticism, denies the existence of the external world in the sense of something that
transcends what is available to a solipsism of the present moment. At most,
realism and idealism debate where the data that we register come from – i.e.
what the external world is. It is not, therefore, a question of whether an external
world exists, and thus not whether an external world exists when nobody is
perceiving it or grasping it in thought. Hence Berkeley's credo does not read
esse est percipi; rather, it is *esse est percipi vel percipi posse*. Neither realism nor
idealism can dispute the condition of objectivity as such, where this states
that truth and holding-true can potentially diverge – hence there is room for
sceptical manoeuvre in the case of both realism and idealism. Whenever we
have reason to suppose that reality as a whole could be totally different from
our understanding of it, scepticism can appear at any time.

47 'The conditions of the *possibility of experience* in general are at the same time
conditions of the *possibility of the objects of experience*' (CPR, B197).

48 Luhmann expresses this idea with his famous doctrine of the 'blind spot' of all
observation qua distinguishing operation: 'No observing (distinguishing and
designating) operation can distinguish and designate itself. For the purpose of
distinguishing observations, it requires a further operation, which operates just
as blindly. The moment of blindness can be eliminated from the observation
just as little as the moment of the boundary. Both phenomena are constitutive
conditions of the operation of observation. All observation therefore generates transparency and intransparency' (*Die Wissenschaft der Gesellschaft*, p. 543,
trans. A. E.). This naturally raises the question of quite how things then stand
with the insight into the necessary finitude of observation itself. Is this finite

too, and, if so, what consequences does this have for its assertability? On this question see chapters 14–15 below.

49 In *Der mentale Zugang Zur Welt*, Willaschek clarifies this point with the example of the compatibility of realism and relativism. Kant, by contrast, infers the structure of reality from the structure of our understanding, construing the former as the absence of the latter. He asserts unequivocally

> that the things that we intuit are not in themselves what we intuit them to be, nor are their relations so constituted in themselves as they appear to us; and that if we remove our own subject or even only the subjective constitution of the senses in general, then all constitution, all relations of objects in space and time, indeed space and time themselves would disappear, and as appearances they cannot exist in themselves, but only in us. (CPR, B59)

However, it would be compatible with Kant's transcendental idealism for the thing in itself to exhibit the same structure as appearances, even if we were unable to detect this. Ultimately, according to Kant, one cannot know anything at all about the thing in itself other than that one can know nothing about it. So it cannot be ruled out that the world is in fact in space and time and is governed by the principle of causality, etc. Yet Kant needs the thesis that causality is a form of understanding that does not pertain to reality in itself in order to make room for the thesis that we can understand ourselves as free qua intelligible (i.e. as thing in itself) – a thesis that can, of course, be motivated only within the context of his practical philosophy. Things would look bleak for intelligible freedom, however, were the thing in itself governed by the same laws as appearance.

50 Wright describes this aptly as follows: 'Cognitive locality is the circumstance that only a proper subset of the kinds of states of affairs which we are able of conceptualizing are directly available, at any given state in our lives, to our awareness. So knowledge of, or warranted opinion concerning, the remainder must ultimately be based on defeasible inference from materials of which we are thus aware' (Wright, 'Warrant for nothing', p. 259). See also Wright, 'Wittgensteinian certainties', p. 52, where he defines 'cognitive locality' as 'the idea of a range of states of affairs and events existing beyond the bounds of her own direct awareness'. Russell identifies the strongest form of scepticism with a solipsism of the moment, which asserts that there is no valid inference from an experience to anything not immediately given in this experience. He formulates the fundamental question to which scepticism draws our attention as follows: 'Is there any valid inference ever from an entity experienced to one inferred?' (Russell, 'Vagueness', p. 92). Russell, however, makes things too easy for himself when he accuses scepticism of being so laconic that it becomes uninteresting (ibid.). He thus precludes scepticism's methodological function from the outset. This serves his concern to develop a naturalised epistemology, something he demanded long before Quine: 'My own belief is that most of the problems of epistemology, in as far as they are genuine, are really problems of physics and physiology' (ibid.).

51 Williams, 'The Agrippan argument', pp. 133f. On the concept of 'entitlement', see also p. 279, n. 27, above.

52 Nietzsche, 'On truth and lies in a non-moral sense', p. 143.

53 Since this trust makes discursive reality possible, it is not itself rationally mediated. On the not yet rational – indeed irrational – operating conditions of modern rationalization, see of course Weber, *The Protestant Work Ethic and the Spirit of Capitalism*.

54 I am here understanding conspicuousness [*Auffälligkeit*] in line with Heidegger. Famously, Heidegger believes that a theoretical attitude to the world can arise only when our frictionless engagement with the world is interrupted, when 'equipment' [*Zeug*] becomes unusable. The ready-to-hand must be discoverable as present-at-hand in order to establish a theoretical attitude towards the world (see *Being and Time* §16). Like Heidegger's conspicuousness of ready-to-hand equipment, the conspicuousness of a discourse calls for repair. The repairs are taken on by the discourse itself as long as the possible impossibility of discourse – i.e. of scepticism – is not yet apparent.

55 PI, §219.

56 RFM, p. 422.

57 Ibid.

58 *Tractatus*, 4.128.

59 PI, §125.

60 Ibid.

61 Hegel, *Difference between Fichte and Schelling's System of Philosophy*, p. 89. Hegel here ascribes to Socrates a method of 'confusion'. Without this method, there could be no philosophy: 'This confusion has the effect of leading to reflection; and this is Socrates' aim. This merely negative side is the central point. It is confusion with which philosophy must begin and which it brings about for itself; one has to doubt everything, one must abandon all presuppositions, in order to win them back as something generated through the concept.'

62 See Derrida, 'Des tours de Babel'.

63 To allay the concerns of opponents of binary oppositions, it may be worth noting at this point that practices allow utterly *neutral* moves, which are neither correct nor incorrect – i.e. are candidates for neither reward nor punishment. Nevertheless, it is true of every neutral move in a practice that it is correct or incorrect *that* it is neutral. We cannot determine neutrality itself without binary oppositions. There are even circumstances that demand neutrality – i.e. that allow a move or series of moves to be executed arbitrarily. Neutral moves should not be excluded from any discourse theory. But what can be excluded is the possibility of a practice that consists exclusively of neutral moves; for this would be a practice in which everything is permitted. Were everything permitted, it would also be permitted to make a move incompatible with everything being permitted – i.e. a move that demands that something ought not to be permitted.

64 While following it in several respects, the basic discourse theory I am outlining here therefore differs from Brandom's theory of normativity. Brandom proceeds from the assumption (contra Wittgenstein) that all moves in the

language game – i.e. in a discourse – have propositional content in virtue of asserting something that is incompatible with other assertions: 'The fundamental [!] sort of move in the game of giving and asking for reasons is making a claim – producing a performance that is propositionally contentful in that it can be the offering of a reason, and reasons can be demanded for it' (*Making it Explicit*, p. 141). Assertions are thus commitments that make a sentence into a possible premise of an inference (see ibid, p. 168). Brandom's inferentialism asserts that the propositional content of a sentence is a function of its inferential role. Consequently, he has to relate everything that can be propositionally contentful – i.e. correct or incorrect – to assertions, which (unlike questions or actions) are the only moves that can be deployed in conditionals. One cannot construct a conditional whose antecedent is, say, a question. Accordingly, Brandom also reduces the linguistic function of questions to the primacy of assertion: 'It is only because some performances function as assertions that others deserve to be distinguished as speech acts. The class of questions, for instance, is recognized in virtue of its relation to possible answers, and offering an answer is making an assertion' (ibid., p. 172).

65 Crispin Wright, however, has suggested ascribing a truth predicate to every discourse. One of the reasons for this suggestion is simply that every discourse allows the construction of statements that we can furnish with a truth predicate. An example from the aesthetic domain would be, say, the statement 'It is true that Picasso's *Les Demoiselles d'Avignons* is beautiful.' Wright therefore opts for a minimal truth predicate, which coincides with the basic difference between correct and incorrect, whereby every discourse can add further determinations to the truth predicate besides its basic norm. Accordingly, truth does not necessarily have to be coupled to representation: there are discourses that require an anti-realist construction. In Wright's view, wherever there is a norm that distinguishes correct from incorrect, there is also a truth predicate. 'Truth', on this account, has no ontological nature but, rather, can be interpreted without remainder as a basic norm that is at work wherever we draw a distinction between correct and incorrect. For this reason, Wright advocates a pluralist theory of truth: it can countenance a multitude of truth predicates, each of which brings with it a range of objectivity conditions, which vary from discourse to discourse. The judgement 'It is true that rhubarb is delicious' has different objectivity conditions to the judgement 'It is true that the table I see is blue.' If we understand 'truth' in Wright's minimalist sense, then it certainly coincides with the distinction between correct and incorrect moves, and the possibility comes into view of ascribing a truth predicate to every discourse and of investigating them accordingly. Yet, for certain discourses, this approach can be misleading, at least on occasion. Take, for example, the judgement 'It is true that Picasso was a better painter than Georges Braque.' There are good reasons for restricting the use of the truth predicate in aesthetic judgements: it can suggest that there are aesthetic facts, which can be mapped by judgements – something that hardly any halfway reflective art critic would accept unrestrictedly. Yet it is less controversial that certain artworks are almost *necessary*, so to speak, at certain times and acquire an epoch-making

status. There is thus a normativity in aesthetic discourse that cannot perhaps be captured with a truth predicate. Such discourses provide a reason to restrict Wright's discourse theory and, instead of 'truth', for introducing a binary code that distinguishes only between correct and incorrect moves within a praxis, without determining this code *de facto* or potentially as truth/false from the outset.

66 Wittgenstein, *Lectures and Conversations on Aesthetics, Psychology and Religious Belief.*

67 On this 'hidden-indexical theory of knowledge sentences', see Schiffer, 'Contextualist solutions to scepticism', pp. 326ff. Schiffer objects to the thesis that knowledge is covertly indexical on the basis that it commits us to an implausible error theory, whereby competent users of the concept of knowledge have a constitutive blindness regarding that very concept. This means, however, that Schiffer has to demand of competent ascribers of knowledge that they know at least that knowledge is not indexical – else they would not even find sceptical paradoxes paradoxical. On this objection, see also Brendel, 'Was Kontextualisten nicht wissen'.

68 By contrast, it is wrong to demand that someone who knows something must be able to state on demand everything with which their knowledge contrasts. The claim that a knower has to defend their knowledge does not presuppose being able to distinguish everything from everything else. This would be an absurd demand. It merely requires that one be able to defend one's knowledge against some given particular alternative. This does not mean that the putative knower must already have excluded the alternative in some inner consultation *before* its explicit presentation.

69 Heidemann interprets the Pyrrhonian *epochê* as the condition in which the sceptic talks 'about his present experience' 'without saying *something determinate*' (*Der Begriff des Skeptizismus*, p. 28). Yet if *epochê* is supposed to go as far as to undercut the difference between correct and incorrect, one could safely dismiss it – the person practicing *epochê* would hardly be comprehensible. But the Pyrrhonian sceptic neither remains silent nor merely babbles on; rather, he withdraws to the safe haven of the norms he inherits from tradition and his upbringing, and he makes no attempt to provide a philosophical justification for them. He thus does have a set of norms at his disposal which inform his action. His statements enjoy the determinacy they do on account of general agreement rather than philosophical justification.

70 See Fumerton, *Metaepistemology and Skepticism*, p. 44:

> a predicate expression 'X' only has meaning if there are things that are both correctly and incorrectly described as being X. Thus, on my reading of Wittgenstein's private language argument, the fundamental objection to private language has nothing much to do with memory. The problem is that a private linguist is the sole arbiter of how similar something must be to a paradigm member of a class to count as similar enough to be described in the same way. But as the sole judge it will not be possible to make a mistake, and where there is no possibility of error there is no possibility of getting it right.

It is only meaningful to talk about the correct application of a rule if it can be contrasted with an incorrect application of the rule.

71 On the concept of 'unexpected harmonies' as the foundational event of all speaking, see Hay, *Die Notwendigkeit des Scheiterns: Das Tragische als Bestimmung der Philosophie bei Schelling*.
72 See CPR, B672–5. Here, Kant means to describe the merely regulative use of Ideas of course. Yet his discussion applies to every empirical concept. For all empirical concepts are 'only a projected unity, which one must regard not as given in itself, but only as a problem; this unity, however, helps to find a principle for the manifold and particular uses of the understanding, thereby guiding it even in those cases that are not given and making it coherently connected' (CPR, B675). The modal status of concepts is virtuality: they are retrospectively generated as unities in order to organise the manifold. The manifold generates its virtual foundation from itself, whereby Kant reverses the classical *ordo rerum*. The many produces the one, which, accordingly, can no longer be the principle of the many.
73 Nietzsche, 'On truth and lies in a non-moral sense', p. 146.
74 Ibid., p. 145.
75 Against this background, Michael Williams wants to be rid of the Platonic epistemic ideal, according to which 'someone who really had knowledge would be able to see every individual thing he knew, including things that are generally taken as individually self-evident, as a necessary component in a complete and fully integrated conception of reality' (*Problems of Knowledge*, p. 39).
76 *Tractatus*, 5.641.
77 Ibid., 5.64.
78 See Brandom, *Making it Explicit*, pp. 18–46; see also Brandom, *Articulating Reasons: An Introduction to Inferentialism*, pp. 45–7.
79 Habermas, *Truth and Justification*, p. 77. See too pp. 16, 27, 61.

Chapter 9 Private Language and Assertoric Content

1 See Hacker, *Insight and Illusion: Wittgenstein on Philosophy and the Metaphysics of Experience*, pp. 215–44. Hacker reconstructs the discussions in the Vienna Circle about Carnap's methodological solipsism and its connection with epistemological foundationalism. It is important to bear in mind that Wittgenstein's late engagement with the problem of solipsism also has an inseparable methodological link with the Vienna Circle's verificationist programme and the solipsism critique of several of its members.
2 On Wittgenstein's 'contemplative solipsism' in the *Tractatus* and his historical predecessors, see Gabriel, *Grundprobleme der Erkenntnistheorie: Von Descartes zu Wittgenstein*, pp. 164ff. According to Monk, Wittgenstein read Kant's *Critique of Pure Reason* together with Ludwig Hänsel in the POW camp in Como. See Monk, *Wittgenstein: The Duty of Genius*, p. 158.

3 See Wright, *Rails to Infinity: Essays on Themes from Wittgenstein's Philosophical Investigations*, p. 226: 'A demonstration of the impossibility of private language will therefore be a demonstration that there is error in any philosophy of mind, or epistemology, which has the consequence that the existence of another consciousness is at best a groundless assumption.'

4 Phenomenalism thus involves the problematic assumption that our phenomenal states do not belong to the world. But if the world is in any sense a totality (everything that is the case, the entirety of being, etc.) then the task of metaphysics, insofar as it investigates the world as world, is to develop a concept of totality that successfully integrates our phenomenal states. We do only partial justice to the problem of the world if we reduce it to a space–time container filled with physical mesoscopic 'objects' to which we refer paradigmatically with singular expressions. Phenomenalism is unable to develop a theory of the world that can consider itself to be part of the world, meaning that the phenomenal subject is excluded from the world. A metaphysical theory of the world as world that is unable in principle to thematise itself within its thematisation of the world ends up losing the world entirely. This is where we find its blind spot: it hypostasises the world as a thing in itself standing over against our cognition. See my opening discussion in Gabriel, *Das Absolute und die Welt in Schellings 'Freiheitsschrift'*.

5 To be sure, the status of protocol sentences was a subject of considerable debate within the Vienna Circle itself. In responding to Neurath's critique of its apparent methodological solipsism, Carnap presented his own position in a way that seems to be able to dispense with phenomenalism (see Carnap, *The Unity of Science*). In an essay from 1931, by contrast, he still insists that protocol sentences describe 'states of affairs' that are 'directly observed' (ibid., p. 43). Here, he explicitly understands the protocol language as 'phenomenal language' or as the 'language of direct experience' (ibid., p. 44). His definition of the simplest sentences of the language shows his phenomenalism especially clearly: 'The simplest statements in the protocol language are protocol statements, i.e. statements needing no justification and serving as foundation for all remaining statements of science . . . [they] refer to the given, and describe directly given experience or phenomena, i.e. the simplest states of which knowledge can be had' (ibid., p. 45). Whether Wittgenstein's private language argument really presents a suitable critique of Carnap's *Aufbau* is a far-reaching question. It seems to me, at any rate, that it does insofar as Wittgenstein shakes the argumentative basis of logical positivism by understanding our relation to the world as socially mediated from the outset. One result of the private language is the idea that there can be no immediate epistemic stance obtaining between mind and world because a purely private mind could not refer to anything determinate.

6 See Kant's *Stufenleiter* of representations in CPR, B376f.:

> The genus is **representation** in general (*repraesentatio*). Under it stands the representation with consciousness (*perceptio*). A **perception** that refers to the subject as a modification of its state is a **sensation** (*sensatio*); an objective

perception is a **cognition** (*cognitio*). The latter is either an **intuition** or a **concept** (*intuitus vel conceptus*). The former is immediately related to the object and is singular; the latter is mediate, by means of a mark, which can be common to several things.

7 CPR, BXXXVI fn.

8 See Koch, *Versuch über Wahrheit und Zeit*, §13.

9 For good reasons, Wittgenstein avoids a detailed discussion of various different elaborations of the solipsistic picture. Aside from a single allusion to Frege (PI, §273) and the polemical opening of the PI with its (clearly abridged) picture of Augustine's philosophy of language, he treats the problem of solipsism as a timeless temptation. 'Wittgenstein's aim was to diagnose a disease of thought to which many have succumbed' (Hacker, *Insight and Illusion*, p. 246).

10 '[N]am quid dolore intimius esse potest?' (AT VII, 77). It is no wonder that Wittgenstein directs his interpretation of pain behaviour against the supposed intimacy of pain. I am not aware, however, that Wittgenstein had Descartes' assertion in mind.

11 Here, I merely want to point out that the concept of representation can also be interpreted in such a way that it requires no commitment to a methodological scepticism. The Platonic–Aristotelian concept of εἶδος, which plays an indispensable role in Aristotle's theory of representation (φαντασία), does not yet presuppose a distinction between representation and cause of representation (in the sense of a pure *causa efficiens*). Likewise for certain medieval concepts of representation, as Dominik Perler shows in 'Wie ist ein globaler Zweifel möglich? Zu den Voraussetzungen des frühneuzeitlichen Außenwelt-Skeptizismus'. Unfortunately, I cannot go into this issue in any further detail here, especially as doing so would require confronting Heidegger's thesis that the Platonic concept of εἶδος bears ultimate responsibility for the modern concept of representation. Yet it bears emphasising that neither Plato nor Aristotle advocates a version of mental representationalism.

12 It is worth underlining here that, in contrast to the theory of Rorty and other critics of representationalism, it is not necessary to assume that the concept of representation is responsible for scepticism. Rather, the converse is the case: representationalism is a result of sceptical reflection and not its origin. This is also argued in Willaschek, *Der mentale Zugang zur Welt*, pp. 97–119.

13 See the extensive discussion in Frede, 'Stoics and skeptics on clear and distinct impressions'.

14 PI, §293.

15 '[G]iving an object a name is essentially the same kind of thing as hanging a label on it' (PG, p. 97).

16 See Hacker, *Insight and Illusion*, p. 225.

17 Note, however, that Wittgenstein does not want to show that one cannot speak to oneself, merely that there is no supposed situation in which there would be no way of rendering the statements of one's private conversation comprehensible to another.

18 One indication that Wittgenstein's argument is aimed against the phenom-

enalist is that it was already deployed by Neurath against Carnap's protocol language (private language!). Consider only the following passage:

> If Crusoe wants to relate what he registered ('protokolliert') yesterday with what he registers today, that is, when he wants to have any sort of recourse to a language, he cannot but have recourse to the inter-subjective language. The Crusoe of yesterday and the Crusoe of today stand to one another in precisely the relation in which Crusoe stands to Friday ... The protocols of one moment must be subject to incorporation in the protocols of the next, just as the protocols of A must be subject to incorporation in the protocols of B. *It is therefore meaningless to talk, as Carnap does, of a private language, or of a set of disparate protocol languages which may ultimately be drawn together.* (Neurath, 'Protocol sentences', p. 205)

Neurath explicitly rejects Carnap's 'methodological solipsism' (pp. 206f.).

19 PI, §309.
20 Wittgenstein, 'Notes for lectures on "private experience" and "sense data"', p. 300.
21 Ibid., p. 282.
22 Habermas's account is therefore on the right lines when he explains that, for Wittgenstein,

> the internal relation of meaning and validity [is] independent of the world-relation of language; he therefore does not connect the rules for the meaning of words with the truth-validity of sentences. Instead, he compares the validity of meaning conventions with the social acceptability of practices and institutions and assimilates the grammatical rules of language games to social norms of action. To be sure, he thereby surrenders every relation to validity that transcends the context of a given language game. Utterances are valid or invalid only according to the standards of the language game to which they belong. It is thus hardly noticed that the relation to truth of fact-stating discourse is also lost. (Habermas, *Postmetaphysical Thinking*, p. 69)

But he thus misses how Wittgenstein throws off the constraints of any kind of solipsism, including a solipsism of 'we', according to which the community is trapped in its language. This is exactly what he seeks to avoid by means of his appeal to second nature. This appeal, however, does ultimately lead to the problem suggested by Habermas's diagnosis (see chapter 14, below). Crispin Wright complains that Wittgenstein advocates an internal realism which threatens 'the idea of truth as an objective of empirical enquiry' – i.e. the relation between language and the world that was central to the *Tractatus*. See Wright, 'Hinge propositions and the serenity prayer', pp. 298ff.
23 I am deliberately replacing the expression 'propositional content' with 'assertoric content' because Wittgenstein's analysis of the determinacy of a discourse is, in my view, incompatible with the assumption of propositions, or Fregean thoughts, as eternal truth-evaluable entities. I discuss this point at greater

length above (pp. 204f.). Due to considerations of space, I am here setting aside the issue of whether Wittgenstein's polemic distorts the concept of the proposition, so that it might still be possible to take propositions into account while sharing Wittgenstein's basic assumptions. In conversation, Crispin Wright has pointed out that, on a Wittgensteinian account, we have to determine the concept of a proposition as 'assertoric content', which is certainly incompatible with a Platonism for which propositions obtain in themselves independently of all discourses. The question of how we can understand or grasp propositions can lead to a rejection of Platonism, as it does in Wittgenstein, but need not lead to a rejection of propositions. That Wittgenstein's analysis of the concept of assertion leads him to reject that of the proposition and to connect content to the function of an assertion in a context, rather than to the grasp of propositions possessing meanings in and of themselves, is also argued by Stanley Cavell. See Cavell, *The Claim of Reason*, pp. 208f.

24 See Putman's critique of the metaphysically empty assumption of a 'ready-made world' in 'Why there isn't a ready-made world'.

25 On the theme of the arbitrariness of grammar in Wittgenstein, see Forster, *Wittgenstein on the Arbitrariness of Grammar*.

26 According to Wittgenstein, the appeal to intuition is far from promising: 'So it must have been intuition that removed this doubt? – If intuition is an inner voice – how do I know *how* I am to obey it? And how do I know that it doesn't mislead me? For if it can guide me right, it can also guide me wrong. (Intuition an unnecessary shuffle.)' (PI, §213**)**.

27 PI, §258.

28 This problem becomes pressing, however, only as long as S wants to establish a language *exclusively* on the basis of her private sensations. The private language argument should not be read as a demonstration that we have no sensations or that we cannot speak about our sensations. It aims to show only that we could not speak about our private sensations if we could not also speak about something public, because the difference between private and public is itself public.

29 PI, §258.

30 Sentences such as 'everything is identical with itself' or 'everything is distinct from everything it is not' are not rules, as they cannot function as norms that fix what is correct and what is incorrect. As long as we cannot determine anything that is *not* the case, we are not dealing with anything like a rule. Rules direct information-processing in doxastic systems by establishing a difference between information to be retained and information to be discarded. Rules that can process any information are therefore not rules at all, as they cannot process any information. The aforementioned sentences are therefore not informative either.

31 PI, §261.

32 On the discriminatory structure of hunger, see Brandom, 'The structure of desire and recognition: self-consciousness and self-constitution.'

33 See PI, §304: '"And yet you again and again reach the conclusion that the sensation itself is a *nothing*." – Not at all. It is not a *something*, but not a *nothing*

either! The conclusion was only that a nothing would serve just as well as a something about which nothing could be said.' Wittgenstein, by his own account, does not want to assert that the sensation is a 'nothing'. Instead, he wants to show that we can avoid the paradox of a sensation language only by assuming the non-propositional – i.e. by recourse to the insight that the function of language is not exclusively that of assertion. The sensation is neither something nor nothing insofar as the sensation language and the intimacy of pain cannot be deployed in an epistemological, and thus assertoric, context. This would already be to treat it as an object, as something or nothing, that we might thematise and designate as though it were an object among possible others.

34 PI, §261.

35 PI, §201.

36 More precisely, the information that S constructs the series '2, 4, 6, 8, 10' is even a confirmation of the hypothesis that S follows the rule +2 *until 10,000 and then +4*. An important rule for formulating sceptical paradoxes works with the confirmation theory that is a branch of probability theory. That is, sceptical paradoxes argue – roughly speaking – by asserting that some piece of information confirms not just our hypothesis H but also its negation, as both H and ~H imply that information. As a result, our hypothesis seems arbitrary.

37 PI, §264.

38 PI, §265.

39 It is no good here invoking the assumption that the grasp of Platonic ideas in finite subjects is realised by an infinite mind, such that finite subjects participate in this encompassing mind whenever they grasp how a particular rule should be followed. For how can a subject determine which process in a finite mind is a manifestation of an infinite mind and which is not? The idea that each manifestation of an infinite mind indicates itself simply begs the question; it just attributes to a finite mind a capacity for grasping the manifestations of the very self-indicating mind that was originally introduced in order to explain the possibility of rule-following. This explanation of rule-following would ultimately have no advantage over the explanation that one always knows that one is following a rule when one is certain one is following it. If this certainty is supposed to be incorrigible, like the grasp of Platonic ideas, we end up with a private language in which everything that seems true is true. No explanatory progress has been made: assuming the manifestation of an infinite mind in a finite mind makes the same argumentative move as the appeal to the certainty. The problem of rule-following, however, was that we have to be able to distinguish between following and contravening a rule. Were every instance of rule-following a matter of a finite mind's grasping an 'idea' thanks to the manifestation of a self-indicating infinite mind, everyone could simply appeal to having grasped the rule qua manifestation. But then we could not have a situation in which two subjects both believe that they have followed the same rule while producing different results; for each could clearly have the impression of witnessing the same manifestation, and it would be impossible to decide which subject had really been the recipient of the infinite mind's

self-revelation. And since the manifestation of a self-indicating mind would in turn be a private procedure, inaccessible to public evaluation, nothing distinguishes it from the bare assertion that one has followed a rule (and, moreover, had done so infallibly). But assume, if only for the sake of argument, not only that we grasp ideas but that we grasp them via an infinite mind's manifestation within a finite mind. We would then clearly face an extraordinary explanatory task whenever we wanted to explain how we are, say, in a position to perform simple addition or to react to the presence of a dog with the word 'dog'. Postulating such manifestations thus either explains nothing at all, or it does explain what it is supposed to, but only by incurring an implausibly excessive explanatory burden. See Rorty, *Philosophy and the Mirror of Nature*, p. 374: 'The dilemma created by this Platonic hypostatization is that, on the one hand, the philosopher must attempt to find criteria for picking out these unique referents, whereas, on the other hand, the only hints he has about what these criteria could be are provided by current practice (by, e.g., the best moral and scientific thought of the day).'

40 Kripke, *Wittgenstein on Rules and Private Language*, p. 54.

41 PI, §218.

42 Neurath expresses this in his famous simile as follows:

> *There is no way of taking conclusively established pure protocol sentences as the starting point of the sciences.* No *tabula rasa* exists. We are like sailors who must rebuild their ship on the open sea, never able to dismantle it in dry-dock and to reconstruct it there out of the best materials. Only the metaphysical elements can be allowed to vanish without trace. Vague linguistic conglomerations always remain in one way or another as components of the ship. If vagueness is diminished at one point, it may well be increased at another. (Neurath, 'Protocol sentences', p. 201)

43 The concept of norms-in-context goes back to Crispin Wright. See Wright, 'Hinge propositions and the serenity prayer', pp. 293f., and 'Wittgensteinian certainties', p. 37.

44 The power of judgment in general is the faculty for thinking of the particular as contained under the universal. If the universal (the rule, the principle, the law) is given, then the power of judgment, which subsumes the particular under it (even when, as a transcendental power of judgment, it provides the conditions a priori in accordance with which alone anything can be subsumed under that universal), is determining. If, however, only the particular is given, for which the universal is to be found, then the power of judgment is merely reflecting. (CJ, 5:179)

Kant's definition of the determining power of judgement is at the very least problematic, given the underlying assumption that a universal (the rule) and a particular (an application) lie ready at hand, waiting to be brought together by the power of judgement. But one aspect of the problem of rule-following is that we are precisely not in a position to state immediately how it is possible to recognise a case *as* a case falling under a rule. This recognition is a condition of our then going on to subsume the particular under the universal, as Kant puts it. It looks as though Kant supposes a stable universal (the realm of rules or concepts), which has to be compared with a variable world of cases of application. But say concepts were universal, in the sense that all applications followed from them, and rule-following were a matter of the power of judgement affording us insight into the inferential relation obtaining between universal and particular: we would then once again have to bargain with superlative, infinite facts (the universal), which need to be brought into contact with the transient, empirical, finite facts. But this kind of gulf between finite and infinite cannot be bridged. Nor should it ever have opened up as part of an explanation of how we can become competent users of simple concepts such as 'dog', 'chair' or 'mountain'. Wittgenstein undermines Kant's attempt to ground our normative nature in a *mundus intelligibilis* by rethinking how we might draw the distinction between is and ought. For Wittgenstein, the ought belongs to human *nature* and does not indicate humanity's transcendence of the sensory world. As we shall discuss extensively in chapter 14 below, the problem of rule-following should ultimately lead to an (admittedly paradoxical) insight into a form of naturalism.

45 B171f. Brandom also points to the parallel between Kant and Wittgenstein in *Making it Explicit*, p. 657. He even assumes a direct influence of Kant on Wittgenstein, which is thoroughly plausible. In the discussion that contains the passage cited in the main text, Kant identifies the power of judgement with 'mother wit'. We might hear this echoed in Wittgenstein's use of 'wit' [*Witz*] in the *Philosophical Investigations*. See PI, §§62, 142, 564, 567.

46 To sum this up: the business of the senses is to intuit; that of the understanding, to think. To think, however, is to unite representations in a consciousness. . . . The unification of representations in a consciousness is judgment. Therefore, thinking is the same as judging or as relating representations to judgments in general. . . . Judgments, insofar as they are regarded merely as the condition for the unification of given representations in a consciousness, are rules. These rules, insofar as they represent the unification as necessary, are *a priori* rules. (P 4:304f.)

47 Of course, the grand master does not break the foundational rules of chess, which regulate the moves of the different pieces; rather, he breaks rules of the form that rooks on open lines are strong, that you should castle in a particular opening, or that you should not sacrifice your rooks in a certain, frequently discussed position.

48 Wolfram Hogrebe's theory of the non-propositional, which he designates as the 'mantic', rests on these considerations. The mantic draws our attention to how we cannot think the non-propositional in and through the propositional, despite Kant's thinking the non-propositional as the power of judgement, and thus in terms of judgement. See Gabriel, 'On Wolfram Hogrebe's philosophical approach'.

49 As Terry Pinkard notes, this places Kant in the proximity of Brandom's thesis that subjects are a normative status and not substances or any other kind of entity that can be an *object* of cognition. See Pinkard, 'Der sich selbst voll-bringende Skeptizismus und das Leben in der Moderne', pp. 48–50. Pinkard rightly argues that concepts are 'rules of judgement' for Kant (ibid., p. 51).

50 Wittgenstein, 'Cause and effect: intuitive awareness', p. 418.

51 I am of course referring to Sellars's position in *Empiricism and the Philosophy of Mind*, p. 44: '[O]ne can have the concept of green only by having a whole battery of concepts of which it is one element' (see also p. 75).

52 I therefore agree in essence with Heidegger's interpretation in *Kant and the Problem of Metaphysics*.

53 On this, see Hogrebe, 'Das dunkle Du'.

54 PI, §201.

55 By *substantial philosophy* I understand any philosophy that does not initially set out looking for a (dis)solution of one or more paradoxes but, rather, introduces its operative concepts as suggested answers to (at least seemingly) pressing problems. As the case of methodological scepticism shows, paradoxes generate the semblance of an urgent problem and so invite us to undertake substantial philosophical theorising. As soon as it can be shown, however, that a philo-sophical problem is merely an instance of a paradox, it is no longer appropriate to try to solve them with substantial philosophy, at least in the case of sceptical paradoxes. Substantial philosophy mostly reacts to the presence of a paradox with what Stephen Schiffer calls a *happy-face solution*:

> A happy-face solution to a paradox does two things, assuming that the propositions comprising the set [of the premises and the conclusion of the paradox, M. G.] really are mutually incompatible: first, it identifies the odd-guy-out, the member of the set that's not true; and second, it shows us why this spurious proposition deceived us, strips from it its patina of truth, so that we're not taken in by it again. (Schiffer, 'Skepticism and the vagaries of justified belief', pp. 178f.)

56 One of the ways in which Kant's concept of the a priori deviates from the contemporary debate around the a priori is that his two criteria for experience-independence are strict necessity and universality:

> At issue here is a mark means of which we can securely distinguish a pure cognition from an empirical one. Experience teaches us, to be sure, that something is constituted thus and so, but not that it could not be otherwise. **First**, then, if a proposition is thought along with its **necessity**, it is an *a priori* judgment; if it is, moreover, also not derived from any proposition except one that in turn is valid as a necessary proposition, then it is absolutely *a priori*. **Second**: Experience never gives its judgments true or strict but only assumed and comparative **universality** (through induction), so properly it must be said: as far as we have yet perceived, there is no exception to this or that rule. Thus if a judgment is thought in strict universality, i.e., in such a way

that no exception at all is allowed to be possible, then it is not derived from experience, but is rather valid absolutely *a priori*. (CPR, B3f.)

57 Meredith Williams also sees Wittgenstein's contextualism as reversing the Kantian order of explanation:

> Wittgenstein inverts the Kantian order of priority. On the Kantian view, our particular applications of a concept are derivative. They are the applications of the schematized concept itself. Thus, the concept as providing or generating the rule of use is prior to particular applications in practice. For Wittgenstein, this representative role is realized only in the context of an ongoing practice of use. Thus, the practice of use is prior to the concept or rule as representative or guiding. (*Wittgenstein, Mind and Meaning: Toward a Social Conception of Mind*, p. 76)

58 On the paradox of analysis and the solution offered here, see Fumerton, 'The paradox of analysis'. The paradox has its roots in antiquity and can be traced back to Plato's *Meno*, where it is formulated as a paradox about knowledge acquisition (see Men. 80d4-e6). Like most classical paradoxes, it is also discussed by Sextus (see AL, 8.331a).

59 On the difference between Wittgenstein and a Kantian metaphysics of experience, see Williams, *Wittgenstein, Mind and Meaning*, pp. 60–81.

60 In Kant's original definition of the power of judgement in the first introduction of the *Critique of the Power of Judgment*, the reference to the concept of representation is still explicit:

> The power of judgment can be regarded either as a mere faculty for reflecting on a given representation, in accordance with a certain principle, for the sake of a concept that is thereby made possible, or as a faculty for determining an underlying concept through a given empirical representation. In the first case it is the reflecting, in the second case the determining power of judgment. To reflect (to consider), however, is to compare and to hold together given representations either with others or with one's faculty of cognition, in relation to a concept thereby made possible. (CPJ, 20:211)

61 On the idea of 'alien reason' in Kant, see Simon, *Kant: Die fremde Vernunft und die Sprache der Philosophie*.

Chapter 10 The Diametrical Opposite of Solipsism

1 The principle of minimal verificationism comes from Roger White. He calls it 'disconfirmability' and formulates it as follows: 'If we know that a certain test cannot yield disconfirmation of our hypothesis, then no result of the test can confirm the hypothesis either' (White, 'Problems for dogmatism', p. 544). The example that follows in the main text is borrowed from the same source,

pp. 543ff. White, however, does not note the bearing of his discussion on the problem of rule-following.

2 '[I]t is impossible to discover that appearances don't match reality when my only guides to reality are those very experiences' (White, 'Problems for dogmatism', p. 546).

3 This is how I understand Kripke's sceptical solution to the problem of rule-following: 'The solution turns on the idea that each person who claims to be following a rule can be checked by others. Others in the community can check whether the putative rule follower is or is not giving particular responses that they endorse, that agree with their own' (Kripke, *Wittgenstein on Rules and Private Language*, p. 101).

4 See the extensive discussion in Luhmann, *Social Systems*, chapter 9.

5 On this topic, see Castoriadis's concept of the social in *The Imaginary Institution of Society*, esp. pp. 101–8.

6 According to Brandom, this problem is a consequence of overestimating I–we sociality. Such overestimation leads to an exaggerated demand that a community agree in all foundational judgement. We therefore have to do justice to an I–you sociality: there must be room for authorities in the community who decide what it means to follow a determinate rule correctly. See Brandom, *Making it Explicit*, p. 39. This solution – i.e. introducing an authority – is, however, generally unconvincing. It ascribes the function of the isolated judging subject to the authority, thus only apparently solving the problem (by *fiat*).

7 Hegel, *Phenomenology of Spirit*, §177.

8   To believe involves a commitment to its being the case that one's truth-taking is regulated by what is in fact true. What performs this regulative function is the answerability of belief to rational criticism. Of course, we sometimes accept something on faith, without any evidence or reasons. But our entitlement to think of any given belief as true, including a belief accepted on faith, depends on its being answerable to rational criticism should we acquire sufficient reason or evidence to suggest it may be false. (Macarthur, 'Naturalism and skepticism', p. 122)

9 Wright, *Truth and Objectivity*, p. 23.

10 Wright, *Rails to Infinity*, pp. 245f.

11 PI, § 101.

12 Wright therefore remarks that the power of Wittgenstein's argument does not even require a demonstration that a private language is impossible, merely that it lacks any epistemic qualification:

What will follow, if Wittgenstein is correct, is not, strictly, that private language is impossible, but that it cannot provide a medium for the formulation of genuine statements, commands, questions, wishes, the framing of hypotheses or any kind of speech act which presupposes the availability in the language of the means for depicting genuine state [sic.] of affairs. It is a further question whether anything so impoverished as to lack all these expressive resources could qualify as a language . . . .. However, since all the lines of thought which attract, or pressure, towards the possibility of private language involve regarding it as a medium for expression of knowledge, there is no comfort for anyone in such a possibility – if possibility it be. (Wright, *Rails to Infinity*, 244f., fn. 14)

13 CPR, B848.
14 CPR, B848f.
15 CPR, B849.
16 Ibid., emphasis M. G.
17 See Brandom, *Tales of the Mighty Dead*, p. 50: 'Concept P is sense dependent on concept Q just in case one cannot count as having grasped P unless one counts as having grasped Q. Concept P is reference dependent on concept Q just in case P cannot apply to something unless Q applies to something.' See above, pp. 28f.
18 Wright, *Rails to Infinity*, pp. 231–3, 242f.
19 This condition applies unrestrictedly. Of course, there are no absolute facts concerning what an individual thinks about herself that are independent of what she thinks about herself. The same can be said of a group or society. But there is, nonetheless, an absolute fact about what an individual thinks about herself.
20 There are, of course, also artefacts or entities, such as states, families and life plans, that are not objective in the same sense as tables and stars. Yet, in these cases too, it remains true that we can refer to such entities only as long as we can make true and false judgement about them. My present aim is not to individuate various ontological regions in terms of various conditions of objectivity, merely to establish *a necessary connection between sociality and objectivity*.
21 See too Koch, 'Absolutes Wissen?', p. 32:

> If this independence of states of affairs from my beliefs did not obtain, then whatever I believe would automatically be true, contrary to that platitude [of the contrast of objectivity, M. G.]. And, conversely: if I were not fallible in my beliefs, their objects would not be anything independent of my act of believing, would not be anything objective. My thoroughgoing fallibility in judgement is accordingly no indication of human weakness but a sign of the objectivity of that to which I relate myself in judgement. The world is not merely my representation. In any case, that is what I claim insofar as I raise objective truth claims. Therefore, Cartesian beliefs of the type 'it seems to be that p' do not concern any objective states of affairs insofar as I am immune to error in having them.

22 PI, §241.
23 This is not to say that the correct/incorrect distinction coincides with the true/false distinction. Correct/incorrect is certainly a condition of the possibility of true/false, but the very way in which it functions as such a condition means

that the two distinctions must be distinguished. From the sociality of objectivity, we cannot derive the idea that everything a community holds true is true; this would simply ground a collective solipsism. Nevertheless, the community can function as an access condition of objectivity.

24 PI, §415.

25 See Baker and Hacker, 'Critical study: on misunderstanding Wittgenstein: Kripke's private language argument'; Blackburn, 'The individual strikes back'. While Blackburn merely objects that, since a community can err just as much as an individual, the community view is liable to private language scepticism in just the same way, Paul Boghossian, in 'The rule-following considerations', has made a still more telling objection. Boghossian distinguishes between an *intentional* and an *extensional* requirement on rule-following. The *intentional requirement* is to define a criterion of normativity – i.e. a condition of correctness – that distinguishes between correct and incorrect applications of a rule. This condition can be fulfilled by the agreement of a community, especially as one can appeal to our habit of mistrusting our own judgement should we find our beliefs conflicting with those of everyone else (or simply of several others) and, conversely, of trusting our judgement when it agrees with that of a sufficiently large body of the community. The problem of the community view lies in its inability to fulfil the *extensional requirement*. This stipulates that our correct and incorrect moves must not be totally independent of the world. Suppose that someone is continually inclined to take cows in a meadow at night for horses. Since he always sees cows in the very same meadow during the day, he comes to wonder whether he does not in fact see the very same cows at night and falsely takes them to be horses. Now, suppose he gathers a group of 17,000 observers who by night take a common stand on the question of whether it is cows or horses standing in the meadow. Nothing prevents us from supposing that they could all believe themselves to be seeing horses when the meadow is really populated with cows.

> The point is that many of the mistakes we make are systematic: they arise because of the presence of features – bad lighting, effective disguises, and so forth – that have a generalizable and predictable effect on creatures with similar cognitive endowments. (This is presumably what makes 'magicians' possible.) But then any of my dispositions that are in this sense systematically mistaken, are bound to be duplicated at the level of the community. (Ibid., p. 536)

Because this objection is in fact decisive against an unqualified community view, Wittgenstein himself added a further factor, namely the 'circumstances' or 'environment' of applying a rule. Without this contextualist addition, the community view is vulnerable to the objection of the possibility of extensional systematic errors. Hence the world comes into play. Without the world, truth would shrink to a *consensus gentium*. Wittgenstein too is unable to understand objectivity entirely without recourse to something independent of our holding-true – including our communal holding-true.

26 See Williams, *Wittgenstein, Mind and Meaning*, p. 165: 'An empirical generalization about what most people do is not the same as a norm standing for what people ought to do.'

27 Truth therefore has both epistemic and non-epistemic facets, and this corresponds to Koch's distinction between phenomenal and normative (i.e. epistemic) aspects of truth on the one hand and a realistic (i.e. non-epistemic) aspect on the other. See Koch, *Versuch über Wahrheit und Zeit*, §§5, p. 71.

28 On this point, see Cavell's criticisms of Kripke. Cavell (e.g. *Philosophy the Day After Tomorrow*, pp. 112ff.) argues that Kripke's solution results in an authoritarian model of education which needs to be replaced with a recognitional model, such that rule-scepticism ultimately points beyond itself to the practical dimension.

29 These considerations are at the centre of Cavell's interpretation of Wittgenstein in *The Claim of Reason*. He sees the *truth or moral of scepticism* in the lesson that our stance towards the world as a whole is not that of propositional knowledge (see, for example, ibid., p. 48). Ultimately, this means for Cavell that '(there is no everything, no totality of facts or things, to be known)' (ibid., p. 239). The assumption of a thus-and-so-determined totality is incompatible with the idea that knowledge is only ever determined discursively. Scepticism therefore sets limits to our reaching out to the whole, because it prevents us from taking seriously the idea that we have justified beliefs about what the whole even is. It is important to note that these reflections do not constitute any objection to metaphysics of a classical provenance: this operated precisely with the idea that totality cannot be an object. For a detailed elaboration of this point, see Gabriel, *Transcendental Ontology*, pp. 2–34.

30 As in Fichte's theory of recognition, we are faced with a kind of recognitional idealism, which de-materialises the status of persons and links it entirely to the stances of other persons. See Bernstein, 'Recognition and embodiment (Fichte's materialism)'.

31 PI,§292.

32 For this reason, all linguistic expressions refer to a symbolic 'always already' that we cannot immediately transcend. See Castoriadis, *The Imaginary Institution of Society*, p. 121.

Chapter 11 McDowell's Disjunctivism as an Anti-Sceptical Strategy

1 See esp. McDowell, *Mind and World* and 'Criteria, defeasibility and knowledge'.

2 McDowell, 'Criteria, defeasibility and knowledge', pp. 470ff.

3 'Indeed, it is arguable that the "highest common factor" model undermines the very idea of an appearance having as its content that things are thus and so in the world "beyond" appearances (as we would have to put it)' (ibid., p. 474).

4 On this, see chapters 6 and 13 of this study.

5 In connection with Reinhold's 'principle of consciousness', that the 'principle

of phenomenality' is 'the highest principle', Wilhelm Dilthey states that, 'accordingly, everything that is present for me is subject to the general condition that it be a fact of my consciousness; every external thing is also given to me only as a connection of facts or processes of consciousness; an object, a thing, is only present for a consciousness and in a consciousness' ('Beiträge zur Lösung der Frage vom Ursprung unseres Glaubens an die Realität der Außenwelt', p. 90). Dilthey thereby encapsulates the theoretical structure of mental representationalism.

6 On the fundamental distinction between 'representational purport' and 'representational success', see Brandom, *Making it Explicit*, p. 72.

7 CPR, B376f.

8 McDowell, 'Criteria, defeasibility and knowledge', pp. 470ff.

9 Ibid., p. 472.

10 McDowell, *Mind and World*, p. 27 *et al.*

11 PI, §95.

12 In this connection, Anton Friedrich Koch speaks of a presentational moment of truth: 'Since truth has an intuitive-presentational aspect, because it is – *also* – unconcealment, veridical appearance, we are in principle entitled to break off regresses in our epistemological justification at some point or other' (*Versuch über Wahrheit und Zeit*, p. 156). On his thesis that the concept of truth has two further moments in addition to its presentational moment, see ibid., §20.

13 McDowell, 'Criteria, defeasibility and knowledge', p. 475; see also McDowell, 'Singular thought and the extent of inner space' and 'Knowledge and the internal'. The disjunctivist theory of perception goes back to Hinton, 'Visual experiences' and *Experiences*. Hinton points to how every assertion that something appears to a subject S to be thus and so is either the assertion that S perceives something or the assumption that S is subject to an illusion, where there is no common factor pertaining to both a perception and an illusion – e.g. a visual experience. If we can give a non-contradictory formulation of disjunctivism, we undermine the assumption that there are sensible representations that are either empty or contentful, such that they are illusions in the first case and perceptions in the second. Of course, removing the assumption of sensible representations facilitates the construction of an anti-sceptical strategy if and only if we can show that scepticism is an implication of the concept of representation, as does seem to be the case for Cartesian scepticism. For a good overview of the positions advocated by a range of authors, see the contributions to Hawthorne and Kovakovich, 'Disjunctivism'; see also Kern, *Sources of Knowledge*, pp. 113ff.; Willaschek, *Der mentale Zugang zur Welt*, pp. 207–88.

14 These example sentences come from McDowell. See 'Criteria, defeasibility and knowledge', p. 472, fn. 2.

15 Aristotle, *Metaphysics* 1073b30f. See, for example, the programmatic commitment to phenomena in *Nichomachean Ethics*, 1145b2-7.

16 On this, see Heidegger, *Being and Time*, pp. 50–54.

17 'When someone has a fact manifest to him, the obtaining of the fact contributes to his epistemic standing on the question. But the obtaining of the fact is precisely not blankly external to his subjectivity, as it would be if the truth about

that were exhausted by the highest common factor' (McDowell, 'Criteria, defeasibility and knowledge', p. 476).

18 Ibid., p. 478.

19 Sellars's analyses of looks-talk operate in the background of McDowell's disjunctivism. See Sellars, *Empiricism and the Philosophy of Mind*, pp. 32–53. Sellars shows that looks-talk is a secondary act insofar as it indicates a subject's withholding judgement. When someone says that something looks to her to be thus and so, she thereby concedes that it is possible that she is having a representation *as though* p, without it being so *that* p. But what is thereby asserted is more complex than the statement that something or other is thus and so – i.e. more complex than any is-talk. Sellars wants to show that is-talk is primary in relation to looks-talk because there cannot be any looks-talk without there being at least some is-talk. Is-talk is therefore irreducible to looks-talk. It follows that the empiricist assumption of a veil of perception separating us from the representable world cannot, at any rate, be justified by assigning any primacy to looks-talk.

20 For a summary presentation of his objections, see Wright, 'Comment on John McDowell's "The disjunctive conception of experience as material for a transcendental argument"'.

21 See Timothy Williamson, 'Past the linguistic turn', p. 110: 'for all that McDowell has shown, there may be necessary limitations on all possible thinkers. We do not know whether there are elusive objects [e.g. perfect hallucinations; M. G.]. It is unclear what would motivate the claim that there are none, if not some form of idealism. We should adopt no conception of philosophy that on methodological grounds excludes elusive objects.'

22 In certain circumstances, we can have direct access to something that indicates a difference between hallucination and perception. This is clear enough in the case of a *fata Morgana*. It suffices to walk up to the spot where one thinks one sees the water's surface in order to establish that one had fallen victim to a perfect hallucination. From having a perfect hallucination, it does not directly follow, though, that one can discover that one is having one, as there could well be perfect hallucinations we cannot discover.

23 Thus Fumerton, in *Metaepistemology and Skepticism*, p. 186: 'If I can reason that there would be nothing to reveal a distinction between what I am acquainted with in hallucinatory and veridical experience, and I can reason that I am not directly acquainted with facts about the physical world in hallucinatory experience, then I can conclude that I am not directly acquainted with such facts in veridical experience.'

24 Macarthur, 'Naturalism and skepticism', p. 111.

25 '[W]hat we pretheoretically assume is the cause of our subjective experiences may be quite different from what actually causes them. The existence of a causal law is no help either if our only basis for its existence presupposes that some of our appearances are caused by the objects that they are apparently about. For what is in question is precisely what justifies such a presupposition' (Ibid., p. 113).

26 McDowell's vision of the logical space of reasons as unbounded is opposed

to the assumption of a boundary between subject and object. This is why he describes *Mind and World* as a 'prolegomenon to a reading of the Phenomenology [of Spirit]' (McDowell, *Mind and World*, p. ix). The second lecture in particular ('The unboundedness of the conceptual') often has deeply Hegelian resonances.

27 McDowell, *Mind and World*, p. 113; likewise McDowell, 'Knowledge and the internal', p. 408, fn. 19. David Macarthur distinguishes between a refutation of scepticism and a quietist response that consists in providing reasons why we need not enter into confrontation with scepticism in the first place. The quietist strategy remains weak, however, if it consists in nothing more than the refusal to dissolve a paradox. See Macarthur: 'Naturalism and skepticism', p. 107. See also Macarthur, 'McDowell, scepticism, and "the veil of perception"'.

28 PI, §201.

29 McDowell, 'Wittgenstein on following a rule', p. 253.

30 McDowell, *Mind and World*, pp. 84–8. In addition, see Bubner, '*Bildung* and second nature'.

31 As does McDowell himself in *Mind and World*, p. 27.

32 'Naturalised Platonism' is how McDowell describes his position (*Mind and World*, p. 91). By this label he understands the thesis that the conceptual is unbounded, such that we cannot ultimately separate nature and concept. This leads to the assumption that as conceptual beings we inhabit a conceptual world, to which we have access thanks to our (second) nature. The conceptual world here need in no sense be transcendent. Rather, McDowell's conceptual world, the logical space of reasons, is the totality of all facts that p. Facts that p, however, can be grasped by conceptual beings precisely because they are not merely natural (in the sense of 'first nature') events, which can exercise an exclusively causal influence upon the sensibility of conceptual beings. McDowell thus assumes that we always already stand in immediate contact with a propositionally structured world, a world that consists not of objects standing in causal-nomological connections but of conceptually graspable facts.

33 McDowell himself believes that Wittgenstein's late philosophy can be best understood on the model of his naturalised Platonism. See *Mind and World*, p. 92. But McDowell's naturalised Platonism implies an 'always already' that Wittgenstein in fact rejects: 'The idea is that the dictates of reason are there anyway, whether or not one's eyes are opened to them; that is what happens in a proper upbringing' (ibid., p. 91). Wittgenstein's later philosophy opposes not only the assumption of a transcendent world of concepts but any *ontological* assumption of a world of concepts to which we have mental access, where such an assumption is introduced to explain the phenomenon of rule-following. Given the private language argument and the supporting rule-following considerations, McDowell's naturalised Platonism is no less questionable than any other variety of semantic Platonism.

34 On the idea of a reconsideration of the facticity of facts in light of the social dimension of the concept of truth, see Wright's discussions in 'Facts and certainty', pp. 429–72, and his reworking of the relevant theses in 'Warrant for nothing'.

35 OC, §156.

36 The social parameter does, however, play an eminent role in McDowell's interpretation of Wittgenstein: he assigns a transcendental function to use and practice insofar as meaning would not be possible without this function. In *Mind and World*, though, it is not clear how he can integrate this communitarian aspect of rule-following into the conception of a world that is in itself as it is grasped in our judgements that it is thus and so. In other words, the Kantianism of *Mind and World* is incompatible with the insight McDowell draws from his Wittgenstein interpretation.

37 PI, §192.

38 See PI, §186.

39 RFM, p. 249. Wittgenstein seems to contradict himself here, as in the *Philosophical Investigations* he insists that 'there is a way of grasping a rule which is *not* an *interpretation*' (PI, §201). Here, I will make no attempt to resolve this contradiction – if there really is one. Applying the principle of charity, we can assume that 'interpretation' has a different meaning in each of the cited passages: the statement from RFM takes aim against the idea of a given, fully conceptually determined rule, whereas the statement in the PI is directed at the regress of rules problem that arises if we always understand rule-following as interpretation.

40 PG, p. 49.

41 Kant had already voiced a similar view about intuition's supposed advantage vis-à-vis discursive comprehension: 'The light dove, in free flight cutting through the air the resistance of which it feels, could get the idea that it could do even better in airless space. Likewise, Plato abandoned the world of the senses because it set such narrow limits for the understanding, and dared to go beyond it on the wings of the ideas, in the empty space of pure understanding' (CPR, B8f).

42 While the debate surrounding the question of whether Robinson Crusoe (i.e. a subject in physical isolation) can follow a rule, even though nobody is around to correct him, is therefore certainly of *empirical* interest, it is not relevant for answering the quite different question of whether a private language is possible. I do not believe that Wittgenstein uses the private language argument to raise the question of how an isolated individual would behave linguistically. However interesting this question might be, it already presupposes the public/private distinction that is simply not available to the private linguist. Neither Robinson Crusoe nor Kaspar Hauser are phenomenalists who would also defend their private rule usage – should they cultivate one – against the public world once they were confronted with it. To determine the impetus of Wittgenstein's argument correctly, we cannot ignore his dialectical opposition to the phenomenalist. Given his distinction between *privately following a rule* and *following a private rule*, Robinson Crusoe is not a real problem for Wittgenstein. Hacker, in *Insight and Illusion*, pp. 252f., rightly locates the solution to the Robinson Crusoe issue in this distinction.

Chapter 12 Stage-Setting and Discourse

1 RFM, p. 414.

2 See Williams, *Wittgenstein, Mind and Meaning*, pp. 188–215.

3 The metaphor of stage-setting can already be found in Rawls's essay 'Two concepts of rules', p. 30: 'That punishment and promising are practices is beyond question. In the case of promising this is shown by the fact that the form of words "I promise" is a performative utterance which presupposes the stage-setting of the practice and the proprieties defined by it.'. (Rawls thereby alludes to Wittgenstein; see ibid., p. 29.) My thanks to Thomas Nagel for directing me to Rawls's essay.

4 Of course, this represents a problem only provided we understand 'nature' as an in-itself wholly meaningless spatiotemporal distribution of particles, whose history would be best described by a function (the world formula) that gives a precise statement of the location of every particle in the universe for every point in time. On this model, natural laws would be the principles governing the distribution of particles in a meaningless universe. Yet 'nature' need not be understood physicalistically. Not every naturalism is physicalist. In *Mind and World*, McDowell has shown that physicalism's concept of nature has to be supplemented by the concept of a normative nature – namely, human nature – if we want to understand how it is possible to conceive of ourselves as rational animals whose intellectual capacities are certainly natural, without having to conceive the subject as an extensionless boundary of the world.

5 However, a more exacting confrontation between scepticism and naturalism is required if we want to ascribe to the latter the explanatory role it has to play in order to help us avoid rule-following scepticism. And unfortunately, as we shall see, a result of this confrontation is that we cannot affirm naturalism as a thesis under sceptical conditions. This is why Wittgenstein oscillates between two different tendencies: on the one hand, he wants to provide 'remarks on the natural history of human beings' (PI, §415; RFM, pp. 92, 352); yet, on the other hand, he rejects this very project: 'We are not doing natural science; nor yet natural history – since we can also invent fictitious natural history for our purposes' (PI II, p. 230). See chapter 14 below.

6 See e.g. PI, §415; PG, p. 94.

7 'The subject does not belong to the world: rather, it is a limit of the world' (*Tractatus*, 5.632). 5.64 is also explicit: 'Here it can be seen that solipsism, when its implications are followed out strictly, coincides with pure realism. The self of solipsism shrinks to a point without extension, and there remains the reality co-ordinated with it.'

8 This point has been developed particularly clearly by Maria Baghramian in *Relativism*, pp. 170, 204.

9 'And now, I think, we can say: Augustine describes the learning of human language as if the child came into a strange country and did not understand the language of the country; that is, as if it already had a language, only not this one. Or again: as if the child could already *think*, only not yet speak. And

"think" would here mean something like "talk to itself"' (PI, §32). Wittgenstein – who, as his many implicit and explicit jabs at Plato reveal, was an attentive reader of the Platonic dialogues – thereby opposes the Platonic conception of discursive thought as the soul's dialogue with itself. See *Tht.* 189e6–190a7; *Soph.* 263e3–15.

10 It is in this point that Meredith Williams quite correctly sees the function of the *Investigations'* opening critique of ostensive instruction for the later private language argument. For the private language argument is opposed to the idea of a private ostensive definition with the help of which the private linguist procures the elementary and supposedly epistemically foundational expressions for her private experiences:

> [O]stensive teaching is a causal process which brings about an association between an object and a sign. Animals as well as human beings are susceptible to this kind of teaching. The result of this teaching (or conditioning) is the ability to parrot, but it does not (in itself) effect an understanding of the sign. For this, ostensive teaching must be coupled with a training in the use of a sign. And the use of a sign is determined by the practice or custom in which the sign is embedded. Thus, ostensive teaching, which helps effect understanding, also presupposes a public language, though the child does not know it. (Williams, *Wittgenstein, Mind and Meaning*, p. 21)

Williams thus widens the community view in the way I am recommending here, bringing in the holistic and contextualist dimension of how rule-following is embedded in a practice that we can access only through instruction: '[T]his [Colin McGinn's] reading ignores Wittgenstein's commitment to the holistic and contextualist features of language mastery and use, the stage setting. Moving a piece on a checkered board only counts as the movement of a pawn – indeed only is the movement of a pawn – within the practice of chess' (ibid., 170f.).

11 See Wittgenstein's example of a coronation: 'A coronation is the picture of pomp and dignity. Cut one minute of this proceeding out of its surroundings: the crown is being placed on the head of the king in his coronation robes. – But in different surroundings gold is the cheapest of metals, its gleam is thought vulgar. There the fabric of the robe is cheap to produce. A crown is a parody of a respectable hat. And so on.' PI, §584; see RFM, p. 95.

12 OC, §105; compare §§140–44.

13 Z, §173.

14 See Schiffer, 'Propositional content.'

15 Of course, Platonic ideas are different from propositions in several respects. An important difference is that ideas are present in everything finite and not simply because we conceive the finite *as though* ideas were present in it. Rather, Plato believes that we can have cognitive access to empirical reality only because it is itself structured by ideas. There is no need for us to invest reality with its intelligibility. Platonic ideas are thus logical-ontological entities in the sense that they structure both the realm of cognition and the realm of being.

Plato, therefore, also ascribes properties to them that nobody would ascribe to propositions – e.g. the property of self-knowledge, which Plato attributes to the ideas a whole, especially in the *Sophist*. Assessing Plato's reasons for the hypothesis of 'Eidos', however, would take us too far afield here.

16 PI, §304.

17 OC, §131.

18 It is nevertheless vital to insist, *pace* Wittgenstein, that there can be no absolute facts within the world, because facts are always only facts for a discourse. Without discourses, there would be no assertoric content whatsoever and thus no possibility of our orienting ourselves to the facts – i.e. seeking knowledge. This insight, however, does introduce second-order absolute facts, as we surely state facts when we state that discourses function in such and such a way. It is impossible to apply contextualism to itself and to give its philosophical insights a discourse-theoretic formulation – that is, not without simply representing a single standpoint that generates equally valid alternatives. The question is therefore whether one can be a contextualist in the way I have been describing that doctrine without representing an inconsistent position, one which has no absolute assertoric content. See chapters 14–15 below.

19   The ultimate source (not ground) for objectivity is, in my opinion, inter-subjectivity. If we were not in communication with others, there would be nothing on which to base the idea of being wrong, or, therefore, being right, either in what we say or in what we think. The possibility of thought as well as of communication depends, in my view, on the fact that two or more creatures are responding, more or less simultaneously, to input from a shared world, and from each other. . . . Without a second person there is, as Wittgenstein powerfully suggests, no basis for a judgement that a reaction is wrong or, therefore, right. (Davidson, 'Indeterminism and antirealism', p. 83)

20 Schopenhauer, *The World as Will and Representation*, p. 209. On this point, see McDowell, 'Wittgenstein on following a rule', p. 254:

Wittgenstein's reflections on rule-following attack a certain familiar picture of facts and truth, which I shall formulate like this. A genuine fact must be a matter of the way things are in themselves, utterly independently of us. So a genuinely true judgement must be, at least potentially, an exercise of pure thought; if human nature is necessarily implicated in the very formation of the judgement, that precludes our thinking of the corresponding fact as properly independent of us, and hence as a proper fact at all.

21 RFM, p. 342.

22 PI, §217.

23 As I have already mentioned, it belongs to certain practices to interact with the world. But *what* it is they interact with – i.e. what the facts are that play a role in the practice – is not something we can determine independently of the practice; for there can be determinations only within a practice that also

contains norms. The idea of a given world with states determined in and of themselves has no place in Wittgenstein's anti-realism.

24 Wittgenstein brings the private linguist to concede that her private objects are neither something nor nothing. They cannot be something, else it would be possible to say what they are. And they should not be nothing, else the private language would be utterly empty. The private language is thus: 'It is not a *something*, but not a *nothing* either! The conclusion was only that a nothing would serve as well as a something about which nothing could be said' (PI, §304).

25 This seems to be the message of PI, §237:

> Imagine someone using a line as a rule in the following way: he holds a pair of compasses, and carries one of its points along the line that is the 'rule', while the other one draws the line that follows the rule. And while he moves along the ruling line he alters the opening of the compasses, apparently with great precision, looking at the rule the whole time as if it determined what he did. And watching him we see no kind of regularity in this opening and shutting of the compasses. We cannot learn his way of following the line from it.

26 See Williams, *Wittgenstein, Mind and Meaning*, p. 177: 'The community is not required in order to police the actions and judgements of all members, but in order to sustain the articulated structure within which understanding and judging can occur and against which error and mistake can be discerned.'

27 On this topic, see the work of John MacFarlane, which attempts to show that introducing a context of assessment is necessary for at least some discourses. See MacFarlane, 'The assessment sensitivity of knowledge attributions', 'Making sense of relative truth', and 'Future contingents and relative truth'. To be sure, MacFarlane's formal semantics of relativism needs to be fleshed out when it comes to the integration into the picture of actually existing agents whose presence is not sufficiently reflected by the introduction of a purely formal parameter into semantics. There is thus a significant gap between MacFarlane's semantic relativism and Wittgensteinian contextualism. It would lead too far afield to go into the details of this difference here. Having said that, MacFarlane's very idea that we need an additional parameter in some contexts is useful as a tool for making sense of Wittgensteinian contextualism, as conceived here.

28 Koch draws our attention to how the 'always already' of objectivity is a temporal mode which corresponds to the past as one of the 'ecstasies' of temporality. The 'always already' absolutises the 'dominance of the realistic aspect' of truth and thus introduces 'the particular danger of naturalising the existent under the governing notion of objectivity' (*Versuch über Wahrheit und Zeit*, p. 537).

29 PI, §115.

Chapter 13 Solipsism's Representations and Cartesian Scepticism

1 See Gabriel, *Grundprobleme der Erkenntnistheorie*, pp. 164ff.

2 This is the reason why Heidegger sees the concept of representation, or the concept of thought as representation, as the origin of the subject–object dichotomy and thus of being's alienation from its world. Heidegger's entire philosophy after *Being and Time* can be read as an abandonment of the concept of representation. In its place he recommends a more detailed consideration of the very earliest Greek philosophy, which is meant to allow us to find our way to overcoming the concept of the world as the totality of the representable. He wants to reach back beyond the Platonic–Aristotelian concept of εἶδος by seeing 'the presupposition which – long prevailing only mediately, in concealment and long in advance – predestined the world's having to become picture' (Heidegger, 'The age of the world picture', here p. 69; also compare Heidegger, 'Plato's doctrine of truth'. But, *pace* Heidegger, we should recall that the concept of representation can also be motivated as the *result* of a sceptical method of justification; it need not be the *presupposition* of the subject–object dichotomy.

3 On this issue, see Russell's famous argument for sense data in Russell, *The Problems of Philosophy*, chs I–V. On arguments for sense data in antiquity and ancient versions of the concept of representation, see Fine, 'Sextus and external world skepticism', 'Descartes and ancient skepticism: reheated cabbage?' and 'Subjectivity, ancient and modern: the Cyrenaics, Sextus, and Descartes'. See also my own discussion in 'Zum Außenweltproblem in der Antike'.

4 Kripke sees Wittgenstein's true achievement as having developed a new form of scepticism together with an anti-sceptical strategy: 'Wittgenstein has invented a new form of scepticism. Personally, I am inclined to regard it as the most radical and original sceptical problem that philosophy has seen to date' (Kripke, *Wittgenstein on Rules and Private Language*, p. 60).

5 See Fogelin, *Pyrrhonian Reflections on Knowledge and Justification*, p. 3. Eusebius already came to the conclusion that Pyrrhonian scepticism represented not a philosophy but an anti-philosophical movement. See *Praep. Evang.* XIV 18, 30 (763d): 'It is evident then that no one in his right mind would approve such a sect [sceptics], or course of argument, or whatever and however any one likes to call it. For I think for my part that we ought not to call it philosophy at all, since it destroys the very first principles of philosophy.' (ἐγὼ μὲν γὰρ οὐδὲ φιλοσοφίαν οἴομαι δεῖν ὀνομάζειν αὐτὴν [viz. τὴν σκηπτικὴν ἀγωγήν, M. G.] ἀναιροῦσάν γε δὲ τὰς τοῦ φιλοσοφεῖν ἀρχάς.)

6 Plato, *Theaetetus*, 158b8-d6. On Plato's dream argument, see Gabriel, *Antike und modern Skepsis*, I.2. It is important to note, however, that the dream argument of the *Theaetetus* merely fulfils the function of helping to refute the thesis that knowledge and perception are identical – i.e. that all knowledge is through perception. The dream argument is meant to show no more than that, since we can be deceived about whether we are currently perceiving anything at all, we need a criterion to distinguish between being in a dream state and being

awake. As this criterion is not itself perceivable, but nevertheless has to be the content of a piece of knowledge, there has to be non-empirical cognition at least of the criterion if we are to secure the thesis that we acquire knowledge through perception. It follows that there cannot just be knowledge through perception, as knowledge through perception depends upon knowledge of its conditions, and this knowledge is not itself empirical.

7 For a more detailed discussion of this point, see Gabriel, 'Der 'Wink Gottes' – Zur Rolle der Winke Gottes in Heideggers Beiträgen zur Philosophie und bei Jean-Luc Nancy'. See also 'Unvordenkliches Sein und Ereignis – Der Seinsbegriff beim späten Schelling und beim späten Heidegger'.

8 I have provided an extensive justification of this reading of Pyrrhonian scepticism elsewhere (in *Skeptizismus und Idealismus in der Antike*).

9 PI, §199.

10 As Stanley Cavell's work on Wittgenstein and scepticism has shown, Wittgenstein precisely sets out to defend the ordinary against the out-of-the-ordinary. Besides *The Claim of Reason*, see also Cavell, *In Quest of the Ordinary: Lines of Skepticism and Romanticism*. See, for example, the summary of his attitude to the ordinary in *The Claim of Reason*, p. 463:

> The wish to be extraordinary, exceptional, unique, thus reveals the wish to be ordinary, everyday. (One does not, after all, wish to become a monster, even though the realization of one's wish for uniqueness would make one a monster.) So both the wish for the exceptional and for the everyday are foci of romanticism. One can think of romanticism as the discovery that the everyday is an exceptional achievement. Call it the achievement of the human.

11 PI, §115.

12 Hiley has shown in detail that Pyrrhonian scepticism attacks a Platonist picture of the position our rationality occupies in the world. See Hiley, *Philosophy in Question: Essays on a Pyrrhonian Theme*, e.g. p. 174:

> The organizing theme of these essays has been the Platonic notion that we can realize our true selves and achieve the good life only by the philosophical project of escape from the contingent and finite into the necessary and eternal, and the Pyrrhonian challenge to that notion which aims to break the connection between knowledge and virtue and return us to the appearances and values of the customary and traditional.

According to Hiley, Rorty and Wittgenstein are the standout Pyrrhonian sceptics of our own age because they not only present philosophical arguments in order to mark out and enrich philosophical knowledge but also aim to retract the axiological primacy assigned to philosophical over ordinary knowledge.

13 *Theaetetus*, 176a8-b1.

14 See above, p. 95.

15 On this, see Williams, *Descartes: The Project of Pure Enquiry*.

16 Nevertheless, the importance he assigned to ethics can be seen in his 'Lecture on ethics', which was first published in 1965 in the *Philosophical Review*. It is remarkable how close Wittgenstein comes to Heidegger in this lecture, a fact of which he was well aware, as a conversation of 30 December 1929 with Moritz Schlick shows:

> To be sure, I can imagine what Heidegger means by being and anxiety. Man feels the urge to run up against the limits of language. Think for example of the astonishment that anything at all exists. This astonishment cannot be expressed in the form of a question, and there is also no answer whatsoever. Anything we might say is a priori bound to be mere nonsense. Nevertheless we do run up against the limits of language. Kierkegaard too saw that there is this running up against something and he referred to it in a fairly similar way (as running up against paradox). This running up against the limits of language is *ethics*. (Waismann, *Ludwig Wittgenstein and the Vienna Circle*, p. 68)

17 OC, §204. Compare Wittgenstein's quotation from Faust: 'In the beginning was the deed.' OC, §402.

18 See Williams, 'Scepticism without theory'.

19 The *locus classicus* of contemporary quietism is Wittgenstein's *Philosophical Investigations*. 'Die eigentliche Entdeckung ist die, die mich fähig macht, das Philosophieren abzubrechen, wann ich will. – Die die Philosophie zur Ruhe bringt, so daß sie nicht mehr von Fragen gepeitscht wird, die sie selbst in Frage stellen. . . . Es gibt nicht eine Methode der Philosophie, wohl aber gibt es Methoden, gleichsam verschiedene Therapien' (PI, §133). Wittgenstein's hope of letting philosophy find peace echoes the sceptics' *ataraxia*. It is no coincidence that Sextus Empiricus, the medical practitioner, understands himself as a doctor of the soul: 'Skeptics are philanthropic, and wish to cure by argument [ἰᾶσθαι λόγῳ], as far as they can, the conceit and the rashness of the dogmatists' (OS, 3.280). For a consistently therapeutic reading of ancient scepticism, see Nussbaum, 'Skeptic purgatives: therapeutic arguments in ancient skepticism'; Cohen, 'Sextus Empiricus: skepticism as a therapy'; Voelke, 'Soigner par le *logos*: la thérapeutique de Sextus Empiricus'.

20 OS, 1.17; AL, 9.49.

21 This is not to say that Sextus himself wanted to ground a kind of empiricism or phenomenalism. On this thesis, see Chisholm, 'Sextus Empiricus and modern empiricism'. And see also Stough, *Greek Skepticism: A Study in Epistemology*, esp. p. 107. Chisholm and Stough's thesis that sceptical phenomenalism implies an epistemological phenomenalism has been convincingly refuted by Bailey in *Sextus Empiricus and Pyrrhonean Scepticism*, esp. pp. 214–55. That Sextus wanted to put a non-metaphysical empiricism, and so something like 'empirical sciences', in the place of metaphysics is an old thesis, which can already be found in Goedeckemeyer, *Die Geschichte des griechischen Skeptizismus*, esp. pp. 283ff.

22 It is important to note that Sextus does not use the expression εἶδος (form/

structure), since it does not automatically admit of a representationalist interpretation. The classical concept of ideas is incompatible with subjective idealism insofar as it was never intended to be anything that could be present only in us and even distort our view of reality. Instead, Plato's postulation of ideas is supposed to explain the fact of the world's knowability. This also distinguishes Platonic ideas from Lockean ideas: while the latter are nothing other than contents of consciousness, the former, by contrast, are neither exclusively subjective nor objective. They are logical (i.e. graspable in thought), while at the same time being ontological forms of reality itself. Thinking is able to comprehend reality because the forms of thinking are the forms of reality. We can label this thesis 'objective idealism' or even idea-realism, because Platonic ideas are in themselves that which they reveal to thought. Plato's problem is therefore less how knowledge is possible as how error (ψεῦδος) is possible. If the forms of thought are the forms of reality itself, the question immediately arises of how our thinking could possibly fall short of reality.

23 AL, 7.194.

24 OS, 2.49.

25 On the problem of the criterion of truth, see the outstanding and still unsurpassed essay by Striker, 'ΚΡΙΤΗΡΙΟΝ ΤΗΣ ΑΛΗΘΕΙΑΣ'; see also his 'The problem of the criterion'. On the systematic problem, see too Huby and Neal, *The Criterion of Truth*. On Sextus' discussion, see Long, 'Sextus Empiricus on the criterion of truth', and also Brunschwig, 'Sextus Empiricus on the *kriterion*: the skeptic as conceptual legatee'.

26 The definitions read as follows: a cataleptic representation 'comes from something real, is imprinted and stamped in accordance with the real object itself, and as such would not come from anything unreal' (ἀπὸ ὑπάρχοντος καὶ κατ' αὐτὸ τὸ ὑπάρχον ἐναπομεμαγμένη καὶ ἐναπεσφραγμένη, ὁποία οὐκ ἂν γένοιτο ἀπὸ μὴ ὑπάρχοντος) (OS, 2.4; AL, 7.248, 426; DL VII, 50).

27 ὥσπερ οὖν τὸ φῶς ἑαυτό τε δείκνυσι καὶ πάντα τὰ ἐν αὐτῷ οὕτω καὶ ἡ φαντασία, ἀρχηγὸς οὖσα τῆς περὶ τὸ ζῷον εἰδήσεως, φωτὸς δίκην ἑαυτήν τε ἐμφανίζειν ὀφείλει καὶ τοῦ ποιήσαντος αὐτὴν ἐναργοῦς ἐνδεικτικὴ καθεστάναι (AL, 7.163).

28 One of the reasons behind post-Kantian idealism's attempts to construct a version of transcendental idealism without the thing in itself is the problem of scepticism. We can discern this motivation in a programmatic remark in Schelling's *Essays in Explanation of the Idealism of the Doctrine of Science* [Abhandlungen zur Erläuterung des Idealismus der Wissenschaftslehre]:

> It is historically demonstrable that the first source of all scepticism was the opinion that there is an original object *outside of us*, whose effect is representation. For as the soul may relate to the object entirely passively or partly actively, so it is certain that the impression has to be different from the object and already modified by the soul's receptivity. Accordingly, the object that acts upon us must be entirely different from the object we intuit. But common sense remains undeterred in its belief that the represented object is also the object in itself, and even the academic philosopher forgets the whole

distinction between appearances and things in themselves as soon as he steps
into real life. (SW, I, 378)

29 This path was recommended most prominently, of course, by Quine, with his
suggestion of a naturalised epistemology. See Quine, 'Epistemology naturalized.'

30 See esp. Schelling, 'Philosophical letters on dogmatism and criticism'. For a
discussion of the scepticism problem in post-Kantianism before Hegel, see the
outstanding study by Paul Franks, *All or Nothing: Systematicity, Transcendental
Arguments, and Skepticism in German Idealism.*

31 See chapter 6 above. The concept of representation can be motivated by the
inference to sense data, and, in this context, it serves as an anti-sceptical strategy: it is supposed to explain how it is possible that we can have true and
false representations of the world, by seeing representations as just neutral
presentations of something to which an extra-mental correlate may or may not
correspond. *How* the concept of representation can be integrated into the construction of a substantial philosophical theory depends upon how the problem
of Cartesian scepticism is dealt with in the specific case.

32 On this topic, see Burnyeat, 'Conflicting appearances'.

33 See Striker, 'ΚΡΙΤΗΡΙΟΝ ΤΗΣ ΑΛΗΘΕΙΑΣ', pp. 53–7.

34 OS, 1.1.

35 This feature of the sceptical method lies behind Sextus' statement that the
Pyrrhonian sceptic occasionally presents obviously weak arguments because
these suffice to undermine weaker positions (see OS, 3.280f).

36 For the subjectivisation of the concept of an 'idea' that was already at work in
the Stoics, see for example, *Stoicorum Veterorum Fragmenta*, I, 65: 'They say that
the content of thought is neither something determinate nor qualia, but quasi
something determinate and quasi qualitative representations of the soul. These
were called "ideas" by the ancients. The Stoics since Zeno say that the ideas
are our representations' (τὰ ἐννοήματά φασι μήτε τινὰ εἶυαι μήτε ποιά,
ὡσανεὶ δέ τινα καὶ ὡσανεὶ ποιὰ φαντάσματα ψυχῆς ταῦτα δὲ ὑπὸ τῶν
ἀπχαίων ἰδέας προσαγορεύεσθαι. . . . οἱ ἀπὸ Ζήνωνος Στωικοὶ ἐννοήματα
ἡμέτερα τὰς ἰδέας ἔφασαν.) On the external world problem in antiquity, see
my discussions in *Skeptizismus und Idealismus in der Antike*.

37 OS, 2.72f. See also AL, 7.357, 383ff. It is worth noting how Sextus draws sceptical consequences not only from the Stoics' mental representationalism but also
from the distinction between primary and secondary qualities that was already
common currency among the ancient atomists. Sextus ascribes to Democritus
in particular the thesis

> that the perceptible cannot even be indicative of itself. For, as we have shown
> many times, those who have inquired into the perceptible, some say that it
> is not grasped by sense-perception as it is by nature [οἵόν ἐστι φύσει]; for
> it is neither white nor black, neither hot, nor cold, nor sweet, nor bitter, nor
> does it have any other such quality, but it seems to exist as such when our
> sense experiences empty effects and tells lies. But some have thought that

some perceptible things do truly exist and others not at all; and others have
testified in favor of the equal reality of all of them. (AL, 8.213; see AL, 7.135;
OS, 1.213f.)

It is therefore false to assume that the conflict between the manifest and scientific images of the world is a modern product. Ancient philosophy continually
operates in light of the possibility that reality could be radically other than
it appears. However, it is important to note that, with the exception of the
sceptics, it was generally assumed that reality is revealed to us in thought.

38 The Latin translation of ὁμοίωσις is *adequatio*. Sextus' arguments here are
evidently directed against the idea of truth as a dyadic relation between the
subjective and the objective, where the latter is understood as an external
world to which we can have access only through our mental representations.
Of course, positing a causal or resemblance relation between representation
and represented is not the sole possibility for interpreting the concept of representation. Another possibility is the Aristotelian assumption that the two
stand in a relation of quasi-identity, where the representation is the same
as the represented, only in another, immaterial, mode of being. What is the
same, on this conception, is the εἶδος, which can be realised both materially
and immaterially. Famously, Aristotle thinks it is the task of the imagination
(φαντασία) to take up the form of material actuality into an immaterial mode
of being. See *De anima* 430a3–5; 432a10. Consequently, one cannot attack the
concept of εἶδος with the same sceptical arguments with which one might
attack the concept of causally engendered sense impressions (πάθος).

39 See Sextus, OS, 2.74.

40 Sellars, 'Phenomenalism', esp. pp. 85f., where he characterises hypothetico-
deductive realism as follows:

> Just as it is reasonable to suppose that there are molecules although we don't
> perceive them, because the hypothesis that there are such things enables us
> to explain why perceptible things (e.g. balloons) behave as they do, so . . . it is
> reasonable to suppose that physical objects exist although we do not directly
> perceive them, because the hypothesis that there are such things enables us
> to understand why our sense contents occur in the order in which they do.

On inference to the best explanation as an anti-sceptical strategy, see Vogel,
'Cartesian skepticism and inference to the best explanation'. Vogel distinguishes various strategies for showing that assuming an external world is the
best explanation for the causal explanation of appearances and tries to give
general criteria that would allow us to formulate an axiological gradation of
explanations. His anti-sceptical strategy then consists in showing sceptical
hypotheses to be poor theories of causality when compared to the non-sceptical
assumption of a causal-nomological world of objects. In executing this strategy,
he asserts that assuming a world of objects (the 'real-world hypothesis') enjoys
an explanatory advantage over against sceptical alternatives insofar as the
latter are 'contrived and unduly indirect' (ibid., p. 666). It follows, conversely,

that the real-world hypothesis can be neither contrived nor unduly indirect. Yet this is hardly the case; the hypothesis of a world of objects is anything but philosophically unencumbered. Likewise, the naïve ontology of individuals (see chapter 3 above) is far from being a natural component of our naïve attitude towards the world. The seemingly natural and self-evident assumption of a world of objects is by no means as naïve as most of its advocates would generally have us believe. One indication of this is that the natural sciences themselves put it into question. Indeed, the supposedly best causal explanation of appearances – i.e. the best physical theories of the world – tend to be incompatible with the hypothesis of a world of objects containing tables, chairs, cats, and the like. We cannot, therefore, draw on the scientific method of inference to the best explanation in order to justify a seemingly natural (naïve) assumption – all of which is more grist to the sceptic's mill.

41 Besides the hypothesis problem, there is of course the Humean–Kantian issue of how it is supposed to be possible to conceive of an external world, which impacts upon us causally, as the result of an inference. See Kern's argument, in *Sources of Knowledge*, pp. 101–3, against every inferentialist theory of perception that assumes a *sotto voce* inference is necessary to explain how we can have perceptual knowledge.

42 See chapter 6 above, on how arbitrarily many concrete hypotheses can serve the formulation of the general Cartesian paradox.

43 For this distinction, see p. 277, n. 19, above.

44 See Sellars, *Empiricism and the Philosophy of Mind*, p. 64.

45 On this topic, see the study by Hoffmann, *Philosophische Physiologie*.

46 See Williams, *Groundless Belief*, p. 48: 'The upshot of this is that the sense-datum theorist is caught in a dilemma. The view that sense-data are simply discovered by introspecting one's perceptual consciousness is highly implausible. But the alternative view – that they are postulated theoretical entities – seems to conflict with the requirement that they be given.'

47 Hogrebe, *Die Wirklichkeit des Denkens*, pp. 30, 33.

48 See OS, 2.100–33.

49 I here follow, in outline at least, Brandom's analysis of representationalism. Like Brandom, I assume that the primary concern of representationalism must be to explain the difference between *representational purport* and *representational success*. See Brandom: *Making it Explicit*, p. 72.

50 See AL, 8, 162–70.

51 James Conant rightly sees that this focus contains the possibility for constructing a genuinely Kantian scepticism. This would attack the conditions of possibility of content/meaning as such without, like Descartes, disturbing the content of our representations and merely robbing them of their worldly origin. See Conant, 'Varieties of scepticism'. According to Conant, therefore, 'Kripkenstein's' rule-following scepticism belongs to a different genus to Cartesian scepticism. Kripkenstein questions the very possibility of meaning, and thus of the propositional content of our representations (or expressions).

52 See e.g. CPR, B68: 'Everything that is represented through a sense is to that extent always appearance, and an inner sense must therefore either not be

admitted at all or else the subject, which is the object of this sense, can only be represented by its means as appearance, not as it would judge of itself if its intuition were mere self-activity, i.e., intellectual.' See also CPR, B155f. See Sturma's argumentation in *Kant über Selbstbewußtsein: Zum Zusammenhang von Erkenntniskritik und Theorie des Selbstbewußtseins*, p. 66f. Sturma arrives at the result that 'Descartes' thesis that the nature of the human mind is better known to us than the objective world is therefore just as false as its alternative' (ibid., p. 67).

53 CPR, B300.

54 CPR, §16. 'For the manifold representations that are given in a certain intuition would not all together be my representations if they did not all together belong to a self-consciousness; i.e., as my representations (even if I am not conscious of them as such) they must yet necessarily be in accord with the condition under which alone they can stand together in a universal self-consciousness, because otherwise they would not throughout belong to me' (CPR, B132f.).

55 CPR, B134.

56 CPR, A112; emphasis M. G.

57 CPR, B404.

58 Nevertheless, Sturma is correct to note that 'Kant argues with the difference between the given and the thought, but not for it' (*Kant über Selbstbewußtsein*, p. 52).

59 '[O]f course we can't get outside our skins to find out what is causing the internal happening of which we are aware. Introducing intermediate steps or entities into the causal chain, like sensations or observations, serves only to make the epistemological problem more obvious' (Davidson, 'A coherence theory of truth and knowledge', p. 144). This means, however, that Davidson accepts the epistemological dilemma in order to give it an anti-representationalist interpretation.

60 Whorf expresses the relation of language and reality using such metaphors as the following: 'It is the grammatical background of our mother tongue, which includes not only our way of constructing propositions but the way we dissect nature and break up the flux of experience into objects and entities to construct propositions about' (*Language, Thought, and Reality: Selected Writings of Benjamin Lee Whorf*, p. 239). The fundamental problem of this form(/ grammar)–content dualism becomes clear as soon as we consider that the flux of experience (in another passage he calls this the 'flux of existence' [ibid., p. 253]) still has to have a *structure* if it is to be divided up into different objects. One cannot divide up anything that lacks structure, even in the minimal sense of a merely spatiotemporal *partes extra partes*. Whorf too has to take account of a structured world beyond language if he is to assert that we structure the world through language. Yet how can he know that it is in-itself unstructured and not, say, exactly as it is represented by the grammar of Hopi? Whorf's linguistic relativism becomes problematic given how much he claims to know about the difference between form and content. See, for example, what is likely the most famous passage of his work:

[W]e dissect nature along lines laid down by our native languages. The categories and types that we isolate from the world of phenomena we do not find there because they stare each observer in the face; on the contrary, the world is presented in a kaleidoscopic flux of impressions which has to be organized by our minds – and this means largely by the linguistic systems in our minds. We cut nature up, organize it into concepts, and ascribe significances as we do, largely because we are parties to an agreement to organize in this way – an agreement that holds throughout our speech community and is codified in the patterns of our language. (Ibid., 213)

A simple operation of self-application also problematises the assumption that our grammars structure the flux of impressions, as this assumption itself belongs to a certain grammar and therefore presupposes a division of the flux of impressions. And, by hypothesis, this division is observable only under certain conditions.

61 Davidson, 'On the very idea of a conceptual scheme', p. 197.
62 One might find an echo here in Borges' famous tale 'The library of Babel'. In one passage, the narrator reflects on his own linguistic usage by considering the fact that all the words and sentences he uses are already written down in some book in the library and, further, that they have completely different meanings in the books than they do on his own lips. But he then goes as far as to try to unsettle the reader by pointing out how all the words he uses to describe this very possibility could be words of another language.

A number n of the possible languages employ the same vocabulary; in some of them, the symbol 'library' possesses the correct definition 'everlasting, ubiquitous system of hexagonal galleries,' while a library – the thing – is a loaf of bread or a pyramid or something else, and the six words that define it themselves have other definitions. You who read me – are you certain you understand my language? ('The library of Babel', here p. 118)

63 See, of course, Quine, *Word and Object*, §7.
64 OC, §156.
65 'What is needed to answer the skeptic is to show that someone with a (more or less) coherent set of beliefs has a reason to suppose his beliefs are not mistaken in the main. What we have shown is that it is absurd to look for a justifying ground for the totality of beliefs, something outside this totality which we can use to test or compare with our beliefs' (Davidson, 'A coherence theory of truth and knowledge', p. 146).
66 Stroud, 'Transcendental arguments', p. 253: '[T]here is a genuine class of propositions each member of which must be true in order for there to be any language, and which consequently cannot be denied truly by anyone, and whose negations cannot be asserted truly by anyone. Let us call this the "privileged class".'
67 Thus ibid., p. 255:

[F]or any candidate S, proposed as a member of the privileged class, the sceptic can always very plausibly insist that it is enough to make language possible if we believe that S is true, or if it looks for all the world as if it is, but that S needn't actually be true. Our having this belief would enable us to give sense to what we say, but some additional justification would still have to be given for our claim to know that S is true. The sceptic distinguishes between the conditions necessary for a paradigmatic or warranted (and therefore meaningful) use of an expression or statement and the conditions under which it is true.

68 See Harrison's thesis, in 'Transcendental arguments and idealism', that all transcendental arguments presuppose idealism in the sense of reference dependence between subject and object. A comprehensive reconstruction of the structure of transcendental arguments can be found in Grundmann, *Analytische Transzendentalphilosophie: Eine Kritik*.

69 Davidson himself thinks he can fend off Cartesian scepticism through a twofold externalism. On the one hand, he advocates a variety of *perceptual externalism*, according to which the content of our perceptions, and all the world-directed judgements derived from it, depend upon which worldly objects causally impinge upon us. On the other hand, he advocates a *social externalism*, according to which the concept of objectivity only arises given the triadic structure of communication (triangulation): the *concept* of an objective (public) world (though not the world itself) is the product of communication between speakers, whose interpretive behaviour commits them to assuming a public world that systematically determines the content of their respective linguistic reactions. See, for example, Davidson, 'Epistemology externalized'. Yet, as the Leibnizian example discussed below will illustrate, this is no strategy for evading Cartesian scepticism. Willaschek raises a similar fundamental objection to externalist anti-sceptical strategies in *Der mentale Zugang zur Welt*, pp. 199f. Another weighty objection is that knowing we have to assume that most of our beliefs are true does not get us any further if we cannot know at the same time *which* of our beliefs are true (on this, see Kern, *Sources of Knowledge*, pp. 106–8). Because we cannot have any a priori criterion for sorting our beliefs into true and false ones, knowing that most of them are true helps us in the individual case just as little as knowing that most lottery numbers are winners if we cannot know which numbers these are. In the case of our beliefs, we cannot engage in any probabilistic reasoning, as it is unclear what it means for most of our beliefs to be true. This assumption, that is, is not based on any statistic and cannot be made more concrete by any statistical enquiry.

70 See Habermas, *Truth and Justification*, p. 16, and pp. 27, 61, *et al*. Habermas also speaks of '[a] shared view of reality as a "territory halfway between" the "worldviews" of different languages is a necessary presupposition of meaningful dialogue *überhaupt*. For the interlocutors, the concept of reality is connected with the regulative idea of a "sum total of all that is knowable"' (p. 57).

71 'The ultimate source (not ground) of objectivity is, in my opinion,

intersubjectivity. If we were not in communication with others, there would be nothing on which to base the idea of being wrong, or, therefore, of being right, either in what we say or in what we think' (Davidson, 'Indeterminism and antirealism', p. 83).

72 The clock analogy can be found in *Third Explanation* of the *New System (Neues System über die Natur, über den Verkehr zwischen den Substanzen und über die Verbindung zwischen Seele und Körper).*

73 See *Monadologie*, §7: 'Les monades n'ont point de fenêtres, par lesquelles quelque chose y puisse entrer ou sortir.'

74 PI, §259.

75 John Foster, in *The Case for Idealism*, has attempted to offer a defence of Berkeleyan idealism (without God). Yet the prospects for combining an idealist ontology with empiricism are decidedly bleak. Wherever we might acquire the information for our information-processing, the source in question has to be operatively external to the processing activity. Hence we cannot perceive whatever we want. Even if we acquired the information from another mind, the question remains: what does the relation between two such minds consist in, and *how* do we in fact process information? An infinite mind could not supply us with any preformed information that we could somehow apprehend independently of the conditions of our information-processing modes of registration. Besides a solipsism of the present moment, every philosophy, be it idealist or realist, is thus committed to an external world independent of the stocks of information each of us respectively possesses at any given time. One cannot (dis)solve sceptical paradoxes by adopting the concept of the external world in a version that is seemingly more conducive to the kind of information we possess as minded creatures – namely, as a kind of communication between pure minds. The sceptical paradoxes arise because finite epistemic beings enjoy a relation to the world to begin with only because they have to make assumptions about the sequence of their informational states that reach beyond the present moment and out to the whole. This structure is initially neutral regarding the question of whether to adopt an idealist or a realist ontology.

Chapter 14 The Failure of Liberal Naturalism's Metatheory

1 McDowell, *Mind and World*, pp. 11, 42, 66. For the accusation of linguistic idealism, see Williams, 'Wittgenstein and idealism'. For a contrary view, see Malcolm, 'Wittgenstein and idealism'.

2 PG, p. 97.

3 This problem is at the basis of Williams's critique in 'Wittgenstein and idealism', p. 376: 'Leaving behind the confused and confusing language of relativism, one finds oneself with a we which is not one group rather than another in the world at all, but rather the plural descendant of that idealist I who also was not one item rather than another in the world.'

4 See, for example, '"There must be some sort of law for reading the chart. –

Otherwise *how would one know* how the table was to be used?" It is part of human nature to understand pointing with the finger in the way we do. The chart does not compel me to use it always in the same way' (PG, p. 14); see also PG, p. 94.

5 PI, II, p. 578.
6 OC, §475.
7 Hume, *A Treatise of Human Nature*, p. 123.
8 Z, §173.
9 See the famous remark in PI, §415: 'What we are supplying are really remarks on the natural history of human beings; we are not contributing curiosities however, but observations which no one has doubted, but which have escaped remark only because they are always before our eyes.' See too PI, II, p. 578; RFM, p. 92.
10 Luhmann, *Social Systems*, pp. 69, 207ff.
11 OC, §505.
12 OC, §509.
13 'I really want to say that a language-game is only possible if one trusts something (I did not say "can trust something")' (OC, §509).
14 See above, pp. 139f.
15 Nature, or the world, as a notion of unity is therefore what Anton Koch calls an ur-state of affairs – i.e. the 'concept of a pre-propositional (pre-discursive), immediately given, original state of affairs' (*Versuch über Wahrheit und Zeit*, p. 105). In a way that is fully in line with our present discussion, Koch shows that all ur-states of affairs are mere conceptions of reflection, which, 'like the Aristotelian concept of prime matter, is the concept of something that cannot be isolated in the actual – a concept of reflection or a limiting concept, which marks an unattainable vanishing point of explanation or analysis, not any stopping point that has already been reached' (ibid.). For his theory of ur-states of affairs, see the entirety of §13 of *Versuch über Wahrheit und Zeit*.

16   Every distinction makes use of the dimension of distinctions. But this is just why the dimension itself cannot be distinguished from anything. It remains the wholly diaphanous background of all semantic contrasts, which cannot itself be contrasted with anything. . . . One obstructs one's access to this dimension when, in having recourse to 'life', one sees these categorial distinctions as primordial, as it were. But life and its elementary technical practices too already employ this dimension of distinctions. (Hogrebe, *Echo des Nichtwissens*, p. 339, trans. A. E.)

17 This, it is worth noting, is Lyotard's point in *La Condition postmoderne: rapport sur le savoir*, esp. pp. 88–97.
18 Paradoxically, this point refers to the 'energy that keeps the "*mobile*" of our explanations in motion' (Hogrebe, *Echo des Nichtwissens*, p. 336). It is only when we bump up against this 'unavoidable boundary of explanation' that we see (in a way that eludes our conceptual grasp) 'how the entire semantic field of both our everyday and scientific self-explanations contains something

external to itself, something it cannot clarify with its own resources. And yet
we have to exploit it as the source of explanatory power. It ensures the cohe-
sion of our explanations' (ibid., p. 337).

19 See Hogrebe's approach, in *Prädikation und Genesis*, which understands metaphysics as a fundamental heuristic.

20 See above, pp. 76f.

21 See chapter 3.

22 '. . . that our relation to the world as such is not one of knowing' (Cavell, *The
Claim of Reason*, p. 48; see also pp. 45, 241, *et al.*).

23 See Nagel, *The View From Nowhere*.

24 See my discussion in Gabriel, 'Endlichkeit und absolutes Ich'.

25 Koch, *Versuch über Wahrheit und Zeit*, §§ 35–42.

26 See chapter 15 below.

27 Famously, this Spinozist principle is 'of infinite importance' for Hegel. See
The Science of Logic, p. 87. On his interpretation, the principle means 'That
determinateness is negation posited as affirmative' (ibid.).

28 Brandom, *Tales of the Mighty Dead*, pp. 183f.

29 For a more extensive discussion of the point, see Gabriel, 'Chôra als différance:
Derridas dekonstruktive Lektüre von Platons Timaios'.

30 See Rorty, 'The world well lost'.

Chapter 15 A Final Attempt to Recover the World

1 Brandom, *Tales of the Mighty Dead*, pp. 207, 221, 225, and 'Sketch of a program
for a critical reading of Hegel: comparing empirical and logical concepts', here
pp. 141, 146, 150, *et al.* According to Brandom, 'experience' is 'the process of
resolving incompatible commitments' (*Tales of the Mighty Dead*, p. 207). But he
thereby robs the *Phenomenology* of its historical dimension. Neither the French
Revolution, nor the shapes of religion, nor (Kantian) morality are empirical
theories that lead to further theories once they have registered their incompatibility with the facts of the 'objective world' in Brandom's sense. Brandom's
Hegel interpretation never really dares to take the step beyond the ontology of
'Perception', for which the world consists of things with properties. History,
conceived as the content of a science of the experience of consciousness, is not
something we can thematise ontologically on Brandomian premises.

2 Again: 'Concept P is *sense dependent* on concept Q just in case one cannot count
as having grasped P unless one counts as having grasped Q. Concept P is *reference dependent* on concept Q just in case P cannot apply to something unless Q
applies to something' (*Tales of the Mighty Dead*, p. 50).

3 For a critical discussion of Brandom's concept of an 'objective idealism', see
Pippin, 'Brandom's Hegel'.

4 At one point, Brandom identifies this with immediacy and thus with the
world, where he glosses 'immediacy' as 'how things really are, what is really
incompatible with what, and what really follows from what' ('Sketch of a
program for a critical reading of Hegel', p. 141).

5 See for example, *Tales of the Mighty Dead*, p. 223, and 'Sketch of a program for a critical reading of Hegel', p. 140. Here, Brandom cites from the introduction to the *Phenomenology* in a way that is unequivocally contrary to its stated intentions, claiming that it is *no* 'way of despair' (*Phenomenology of Spirit*, §78) of natural consciousness (see 'Sketch of a program for a critical reading of Hegel', p. 148). Hegel, however, explicitly means to show that, at the end of its experience, the natural consciousness attains an insight into its own 'untruth' (*Phenomenology*, §78), which consists in seeing how 'the supreme reality is what is in truth only the unrealized Notion' (ibid.). This untruth consists, for example, not in consciousness believing it can establish a coherent system of beliefs about the world but in how consciousness is convinced that its beliefs are directed towards something ontically prior to it. Brandom, by contrast, presents himself as an advocate of natural consciousness from the start and simply takes over its concept of the world. In the *Phenomenology*, determinate negation does not stand for a kind of holism but is explicitly introduced as an operative concept – indeed, as the very motor of the history of consciousness:

> This is just the skepticism which only ever sees pure nothingness in its result and abstracts from the fact that this nothingness is specifically the nothing- ness of that *from which it results*. For it is only when it is taken as the result of that from which it emerges, that it is, in fact, the true result; in that case it is itself a *determinate* nothingness, one which has a *content*. The skepticism that ends up with the bare abstraction of nothingness or emptiness cannot get any further from there, but must wait to see whether something new comes along and what it is, in order to throw it too into the same empty abyss. (*Phenomenology*, §78; see also *Science of Logic*, p. 10)

6 The process on the subjective side of certainty that corresponds to the relation of incompatibility of facts or properties on the objective side of truth is resolv- ing incompatible commitments by revising or relinquishing one of them. . . . [O]bjectively incompatible properties cannot characterize the same object (objectively incompatible facts cannot characterize the same world), while subjectively incompatible commitments merely ought not to characterize the same subject. (Brandom, *Tales of the Mighty Dead*, p. 193)

7 Ibid., p. 208.
8 Hegel, *Science of Logic*, p. 367.
9 Ibid., pp. 51; 8, 108; 366f. *et al.*
10 Ibid., p. 749.
11 Brandom, *Tales of the Mighty Dead*, p. 185.
12 See chapter 14 above.

> Strong individuational semantic holism asks us to think of conceptual con- tents – that is, for Hegel, whatever is in any coherent sense determinate – as forming a holistic relational structure. Such a structure would consist of a domain and set of relations of material exclusion defined on that domain.

But, further, it asks us to understand the domain elements themselves as constituted by the relations of material exclusion it stands in to other domain elements. The relata are in a sense dissolved into the relations between them ... The intelligibility of the relations themselves is threatened. (Brandom, *Tales of the Mighty Dead*, p. 187)

13 Hegel, *Science of Logic*, p. 387.
14 Brandom, *Tales of the Mighty Dead*, pp. 204, 206.
15 Sellars, *Empiricism and the Philosophy of Mind*, p. 14.
16 Hegel, *Science of Logic*, pp. 346–50.
17 This residue is especially clear in a passage where Brandom opposes the world and the social-semantic dimension in the sense of an ontological naturalism: 'Our activity institutes norms, imposes normative significances on a natural world that is intrinsically without significance for the guidance or assessment of action. A normative significance is imposed on a nonnormative world, like a cloak thrown over its nakedness, by agents performing preferences, issuing orders, entering into agreements, praising and blaming, esteeming and assessing' (Brandom, *Making it Explicit*, p. 48).
18 See Brandom, 'Sketch of a program for a critical reading of Hegel'.
19 Hegel, *Science of Logic*, p. 346.
20 Ibid., p. 347.
21 See Koch, 'Sein – Wesen – Begriff', p. 18: 'It is a realist "platitude" that our holding-true does not guarantee truth. Insofar as our truth claims are claims to objective validity, they include the independence of being-the-case from our acts of judgement, and thus our fallibility in judgement.'
22 CPR, B309ff.; see pp. 57f. above.
23 Hegel, *Science of Logic*, p. 348.
24 Koch, 'Die Selbstbeziehung der Negation in Hegels Logik', p. 15.

25   Being as entirely abstract, immediate self-reference is nothing but the abstract moment of the concept; it is its moment of abstract universality that also provides what is required of being, namely that it be outside the concept, for inasmuch as universality is a moment of the concept, it is also its difference or the abstract judgment wherein the concept opposes itself to itself. . . . The consequence of a philosophizing that in regard to being fails to rise above the senses is that, in regard to the concept, it also fails to let go of merely abstract thought; such thought stands opposed to being. (*Science of Logic*, p. 627)

26 Thus Koch, 'Die Selbstbeziehung der Negation in Hegels Logik', p. 10.
27 On this, see Gabriel, 'Hegel und Plotin' and 'The dialectic of the absolute'.
28 See pp. 176f. above.
29 Hegel, *Phenomenology of Spirit*, §47.

References

Sigla used in the text

René Descartes

AT: *Oeuvres*, ed. Charles Adam and Paul Tannery, 11 vols (Paris: Cerf, 1897–1913).

Immanuel Kant

References to the *Critique of Pure Reason* are to the standard A and B pagination of the first and second editions. Otherwise, all references to Kant are to the volume and page number of *Kants gesammelte Schriften*, ed. Deutschen (formerly Königlichen Preussischen) Akademie der Wissenschaften, 29 vols (Berlin: Walter de Gruyter, 1902).

CPR: *Critique of Pure Reason*, trans. and ed. Paul Guyer and Allen Wood (Cambridge: Cambridge University Press, 1998).

P: *Prolegomena to Any Future Metaphysics that Will be Able to Come Forward as Science: With Selections from the Critique of Pure Reason*, trans. and ed. Gary C. Hatfield (Cambridge: Cambridge University Press, 2004).

CJ: *Critique of the Power of Judgment*, trans. and ed. Paul Guyer and Eric Matthews (Cambridge: Cambridge University Press, 2000).

Sextus Empiricus

AL: *Against the Logicians*, trans. and ed. Richard Bett (Cambridge: Cambridge University Press, 2005); cited by book and page number.

OS: *Outlines of Scepticism*, trans. and ed. Julia Annas and Jonathan Barnes (Cambridge: Cambridge University Press, 2000); cited by book and page number.

Ludwig Wittgenstein

OC: *On Certainty*, trans. Denis Paul and G. E. M Anscombe, ed. G. E. M. Anscombe and G. H. von Wright (Oxford: Blackwell, 1969); cited by section number.

PI: *Philosophical Investigations*, trans. G. E. M. Anscombe (Oxford: Blackwell, 1974); cited by section number.

RFM: *Remarks on the Foundations of Mathematics*, trans. G. E. M. Anscombe, ed. G. H. von Wright, Rush Rhees and G. E. M. Anscombe (Oxford: Blackwell, 1978); cited by page number.

PG: *Philosophical Grammar*, trans. Anthony Kenny, ed. Rush Rhees (Oxford: Blackwell, 1974); cited by page number.

Z: *Zettel*, ed. G. E. M. Anscombe and G. H. von Wright, trans. G. E. M. Anscombe (Oxford: Blackwell, 1967); cited by section number.

Books, book chapters and articles

Abel, Günther, *Interpretationswelten: Gegenwartsphilosophie jenseits von Essentialismus und Relativismus* (Frankfurt am Main: Suhrkamp, 1993).

Adorno, Theodore W., *Negative Dialectics*, trans. E. B. Ashton (London: Continuum, 1983).

Aristotle, *De anima*, ed. W. Jaeger (Oxford: Clarendon Press, 1956).

—— *Metaphysics*, trans. C. D. C. Reeve (Indianapolis: Hackett, 2016).

—— *Nichomachean Ethics*, trans. W. D. Ross (Oxford: Oxford University Press, 1959).

Baghramian, Maria, *Relativism* (London: Routledge, 2004).

Bailey, Alan, *Sextus Empiricus and Pyrrhonean Scepticism* (Oxford: Clarendon Press, 2002).

Baker, G. P., and Hacker, P. M. S., 'Critical study: on misunderstanding Wittgenstein: Kripke's private language argument', *Synthese* 58 (1984): 407–50.

Bernstein, Jay M., *The Fate of Art: Aesthetic Alienation from Kant to Derrida and Adorno* (Cambridge: Polity, 1992).

—— 'Hegel's ladder: the ethical presuppositions of absolute knowing,' *Dialogue* 39 (2000): 803–18.

—— 'Recognition and embodiment (Fichte's materialism)', in Espen Hammer (ed.), *German Idealism: Contemporary Perspectives* (London: Routledge, 2007), pp. 183–205.

Blackburn, Simon, 'The individual strikes back', *Synthese* 58 (1984): 281–301.

Boghossian, Paul A., *Fear of Knowledge: Against Relativism and Constructivism* (Oxford: Oxford University Press, 2006).

—— 'The rule-following considerations', *Mind* 98 (1989): 507–49.

Borges, Jorge Luis, 'The library of Babel', in *Collected Fictions*, trans. E. Hurely (London: Penguin, 1999).

Brandom, Robert, 'Animating ideas of idealism', in *Reason in Philosophy: Animating Ideas* (Cambridge, MA: Harvard University Press, 2009).

—— *Articulating Reasons: An Introduction to Inferentialism* (Cambridge, MA: Harvard University Press, 2000).

—— *Making it Explicit: Reasoning, Representing, and Discursive Commitment* (Cambridge, MA: Harvard University Press, 1994).

—— 'Sketch of a program for a critical reading of Hegel: comparing empirical and logical concepts', *Internationales Jahrbuch des Deutschen Idealismus* 3 (2005), pp. 131–61.

—— 'The structure of desire and recognition: self-consciousness and self-constitution', *Philosophy & Social Criticism* 33 (2007): 127–50.

—— *Tales of the Mighty Dead: Historical Essays in the Metaphysics of Intentionality* (Cambridge, MA: Harvard University Press, 2002).

Brendel, Elke, 'Was Kontextualisten nicht wissen', *Deutsche Zeitschrift für Philosophie* 51 (2003): 1015–32.

Brunschwig, Jacques, 'Sextus Empiricus on the *kriterion*: the skeptic as conceptual legatee', in J. M. Dillon and A. A. Long (eds), *The Question of 'Eclecticism'* (Berkeley: University of California Press, 1988), pp. 145–75.

Bubner, Rüdiger, '*Bildung* and second nature', in Nicholas H. Smith (ed.), *Reading McDowell: On Mind and World* (London: Routledge, 2002): 209–16.

Burge, Tyler, 'Perceptual entitlement', *Philosophy and Phenomenological Research* 67/3 (2003): 503–48.

Burnyeat, Myles, 'Conflicting appearances', *Proceedings of the British Academy* 65 (1979): 69–111.

—— 'Protagoras and self-refutation in later Greek philosophy', *Philosophical Review* 85/1 (1976): 44–69.

—— 'Protagoras and self-refutation in Plato's *Theaetetus*', *Philosophical Review* 85/2 (1976): 172–95.

—— 'The sceptic in his place and time', in Myles Burnyeat and Michael Frede (eds), *The Original Sceptics: A Controversy* (Indianapolis: Hackett, 1997), pp. 92–126.

Carnap, Rudolf, *The Unity of Science*, trans. M. Black (Bristol: Thoemmes Press, 1995).

Cassam, Quassim, *The Possibility of Knowledge* (Oxford: Clarendon Press, 2007).

Castoriadis, Cornelius, *The Imaginary Institution of Society*, trans. Kathleen Blaney Mclaughlin (Cambridge: Polity, 1987).

—— 'The logic of magmas and the question of autonomy', in David Ames Curtis (ed.), *The Castoriadis Reader* (Oxford: Blackwell, 1997), pp. 290–318.

Cavell, Stanley, *The Claim of Reason: Wittgenstein, Skepticism, Morality, and Tragedy* (Oxford: Oxford University Press, 1979).

—— *Disowning Knowledge in Six Plays of Shakespeare* (Cambridge: Cambridge University Press, 1987).

—— *In Quest of the Ordinary: Lines of Skepticism and Romanticism* (Chicago: University of Chicago Press, 1988).

—— *Philosophy the Day After Tomorrow* (Cambridge, MA: Harvard University Press, 2006).

Chisholm, Roderick M., 'Sextus Empiricus and modern empiricism', *Philosophy of Science* 8/3 (1941): 371–84.

Cohen, Avner, 'Sextus Empiricus: skepticism as a therapy', *Philosophical Forum* 15/4 (1984): 405–24.

Cohen, Stewart, 'Contextualism and skepticism', *Philosophical Issues* 10/1 (2000): 94–107.

—— 'Contextualism and unhappy-face solutions: a reply to Schiffer', *Philosophical Studies* 119/1–2 (2004): 185–97.

—— 'Knowledge, speaker and subject', *Philosophical Quarterly* 55/219 (2005): 199–212.

Conant, James, 'The search for logically alien thought: Descartes, Kant, Frege, and the *Tractatus*', *Philosophical Topics* 20/1 (1991): 115–80.

—— 'Varieties of scepticism', in D. McManus (ed.), *Wittgenstein and Scepticism* (London: Routledge, 2004), pp. 97–135.

Davidson, Donald, 'A coherence theory of truth and knowledge', in *Subjective, Intersubjective, Objective* (Oxford: Clarendon Press, 2001), pp. 137–53.

—— 'Epistemology externalized', in *Subjective, Intersubjective, Objective* (Oxford: Clarendon Press, 2001), pp. 193–204.

—— 'Indeterminism and antirealism', in *Subjective, Intersubjective, Objective* (Oxford: Clarendon Press, 2001), pp. 69–84.

—— 'On the very idea of a conceptual scheme', in *Inquiries into Truth and Interpretation* (Oxford: Clarendon Press, 2001), pp. 183–98.

De Caro, Mario, and Macarthur, David (eds), *Naturalism in Question* (Cambridge, MA: Harvard University Press, 2004).

DeRose, Keith, 'Solving the skeptical problem', *Philosophical Review* 104 (1995): 1–52.

—— 'The ordinary language basis for contextualism and the new invariantism', *Philosophical Quarterly* 55/219 (2005), pp. 172–98.

Derrida, Jacques, 'Des tours de Babel', in J. F. Graham (ed.), *Difference in Translation* (Ithaca, NY: Cornell University Press, 1985), pp. 165–205.

Descartes, René, *Meditations on First Philosophy*, trans. Michael Moriarty (Oxford: Oxford University Press, 2008).

Dilthey, Wilhelm, 'Beiträge zur Lösung der Frage vom Ursprung unseres Glaubens an die Realität der Außenwelt', in K. Gründer (ed.), *Gesammelte Schriften* (Göttingen: Vandenhoeck & Ruprecht, 1957), vol. 5, pp. 90–138.

Diogenes Laertius, *Lives of Eminent Philosophers*, trans. R. D. Hicks, 2 vols (Cambridge, MA: Harvard University Press, 1991).

Dretske, Fred, 'The case against closure', in Matthias Steup and Ernest Sosa (eds), *Contemporary Debates in Epistemology* (Oxford: Oxford University Press, 2005), pp. 13–26.

—— 'Entitlement: epistemic rights without epistemic duties', *Philosophy & Phenomenological Research* 60 (2000): 591–606.

—— 'Epistemic operators', *Journal of Philosophy* 67/24 (1970): 1007–23.

Dworkin, Ronald, 'Objectivity and truth: you'd better believe it', *Philosophy & Public Affairs* 25 (1996): 87–139.

Engelhard, Kristina, *Das Einfache und die Materie: Untersuchungen zu Kants Antinomie der Teilung* (Berlin: Walter de Gruyter, 2005).

Fichte, Johann Gottlieb, 'Review of *Aenesidemus*', in *Early Philosophical Writings*, trans. Daniel Breazeale (Ithaca, NY: Cornell University Press, 1988), pp. 59–78.

Fine, Gail, 'Descartes and ancient skepticism: reheated cabbage?', *Philosophical Review* 109 (2000): 195–234.

—— 'Sextus and external world skepticism', in *Oxford Studies in Ancient Philosophy* 24 (2003): 341–85.

—— 'Subjectivity, ancient and modern: the Cyrenaics, Sextus, and Descartes', in Jon Miller and Brad Inwood (eds), *Hellenistic and Early Modern Philosophy* (Cambridge: Cambridge University Press, 2003), pp. 192–231.

Flintoff, Everard, 'Pyrrho and India', *Phronesis* 25 (1980): 88–108.

Fogelin, Robert, 'Contextualism and externalism: trading in one form of skepticism for another', *Noûs* 34 (2000): 43–57.

—— *Pyrrhonian Reflections on Knowledge and Justification* (Oxford: Oxford University Press, 1994).

—— 'The skeptics are coming! The skeptics are coming!', in W. Sinnott-Armstrong (ed.), *Pyrrhonian Skepticism* (Oxford: Oxford University Press, 2004), pp. 161–73.

—— 'Wittgenstein and classical scepticism', in Robert Fogelin (ed.), *Philosophical Interpretations* (Oxford: Oxford University Press, 1992), pp. 214–32.

Forster, Michael N., *Hegel and Skepticism* (Cambridge, MA: Harvard University Press, 1989).

—— *Kant and Skepticism* (Princeton, NJ: Princeton University Press, 2008).

—— *Wittgenstein on the Arbitrariness of Grammar* (Princeton, NJ: Princeton University Press, 2004).

Foster, John, *The Case for Idealism* (London: Routledge & Kegan Paul, 1982).

Foucault, Michel, *Archaeology of Knowledge*, trans. A. M. Sheridan Smith (New York: Pantheon Books, 1972).

Franks, Paul, *All or Nothing: Systematicity, Transcendental Arguments, and Skepticism in German Idealism* (Cambridge, MA: Harvard University Press, 2005).

Frede, Michael, 'Stoics and skeptics on clear and distinct impressions', in Michael Frede (ed.), *Essays in Ancient Philosophy* (Oxford: Clarendon Press, 1987), pp. 151–76.

Fumerton, Richard A., *Metaepistemology and Skepticism* (Lanham, MD: Rowman & Littlefield, 1995).

—— 'The paradox of analysis', *Philosophy and Phenomenological Research* 43 (1983): 477–97.

Gabriel, Gottfried, *Grundprobleme der Erkenntnistheorie: Von Descartes zu Wittgenstein* (Paderborn: Mentis, 1993).

Gabriel, Markus, *Das Absolute und die Welt in Schellings 'Freiheitsschrift'* (Bonn: Bonn University Press, 2006).

—— *Antike und moderne Skepsis: Zur Einführung* (Hamburg: Junius, 2008).

—— 'The art of skepticism and the skepticism of art', *Philosophy Today* 53 (2009): 58–70.

—— 'Der ästhetische Wert des Skeptizismus beim späten Wittgenstein', in G. Gebauer, F. Goppelsröder and J. Volbers (eds), *Philosophie als Arbeit an Einem selbst* (Munich: Fink, 2009), pp. 207–22.

—— 'Chôra als *différance*: Derridas dekonstruktive Lektüre von Platons *Timaios*', in G. Fitzi (ed.), *Platon im Diskurs* (Heidelberg: Winter, 2006), pp. 51–66.

—— 'The dialectic of the absolute – Hegel's critique of transcendent metaphysics', in Nectarios G. Limnatis (ed.), *The Dimensions of Hegel's Dialectic* (London: Bloomsbury, 2009), pp. 76–96.

—— 'Endlichkeit und absolutes Ich – Heideggers Fichtekritik', *Fichte-Studien* 37 (2013): 241–61.

—— 'Hegel und Plotin', in Dietmar H. Heidemann and Christian Krijnen (eds), *Hegel und die Geschichte der Philosophie* (Darmstadt: WBG, 2007), pp. 70–83.

—— 'Kunst und Metaphysik bei Malewitsch: Das schwarze Quadrat als Kritik der platonischen Metaphysik der Kunst', in Markus Gabriel and Jens Halfwassen (eds), *Kunst, Metaphysik und Mythologie* (Heidelberg: Winter, 2008), pp. 257–77.

—— *Der Mensch im Mythos: Untersuchungen über Ontotheologie, Anthropologie und Selbstbewußtseinsgeschichte in Schellings 'Philosophie der Mythologie'* (Berlin: Walter de Gruyter, 2006).

—— 'On Wolfram Hogrebe's philosophical approach', trans. Adam Knowles, *Graduate Faculty Philosophy Journal* 31/2 (2010): 201–18.

—— *Sinn und Existenz: Eine realistische Ontologie* (Frankfurt am Main: Suhrkamp, 2016).

—— *Skeptizismus und Idealismus in der Antike* (Frankfurt am Main: Suhrkamp, 2009).

—— *Transcendental Ontology: Essays in German Idealism* (London: Continuum, 2011).

—— 'Unvordenkliches Sein und Ereignis: Der Seinsbegriff beim späten Schelling und beim späten Heidegger', in Lore Hühn and Jörg Jantzen (eds),. *Heideggers Schelling-Seminar (1927/28)* (Stuttgart-Bad Cannstatt: Frommann-Holzboog, 2011), pp. 81–112.

—— 'Die Wiederkehr des Nichtwissens: Perspektiven der zeitgenössischen Skeptizismus-Debatte', *Philosophische Rundschau* 54/2 (2007): 148–176.

—— 'Der "Wink Gottes": Zur Rolle der Winke Gottes in Heideggers *Beiträgen zur Philosophie* und bei Jean-Luc Nancy', *Jahrbuch für Religionsphilosophie* 7 (2008): 145–73.

—— 'Zum Außenweltproblem in der Antike: Sextus' Dekonstruktion des mentalen Repräsentationalismus und die skeptische Begründung des Idealismus bei Plotin', in *Bochumer philosophisches Jahrbuch für Antike und Mittelalter* 12 (2007): 15–43.

Goedeckemeyer, Albert, *Die Geschichte des griechischen Skeptizismus* (Aalen: Scientia-Verlag, [1905] 1968).

Goodman, Nelson, *Ways of Worldmaking* (Indianapolis: Hackett, 1978).

Grentier, Jean, 'Sextus et Nagarjuna', *Revue Philosophique de la France et de l'Étranger* 95 (1970) : 67–75.

Grundmann, Thomas, *Analytische Transzendentalphilosophie: Eine Kritik* (Paderborn: Mentis, 1994).

Grundmann, Thomas, and Stüber, Karsten, *Philosophie der Skepsis* (Paderborn: Mentis, 1996).

Haas-Spohn, Ulrike, *Versteckte Indexikalität und subjektive Bedeutung* (Berlin: De Gruyter, 1995).

Habermas, Jürgen, 'Actions, speech acts, linguistically mediated interactions and the lifeworld', in Guttorm Fløistad (ed.), *Philosophical Problems Today* (Dordrecht: Springer, 1994).

—— *Postmetaphysical Thinking*, trans. William Mark Hohengarten (Cambridge, MA: MIT Press, 1992).

—— *Truth and Justification*, trans. Barbara Fultner (Cambridge, MA: MIT Press, 2003).

Hacker, Peter, *Insight and Illusion: Wittgenstein on Philosophy and the Metaphysics of Experience* (Oxford: Oxford University Press, 1986).

Harrison, Ross, 'Transcendental arguments and idealism', in Godfrey Vesey (ed.), *Idealism: Past and Present* (Cambridge: Cambridge University Press, 1982), pp. 211–24.

Hawthorne, John, 'The case for closure', in Matthias Steup and Ernest Sosa (eds), *Contemporary Debates in Epistemology* (Oxford: Oxford University Press, 2005), pp. 26–43.

Hawthorne, John, and Kovakovich, Karson, 'Disjunctivism', *Aristotelian Society Supplementary* 80/1 (2006): 145–83.

Hay, Katia, *Die Notwendigkeit des Scheiterns: Das Tragische als Bestimmung der Philosophie bei Schelling* (Munich: Karl Alber, 2012).

Hegel, George Wilhelm Friedrich, *Difference between Fichte and Schelling's System of Philosophy*, trans. H. S. Harris and Walter Cerf (Albany: State University of New York Press, 1977).

—— *Lectures on the History of Philosophy 1825–6*, Vol. 2: *Greek Philosophy*, trans. and ed. R. F. Brown (Oxford: Oxford University Press, 2006).

—— *Phenomenology of Spirit*, trans. A. V. Miller (Oxford: Oxford University Press, 1977).

—— *The Science of Logic*, trans. George di Giovanni (Cambridge: Cambridge University Press, 2015).

Heidegger, Martin, 'The age of the world picture', in *Off the Beaten Track*, ed. and trans. Julian Young and Kenneth Haynes (Cambridge: Cambridge University Press, 2002), pp. 57–85.

—— *Being and Time*, trans. John Macquarrie and Edward Robinson (Oxford: Blackwell, 1962).

—— *Der deutsche Idealismus (Fichte, Schelling, Hegel) und die philosophische Problemlage der Gegenwart* (Frankfurt am Main: Klostermann, 1997).

—— *Kant and the Problem of Metaphysics*, trans. Richard Taft (Bloomington: Indiana University Press, 1990).

—— 'Plato's doctrine of truth', in *Pathways*, trans. W. McNeill (Cambridge: Cambridge University Press, 1998), pp. 155–82.

Heidemann, Dietmar, *Der Begriff des Skeptizismus: Seine systematischen Formen, die pyrrhonische Skepsis und Hegels Herausforderung* (Berlin: Walter de Gruyter, 2007).

—— 'Metaphysik und Realismus in der Erkenntnistheorie', in K. Gloy (ed.), *Unser Zeitalter: Ein postmetaphysisches?* (Würzburg: Königshausen & Neumann, 2004), pp. 277–90.

Hiley, David R., *Philosophy in Question: Essays on a Pyrrhonian Theme* (Chicago: University of Chicago Press, 1988).

Hinton, John Michael, *Experiences* (Oxford: Clarendon Press, 1973).

—— 'Visual experiences', *Mind* 76 (1967): 217–27.

Hoffmann, Thomas S., *Philosophische Physiologie* (Stuttgart-Bad Cannstatt: Frommann-Holzboog, 2003).

Hogrebe, Wolfram, *Ahnung und Erkenntnis: Brouillon zu einer Theorie des natürlichen Erkennens* (Frankfurt am Main: Suhrkamp, 1996).

—— 'Das dunkle Du', in *Die Wirklichkeit des Denkens: Vorträge der Gadamer-Professur*, ed. Jens Halfwassen and Markus Gabriel (Heidelberg: Winter, 2007).

—— *Echo des Nichtwissens* (Berlin: Walter de Gruyter, 2006).

—— 'Erkenntnistheorie ohne Erkenntnis', *Zeitschrift für philosophische Forschung* 38 (1984): 545–59.

—— *Prädikation und Genesis: Fundamentalheuristik im Ausgang von Schellings 'Die Weltalter'* (Frankfurt am Main: Suhrkamp, 1989).

—— *Die Wirklichkeit des Denkens: Vorträge der Gadamer-Professur*, ed. Jens Halfwassen and Markus Gabriel (Heidelberg: Winter, 2007).

Huby, Pamela, and Neal, George (eds), *The Criterion of Truth* (Liverpool: Liverpool University Press, 1989).

Hume, David, *A Treatise of Human Nature* [1738], ed. David Fate Norton and Mary J. Norton (Oxford: Clarendon Press, 2000).

Hüppauf, Bernd-Rüdiger, and Vieweg, Klaus, *Skepsis und literarische Imagination* (Munich: Fink, 2003).

Husserl, Edmund, *The Crisis of European Sciences and Transcendental Phenomenology*, trans. David Carr (Evanston, IL: Northwestern University Press, 1970).

Janich, Peter, 'Szientismus und Naturalismus: Irrwege der Naturwissenschaft als philosophisches Programm?', in G. Keil and H. Schnädelbach (eds), *Naturalismus: Philosophische Beiträge* (Frankfurt am Main: Suhrkamp, 2000), pp. 289–309.

Jaspers, Karl, *General Psychopathology*, trans. J. Hoenig and Marian W. Hamilton (Baltimore: Johns Hopkins University Press, 1997).

Kant, Immanuel, *Correspondence*, trans. Arnulf Zweig (Cambridge: Cambridge University Press, 1999).

Kaplan, David, 'Demonstratives', in *Themes from Kaplan*, ed. Joseph Almog, John Perry and Howard Wettstein (Oxford: Oxford University Press, 1989), pp. 481–563.

Kern, Andrea, *Sources of Knowledege*, trans. Daniel Smythe (Cambridge, MA: Harvard University Press, 2017).

—— 'Understanding scepticism: Wittgenstein's paradoxical reinterpretation of sceptical doubt', in Denis McManus (ed.), *Wittgenstein and Scepticism* (London: Routledge, 2004), pp. 200–17.

—— 'Warum kommen unsere Gründe an ein Ende? Zum Begriff endlichen Wissens', *Deutsche Zeitschrift für Philosophie* 52 (2004): 25–43.

Kersting, Wolfgang, 'Plädoyer für einen nüchternen Universalismus', *Information Philosophie* 1 (2001): 8–22.

Kjellberg, Paul, 'Skepticism, truth, and the good life: a comparison of Zhuangzi and Sextus Empiricus', *Philosophy East and West* 44 (1994): 111–33.

Koch, Anton Friedrich, 'Absolutes Wissen?', *Prima Philosophia* 12 (1999): 29–40.

—— 'Sein – Wesen – Begriff', in A. F. Koch, A. Oberauer and K. Utz (eds), *Der Begriff als die Wahrheit: Zum Anspruch der Hegelschen 'Subjektiven Logik'* (Paderborn: F. Schöningh, 2003), pp. 17–30.

—— 'Die Selbstbeziehung der Negation in Hegels Logik', *Zeitschrift für philosophische Forschung* 53 (1999): 1–29.

—— *Versuch über Wahrheit und Zeit* (Paderborn: Mentis, 2006).

Kripke, Saul A., *Wittgenstein on Rules and Private Language: An Elementary Exposition* (Oxford: Blackwell, 1982).

Leibniz, Gottfried Wilhelm, *Philosophische Schriften*, 4 vols (Frankfurt am Main: Suhrkamp, 1996).

Lewis, David, 'Elusive knowledge', *Australasian Journal of Philosophy* 74 (1996): 549–67.

Long, A. A., 'Sextus Empiricus on the criterion of truth', *Bulletin of the Institute of Classical Studies* 25 (1978): 35–49.

Luhmann, N., *Social Systems*, trans. John Bednarz Jr and Dirk Baecker (Stanford, CA: Stanford University Press, 1995).

—— *Die Wissenschaft der Gesellschaft* (Frankfurt am Main: Suhrkamp, 1992).

Lyotard, J.-F., *La Condition postmoderne: rapport sur le savoir* (Paris: Minuit, 1979).

Macarthur, David, 'McDowell, scepticism, and "the veil of perception"', *Australasian Journal of Philosophy* 81 (2003): 175–90.

—— 'Naturalism and skepticism', in Mario De Caro and David Macarthur (eds), *Naturalism in Question* (Cambridge, MA: Harvard University Press, 2004), pp. 106–24.

McDowell, John, 'Criteria, defeasibility and knowledge', *Proceedings of the British Academy* 68 (1982): 455–79.

—— 'Having the world in view: Sellars, Kant, and intentionality', *Journal of Philosophy* 95/9 (1998): 431–91.

—— 'Knowledge and the internal', in John McDowell, *Meaning, Knowledge, and Reality* (Cambridge, MA: Harvard University Press, 1998), pp. 395–413.

—— *Mind and World* (Cambridge, MA: Harvard University Press, 1996).

—— 'Singular thought and the extent of inner space', in John McDowell, *Meaning, Knowledge, and Reality* (Cambridge, MA: Harvard University Press, 1998), pp. 228–59.

—— 'Wittgenstein on following a rule,' in John McDowell, *Mind, Value, and Reality* (Cambridge, MA: Harvard University Press, 1998), pp. 221–62.

MacFarlane, John, 'The assessment sensitivity of knowledge attributions', in Tamar S. Gendler and John Hawthorne (eds), *Oxford Studies in Epistemology*, Vol. 1 (Oxford: Oxford University Press, 2005), pp. 197–233.

—— 'Future contingents and relative truth', *Philosophical Quarterly* 53 (2003): 321–36.

—— 'Making sense of relative truth', *Proceedings of the Aristotelian Society* 105 (2005): 321–39.

Mackie, John L., *Ethics: Inventing Right and Wrong* (Harmondsworth: Penguin, 1977).

Malcolm, Norman, 'Wittgenstein and idealism', in G. Vesey (ed.), *Idealism: Past and Present* (Cambridge: Cambridge University Press, 1982), pp. 249–67.

Marquard, Odo, *Skeptische Methode mit Blick auf Kant* (Freiburg: Alber, 1978).

Matilal, B. K., 'Scepticism and mysticism', *Journal of the American Oriental Society* 105/3 (1985): 479–84.

Meja, Volker, and Stehr, Nico (eds), *Der Streit um die Wissenssoziologie*, Vol. 1: *Die Entwicklung der deutschen Wissenssoziologie*; Vol. 2: *Rezeption und Kritik der Wissenssoziologie* (Frankfurt am Main: Suhrkamp, 1982).

Monk, Ray, *Wittgenstein: The Duty of Genius* (London: Vintage, 1991).

Moore, G. E., 'A defence of common sense' in G. E. Moore, *Philosophical Papers* (London: Allen & Unwin, 1959), pp. 32–59.

—— 'Proof of an external world', in G. E. Moore, *Philosophical Papers* (London: Allen & Unwin, 1959), pp. 127–50.

Nagel, Thomas, *The View from Nowhere* (Oxford: Oxford University Press, 1986).

Neurath, Otto, 'Protocol sentences', trans. George Schick, in A. J. Ayer (ed.), *Logical Positivism* (New York: Free Press, 1959), pp. 199–208.

Nietzsche, Friedrich, 'On truth and lies in a non-moral sense', in *The Birth of Tragedy and Other Writings*, ed. Raymond Geuss and Ronald Speirs (Cambridge: Cambridge University Press, 1999).

Novalis, 'When numbers and figures' (original German with English trans. by David Wood), *Philosophical Forum* 33/3 (2002): 324–5.

Nozick, Robert, *Philosophical Explanations* (Cambridge, MA: Harvard University Press, 1981).

Nussbaum, Martha C., 'Skeptic purgatives: therapeutic arguments in ancient skepticism', *Journal of the History of Philosophy* 29 (1991): 521–57.

Palmer, Anthony, 'Scepticism and tragedy: crossing Shakespeare with Descartes', in Denis McManus (ed.), *Wittgenstein and Scepticism* (London: Routledge, 2004), pp. 260–77.

Peacocke, Christopher, *The Realm of Reason* (Oxford: Clarendon Press, 2004).

Perler, Dominik, *Repräsentation bei Descartes* (Frankfurt am Main: Klostermann, 1996).

—— 'Wie ist ein globaler Zweifel möglich? Zu den Voraussetzungen des frühneuzeitlichen Außenwelt-Skeptizismus', *Zeitschrift für philosophische Forschung* 57 (2003): 481–512.

—— *Zweifel und Gewissheit: Skeptische Debatten im Mittelalter* (Frankfurt am Main: Klostermann, 2006).

Pinkard, Terry, 'Der sich selbst vollbringende Skeptizismus und das Leben in der Moderne', in Bernd-Rüdiger Hüppauf and Klaus Vieweg (eds), *Skepsis und literarische Imagination* (Munich: Fink, 2003), pp. 45–62.

Pippin, Robert B., 'Brandom's Hegel', *European Journal of Philosophy* 13/3 (2005): 381–408.

Prauss, Gerold, *Kant und das Problem der Dinge an sich* (Bonn: Bouvier, 1977).

Pritchard, Duncan, 'Scepticism and dreaming', *Philosophia* 28 (2001): 373–90.

—— 'Wittgenstein's *On Certainty* and contemporary anti-scepticism', in D. Moyal-Sharrock and W. H. Brenner (eds), *Readings of Wittgenstein's On Certainty* (Basingstoke: Palgrave Macmillan, 2005), pp. 189–225.

Pryor, James, 'The skeptic and the dogmatist', *Noûs* 34 (2000): 517–49.

—— 'There is immediate justification', in Matthias Steup and Ernst Sosa (eds), *Contemporary Debates in Epistemology* (Oxford: Blackwell, 2005), pp. 181–201.

—— 'What's wrong with Moore's argument?', *Philosophical Issues* 14 (2004): 349–78.

Putnam, Hilary, 'Why there isn't a ready-made world', in Hilary Putnam, *Realism and Reason: Philosophical Papers*, Vol. 3 (Cambridge: Cambridge University Press, 1992), 205–28.

Quine, Willard van Orman, 'Epistemology naturalized', in *Ontological Relativity and Other Essays* (New York: Columbia University Press, 1969), pp. 69–90.

— *Word and Object* (Cambridge, MA: MIT Press, 1960).

Rawls, John, 'Two concepts of rules', *Philosophical Review* 64 (1955): 3–32.

Rorty, Richard, *Philosophy and the Mirror of Nature* (Princeton, NJ: Princeton University Press, 1979).

— 'The world well lost', *Journal of Philosophy* 69/19 (1972): 649–65.

Russell, Bertrand, *The Problems of Philosophy* (Oxford: Oxford University Press, 2001).

— 'Vagueness', *Australasian Journal of Psychology and Philosophy* 1 (1923): 84–92.

Schaffer, Jonathan, 'Contrastive knowledge', in Tamar Gendler and John Hawthorne (eds), *Oxford Studies in Epistemology*, Vol. 1 (Oxford: Oxford University Press, 2005), pp. 235–71.

— 'From contextualism to contrastivism in epistemology', *Philosophical Studies* 119 (2004): 73–103.

— 'Skepticism, contextualism, and discrimination', *Philosophy and Phenomenological Research* 69 (2004): 138–55.

Schelling, F. W. J., 'Philosophical letters on dogmatism and criticism', trans. Bruno Gaetano, in *A Schelling Reader*, ed. Benjamin Berger and Daniel Whistler (London: Bloomsbury, 2019).

— *Sämmtliche Werke*, ed. K. F. A. Schelling, 14 vols (Stuttgart, 1856–61).

Schiffer, Stephen, 'Contextualist solutions to scepticism', *Proceedings of the Aristotelian Society* 96 (1996): 317–33.

— 'Propositional content', in Ernest Lepore and Barry C. Smith (eds), *Oxford Handbook of Philosophy of Language* (Oxford: Clarendon Press, 2006), pp. 267–94.

— 'Skepticism and the vagaries of justified belief', *Philosophical Studies* 119 (2004): 161–84.

Schopenhauer, Arthur, *The World as Will and Representation*, trans. Christopher Janaway (Cambridge: Cambridge University Press, 2010).

Sellars, Wilfrid, *Empiricism and the Philosophy of Mind* (Cambridge, MA: Harvard University Press, 2000).

— 'Phenomenalism', in *Science, Perception and Reality* (Atascadero, CA: Ridgeview, 1991), pp. 60–105.

— 'Philosophy and the scientific image of man', in *Science, Perception and Reality* (Atascadero, CA: Ridgeview, 1991), pp. 1–40.

Simon, Josef, *Kant: Die fremde Vernunft und die Sprache der Philosophie* (Berlin: Walter de Gruyter, 2003).

Sinnott-Armstrong, W. (ed.), *Pyrrhonian Skepticism* (Oxford: Oxford University Press, 2004).

Sluga, Hans, 'Wittgenstein and Pyrrhonism', in Walter Sinnott-Armstrong (ed.), *Pyrrhonian Skepticism* (Oxford: Oxford University Press, 2004), pp. 99–117.

Stack, Michael, 'Self-refuting arguments', *Metaphilosophy* 14 (1983): 327–35.

Stalnaker, Robert, *Context and Content: Essays on Intentionality in Speech and Thought* (Oxford : Oxford University Press, 1999).

Stoicorum veterum fragmenta, ed. H. von Arnim (Leipzig: Teubner, 1903–24).

Stough, Charlotte, *Greek Skepticism: A Study in Epistemology* (Berkeley: University of California Press, 1969).

Strawson, Peter F., *The Bounds of Sense: An Essay on Immanuel Kant's Critique of Pure Reason* (London: Methuen, 1966).

—— *Skepticism and Naturalism: Some Varieties* (New York: Columbia University Press, 1985).

Striker, Gisela, 'ΚΡΙΤΗΡΙΟΝ ΤΗΣ ΑΛΗΘΕΙΑΣ', in *Essays on Hellenistic Epistemology and Ethics* (Cambridge: Cambridge University Press, 1996), pp. 22–76.

—— 'The problem of the criterion', in Stephen Everson (ed.), *Epistemology* (Cambridge: Cambridge University Press, 1990), pp. 150–69.

Stroud, Barry, *The Significance of Philosophical Scepticism* (Oxford: Oxford University Press, 1984).

—— 'Transcendental arguments', *Journal of Philosophy* 65 (1968): 241–56.

Sturma, Dieter, *Kant über Selbstbewußtsein: Zum Zusammenhang von Erkenntniskritik und Theorie des Selbstbewußtseins* (Hildesheim: Olms, 1984).

Taylor, C. C. W., *The Atomists: Leucippus and Democritus* (Toronto: University of Toronto Press, 2016).

Trendelenburg, Friedrich Adolf, 'Über eine Lücke in Kants Beweis von der ausschließlichen Subjectivität des Raumes und der Zeit', in *Historische Beiträge zur Philosophie*, Vol. 3 (Berlin, 1867), pp. 215–76.

Tymoczko, Thomas, and Vogel, Johnathan, 'The exorcist's nightmare: a reply to Crispin Wright', *Mind* 101 (1992): 543–52.

Unger, Peter, *Ignorance: A Case for Scepticism* (Oxford: Clarendon Press, 1975).

Voelke, A.-J., 'Soigner par le *logos*: la thérapeutique de Sextus Empiricus', in A.-J. Voelke (ed.), *Le scepticisme antique: perspectives historiques et systématiques* (Geneva: Cahiers de la Revue de Théologie et de Philosophie, 1990), pp. 181–94.

Vogel, Jonathan, 'Cartesian skepticism and inference to the best explanation', *Journal of Philosophy* 87 (1990): 658–66.

Waismann, Friedrich, *Ludwig Wittgenstein and the Vienna Circle*, ed. B. F. McGuinness (Oxford: Blackwell, 1979).

Watson, R. A., 'Sextus and Wittgenstein', *Southern Journal of Philosophy* 7/3 (1969): 229–37.

Weber, Max, *The Protestant Work Ethic and the Spirit of Capitalism*, trans. Talcott Parsons (London: Routledge, 2001).

—— 'Science as a vocation', in *The Vocation Lectures*, trans. Rodney Livingstone, ed. David Owen and Tracy B. Strong (Indianapolis: Hackett, 2004).

White, Roger, 'Problems for dogmatism', *Philosophical Studies* 131/3 (2006): 525–57.

Whorf, Benjamin Lee, *Language, Thought, and Reality: Selected Writings of Benjamin Lee Whorf*, ed. John B. Carroll (Cambridge, MA: MIT Press, 1956).

Willaschek, Marcus, *Der mentale Zugang zur Welt: Realismus, Skeptizismus und Intentionalität* (Frankfurt am Main: Klostermann, 2003).

Williams, Bernard, *Descartes: The Project of Pure Enquiry* (London: Routledge, 2005).

—— 'Wittgenstein and idealism', in *The Sense of the Past: Essays in the History of Philosophy* (Princeton, NJ: Princeton University Press, 2006), pp. 361–79.

Williams, Meredith, *Wittgenstein, Mind and Meaning: Toward a Social Conception of Mind* (London: Routledge, 1999).

Williams, Michael, 'The Agrippan argument and two forms of skepticism', in Walter Sinnott-Armstrong, *Pyrrhonian Skepticism* (Oxford: Oxford University Press, 2004), pp. 121–45.

—— *Groundless Belief* (Princeton, NJ: Princeton University Press, 1999).

—— *Problems of Knowledge: A Critical Introduction to Epistemology* (Oxford: Oxford University Press, 2001).

—— 'Scepticism without theory', *Review of Metaphysics* 41 (1988): 547–88.

—— *Unnatural Doubts: Epistemological Realism and the Basis of Scepticism* (Princeton, NJ: Princeton University Press, 1996).

Williamson, Timothy, *Knowledge and its Limits* (Oxford: Oxford University Press, 2000).

—— 'Past the linguistic turn', in Brian Leiter (ed.), *The Future for Philosophy* (Oxford: Clarendon Press, 2004), pp. 106–28.

Wittgenstein, Ludwig, 'Cause and effect: intuitive awareness', *Philosophia* 6 (1976): 409–25.

—— 'Lecture on ethics', *Philosophical Review* 74/1 (1965): 3–12.

—— *Lectures and Conversations on Aesthetics, Psychology and Religious Belief*, ed. Cyril Barrett (Berkeley: University of California Press, 2007).

—— 'Notes for lectures on "private experience" and "sense data"', *Philosophical Review* 77 (1968): 275–320.

Wright, Crispin, '(Anti-)sceptics simple and subtle: G. E. Moore and John McDowell', *Philosophy and Phenomenological Research* 65 (2002): 331–49.

—— 'Comment on John McDowell's "The disjunctive conception of experience as material for a transcendental argument"', in Adrian Haddock and Fiona MacPherson (eds), *Disjunctivism: Perception, Action, Knowledge* (Oxford: Oxford University Press, 2007).

—— 'Contextualism and scepticism: even-handedness, factivity and surreptitiously raising standards', *Philosophical Quarterly* 55/219 (2004): 236–62.

—— 'Facts and certainty', *Proceedings of the British Academy* 71 (1985): 429–72.

—— 'Hinge propositions and the serenity prayer', in Winfried Löffler and Paul Weingartner (eds), *Wissen und Glauben – Knowledge and Belief: Proceedings of the 26th International Wittgenstein-Symposium 2003* (Vienna: Öbv & Hpt, 2004), pp. 287–306.

—— 'On Putnam's proof that we are not brains-in-a-vat', in Peter Clark and Bob Hale (eds), *Reading Putnam* (Oxford: Blackwell, 1994), pp. 216–41.

—— *Rails to Infinity: Essays on Themes from Wittgenstein's* Philosophical Investigations (Cambridge, MA: Harvard University Press, 2001).

—— 'Scepticism and dreaming: imploding the demon', *Mind* 100 (1991): 87–116.

—— 'Some reflections on the acquisition of warrant by inference', in Susana Nuccetelli (ed.), *New Essays on Semantic Externalism and Self-Knowledge* (Cambridge, MA: MIT Press, 2003), pp. 57–77.

—— *Truth and Objectivity* (Cambridge, MA: Harvard University Press, 1992).

—— 'Warrant for nothing (and foundations for free)?', *Aristotelian Society Supplementary* 78/1 (2004): 167–212.

—— 'Wittgensteinian certainties', in Denis McManus (ed.), *Wittgenstein and Scepticism* (London: Routledge, 2004), pp. 22–55.

Zimmermann, Rolf, *Der 'Skandal der Philosophie' und die Semantik: Kritische und systematische Untersuchungen zur analytischen Ontologie und Erfahrungstheorie* (Freiburg: Alber, 1981).

Index